CW01500206

Contents

Foreword

The B-24 Liberator is probably most well known as a bomber in the iconic photos of them flying through the smoke and flames of the burning Ploiești oil fields.

Although the Douglas C-47 Skytrain (the military version of the DC-3) is deservedly celebrated as the most important twin-engine transport aircraft of the war, virtually unknown and as important was the early use of the four-engine Consolidated B-24 Liberator bomber as a passenger and cargo carrier. Since the B-24's boxy fuselage had more interior room than the cigar-shaped B-17 fuselage, it could be more easily be converted into a transport.

These early Liberators operated America's and Britain's early diplomatic missions and then were to be flown extensively by the Atlantic Ferry Organization and transport commands on missions that opened the world to air transport as never before. Several B-24s were converted for VIP personal and diplomatic use, which included Harriman's Moscow round-the-world diplomatic mission and those used by Churchill and Eisenhower to 'get around'.

During early 1942, to meet the need for a cargo and personnel transport that had longer transoceanic range and improved high-altitude performance than the C-47, the C-87 was hastily designed as a B-24 derivative and placed into production. By installing a built-up floor section that replaced the bomb bay doors, the C-87 could carry 6 tons of cargo loaded through a cargo door cut into the side of its fuselage or through a special hinged door in its nose.

Most C-87s were operated by the US Ferrying and Air Transport Commands, and by the late summer of 1943 they were extensively operating regular routes from the United States to the world's most remote areas. To meet this increased requirement for air transport, the ATC was forced to turn to four commercial airlines for help operating the system. Of the 287 purpose-built C-87s, 24 were transferred to the RAF under Lend-Lease for RAF Ferry and Transport Command. The C-87 would remain as a prime mover until the dedicated C-54 Skymaster four-engine transport came into service.

The 208 C-109s were fuel tanker conversions of completed B-24 bombers that had all armament removed and extra fuel tanks added to carry fuel from India for B-29s based in China. The US Navy used 39 of its 739 Liberator Privateer variant as a RY-3 transport.

Due to the lack of C-47s after D-Day, conventional B-24s were again converted for transporting vital supplies and bulk fuel to troops in France. Once Allied troops broke out of the Normandy Beachhead, converted Liberators flew *Trucking* supply drop operations delivering emergency fuel and supplies to Patton's fuel-starved armies racing across France. Later these B-24s supplied the ill-fated *Market Garden* paratroopers. At the end

The B-24 Liberator Haulers

The B-24 Liberator Haulers

Transport and Personnel Variants During WW2

William Wolf

AIR WORLD

First published in Great Britain in 2024 by
Air World
An imprint of Pen & Sword Books Limited
Yorkshire – Philadelphia

Copyright © William Wolf 2024

ISBN 978 1 39903 161 5

The right of William Wolf to be identified as
Author of this Work has been asserted by him in accordance
with the Copyright, Designs and Patents Act 1988.

A CIP catalogue record for this book is
available from the British Library

All rights reserved. No part of this book may be reproduced or
transmitted in any form or by any means, electronic or mechanical
including photocopying, recording or by any information storage and
retrieval system, without permission from the Publisher in writing.

Typeset by Mac Style
Printed in the UK by CPI Group (UK) Ltd, Croydon, CR0 4YY.

Pen & Sword Books Limited incorporates the imprints of After the Battle,
Atlas, Archaeology, Aviation, Discovery, Family History, Fiction, History,
Maritime, Military, Military Classics, Politics, Select, Transport, True Crime,
Air World, Frontline Publishing, Leo Cooper, Remember When, Seaforth
Publishing, The Praetorian Press, Wharncliffe Local History, Wharncliffe
Transport, Wharncliffe True Crime and White Owl.

For a complete list of Pen & Sword titles please contact

PEN & SWORD BOOKS LIMITED
47 Church Street, Barnsley, South Yorkshire, S70 2AS, England
E-mail: enquiries@pen-and-sword.co.uk
Website: www.pen-and-sword.co.uk
or
PEN AND SWORD BOOKS
1950 Lawrence Rd, Havertown, PA 19083, USA
E-mail: uspen-and-sword@casematepublishers.com
Website: www.penandswordbooks.com

This book is dedicated to all the men and boys who flew, crewed, and serviced the B-24, giving up their youth and often their lives to keep America free and the world safe again.

of the war, six *Trolley Missions* provided 8AF ground personnel with an opportunity of flying over areas that had been bombed by the 8AF.

These Liberator progenies served as America's most important four-engine transport until the dedicated C-54 Skymaster transport came into service.

Acknowledgments

My lifelong hobby has been Second World War aerial combat and over the past 40 years I have collected over 27,000 books and magazines, along with hundreds of reels of microfilm on the subject. I probably have nearly every relevant book written on Second World War aviation and complete collections of every aviation magazine published since 1939. Also included in my collection are hundreds of aviation unit histories; intelligence reports; pilot, crew, flight, and training manuals; and technical, structural, and maintenance manuals for aircraft ordnance, armament, engines, and equipment. My microfilm collection, equaling 2.5 million pages, includes vintage intelligence reports; hundreds of USAF, USN and USMC group and squadron histories and After Combat Reports; complete Japanese Monograph series; complete US Strategic Bombing Surveys as well as complete USAF Historical Studies. Over the years I have been fortunate to meet many fighter aces, other pilots, and fellow aviation buffs who have shared stories, material, and photographs with me (I have over 5,000 photos of fighter aces alone). I have made many multi-day expeditions to various military libraries, museums, and photo depositories with my copy machine and camera accumulating literally reams of information and thousands of photographs. I also had a photo darkroom where I developed thousands of rare photos from microfilm negatives.

The author wishes that every person who contributed photos and materials during the past 40 years could be specifically mentioned. Over the years the origin of many of the thousands of photos I have been lent to copy, have copied or I have collected have become obscured. Most are from military and government sources, but many are from private individuals, and although I have made best endeavors to properly credit all images, I apologize in advance if some of the photos are miscredited. Also, some of the photos are not of the best quality because of their age and sources, especially those copied from microfilm and contemporary publications, at a time before digital cameras and Photoshop, but are used because of their singularity and historical importance.

Many thanks go to a helpful and talented Pen & Sword editor, who reads through my manuscript with a 'fine tooth comb' and patiently places the hundreds of photos and drawings I submit for each book.

A belated thank you goes to Judy Endicott of the Albert F. Simpson Historical Research Center, Maxwell AFB, Alabama. Ms Endicott was of great help during my three-week expedition to that facility in the mid-1980s to collect materials and photos that I have used in this and past books. Thanks also go to the personnel on my numerous visits to the Air Force Museum Archives at Wright-Patterson, Dayton, Ohio, and also to the Library of Congress, National Archives, and the Ferndale Photographic facility,

Washington, D.C. which I visited over the past 40 years to copy thousands of photos and documents.

For yet another time, thanks go to my persevering wife, Nancy, who allows me to spend many hours researching and writing and patiently (mostly) waits while I browse bookstores and visit air museums in search of new material and photos. Also, I thank her because her car sits out in the hot Arizona sun while my Second World War library luxuriates in the remodeled, air-conditioned three-car garage.

Author Bill Wolf.

Caption Credit and Other Abbreviations

AAF:	Army Air Force
AFSHRC:	Albert F. Simpson Historical Research Center
ATSC:	Air Technical Service Command (Logistics Planning Division)
Author:	Author's Collection
CAF:	Commemorative Air Force/AZ Wing
LoC:	Library of Congress
NARA:	National Archives and Records Administration
NACA:	National Advisory Committee for Aeronautics
NASM:	National Air and Space Museum
NMUSAF:	National Museum of the US Air Force
PASM:	Pima Air and Space Museum

RAF:	Royal Air Force
USAF:	United States Air Force
USCG:	United States Coast Guard
USMC:	United States Marine Corps
USN:	United States Navy
USSBS:	US Strategic Bombing Survey

Inflation Adjustor

$1 in 1941–45 = 2024 $

1941 = $21.38

1942 = $19.27

1943 = $18.19

1944 = $17.89

1945 = $17.50

Chapter 1

US and UK Liberators Become Essential for Transport Conversion

O nce the war began and German U-boats were preventing vital materials from arriving to and leaving from the American east coast ports; America found itself with a very heterogeneous assortment of transport aircraft; instead of a standardized, interchangeable air transport fleet that was essential for logistical planning and scheduling, along with aircraft crewing and maintenance. However, at this dismal junction in the war, there was a critical shortage of aircraft of all types including the B-24 and the future ubiquitous C-47 (DC-3) transport, and an urgent need for transport aircraft arose that led to the development of several derived from the *Liberator*.

Consolidated Aircraft Corporation received an order to expedite converting its B-24 bomber into a dedicated transport as the Liberator's long-range, spacious (by 1942 standards) fuselage, and straightforward loading features had been recognized as suitable for transport duties. Some LB-30s and early B-24s had been modified to improve their passenger- and cargo-carrying provisions but these changes were usually impromptu, in the field, modifications and varied from aircraft to aircraft. During the evacuation of Java in early 1942, the LB-30 Liberator was used to carry essential personnel and crucial cargo in its large fuselage while additional cargo was packed between the racks where bombs had once been carried. Early in the war a single test B-24D was experimentally modified by gutting its interior so that knocked down P-39 Airacobras could be transported to the South Pacific but the project, while feasible, was abandoned.

LB-30 Transports: British and American

Roosevelt's 'Arsenal of Democracy' was ready to supply its latest American warplanes to 'friendly countries' with the proviso that they, in turn, furnish information on their operational use and service improvements. The XB-24 bomber prototype made its first flight on 29 December 1939, and with the war in Europe a reality, orders were received by Consolidated from the French and British as well as the US Army Air Corps. The beleaguered French government placed a rush order for 60 B-24s with options for 120 more, while the British contracted for 164. However, when France fell in June 1940, its order was transferred to the British. B-24s under these foreign orders were designated as model LB-30s and were carried on the AAF register as LB-30s with their British serials. Thus, prior to the beginning of Lend-Lease, the first models to be produced were paid for by the British with hard cash and delivered as LB-30As, being the 30th design in Consolidated's Land Bomber (LB) series or LB-30.

During November 1941, a Consolidated LB-30 (AL527) crew, cruising at 13,000ft from San Diego's Lindbergh Field, arrived at Hickam Field, O'ahu, Hawaii, after completing a proving flight of 12 hours 15 minutes, setting a route record for a land-based aircraft. Aided by the usual west to east, tail winds, the return trip to in San Diego was flown in 11 hours 40 minutes, demonstrating the Liberator's long-range bomber and transport capabilities. Early in the war, Consolidated had ferried numerous larger aircraft to England and the Pacific but a new and more efficient method was needed for the ferry crews to finish their round trip as previously they had booked passage on any available sea vessel, losing invaluable crew duty time.

LB-30 Transport Conversion

From its beginning the LB-30 proved the superiority of a four-engine land plane over the large seaplanes that had once ruled the long-distance, over-water routes during the 1930s. The LB-30 was much faster and by taking off from a runway did not have to contend with the drag of a water take-off; thus, giving it a longer range and the ability to carry a heavier load.

LB-30 transport conversion was relatively involved and time-consuming, with these procedures completed adhering to civil aeronautics requirements with post-war civilian marketability in mind. Internally, about 2,000ft of metal hydraulic, vacuum, and fuel lines were removed and replaced with new Duralumin tubing. Electrical wiring was removed,

Prior to the beginning of Lend-Lease the first Liberators to be produced were paid for by the British with hard cash and delivered as LB-30As. (*RAF*)

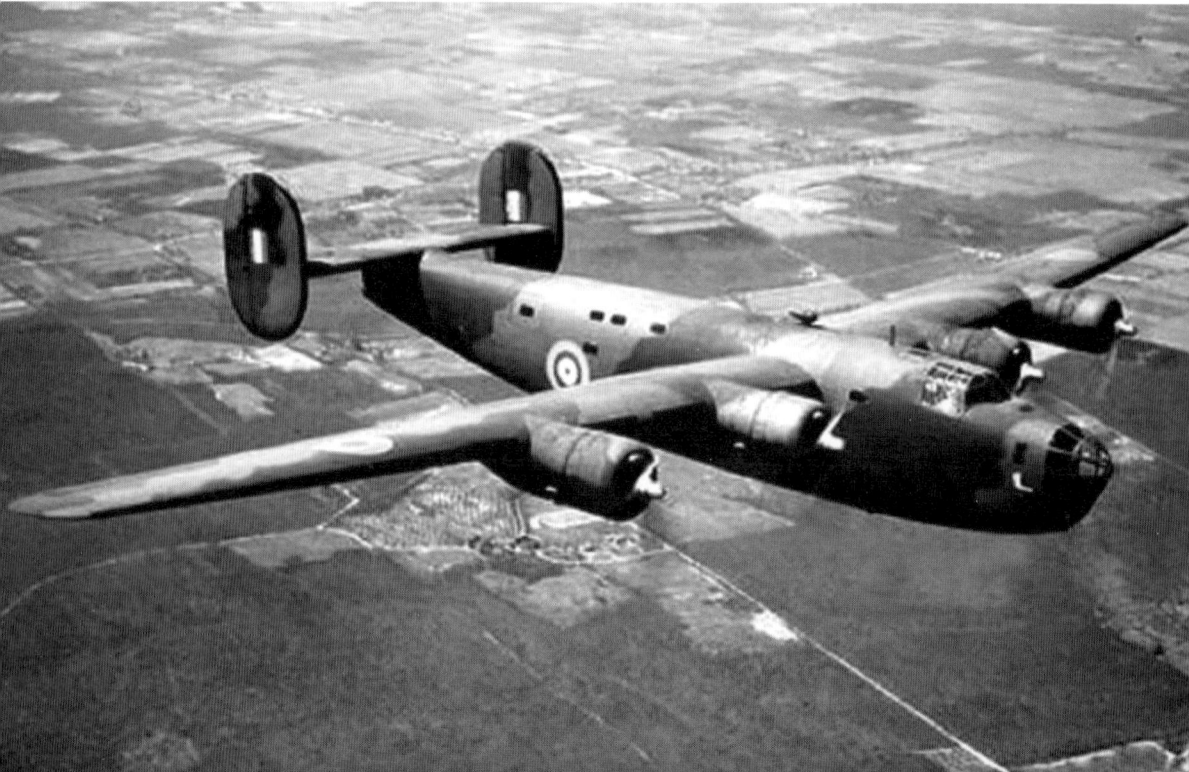

Reuben Fleet (R) with a RAF LB-30 Liberator, basically a B-24A, having a 3ft-longer nose section, increasing the length from 63ft 9in. This Fleet inspiration would be important by adding area to the Liberator's cramped nose line. (*CAC/AAF*)

and replacement wiring was housed in conduit for greater protection. Instruments and cockpit controls were inspected and overhauled or replaced when required. Existing control cables extending to the wings and tail were replaced with new cables. The new cables extending to the tail had to be rerouted from along the sides of the fuselage to an overhead direction to protect the cables when loading cargo up against the sides of the fuselage.

A 'canoe' was fabricated to replace the bomb bay doors, bulkheads, and catwalk keel, which were removed from the jigged LB-30 Liberator transport conversions (LB-30 AL529 shown here with ladder leading into interior through the canoe floor). (*RAF*)

A 'canoe' with 17 bulkheads and 19 stringers, skinned in aluminum, was fabricated to replace the bomb bay doors, bulkheads, and catwalk keel, which were removed from the jigged Liberators. To further strengthen the fuselage integrity, the 0.040in skin sheets were removed from portions of the fuselage sides and replaced with thicker 0.064in sheets, into which seven windows were cut into each side of the fuselage. A few of the fuselage bulkheads were removed and replaced with stronger construction. Heavy longeron members were added to the upper and lower structure of the aft fuselage to carry loads around the large new cargo door opening cut into the side of the fuselage. Some structures such as the outer wing panels and the stabilizer were reinforced to correspond to the increased strength of later-model production B-24s. Four new Pratt & Whitney R-1800 engines were installed, and the bomber-style, self-sealing rubber fuel cells were removed. Also, the wing cavity was sealed to make an integral fuel tank.

LB-30 'passenger compartments' AKA bomb bays (shown here on the Atlantic Return Ferry route) were notoriously cold and crowded, especially when seated on the drafty metal bomb bay floor. (*RAF*)

RAF Liberator II/LB-30s

Liberator II was the RAF designation assigned to a version of the LB-30 Liberator ordered in 1941 directly from the Consolidated production line rather than being diverted from USAAC production orders. It was designed specifically to meet British requirements and had no direct USAAF counterpart. The British ordered 165 under RAF serials AL503/AL667, but only 140 were built and they would serve with 3 Coastal Command and 2 Bomber Command squadrons.

The Liberator II/LB-30 differed from the previous Liberator I (which was basically a B-24A) primarily in having a longer nose section, increasing the length by 3ft from 63ft 9in. This stretched nose had been personally specified by Consolidated founder Reuben Fleet very early in the Liberator's development when he described to his engineering team that his 'gut feeling' was that the nose was too short. Fleet's instinct proved to be correct as the longer nose added extra area, which was to become more important as more and more equipment had to be added to the bomber version. It was also felt by a few that the longer nose made the Liberator more aesthetically appealing!

LB-30s in Service

Atlantic Ferry Organization (ATFERO)

Former RAF officer Capt. Donald Bennett was a specialist in long-distance flying, having in July 1938 piloted the *Mercury* aircraft of the Short Mayo Composite flying boat across the Atlantic. Later, as Air Vice Marshal and Commander of the Pathfinder Force, he led the first transatlantic aircraft delivery flight on 10 November 1940. Bennett took off from Gander, Newfoundland, leading seven Lockheed Hudsons, that were to fly in formation and remain within sight of each other as only one aircraft had a navigator. Unfortunately, weather conditions deteriorated towards the end of the flight. The first four Hudsons arrived at Aldergrove, Northern Ireland, after an 11-hour flight, while the other three became lost but found their way and landed an hour later. Bennett's flight established that larger aircraft, such as the Liberator, could be flown directly to the UK, and an organization was established to this purpose using civilian pilots. A transatlantic program was initiated by the Ministry of Aircraft Production (MAP) under its minister, the inimitable Lord Beaverbrook. A Canadian by origin, Beaverbrook reached an agreement with Sir Edward Beatty, a friend, and Chairman of the Canadian Pacific Railway Company (CPR), to provide ground facilities and support while MAP would provide civilian crews and management. During 1941, MAP relieved CPR and placed the operation under the Atlantic Ferry Organization (ATFERO) headed by Montreal banker Morris Wilson. ATFERO hired the pilots, planned the routes, selected the airports, and established weather and radio-communication stations. Wilson hired civilian pilots to fly the aircraft to the UK, after which these pilots were ferried back in converted RAF Liberators.

Improving weather conditions in spring 1941 and increasing aircraft production made possible an increase in transatlantic aircraft deliveries The first eastbound flight from Montreal was flown by Capt. Donald Bennett in AM258 on 4 May 1941, while the first westbound return flight from Prestwick, Scotland, was to be flown by Capt. Youell that same day but was delayed both by the Luftwaffe fighters in the vicinity and then by weather. It did not arrive in Montreal until 9 May. However, ATFERO experienced considerable difficulty in recruiting enough pilots and other crew members to maintain its schedules. At the time the US War Department was trying to assist the British in securing additional pilots in the US, while the besieged British were forced to withdraw some valuable pilots from combat units for ferrying duty. A solution to the problem was made possible by the Lend-Lease Act as on 21 April General Henry 'Hap' Arnold proposed that the USAAC assume responsibility for the ferrying of British aircraft from the American factories (B-24s from San Diego) to Montreal by American military and civilian pilots who would be employed by the factories, but the civilian pilots would continue flying the ferry flights to the UK.

BOAC

Although early flights were operated by ATFERO and MAP, by May 1941, with the production of aircraft and the need for them quickly surpassing the availability of aircrew, British Overseas Airways Corporation (BOAC) agreed to operate a Return Ferry Service to fly crews back to Montreal from the UK. Many more aircraft could then be ferried without increasing the number of flyers involved by quickly returning airmen to the western Canadian terminus to pick up new delivery aircraft. BOAC was enlisted to assist and provide a nucleus of experienced pilots and management personnel and to begin operations to the requirements of the Air Officer Commanding, No. 45 Group, Ferry Command, RAF. The BOAC flight crews were to wear their civilian uniforms and were protected by the Geneva Convention. Throughout the war these BOAC Liberators were painted in daytime RAF camouflage with full civilian markings. The BOAC 'Speedbird' logo was applied to the forward fuselage, aft of the Union Flag; the registration letters were located under the port wing; with three digits of the serial number and Transport Command code letters applied to the nose.

As the situation in the Mediterranean became more and more precarious, pressure mounted on the need to deliver men and supplies to the North African and Middle Eastern war zones and to West Africa. To deliver these to the Middle East from England, the RAF began making direct Liberator flights from Lyneham to Cairo, Egypt. To supplement these flights, BOAC was requested to inaugurate similar flights with Liberators loaned from the North Atlantic Ferry Service. On 24–25 January 1942, a Liberator Mk.I (AM918/G-AGDR) operated the first non-stop flight from the UK to Cairo. However, on the return of the first flight from Cairo on 15 February 1942, this Liberator, under the command of BOAC Capt. Page, was mistakenly shot down off the English south coast by a Polish-flown Spitfire with the loss of all on board. It was not until July that the operation was resumed with Liberators assigned to the BOAC in RAF markings but assigned civilian registrations. These Liberators were flown to Egypt by BOAC crews, circumventing Luftwaffe-protected Europe, normally with a stop at Gibraltar.

These flights continued until mid-December but by the end of 1942, BOAC inaugurated another new route that crossed Nazi-held territory to Moscow ('X-Base'). Although there was no direct air communication with the USSR from Britain, there was indirect routing through Cairo to Tehran, Iran, where a connection was made with the Russian flights to Kuybyshev (modern-day Samara) located at the confluence of the Volga and the Samara rivers. The advantages of a direct flight were obvious, and Britain was dedicated to establishing one. Early in 1942 a Liberator was detached from the Return Ferry Service and Capt. Percy and his BOAC crew were chosen to organize the direct flight. It was obviously impossible to avoid enemy territory, as the route selected was from Prestwick north to the Arctic Circle and then east crossing the northern coast of Norway, over Sweden then south across Finland to Riga, Latvia. It continued over German-occupied Russia and then actually flew over the German–Russo front line to Yaroslavl, and finally south to the designated airfield of Ramenskoye, outside Moscow. These flights were to fly over German-held territory during darkness as much as possible, and preferably in cloudy conditions. The first BOAC exploratory flight left Prestwick on 21 October piloted by Capt. Percy, with a crew of four and eight passengers plus mail and urgent freight. After flying 13 hours 9 minutes in extremely low temperatures, the aircraft arrived at Ramenskoye at the planned time. By the end of the year only one further round trip flight had been flown and then seven more round trips were completed successfully despite the hazards. Service on this route ceased in April 1943 with the onset of the long daylight hours in the northern latitudes.

BOAC Liberator transport conversions operated flights between Leuchars, Scotland, and Stockholm, in neutral Sweden, during the war, transporting back to the UK materials in short supply, such as precision ball bearings. Operations on this route will be described later.

Between August 1941 and February 1945, ten BOAC Liberators were lost. During January 1945 all BOAC Liberators were returned to the RAF, with seven converted in 1946 as commercial transports with all camouflage paint removed and BOAC markings applied.

These conversions included:

AL507	G-AHYC
AL514	G-AGIP
AL522	G-AHYD
AL529	G-AHYE
AL592	G-AHYF
AL603	G-AHYG
AL627	G-AHYJ

In March 1941 Liberators were the only aircraft capable of flying the 3,000-mile non-stop route between Prestwick and Montreal. Initially four Liberators were provided to

The British Overseas Airways Corporation (BOAC) was enlisted to assist and provide a nucleus of experienced pilots and management personnel. Throughout the war these BOAC Liberators were painted in daytime RAF camouflage with full civilian markings and the BOAC *Speedbird* logo applied to the forward fuselage. AL520 is seen at a snowy Montreal Dorval Airport. (*BOAC*)

BOAC LB-30s were much more comfortable as the company realized its airline roots by installing bench seating. (*BOAC*)

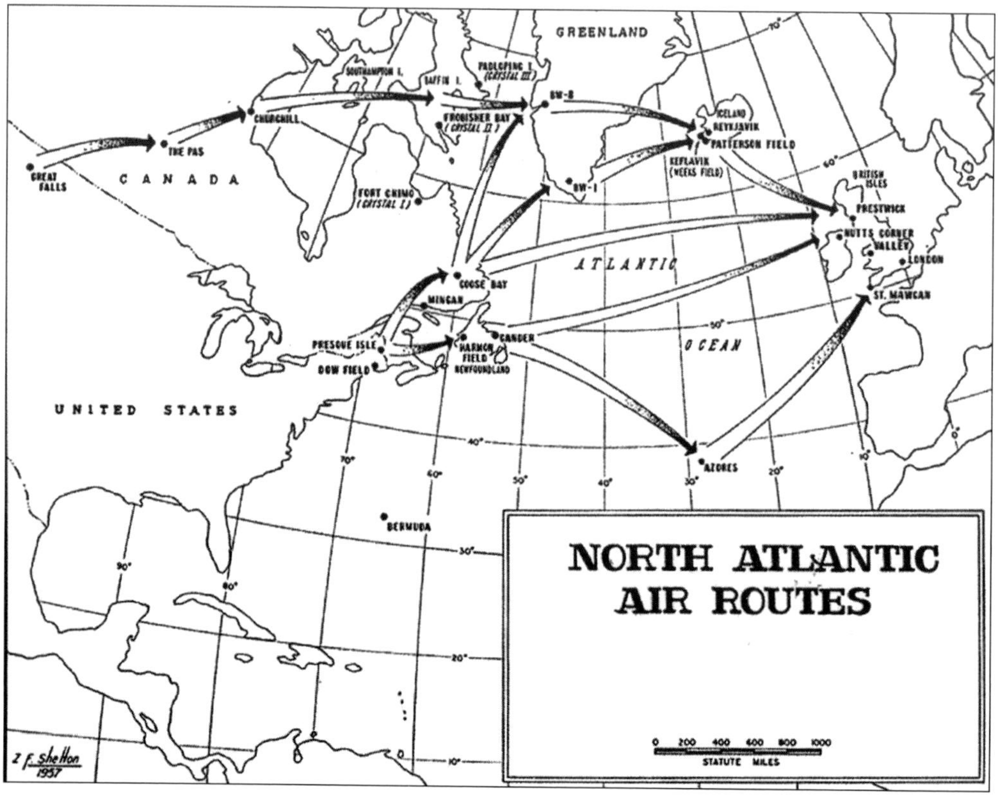

The first BOAC LB-30 arriving at snowy Gander, Newfoundland, on 9 May 1942. The base was to become the regular east–west and west–east refueling stop from Montreal. (*BOAC*)

the RAF (AM258 through 261) at Dorval Airport near Montreal, for preparation and modification. The Return Ferry Service Liberators carried no armament, and their glazed noses were later covered with doped fabric. The flight crew stations continued much the same as those for Coastal Command Liberators, but the first passenger accommodation was very spartan, consisting of mattresses and blankets on boards laid over the bomb bay floor. Because no cabin heating was available, the passengers had to suffer temperatures as low as -40°F (-40°C). Later, combustion heaters were installed and some oxygen tanks with rubber tubes that the passengers could suck on at higher altitudes. Eventually 14 seats were installed aft of the bomb bays, where the racks for freight had been installed. The final heating system tapped heat off the engine exhausts, with the warm air circulated around the passenger area and dumped overboard through a simple valve system. The prevailing westerly winds increased the return trip time from Scotland to Montreal to 15 hours.

While the Return Ferry Service had lost 43 aircrew in 2 terrible crashes in Scotland within 5 days during August 1941, during 1942 the BOAC made 136 Liberator flights between Prestwick and Montreal without encountering any serious problems. Gander was used as a regular refueling point, although some flights were routed through Reykjavik, Iceland or through Goose Bay, Labrador, but as experience was gained an assortment of routings through Iceland and alternates in Canada were used.

RAF Ferry Command (RAFFC)

RAF Ferry Command was formed on 20 July 1941 by the raising ATFERO to Command status, with the RAF assuming responsibility for the delivery operation it had initially opposed. The civilian organization was retained but with a veneer of military officers under Air Chief Marshal Sir Frederick Bowhill. Bowhill, who had initially been an early opponent of transatlantic ferry operations, had previously served as the Air Officer

Commanding-in-Chief (AOC) at RAF Coastal Command and had distinguished himself by his significant help in the identification of the likely position of the German battleship *Bismarck* that led to its sinking. After serving admirably with RAFFC, Bowhill retired from this position a year later but on 25 March 1943 became AOC of Transport Command, serving with distinction in that capacity until the end of the war.

The new Ferry Command retained the substantial civilian component of its Atlantic Ferry Organization predecessor engaging, about 1,000 personnel in Montreal, Newfoundland, and Bermuda, including 400 aircrew, of whom 207 were civilians, mostly Canadian and American. Ferry Command, in co-operation with the RCAF, developed a training organization at Debert, Nova Scotia, and North Bay, Ontario. As the war progressed, the Command delivered an assortment of aircraft types overseas, to the UK, but sometimes to Russia (via Iran), through Africa to India and even to Australia flying multiple aircraft deliveries that were abandoned in favor of individual flights. Airfields established in Greenland and Iceland alleviated many problems concerning weather conditions, fuel capacity, and crew fatigue. These problems were further eased early in 1942 with the decision to construct a large base at Goose Bay, Labrador.

Ferry operations had initially been flown from St Hubert, south-east of Montreal, but this field was congested due to a RCAF flying school located there and during September 1941, Ferry Command moved to the Dorval airport (now Pierre Elliott Trudeau International Airport), which had just opened on 1 September with three paved runways.

Once the aircraft were ferried eastward their aircrews needed to return to North America for another delivery and the new long range, four-engine Consolidated Liberator, which arrived during March 1941, appeared to solve the aircrew return transport problem. However, the first Liberators intended for British service became highly valued by both the RAF and the Ministry of Aircraft Production (MAP). The MAP prevailed and the first British Liberators ferried crews back to Canada. The Return Ferry Service tragically initiated its flights by having two Liberators crash in Scotland during August 1941, killing a total 43 civilian pilots, radio operators and flight engineers plus one passenger en route back to Canada (18 Canadians, 18 Americans, seven British and one Australian). After this inauspicious beginning, return flights would become routine, though never easy. The Liberator bomb bays-cum-passenger-compartments were very cold and cramped, with certainly no first class for VIPs and every passenger suffering identical discomforts.

ACM Sir Frederick Bowhill, first Commander-in-Chief of the RAF Ferry Command. (*RAF*)

RAF Transport Command

On 25 March 1943, RAF Transport Command was established, and Ferry Command became No. 45 Group within the larger organization with various wings directing their geographic operations: No. 112 Wing at Dorval handling North Atlantic operations and No. 113 Wing at Nassau, Bahamas, directing flights through the Central and South Atlantic. Sir Frederick Bowhill returned from retirement to assume command. Late in the war 280 and 300 Wings were formed at San Diego, California, and Sydney, Australia, respectively, to direct what was expected to become a emergent delivery system to the Pacific. The establishment of RAF Transport Command came with the increased delivery of cargos as well as aircraft. Liberator use would continue but also marked the ascendancy of the C-47 Dakota for both cargo and passenger transport and the dropping of paratroopers. Transport Command controlled all transport aircraft of the RAF and was established on 25 March 1943 by renaming Ferry Command.

Winston Churchill's LB-30 *Commando*

The most famous Liberator II was *Commando* (AL504), which served as Prime Minister Winston Churchill's personal transport. Originally it was delivered as the second of 139 VLR (Very Long Range) Liberator IIs received by the RAF, intended to be used by Coastal Command on maritime and anti-submarine patrol duty. During July 1942, shortly after delivering this Liberator to the UK, American volunteer pilot William Vanderkloot met Sir Charles Portal, Chief of the Air Staff, to discuss a safe, direct air route from England to Cairo, avoiding the hazards from land-based enemy aircraft over North Africa and Sicily. During the 1930s Vanderkloot had been a pilot for Trans World Airlines but went to Montreal in mid-1941 to volunteer with RAF Ferry Command to transfer long-range aircraft to Great Britain. After flying to numerous exotic destinations during his 18 months with Ferry Command, Vanderkloot had gained a reputation as an excellent navigator, which was brought to the attention of Portal. In his interview with Portal, Vanderkloot told him that he could make the trip to Cairo with one stop in Gibraltar by first flying east, remaining over the Mediterranean in the afternoon and then, after sundown, turning sharply south, flying over Spanish and Vichy Africa during the night before turning east again toward the Nile and approaching Cairo from the south. Thus, the danger from land based enemy aircraft in enemy-occupied North Africa and Sicily would be avoided without having to fly halfway around Africa. Portal was impressed and the next day had Vanderkloot meet Winston Churchill at No. 10 Downing Street. Reportedly, Churchill, wearing a robe and slippers, offered him a drink, which began an association during which Vanderkloot would fly Churchill on diplomatic missions to Russia, North Africa, and the Middle East. Meanwhile, the Liberator Vanderkloot had delivered to Prestwick was assigned as a VIP transport. It had all armament removed and the fuselage was modified to accommodate luxurious seating, berths, and an electric flight kitchen but maintained the standard Liberator nose and tail configuration. After his successful scouting flight and meeting with Churchill, Vanderkloot began flying the Prime Minister and other English VIPs on important secret diplomatic trips. On these the usual crew was the American co-pilot John Ruggles, and the Canadian flight engineers John Affleck and Ronald Williams, and radio operator Russell Holmes. Usually accompanying Churchill were his doctor and valet.

Vanderkloot flew Lord Mountbatten to England in June 1942; carried the Prime Minister and Chief of the Imperial General Staff Alan Brooke to Egypt in August 1942 to replace Claude Auchinleck as Commander of the British Army in North Africa with Bernard Montgomery; then transported Churchill to high-level talks in Moscow with Joseph Stalin during the second Moscow Conference during August 1942. He also flew Churchill to the Casablanca Conference and to Turkey to determine that country's wartime intentions during January–February 1943. After these extended trips, Churchill was never to be a *Commando* passenger again, swapping *Commando* for *Ascalon*, an Avro York transport aircraft (LV633) using an all-British crew. The York used the wings and tail arrangement from the Lancaster bomber and became the standard aircraft for use by King George VI and Prime Ministers Winston Churchill and Anthony Eden. *Ascalon* was the sword used by Saint George to slay the dragon,

Although *Commando* was the pride of Ferry Command, the converted bomber was certainly considered primitive compared to today's luxurious airliners. In his Second World War history *The Hinge of Fate* (Houghton Mifflin, 1950), Churchill described his flight to Cairo:

> This was a very different kind of travel from the comforts of the Boeing Flying boats. The bomber was at this time unheated, and razor-edged draughts cut through many chinks. There were no beds, but the two shelves in the after cabin enabled me and Sir Charles Wilson, my doctor, to lie down. There were plenty blankets for all. We flew low over the South of England in order to be recognized by our batteries, who had been warned but who were also under Alert conditions.

Pilot William Vanderkloot relates in *The Man Who Flew Churchill* (by Bruce West, McGraw Hill, 1975):

> Meals aboard *Commando* consisted of quite plain fare, mostly box lunches packed in England before departure. The aircraft's quite austere living facilities didn't permit the preparation of much hot food while aloft …
>
> *Commando's* cabin was fitted with two fairly comfortable rear berths and eight seats. Even though the berths might have been soft enough to lull the travellers into slumber, the chill drafts which somehow always managed to sneak through the pitch black hide of *Commando* did cause, from time to time, the prime minister to toss about a bit …
>
> Housekeeping equipment aboard the converted Liberator was simple but fairly effective. The small cooking stove was situated immediately under the astro hatch,

located in the top of the cabin and usually opened while making navigational shots upon the stars. But this hatch also came in quite handy while carrying out other chores. Sometimes, while in flight, the hatch would be lifted to serve as part of an ingenious kind of makeshift vacuum cleaner. By simply extending one end of a length of hose up into the slipstream, the brisk suction created at the other end could be used to tidy up *Commando's* cabin.

Sir Charles Wilson, passenger and Churchill's doctor, wrote in his diary:

Two mattresses had been dumped in the after cabin, and I passed the night in comfort. The P.M. was less happy; he dislikes draughts, and after all it is rather a feckless way of sending him over the world when he is approaching his seventieth year. However, he soon forgot his discomforts in sound sleep, and when we got to Gibraltar this morning, he was ready for anything.

It was after this initial journey in *Commando* that Churchill's Aide-de-Camp, Cdr Charles Thompson, sent the following note to Vanderkloot:

Dear Van,
The P.M. has asked me to write you to say will you make sure that the wind-proofing of the aircraft around the beds is completed before your next trip. He suggests that the way you have fixed the blankets is all right as far as it goes, but that similar protection should be fixed round the head ends of the beds as well as up to the roof. He also suggests that some kind of windproof fabric might be better than blankets. *Commando's* air conditioning was indeed a little too adequate even for an inveterate cigar-smoker. The sleeping compartment also had a small cupboard between the heads of the two bunks, and an adjustable reading lamp which sat near a recess in the top of a cabinet that was large enough to contain a bottle of brandy, in case it was needed to help chase away the chills.

During September 1943 this Liberator II was withdrawn from VIP service and flown to Tucson, Arizona, where it underwent major modifications and emerged as a one-off transport, lengthened by 7ft, with single tail fin, extended fuselage, and upgraded engines. AL504 flew again in March 1944 as the trial version of the USN's Consolidated RY Liberator Express transport. Vanderkloot and the crew then continued to fly it, serving with No. 45 Group Communications based at Dorval, near Montreal. For his service Churchill personally awarded Vanderkloot the Commander of the Order of the British Empire. Post-war, Vanderkloot headed the aviation branch of the Johns Manville Corporation, New York, piloting executive jets and helicopters until he retired in 1970.

The aircraft was well maintained and proved extremely reliable, and it had been flown from Montreal to Sydney on 5 November 1944 by Air Commodore C.J. Powell, (RAF Senior Air Staff Officer) RAF Transport Command. On 26 March 1945, flown by Wing

Commander William Biddell, the aircraft took off from RAF Northolt, London, at 2300 to fly to Ottawa, Canada, with a refueling stop at Lajes Field in the Azores. On board were various notables including the Under-Secretary of State for Air Rupert Brabner, his deputy Sir John Abraham, and the Air Member for Training, Air Marshal Sir Peter Roy Maxwell Drummond, to attend a ceremony marking the closure of the British Commonwealth Air Training Plan. The aircraft failed to arrive at Lagens and no sign of it was ever found.

Churchill's LB-30 *Commando*

The most famous Liberator II was *Commando* (AL504), which served as Prime Minister Winston Churchill's personal transport. (*RAF*)

Commando crew (L-R): Radio officer Russell Holmes; co-pilot Capt. John Ruggles; pilot Capt. William Vanderkloot; flight engineer Ronald Williams, and flight engineer John Affleck. (*RAF*)

The Prime Minister poses with his signature cigar from *Commando*'s cockpit at the time of the Casablanca Conference, January 1943. *Commando*'s nose displays a Turkish flag, denoting Churchill's participation in the Cairo (Sextant) Conference in November 1943, and a Soviet Hammer and Sickle emblem denoting the second Moscow Conference in August 1942. (*RAF*)

Staff seating. (*CAC/NMUSAF*)

Churchill's private corner. (*CAC/NMUSAF*)

Churchill in RAF uniform, accompanied by Air Chief Marshal Sir Charles Portal, Chief of the Air Staff, leaving *Commando* at RAF Lyneham, Wiltshire, on their return from the Casablanca Conference. (*NA*)

W. Averell Harriman representing President Roosevelt (center), with Winston Churchill, and Vyacheslav Molotov departing *Commando* in Moscow, August 1942, on their way to meet Stalin to participate in a series of conversations concerning the future conduct of the war. (*NA*)

Refurbished *Commando* at Northolt, Middlesex, on returning to the UK, following extensive modification and a complete overhaul by Consolidated at San Diego. The fuselage was extended by 7ft, and equipped with a RY-3 Navy single tail fin, and upgraded engines. (*CAC/AAF*)

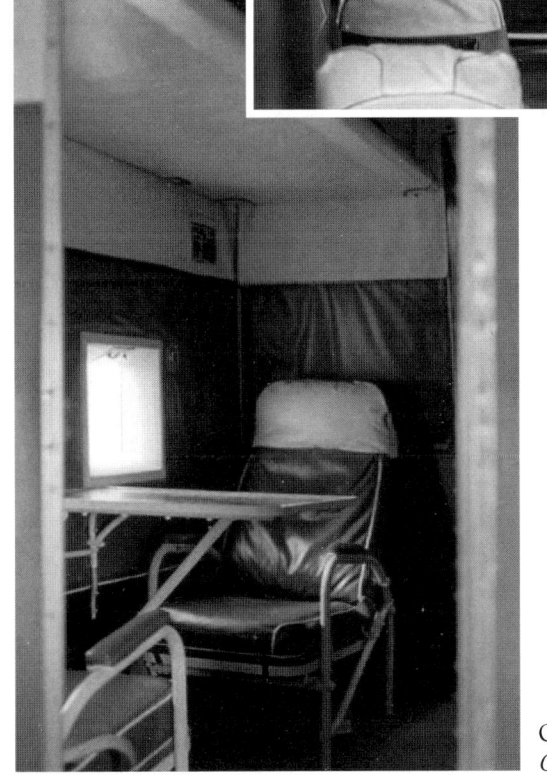

The main cabin interior was furnished to accommodate 20 passengers with bunks and a steward's galley. This view shows the main cabin with the bunks stowed. (*CAC/NMUSAF*)

Conference/desk area at the rear of *Commando*. (*CAC/NMUSAAF*)

US Ferrying Command and Air Transport Command Liberator Use

On 14 December 1941 a meeting was convened to include the US Army Air Corps' fledgling Ferrying Command; the Navy's Air Transport Service (NATS) established only two days earlier; Office of Production Management (OPM), Civil Aeronautics Board (CAB), and the Air Transport Association (ATA), which represented the airlines; Pan American and Transcontinental & Western Airways. In case of an expansion of the newly declared war with Japan, it was realized that distant parts of the world (China, the Philippines, and Australia) would be cut off from men and supplies from both the UK and America, as had been Russia and England by the Nazis. The members attending the meeting considered America's meager four-engine air transport resources: 11 crudely converted Ferrying Command B-24A bombers, a Boeing Clipper that the War Department had purchased from Pan Am – which could be supplemented by eight more and two Martin Flying Boats owned by Pan Am, and five TWA Boeing Stratoliners. America's domestic airlines were equipped exclusively with intermediate and short-range aircraft, mainly Douglas DC-3s and Lockheed Lodestars.

From 1926 until 1942, the Air Corps' logistical duties were assigned to the Office of the Chief of the Air Corps Materiel Division, headquartered at Wright Field, Ohio, and with four major depots distributed over the United States. During the early 1930s, the AAC began investigating the systematic use of air transport for the distribution of aviation supplies. In 1932 the Materiel Division established a provisional 1st Air Transport Group with four transport squadrons, each equipped with Bellanca Aircruisers and Douglas DC-2s, assigned to one of the four major air depots to transport supplies and spare parts from one depot to another. The group was redesignated the 10th Transport Group in 1937, under the control of the GHQ Headquarters. During the late 1930s the AAC found that it did not have sufficient transport aircraft to support its growing operations, with the GHQ Air Force's 10th Transport Group remaining as the only dedicated AAC airlift unit at that time.

During May 1938, GHQ Air Force conducted maneuvers in the north-eastern United States, during which the First Wing moved 42 aircraft and 945 men from stations in California to different fields in New England using 16 converted bombers as transports. Although this deployment of forces was impressive for its time, it would be totally insufficient for the impending global war.

Once war broke out in Europe in September 1939, the Allied combatants found they needed American aircraft to supplement their air forces and initially British or contracted American pilots were engaged to ferry these to Britain. Overwater delivery of American-built aircraft to England began in November 1940, when a Canadian company began transatlantic deliveries of aircraft that had been flown to Montreal by factory-employed delivery pilots. In March 1941, Congress passed the Lend-Lease Act, in which America affirmed its intention to provide military equipment to the 'unnamed countries' (but unabashedly the British) that were already engaged in war against the Axis nations. However, the increase in Lend-Lease Act aircraft deliveries would cause a shortage of factory pilots, and to contend with the problem the Army Air Corps established its Ferrying Command (ACFC) under the command of Brig. Gen. Robert Olds, the former commander of the 2nd Bombardment Group. On 29 May 1941, Northeast Airlines was contracted to provide pilots to make the domestic deliveries of Lend-Lease aircraft from American factories to US east coast or Canadian embarkation points, from where British pilots flew them to across the North Atlantic to England. After Pearl Harbor the ACFC also contracted Pan American Airways to provide pilots to ferry aircraft to British forces in the Middle East via South America and Africa. The ACFC afforded Army pilots experience flying the latest combat equipment and freed civilian factory pilots to join the British organization responsible for transatlantic deliveries from North America to England.

Brig. Gen. Robert Olds was appointed as the first commander of the Ferrying Command. (*AAF*)

Meanwhile, because for several months of the year, winter weather prohibited flights over the North Atlantic, the Ferrying Command looked to establish new routes from the US. A South Atlantic route was surveyed and established; originating in Miami and then routing over the Caribbean to British Guyana and Brazil, then over the Atlantic to Ascension Island, on to the west coast of Africa, then crossing the African continent to Cairo. The Ferrying Command also inaugurated a flying boat service to West Africa using Pan Am aircraft that had been withdrawn from Pacific service. In addition to the Pan American ferry service, the War Department also established a military-operated transport service to Cairo, again using converted B-24s.

Before Pearl Harbor, the USAAC had ordered the conversion of most of its initial order of B-24As to fill the transport role and had used them to open the first overseas routes. On 1 July 1941, famed AAC test pilot (Boeing XB-15/B-17), Lt Col Caleb Haynes, co-pilot Capt. James Rothrock, navigator 1Lt John Montgomery, and five other passengers were assigned to fly one of the first B-24A bombers that Consolidated delivered to the Army on a secret flight to test a North Atlantic air route to Great Britain. The transformed B-24A had been 'converted' to ferry status by removing armament (except the tail gun) and laying down a plywood floor and installing basic seating in the bomb bay. During the flight the crew was extremely uncomfortable due to the bitter cold and ineffective heaters that often became inoperative. Because the Liberator rear fuselage was notorious for harboring inflammable gasoline fumes, smoking was only allowed one at a time on the flight, which probably became a chimney. Haynes took off from Bolling Field, Washington DC, and refueled at Montreal and then again at Gander

Lake, Newfoundland, before arriving at Prestwick, Scotland, delivering the B-24 on its first transatlantic flight. Prestwick, just outside Glasgow, had been chosen as the terminus because of its 'relatively' good weather but on arrival Haynes was forced to circle the field for 2½ hours and then make an almost blind landing. On the return flight the scheduled refueling stop at Newfoundland had to be bypassed due to bad weather. The crew were awarded DFCs for the classified flight in a secret ceremony.

The new service, soon labeled 'the Arnold Line', was flown by 22 converted B-24s with the passengers seated in the bomb bays for the next three and a half months, until winter weather over the North Atlantic halted the flights in October. These flights were not without incident as on the second one a Liberator was intercepted by a roving Luftwaffe Dornier, which was driven off by the tail gunner. On another flight Liberator pilot 1Lt William Vickers descended through thick overcast, only to find himself over an Allied convoy that immediately opened fire on his aircraft.

Soon, Haynes was assigned the task of scouting and establishing another air route that was to cross the southern Atlantic from the US during the winter months when bad weather precluded flights across the North Atlantic. On 31 August 1941, with Maj. Curtis LeMay as his co-pilot and Chief of the Air Corps Maj. Gen. George Brett as a passenger, Haynes took off from Bolling Field to begin the first 26,000-mile round trip to Egypt and then beyond, carrying Brett to Basra, Iraq. The flight was a secret mission to investigate possible Lend-Lease air routes to Russia. On 7 October, Haynes and LeMay retraced their flight to land back in the US, proving the southern route to be satisfactory. Ther UK then agreed to purchase 16 LB-30s to be delivered via this route to Cairo, with four completing the trip before the remainder were redirected into American service (another was damaged beyond repair in a crash). Hayne's flights in 1941 gave

Before Pearl Harbor, the AAC ordered the conversion of most of its initial order of B-24As to fill the transport role and used them to open the first overseas routes. The US flag was applied to demonstrate US pre-Pearl Harbor neutrality. (*AAC*)

Maj. Curtis LeMay (L) and Lt Col Caleb Haynes (2L) map their August 1941 26,000-mile round trip to Egypt and then beyond to Basra, Iraq, on a special mission to investigate possible Lend-Lease air routes to Russia. (*AAC*)

America an advantage in developing viable air routes for its military forces that began in 1942, when these routes were adapted for year-round movement of aircraft, units, supplies and materials to the combat theaters.

The Record B-24 Post-Harriman Russia Mission Flights

During September 1941, W. Averell Harriman, Roosevelt's special envoy to Europe, was to arrive in Moscow with an Anglo-American Commission to discuss Lend-Lease. While Harriman was going to cross the Atlantic by ship and then continue to Russia, it was decided to fly some of the participants there and thus also to have an American aircraft available while the Commission was in Russia. Two modified passenger-carrying Ferrying Command B-24s, carrying the Ferrying Command US/British markings of an RAF roundel and a large US flag on the forward fuselage, were piloted by Maj. Alva Harvey (B-24 40-2373) and 1Lt Louis Reichers (B-24 40-2374). On President Roosevelt's 'Special War Supply Mission', Harvey's crew was made up of Air Corps personnel including Lt Montgomery (co-pilot), Lt Hutchins (navigator), Sgts Green and Moran (mechanics), and Sgt Drew (radio operator).

Previously, during April 1924, a young Sgt Alva Harvey was the mechanic on the *Seattle*, one of four Douglas World Cruisers of the US Army Air Service under the command of Maj. Frederick Martin (the *Seattle* pilot), which departed from Sand Point Airfield near Seattle, Washington, flying westward to circumnavigate the globe. However, the *Seattle* crashed into an Alaskan mountain, with Harvey and Martin surviving more than a week, plodding in freezing temperatures before finding a fish cannery settlement. Three World Cruisers returned to Sand Point on 28 September 1924 to become the first aircraft to fly round the world.

Reichers' and Harvey's orders were to fly the now established, routine itinerary across the North Atlantic from Washington DC to Prestwick, Scotland, arriving there on 15 September 1941, and then to wait there to be issued special mission orders, which were to fly to Moscow. Soviet Ambassador Constantin Oumansky, returning from the US, was to be one of the passengers and was to act as liaison with the Russian authorities. US representative to Moscow W. Averell Harriman flew to Moscow with Churchill in his B-24 *Commando*. The route for the secret mission to Moscow was selected carefully: it was decided that the two Liberators would fly north around Norway to Archangel and then south to Moscow, rather than flying directly over German-held territory. The chance of Luftwaffe interception, even on a high-altitude, night flight was only one consideration in this decision as equally important was that the Russians could not guarantee that any aircraft heading in from enemy Germany would not be attacked by their notoriously trigger-happy AA gunners and interceptors, who were not known for

Maj. Alva Harvey piloted one of the two B-24s on a 3,150-mile non-stop flight from the US to Moscow on the Harriman mission and then continued on another record-setting flight, flying 27,238 miles around the world in 117 hours of actual flying time covering 37 days. (*AAC*)

1Lt Louis Reichers flew the second B-24 to Moscow and returned to the US via Iran, across Africa, the South Atlantic to Brazil and on north to Bolling Field, Washington. (*AAC*)

Reichers' B-24D (40-2374) Number 74 during the return flight from Moscow. (*AAC*)

their aircraft identification expertise. Harvey took off from Prestwick on 23 September at 2120, with Reichers following ten minutes later. Near the Shetland Islands they were intercepted by patrolling British aircraft but were recognized after they fired the colors of the day. They continued their flight in the cold, dark night, remaining 200 miles off the coast of Norway and then crossing the Barents Sea far north of the Arctic Circle. They arrived over Archangel in daylight but as it was overcast and there was snow and sleet in the area, they decided fly on non-stop to Moscow. Nearing Moscow, although the Liberator's radios were functioning the pilots were unable to raise any response from any Russian station. Harvey chose an airfield and landed, without any directives or apparent recognition of his presence. However, once on the ground, Russian officers came to meet him and shortly he and his crew were feted with the preordained Russian welcome of caviar and unrestrained vodka toasts. Reichers likewise chose a landing field and was greeted in the same manner. The two Liberator pilots had successfully completed non-stop flights of 3,150 miles under trying and even dangerous circumstances: their accomplishment ranking among the great, though unacknowledged, long-distance flights of history.

Reichers' Return Flight

Reichers remained in Moscow for 11 days and Harvey for another week while they were entertained but kept under strict constant surveillance while their aircraft were examined thoroughly. Brig. Gen. Robert Olds had foreseen the opportunity that these Moscow flights presented for further long-range flight investigation. When the Harriman mission was completed, Reichers left on 2 September, on an equally noteworthy part of his continued journey back to the US; setting his initial course to Baku (Azerbaijan) on the Caspian Sea and then to Habbaniyah, Iraq. The only glitch on the route was an encounter with the Caucasus Mountains, which were substantially higher than his map data indicated. From Iraq he flew on to Cairo, and then south, exploring the area over which Pan American Airways established a new route.

In June 1941, Pan American had organized a special department to make deliveries of British-purchased Douglas DC-3 transports to Africa. Flown by Pan American Airways crews, the first transports left Florida for Africa on 21 June. At the time it was determined that Pan American, as well as other US airlines, would play a major role in the Ferrying Command and the subsequent Air Transport Command for the duration. Under an agreement reached with the War Department and the British, Pan Am assumed responsibility for establishing ferry and transport routes to Africa, and also for operating a trans-African transport route that had been previously established by the British. Speedy aircraft delivery from the US to British combat units in Africa was the primary purpose of the new service, with air transport of cargo and personnel secondary. As it transpired, Pan Am would only deliver a dozen aircraft, all transports, prior to Pearl Harbor.

Reichers' flight had continued satisfactorily until he arrived at El Fasher on the edge of the Sudan during the Ramadan holiday, during which the Mohammedan radio operators had celebrated the night before and were sleeping during its fast day and were unavailable. Reichers landed successfully on the strange field and searched for 2,500 gallons of fuel, which was stored in 4-gallon tins, which had previously required over a month for 100 camels working steadily between El Fasher and Khartoum to deliver. After their arrival the tins were scattered widely and buried for safety in case of attack. Five hundred tins were unearthed, and each lifted on to the Liberator's wing and their fuel poured into the tanks individually. Once refueled, Reichers stopped at Takoradi on the African Atlantic coast, and found that no weather information was available for his long and arduous flight across the Atlantic to Natal, Brazil. Being advised that the weather was 'generally good at that time of year', on that basis he took off to cross the Atlantic for Brazil. When he reached the Brazilian mainland at Natal, he found one runway under repair and that using the other one would involve landing in a high crosswind, so, instead, he flew on to Fortaleza, where he landed on a rough field. His next stop was Belém and the established Pan American facility there. After that he continued uneventfully to Washington DC, gathering invaluable information about the little-known, but soon to be important, areas he had just flown over.

Harvey's Return Flight

Maj. Harvey's return flight was even more notable than Reichers', as Brig. Gen. Olds, acting on his own initiative, had ordered Harvey to continue around the world via India, wanting him to investigate the air routes in that easterly direction. Harvey's route took him from Habbaniyah to Karachi at the western edge of India, and then to Calcutta, where he found that the runway at Dum Dum Airfield near Calcutta was only 2,400ft long, supposedly an impossible length for landing a B-24. Using great skill, he made his landing but then, on taxiing, found that the wheels of his heavy aircraft were sinking into the soft taxiway surface. Harvey noticed the concrete compass rose compass-testing area and parked on it. The next day Harvey departed for Rangoon, then continued to

Singapore; Darwin, Australia; Port Moresby, Papua New Guinea; Wake Island, Hickam Field near Honolulu, and March Field, California, and finished by returning to Bolling Field, Washington DC, via Fort Worth, Texas, for another record-setting flight flying 27,238 miles in 117 hours of actual flying time covering 37 days.

Itinerary for the Harvey's Round-the-World Flight

Departed from Washington DC (13 September 1941)
Montreal, Canada
Newfoundland, Canada
Prestwick, Scotland (over northern tip of Norway and Finland)
Moscow, Soviet Union
Habbaniyah, Iraq
Karachi, Pakistan
Calcutta, India
Rangoon, Burma
Singapore
Port Darwin, Australia
Port Moresby, Papua New Guinea
Wake Island
Honolulu, Hawaii
March Field, California
Fort Worth, Texas
Arrived at Washington DC (30 October 1941)

Haynes' explorations and Reichers' epic flight were followed by regular Ferrying Command services across the North Atlantic from 14 November and this continued until the outbreak of war, when the Command was operating 11 converted B-24s that had been loaned by the Army Air Corps Combat Command. After the Pearl Harbor attack, flight schedules were no longer regular and were down to urgent need.

Meanwhile, after 22 round trips had been flown in three and a half months, or about one every five days, operations over the North Atlantic had to be suspended on 18 October, as winter weather made the crossing virtually impossible owing to the then undeveloped state of the route. By that time the ACFC was making some progress in securing the communications, weather reports, and other aids, as well as the construction of bases across the North Atlantic, which would eventually make year-round crossing routine.

Project X: First Heavy Bomber Ferrying

Project X, the movement of heavy bombers to the Far East, became the first major foreign ferrying mission of the war and the first overseas movement of tactical units in which the Ferrying Command had taken a part. Not until the air echelon of the Eighth Air Force began its movement to Britain in June 1942 would the Army Air Forces commence an overseas ferrying operation of greater size and complexity. Although 80 four-engine bombers were originally earmarked for the project, fewer left the US and even fewer arrived in the Far East. Original orders directed all flights to proceed first to MacDill Field near Tampa, Florida, for final staging prior to take-off but a few bombers were diverted to Hamilton Field, California, and were dispatched over the new South Pacific route, which was opened on a small scale after mid-January 1942.

Project X comprised two separate echelons of heavy bombers. The first of these ordered to the MacDill Field on 6 December for staging was made up of 15 LB-30s repossessed from the British and manned by crews of the 7th Bombardment Group. Only six of these Liberators under the command of Maj. Austin Straubel actually staged through MacDill Field, the others being ultimately diverted to the Pacific route. Travel orders were issued on 19 December 1941, and within a few days aircraft and crews began to arrive at Tampa to prepare for the long overseas flight. The second and more important contingent was made up of a projected 65 B-17 bombers, most of which were in the process of manufacture and were to move to the Sacramento Air Depot in small groups as they became available. However, orders were issued on 23 December for the transfer of the 65 Fortresses to the Philippines along with the LB-30s along the route Tampa/MacDill–Trinidad–Belem–Natal–Accra–Khartoum–Cairo–Habbaniyah–Karachi. At Karachi the Straubel's LB-30s were to be transferred to the US Army Forces in the Far East.

Ferrying Command was assigned specified responsibilities for the final processing for the staging of the Third Air Force heavy bombers and crews at MacDill Field. During late December 1941 Ferry Command sent long-distance flight veteran 1Lt Louis Reichers, who had just completed his record post-Harriman Moscow Conference flight, and another officer to MacDill Field to assist in loading the LB-30s for their long-distance overseas flight in accordance with established weight and balance specifications. Reichers found that the LB-30s being processed were overloaded with all types of miscellaneous and excess equipment and removed an average of more than 3,000lb from each Liberator. He then arranged to ship much of this excess via the Pan American Transport Service. All aircraft were pared down to just below the absolute maximum weight allowed for safe flying. The LB-30 crews were inexperienced and untrained in long-distance flight and Reichers was the natural choice to establish a training school at MacDill assisted by specialists in the various crew positions, all of whom had had transatlantic flying experience with the B-24 shuttle services to Great Britain and Cairo.

The training and briefing of the crews and preparing the aircraft for their overseas journey was only the first phase in the complex task of moving *Project X* to the Far East. Control officers, often new and inexperienced, were to be stationed along the route to provide the logistics for the project. The most difficult part of the project were shortages of fuel and oil, primitive refueling and maintenance facilities, and an inadequate weather and communications network. The problem of providing a sufficient supply of gas and oil at refueling points was overwhelming, as an estimated 500,000 to 1,000,000 gallons of 100 octane gasoline with proportionate amounts of lubricating oil were required at each of a dozen control points. Nearly all the gasoline had to be shipped and stored in bulk, which required that the shipment of material for bulk tank construction precede that of the gasoline itself. The speed with which the *Project X* movement was being undertaken made it impossible for the Ferrying Command to accumulate an adequate supply of spare parts at intermediate bases, which would become the single issue most responsible than any other for the numerous delays en route. Except for the few spares carried by each LB-30 and some Liberator parts stocked by the RAF at Cairo, all spare parts had to be shipped from the US. Selective cannibalization enabled some of the grounded Liberators to continue on their way but those that had been raided of a part and those suffering major damage had to wait for replacements to be transported by air, when possible, or by water. The small amount of air cargo space available at the time, the priority given to high-ranking military personnel traveling by air, and the almost total lack of transport aircraft capable of carrying complete engine assemblies made the movement of supplies by air very difficult. Some spares were shipped to West Africa by sea and then distributed to intermediate bases in Africa and India by Pan American aircraft. The shortage of maintenance crews at most points forced the combat crews to do their own maintenance after long and fatiguing flights or this was carried out by local Pan American maintenance crews, if available. In February Ferrying Command sent trouble-shooting crews along the route to make special or major repairs that were beyond the capabilities of the Liberator or Pan American crews.

Meanwhile, in early January 1942 three B-17s of *Project X* left Hickam Field, Hawaii, for Australia and finally arrived in company with another B-17 at Malang, Java, on 14 January, three hours ahead of LB-30 AL576, each completing their portion of a halfway around the world flight. This Pacific portion of *Project X* would later be flown by the first Australian Catalina ferry crews, followed later by the transports of Consairway, the USAAF Ferrying and Transport Commands, RAF Transport Command, and USAAF and RAAF Liberator ferry crews.

The staging of *Project X* aircraft and crews at MacDill Field had extended over a period of about two months. During that time some 58 heavy bombers of the projected 80 departed for the Far East over the south-eastern route, while eight flew out over the South Pacific route. Despite many problems and delays along the route, by late February, 44 of the 66 bombers were delivered to the Southwest Pacific Area over both routes. Others were diverted to the Tenth Air Force in India after the route from India to Australia was closed; some had served as a source of spare parts to help the others get through. Seven of the B-17s never arrived in India and none of the bombers reached the Philippines, but most were employed in Australia or on other fronts. *Project X* was considered a success when allowing for its pioneering character, the inexperienced and poorly trained crews, and the necessity of building a complete ferrying organization through the South Atlantic and across Africa and India even while the aircraft movement was in progress. By assuming most of the responsibility for *Project X*, the Ferrying Command acquired considerable valuable experience that would prove useful as its ferrying duties increased as the war in Europe and in the Pacific intensified.

Project X, the ferrying of heavy bombers to the Far East, became the first major foreign ferrying mission of the war and the first overseas movement of tactical units in which the Ferrying Command had a part. A rare photo of a LB-30 being refueled at primitive African base. (*AAC*)

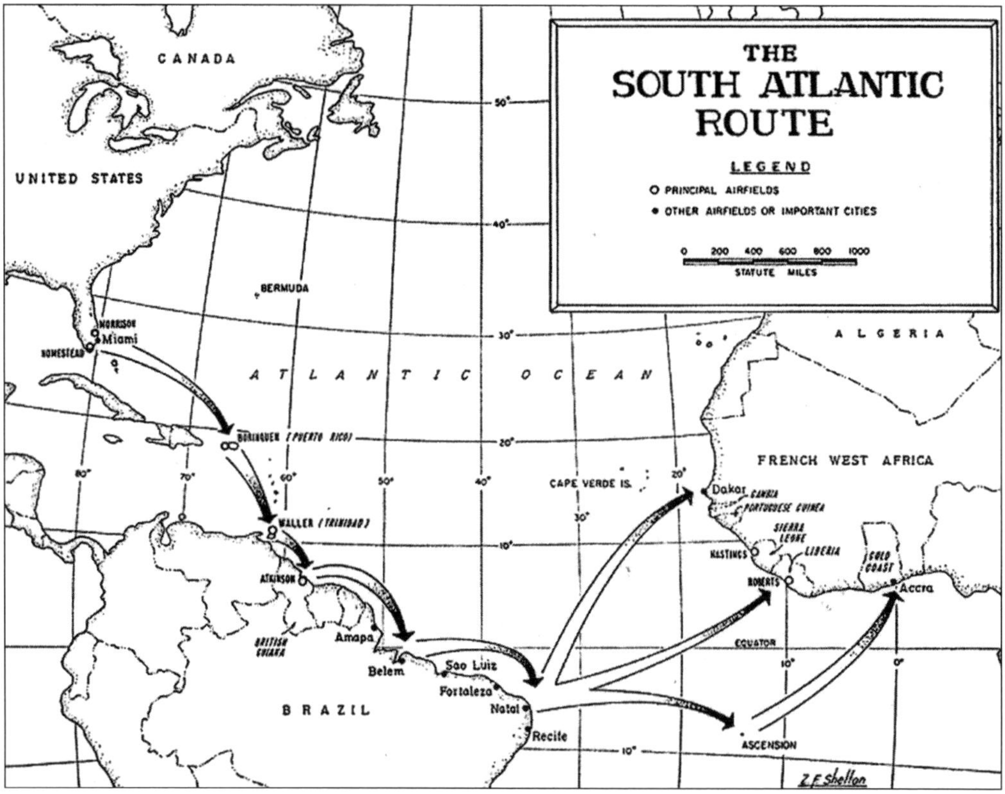

Formation of the Air Transport Command (ATC)

After Pearl Harbor, a narrow perception continued concerning the role of long-range air transportation in the new intercontinental war. No one had anticipated the huge network of long-range transport routes supporting the daily movement of hundreds of tons of supplies and thousands of passengers that would extend across continents and that daily flights to such remote areas as the Alaska, Australia, the Philippines, India, and China would become commonplace. Fearing the fragmentation of the airline industry due to competing contracts from the innumerable military agencies, L.W. 'Larry' Pogue, Chairman of the Safety Agency for Civil Aviation of the Civil Aeronautics Board, wrote to President Roosevelt advocating the establishment of an independent air transportation organization separate from both the Army and the Navy. Pogue advocated an independent government airline that would function outside both the War and Navy Departments. A second option of the 'Pogue Plan' was the establishment of a War Department command to assume responsibility for all the Army's air transportation requirements. Arnold believed that at the minimum all Army air transportation should be unified under one command and presented the question to a board of officers. On 20 June 1942, before the board could make an official report, Arnold, not surprisingly, chose the second Pogue option, which was issued as General Order #8, and would restructure the Ferrying Command into the Air Transport Command (ATC). The ATC was to be a new organization responsible for all aircraft ferrying and for all air transportation of the War Department 'except those served by the Troop Carrier Command', which had been established by the same order. The duties of the Ferrying Command were assumed by the new ferrying division of the Air Transport Command. The Navy had formed its own air transport command, Naval Air Transport Service (NATS), on 12 December 1941.

The new ATC was established as a military airline, and, in fact, drew very heavily upon the airlines for personnel, both aircrews and administrative. The ATC commander was Brig. Gen. Harold George, a veteran military officer who had been known as an expert in bombardment rather than air transport, while his Executive Officer and Chief of Staff was Col Cyrus Smith, who in civilian life was President of American Airlines and would be largely responsible for the development of the new military airline. The Air Transportation Division was commanded by Col Robert Smith, who was Vice President of Braniff Airlines, and he was joined by dozens of other airline personnel who had served in executive positions throughout the new Air Transport Command.

Finding pilots for the expanding Air Transport Command was even more difficult than finding aircraft. Prior to the war, the Ferrying Command had utilized combat pilots on loan from the Air Force Combat Command. These pilots served 30-to-90-day periods to gain experience flying the combat planes being delivered to the British, a policy that could not continue. The outbreak of war led to a recall of these experienced pilots to their

L.W. 'Larry' Pogue, Chairman of the Safety Agency for Civil Aviation of the Civil Aeronautics Board, advocated the establishment of an independent air transportation organization separate from both the Army and the Navy. (*NA*)

Col Cyrus Smith, George's ATC Executive Officer, who previously in civilian life was the President of American Airlines. (*AAC*)

On 20 June 1942 Gen. Hap Arnold ordered that the Ferrying Command be formed into the Air Transport Command (ATC), a new organization responsible for all aircraft ferrying and for all air transportation of the War Department. (*AAC*)

parent units as their squadrons prepared for combat operations overseas.

With America's entry into the war, the need for air transportation increased dramatically and the return of Ferrying Command personnel to the US after overseas deliveries was a major consideration. To begin, the Command set up scheduled routes between the US and Australia using five LB-30 Liberators that had been converted into transports. The airline was operated under contract with crews provided by Consolidated Aircraft, which had previously established a ferry route for deliveries of twin-engine bombers to the Dutch in the East Indies. Also, three of Ferrying Command's converted B-24s were taken off the Cairo run and sent to the Southwest Pacific, where they were assigned to the Allied Air Transport Command

Brig. Gen. Harold George, first ATC Commander. (*AAC*)

in Australia and used to transport ammunition to the Philippines and move personnel throughout Asia. All three were lost within a few months, two to enemy action and one to a forced landing in the sea.

Effective 1 July 1942, the mission of the ATC was to ferry new aircraft from the factories to commands located worldwide; and provide global air transport for personnel, materiel, and mail (except for those agencies served by Troop Carrier Command). The ATC operated over fixed routes spanning 35,000 miles within the Zone of the Interior (ZI/Continental US) and over 95,000 miles overseas. The organization had more than 200 bases under its command along with worldwide communications and weather facilities. The ATC was divided into wings (later divisions) serving specific geographic areas. These wings were designated the 23rd through the 27th; however, on 5 July 1942 it was decided to name the wings by geographical area to preclude typographical errors from causing vital cargo to be misrouted.

Wings	Activated
India-China	1 December 1942
European	14 January 1943
North Atlantic	12 July 1943
South Atlantic	12 July 1943
Pacific	12 July 1943
African-Middle East	12 July 1943
Caribbean	12 July 1943
North African	13 December 1943

Liberators and Ferrying the South Pacific Route

The situation in the Pacific became dire for the Allies by early 1942 with the Japanese advancing rapidly south toward the rich oil resources of the Dutch East Indies and then with the intention of expanding into the South Pacific. America urgently needed to send heavy bombers and transport aircraft to the East Indies and the Philippines. A secure route was needed from Hawaii through the South Pacific to Australia as the air route across the Atlantic, Africa, and Asia was too long and would result in significant attrition.

During late 1941, an accelerated program was begun to prepare adequate airfields and place defensive air squadrons on Christmas Island, Palmyra Atoll, Canton Island, Fiji (Nandi), and New Caledonia (La Tontouta) for landplane routes. The route would mostly parallel Pan American Airways' pre-war Foreign Air Mail-19 (FAM-19) seaplane route, awarded to Pan Am on 12 July 1940 and first flown by J.H. Tilton in a Boeing 314 from San Francisco across the Pacific via Hawaii to New Zealand, and later from Los Angeles to Australia.

The first four-engine B-17 bombers bound for Java flew the Hickam Field Oahu, Hawaii, to Sydney route during the first two weeks of 1942, detouring to the Naval Air Station on Palmyra because the Christmas Island Airfield was nearly ready. However, even after Ferrying Command developed and was renamed Air Transport Command, undertakings in the SWPA never attained the size and scope as they were in other theatres. At the time air bases were controlled by the 7AF outside Hawaii and by the 5AF in Australia, which flew much of their transport. The Directorate of Air Transport managed and controlled SWPA air transport and assumed that it could have the same control on ATC cargoes and priorities as it had over 5AF units and opposed any expansion of ATC services beyond the main San Francisco–Amberley, Australia, route which was operated almost wholly through the contracted civil airlines. Moreover, the ATC's substantial obligations in other theatres depleted it of aircraft or personnel for the Pacific duty.

In February 1943 ATC began a service from Espiritu Santo to Auckland, New Zealand, and in March 1943, a comprehensive plan was proposed, recommending the use of C-87 or C-54 transports. During July a route from Port Moresby, New Guinea, to Sydney for troop furloughs was established but it was not until the end of 1943 that the ATC began to actively engage in expansion in the Pacific. By 31 December 1943 this had been refined to a C-87 or C-54 route from Bangalore, India, to Amberley via two refueling points, Sigiriya, Ceylon, and Corunna Downs, Western Australia. By February 1944 C-54As and their selected crews of the Southwest Pacific Wing of the Pacific Division were established at Nadzab, New Guinea; with its regular flights beginning on 23 June 1944 operated by C-54 Skymasters and Liberator use no longer required in the SWPA.

B-24As in the Pacific

During June–July 1941 and immediately after manufacturing the Liberator I (LB-30B), Consolidated produced nine B-24As (40-2369/2377) for the AAF that were substantially the equivalent of the RAF Liberator Is with the short nose. Most were assigned to transport duties and five (40-2369, 40-2370, 40-2373, 40-2374 and 40-2376) assigned to the 7BG/11BS operated in the Australia/Pacific area during 1941–42, painted in neutrality markings with a large US flag on both sides of the nose and the last two numbers of their serial painted on each side of the vertical fin. At least three 40-2370, 40-2373, and 40-2376 had joined the LB-30s on the African route before the Pacific War but were then taken off the Washington–Cairo route and were flown to Australia to supply ammunition to MacArthur in the Philippines. Two, 40-2375 and -2376, were in Cairo on 7 December 1941 with 40-2375 transporting Gen. George Brett on a flight to India, China, Singapore, and then to Java and Australia. Aircraft 40-2376 remained in Cairo until 22 December and then was ordered to Java, while 40-2370 left Bolling Field, Washington DC, on 20 December and arrived at Darwin, Australia, on 7 January to join the Philippines/Java transport service. The quantity of ammunition transported to the Philippines did not reach predicted goals, but significant quantities of essential supplies were flown from Darwin to MacArthur's forces.

The fate of three of the five B-24As was finalized on 3 March 1942 at Broome Airfield, Australia. On that day an overloaded 40-2374 took off during a Japanese air

40-2369 was one of two surviving members of nine B-24As to fly supply and rescue missions from the Philippines and Java. (*AAC*)

raid and was shot down, killing the two pilots and 19 passengers aboard. Meanwhile, on the same day 40-2373 had also landed at Broome to deliver medical supplies and doctors to treat the wounded from the Japanese air raid earlier in the day. Then loaded with evacuees, this bomber also took off fully loaded with evacuees to escape the Japanese attack but ran off the runway damaging its landing gear but without injury to anyone aboard. Although it could have been repaired, orders were issued to destroy the bomber, fearing an eminent Japanese landing. Interestingly, both aircraft were flown on the Harriman Russia mission: 40-2373 by Maj. Alva Harvey and 40-23741 by Lt Louis Reichers. Aircraft 40-2370, *Arabian Knight*, was parked at Broome Airfield fully fueled during the Japanese air raid and was strafed and set on fire. Soon afterwards it exploded and was destroyed on the runway.

Aircraft 40-2376 flew a number of supply and rescue flights during the Allied evacuation from the Philippines and Java. On 4 May 1942, the B-24, named *Old Bag of Bolts*, arrived over Mindanao. As the bomber flew toward the field the weather deteriorated until the crew encountered a violent tropical storm and ran out of fuel, successfully ditching off Yu Island. The crew was rescued by the submarine USS *Porpoise* (SS-172) and were returned to Darwin. Aircraft 40-2369 and 40-2375 survived the early dangerous duty while the Japanese were overrunning the Pacific to later serve with Consairway and they survived the war.

Consairway

During late 1941, Consolidated needed to return its own crews back to the US from Pacific bases as the company employed 55 pilots and crewmen to deliver AAF Catalinas from its San Diego factory across the Central Pacific (Hawaii–Midway–Wake–Port Moresby–Darwin–Manila) for delivery to the AAF in the Philippines. After delivering their aircraft these crews returned via a sea voyage, requiring as much as six weeks. In

November 1941, more than a dozen company crew became stranded in Honolulu, causing Consolidated pilot Richard McMakin to appropriate an RAF LB-30 (AL504) in San Diego, add some boards for seats in the bomb bay, and return with the crews in a 24-hour round trip. Several weeks later McMakin, flying the same LB-30, surveyed a route to Australia, returning in just over five days with 16 crewmen. McMakin would later become the manager of Consairway and led the way in acquiring aircraft, mostly from the British-contracted LBs that Consolidated reconditioned and modified for transport requirements. When a well-used LB-30 bomber was first received at the Consairway overhaul hangar, the outside oil stains and gunge needed to be removed with a cleaning solvent, with the engine cowlings in particular need of cleaning. All gasoline and oil was drained from the tanks and engines. The coat of camouflage paint was coated with paint stripper to blister and peel the paint, after which compressed air was used to blow away the flaking coating to expose the underlying bare aluminum natural finish. After an estimated 50 man-hours, 175lb of paint coating was removed and then the exposed aluminum was polished to improve, not only the aesthetics, but performance and diminish radio static interference. In early modifications wooden plank seats were installed in the bomb bays but later more comprehensive modifications produced a better but still austere 20-seat cabin.

On 16 April 1942 Consolidated received approval to form a company-operated separate subsidiary Air Division using its own aircraft (Liberator LB-30s, B-24Ds, and C-87s). The new company was named Consolidated Airways Corporation, which then became known as 'Consairway,' a contraction of Consolidated Airways, with Richard McMakin at its head. Consairway's Transport Division comprised of very experienced volunteer pilot/captains and air and ground crews. The new airline began its supplementary transport service on 23 April 1942 when an LB-30 (AL598) left Hamilton Field, California, for Williamtown, Australia. LB-30 AL598 returned to Hamilton Field, on 4 May 1942, after completing the 15,000-mile trip in 11 days. As the tempo of deliveries soon outstripped the supply of available military pilots, the AAC Ferry Command contracted with Consairway to supplement the ferrying service by returning ferrying pilots from the South Pacific using Consolidated LB-30s, with these returning pilots given first priority over mail, freight, and even most VIPs. During that May, the initial 15 trips carried 120 passengers, nearly a ton of mail, and almost 13 tons of freight.

By December 1942, Consairway was operating regularly scheduled trans-Pacific flights between Hamilton Field and Amberley, Queensland. Williamtown had been the Pacific terminus until December, when runway improvements at Amberley were completed and Air Transport Command Pacific Wing Station 3 was established. Thirteen weekly flights were being flown by Consairway when United Airlines began its Pacific operations. Until mid-October 1942, Consairway used the same aircraft and crew to fly from the US to Australia and return but from about mid-January 1943, one aircraft and crew flew south, and another flew the return service. The landing fields from Honolulu to Australia were Canton Island in the Phoenix Islands, Nandi (Nadi) on Viti Levu of the Fiji Island group, and Plaines des Gaiacs in New Caledonia. During the early operations these fields were crude and rough, with no landing lights, or weather forecasts.

Richard McMakin led the way as a pilot on Consolidated's initial Pacific routes in late 1941 and during April 1942. When Consolidated formed a company-operated separate subsidiary air division, Consairway, he became its manager. (*Consairway Flight Deck*)

Consairway LB-30 as depicted in a PR drawing. (*Consairway Flight Deck*)

During November 1943 Consairway operations and maintenance was transferred from San Diego to Fairfield-Suisun AAB (now Travis AFB) outside San Francisco. From February to April 1944, Consairway flew the triangular service connecting Guadalcanal and Townsville with Amberley. During August, the western terminus for the trans-Pacific flights moved to Nadzab, New Guinea; in November to Biak; and finally, to Guam in August 1945. The maintenance facilities at Amberley reduced the lay-over time to eight hours, which by the end of 1944 had aircraft averaging over 13 flying hours in each 24.

Consairway B-24A (40-2375), displaying the company logo on its fuselage, had flown in the Pacific during the very early war, transporting Gen. George Brett. (*Consairway Flight Deck*)

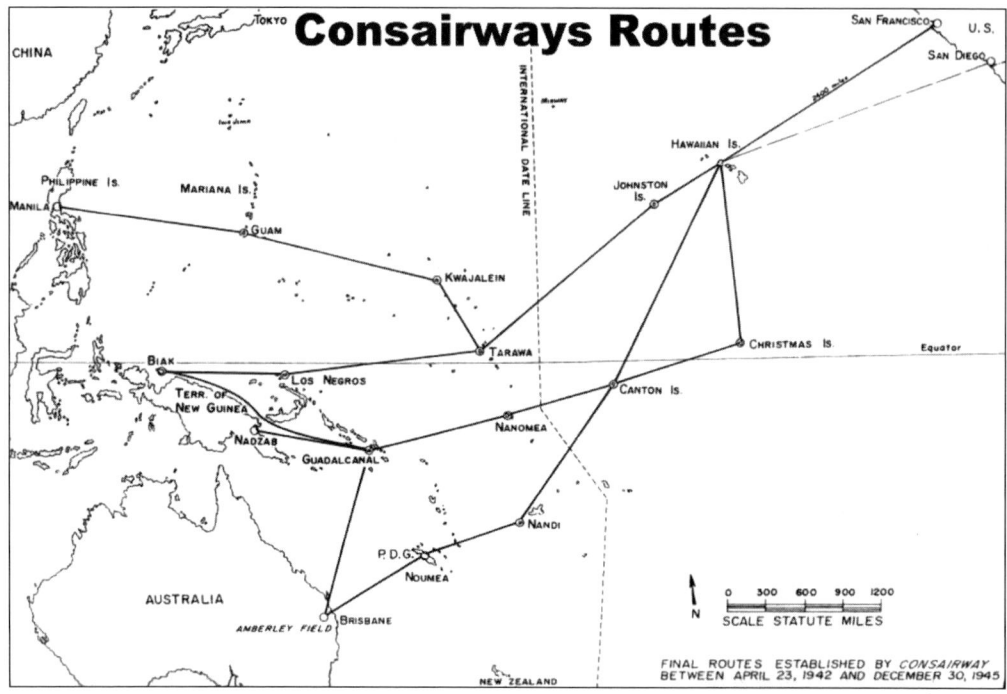

At its December 1945 zenith for its Pacific operations, Consairway inventoried a total 85 flight crews operating 26 aircraft: among them 14 RLB-30s, one B-24A (40-2369), two C-87s (41-24029 and 41-11706), along with a single C-47. During maximum operations, Consairway flew schedules averaging 16 hours out of every 24, which marked the maximum flight time accomplishment of any component of the Air Transport Command, contract carrier or military. Consairway employed more than 1,000 personnel at 16 different bases: San Diego, Hamilton, Fairfield, Hickam, Canton, Christmas, Johnston, Nandi, Plaines des Gaiacs, Amberley, Biak, Nadzab, Guadalcanal, Tarawa, Manila and Guam. Only three aircraft were lost: C-87 (41-11706), captained by Hugh Prince, crashed on Florida Island in June 1944, and LB-30 (AL640), piloted by Norman Fisher, ditched between Hawaii and the mainland after running out of fuel on 3 November 1945. B-24A (40-2372) caught fire and was destroyed in the Amberley hangar on 20 July 1943 during a 50-hour inspection. After the war, on 28 November 1945, Consairway was officially notified that the ATC was opposed to authorizing the airline to carry passengers in the Pacific, nor could they fly transcontinental passenger routes. The ATC terminated Consairway's contract on 1 January 1946 and the company airline concluded operations. After the war, a number of these LB-30s went into civil service with operators including Morrison-Knudsen Construction, which flew two LB-30s in Alaska.

Air Transport Command Pacific Routes

The AAC Ferry Command (AACFC) was combined with other AAF groups and re-designated as the Air Transport Command (ATC) on 20 June 1942. The newly created

ATC was assigned to ferry all aircraft worldwide, transport personnel, material, and mail for all War Department agencies (except troop carrier units), and control, operate, and maintain facilities on air routes outside of the US. It also carried civilian mail on a space-available basis. Although the ATC was to conduct all transport, the Navy continued operating its Naval Air Transport Service (NATS), which had been created just after Pearl Harbor. Conferences were held and an agreement was reached to coordinate Army and Navy services, but this did not occur in practice until mid-1944. The ATC began with five Pacific Wings, including the South Pacific Wing for operations from the west coast. The Alaskan Wing was added in October 1942. The South Pacific Wing divided into the Pacific and West Coast Wings in early 1943. The West Coast Wing's operations were limited to between the West Coast and Hawaii. The wings were recombined by the end of 1943 to better coordinate service. With the ATC continuation of AACFC South Pacific routes, transport and ferrying operations continued to accelerate, and the ATC needed to contract United Airlines to supplement the transport service. United flights from Hawaii to Australia began on 23 September 1942. Beginning 15 June 1943, the main route from Hickam to Australia was changed to Hickam–Canton–Plaines des Gaiacs (New Caledonia)–Amberley Field (Brisbane). Every fifth southbound flight flew the old Hickam–Christmas–Tutuila–Nandi route, bypassing Canton Island.

Consairway and United continued as operators with 14 trips scheduled each week between California and Australia using 15 Liberator types (B-24, LB-30, and C-87) and Douglas C-54 (reinforced DC-4) Skymaster transports. The pace of operations accelerated as, effective on 6 October 1943, all Australian routes originated from Hamilton Field (San Francisco). The original route was flown on 11 monthly trips and the route through Canton Island 14 trips weekly. A third route was added with four weekly trips. On this route, southbound flights followed Hamilton–Hickam–Canton–Plaines des Gaiacs–Amberley, and northbound flights also stopped at Nandi. Consairway and United continued as operators on all these routes. Another South Pacific route, the so-called 'Milk Run Route', was opened in April 1943 and served additional South Pacific islands on an alternate, more southerly ferrying, route. The 'Milk Run' carried supplies and mail to Army and Navy personnel on the route and regular service ended in August 1944. ATC crews in C-87s flew the route Hickam Field–Christmas Island–Penrhyn Island (Cook Islands)–Bora Bora (Society Islands)–Aitutaki (Cook Islands)–NAS Tutuila (American Samoa)–Nandi every seven to ten days.

Two Intra-Theater Rest & Recreation Shuttle Routes were established during 1943 to ferry personnel to Australia and New Zealand for rest and recreation and also carried mail.

The Auckland–Espiritu Shuttle (initially via Plaines des Gaiacs) began in February 1943, transporting Army infantry and Marine personnel stationed on Guadalcanal and adjoining islands to New Zealand. It was operated by United Airlines with C-87 Liberator Express transports. The Auckland–Espiritu route was extended northwards in January 1944 to Guadalcanal and was flown by ATC pilots when two additional C-87s became available. This service supplemented the South Pacific Combat Air Transport Command (SCAT) service, which began in Guadalcanal in late 1942 evacuating wounded to Espiritu Santo and Nouméa (New Caledonia).

The 'Sacktime' Shuttle, carrying soldiers stationed in the New Guinea area to Australia, was operated from July 1943 with five C-47s flown by ATC crews on the route Port Moresby (New Guinea)–Townsville–Sydney. The route was later extended to Nadzab Airfield, near Lae on the north-eastern coast of New Guinea. Eventually non-ATC transport replaced the ATC. On 23 February 1944, the ATC began altering its emphasis from the South Pacific routes northwards to the Solomon Islands and New Guinea with three routes developing: the Hamilton–Amberley route via Hickam; the Canton–Nandi–Plaines des Gaiacs flown eleven times weekly by Consairway; and two new Hamilton-Townsville (Australia) routes via Hickam–Canton–Guadalcanal flown 14 times weekly by United. On half of these routes, Port Moresby (New Guinea) would be scheduled as a stop between Guadalcanal and Townsville.

The Hamilton–Townsville route was discontinued by early November 1944. The remaining South Pacific Hamilton–Amberley route was then flown twice weekly by ATC C-54 transports via Christmas–Canton–Nandi–Tontouta. In December, Consairway assumed the route, flying LB-30 transports, until at least April 1945.

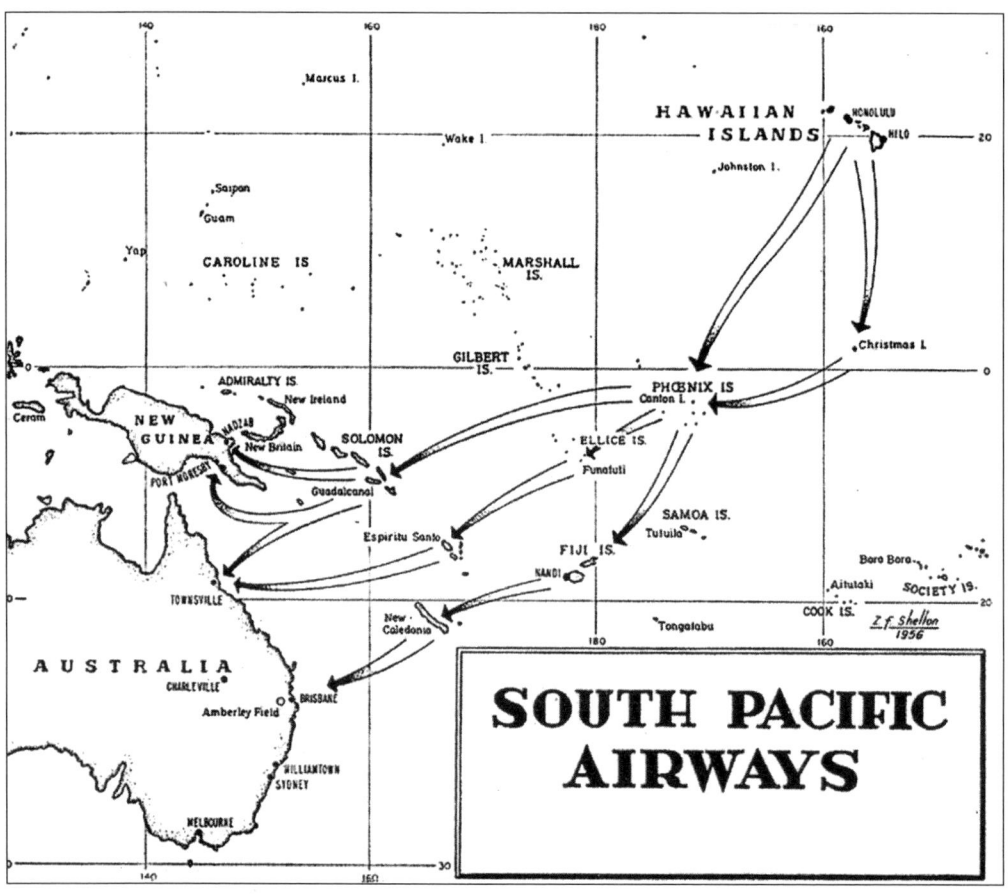

QANTAS

Between June 1944 and November 1950, at least four ex-BOAC Liberator IIs served with Australian QANTAS Empire Airways Ltd. QANTAS was formed in 1920 as Queensland And Northern Territory Aerial Services Ltd under co-founder and manager Hudson Fysh. In 1934, QANTAS and Britain's Imperial Airways Ltd jointly formed QANTAS Empire Airways Ltd (QEA) to operate the Australia–Singapore segment of the Australia–United Kingdom air route, with Fysh as general manager. As the successor to Imperial Airways, BOAC inherited Imperial's 50 per cent shareholding in QANTAS Empire Airways and its Liberators.

After the Japanese captured Java in March 1942, the only air connection Australia had across the Pacific was operated by Consairway, the Air Transport Command, and United Airlines. During February 1942, Hudson Fysh had contacted BOAC broaching tentative plans for an Indian Ocean service to be flown with Consolidated PBY Catalinas, refueling at Cocos Island. However, when Cocos came within range of Japanese patrol aircraft, the proposal was cancelled but was revived in October when it was shown that these flights could be made non-stop.

During March 1943 Fysh traveled on a Consairway Liberator from Amberley, headed for London via the US. In London Fysh was able to outmaneuver RAF/BOAC politics and QANTAS was chosen by BOAC as their agent to operate the requested Indian Ocean service. When Fysh returned to Australia in August he was able to do so by a PBY-5 Catalina from the inland Koggala Lake near Galle, Ceylon, to Swan River, Perth. In March 1943, Capt. W.H. Crowther, head of QANTAS Western Operations Division, was informed that his requested LB-30 Liberators were not available and the operation would have to continue flying Catalinas. The five 'civilianized' Consolidated PBY Catalinas flew the 3,513-nautical mile non-stop Indian Ocean route in radio silence, at times with an all-up-weight of 35,400lb, which was over 8,000lb over design. Cargo capacity was only 1,100lb with nearly 7 tons of fuel, so passengers and mail had to be controlled rigorously. The first Catalina flight was on 10 July 1943 but a year after its Catalina service began the QANTAS air fleet became short of aircraft after many of its aircraft had been impounded into war service and suffered losses through attrition and accidents. The company applied to the British Air Ministry for additional transport aircraft. The Air Ministry approved the transfer of two ex-RAF LB-30 Liberators: AL619 and later AL547 from BOAC for use on the Indian Ocean route. Liberator AL619 was built by Consolidated, San Diego, was acquired by the British Purchasing Commission in April 1942 and was mainly flown by 511 Squadron at Lyneham in Transport Command until 9 May 1944. It was then registered G-AGKT with BOAC at Lyneham. On 15 May 1944 it was officially taken on charge by the BOAC and flown to Australia later the same month. On 3 June 1944 it was registered to QANTAS Empire Airways at Mascot, Sydney. This Liberator arrived at Guildford, Western Australia, on 3 June 1944 and then was sent to QEA's Brisbane/Archerfield workshops, where it was modified by the removal of the British-installed long-range fuel tanks from the bomb bay and rubber tanks installed in the wings, which permitted a payload of 5,500lb, including the weight of 15 passengers, all of which was five times the capacity of the Catalina. Seven additional passenger seats were added in the bomb bay. Both QANTAS Liberators would appear in natural metal finish with black registration letters underlined in blue and white.

G-AGKT was to be piloted by QANTAS' Catalina pilot Capt. O.P. Jones, who was unfamiliar with the Liberator's retractable undercarriage. Jones and his crews had previously participated in a five-day conversion program at 7 OTU, RAAF Tocumwal, NSW, and by the time G-AGKT arrived, five captains and three first officers had qualified.

The original Catalina route plan to stage the flight to Ceylon through Exmouth Gulf on the north-west Australian coast was implemented for the Liberator operations, which allowed a refueling stop at Learmonth, Western Australia. Overwater flight was reduced, while the higher cruising speed of the Liberator cut the flight time by approximately 10 hours. The first QANTAS Perth–Colombo Liberator service to Ceylon left Swan River on 17 June, when G-AGKT, piloted by Capt. O.P. Jones, with a take-off weight of 58,000lb. Including the 3-hour 40-minute refueling flight to Learmonth, the Liberator arrived at RAF Ratmalana, Ceylon 12 hours 33 minutes later. The return flight on 21 June was flown in 17 hours 21 minutes. The frequency of the service was planned to be once every ten days.

A second Liberator, G-AGKU (ex-RAF LB-30 AL547), was delivered on 14 August 1944 and also flown to Archer Field for modification. After G-AGKU went into service on 24 September, G-AGKT was flown to Archer Field for similar modifications on 19 September. In service G-AGKU suffered numerous nose wheel problems that kept it out of service. In the meantime, G-AGKT had its modifications completed by 12 October and was able to resume services. Spare parts became a problem for QANTAS but in 1944, the 380th Bomb Group was moving to Biak, New Guinea, and it offered QANTAS many unwanted items that helped alleviate the problem. Initially operating services were every 10 days but by January 1945 the two Liberators increased frequency to four crossings per week. The 200th flight was made by August and shortly afterward the 2,000th passenger was transported. The last wartime Liberator flight before they

G-AGKT (previously RAF AL619) was the first of four QANTAS Liberators and received during June 1944. (*QANTAS*)

The 3,500-nautical mile non-stop Australia to Ceylon flight across the Indian Ocean permitted a payload of 5,500lb, including the weight of 15 passengers. (*QANTAS*)

G-AGTI (ex-AL541) was QANTAS Empire Airways' third Liberator and flew the 'Kangaroo Service' denoted by the airline logo on the forward fuselage. (*QANTAS*)

were replaced by Lancastrians was flown on 18 July 1945, the entire time without loss. After V-J Day, on 28 November 1945, the third LB-30 Liberator, G-AGTI (ex-AL541), was received. During October QANTAS made its first flight to Singapore since February 1942 and by February 1946 commenced scheduled landplane operations when the Short Empire Service was cancelled. The final Liberator, G-AGTJ (AL524), was overhauled by Scottish Aviation at Prestwick Airport, Scotland, to QANTAS requirements and was to be ferried to Australia during March 1946, giving QANTAS four ex-RAF LB-30/ Liberator IIs in service. The QANTAS Liberators subsequently made 327 Indian Ocean crossings on what the airline called its 'Kangaroo Service', denoted by the QANTAS logo on the forward fuselage that carried a kangaroo surrounded by these words and another kangaroo straddling the words 'QANTAS-EMPIRE AIRWAYS'. The first two Liberators were scrapped during 1947 at Mascot, Sydney, while the other two remained on the civilian registry until 1950, when they, too, were scrapped.

Chapter 2

C-87 Liberator Express

Both the Douglas C-47 Skytrain and the Curtiss C-46 Commando were excellent transport designs, but whose twin engines placed them at a disadvantage on long overwater flights and gave them a smaller long-range cargo capacity. While four-engine aircraft offered a safety margin and increased payload, there were no suitable four-engine transport aircraft available in mid-1942. The Douglas' C-54 Skymaster, the military designation of the DC-4, continued under development and would not arrive into service in large numbers until sometime during 1943. Boeing's C-75 was converted from TWA's 307 Stratoliner commercial versions beginning in February 1942 but its troubled three-year conversion time and its small 4,500lb payload made it unsuitable for long-range transport service. By the time it was ready the AAF had sufficient long-range transports and no longer needed the C-75s, selling them back to TWA. Lockheed's C-69 Constellation was suitable but that company's commitment to P-38 fighter production limited its delivery and only a small number would see service in the last year of the war. Until the C-54 arrived, the only choice for a four-engine transport was the C-87 conversion of the versatile B-24D. The factory-produced C-87 Liberator Express was available and was able to transport a payload of 7,500 to 9,400lb over 3,250 miles and, therefore, was the expedient that inaugurated ATC's long-range transport service. These four-engine transports were placed into immediate service as they rolled off the Consolidated assembly lines and were soon a regular resident at military airfields over the globe. By the late summer 1943, the ATC was operating them regularly on routes from America and to the most remote areas of the earth.

During early 1942 while the to-be-renowned twin-engine Douglas C-47s transport was establishing itself in combat theaters around the world, Consolidated began to work on its prototype four-engine C-87 transport. For the initial C-87 conversion prototype, a B-24D (42-40355) that had been damaged during crash landing in the Arizona desert that killed six of the 34 passengers became available. On 10 March, after makeshift repairs, it was flown, gear down, to San Diego, where, under the direction of Consolidated's iconic engineer, Isaac 'Mac' Laddon, the conversion began. Laddon stated: 'There wasn't time for drawings. Col. (Carl) Brandt, the Air Force factory representative, and I did it mostly by waving our arms and pointing to show where we wanted equipment taken out, a deck laid, or an opening cut.'

Meanwhile, Ford entered the transport conversion competition with its 'Ford Utility Transports', B-24E-FO transport conversions of 42-6976 and 42-6985. A B-24E, 42-6976, characterized Ford's concept of a passenger/cargo Liberator configuration as its prototype version, beginning as an assortment of B-24 spare parts. It was not delivered until 12 November 1942, by which time the Consolidated Laddon/Brandt version was already in production at Fort Worth. The Ford Utility Transport seems to have then been abandoned as the new, huge Willow Run Plant was having production problems.

C-87 Liberator Express Specifications

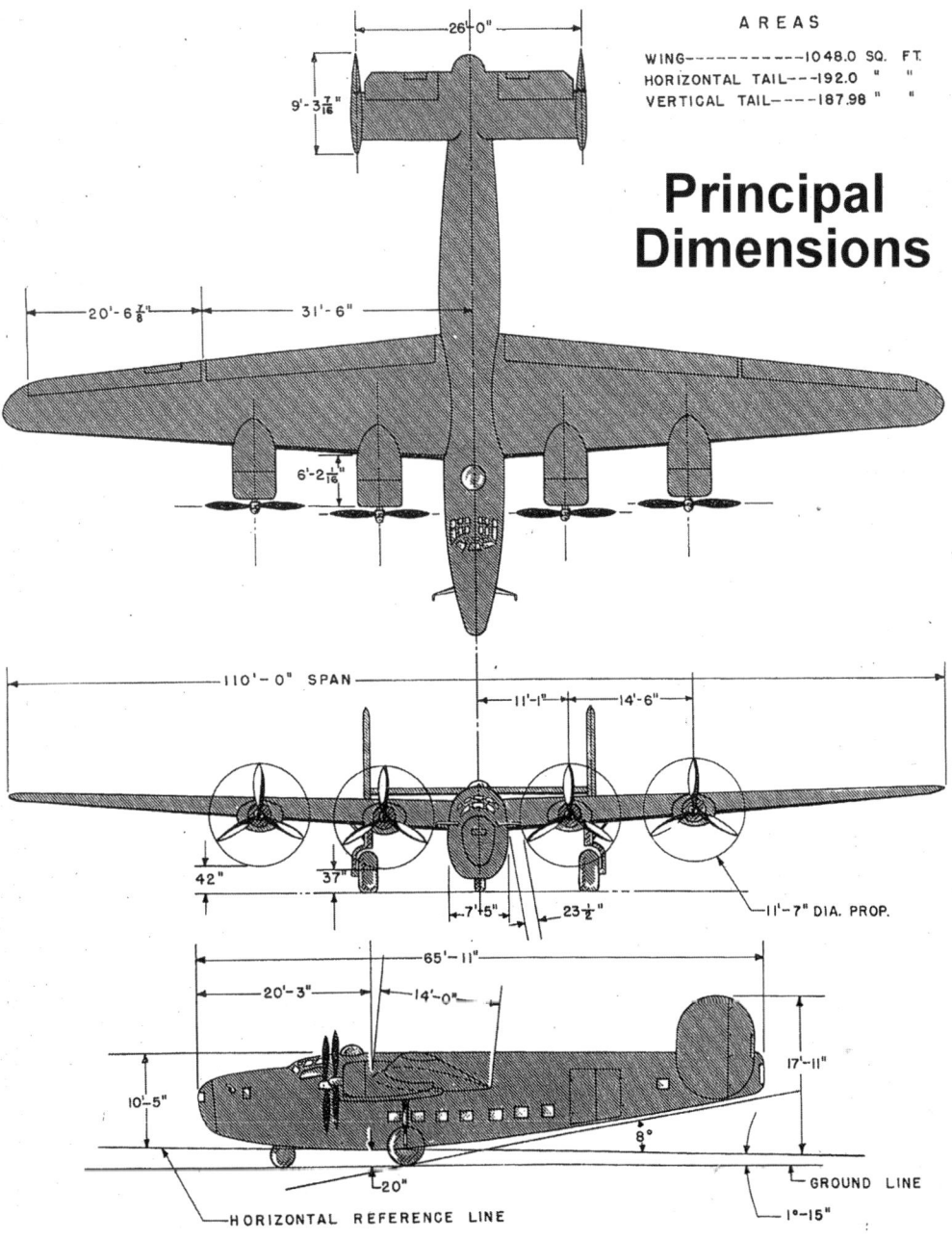

AREAS

WING----------1048.0 SQ. FT.
HORIZONTAL TAIL---192.0 " "
VERTICAL TAIL----187.98 " "

Principal Dimensions

DESCRIPTION, DIMENSIONS, AND LEADING PARTICULARS

1. DESCRIPTION.

a. GENERAL. — The C-87 series airplanes (Navy Model RY-1) are mid-wing monoplanes of all-metal construction.

b. The full cantilever wing is built in three main sections. The center section, which carries the four nacelles, is permanently fastened to the fuselage. The outer panels and wing tips are detachable, as are all leading and trailing edge sections.

c. The fuselage of all metal, semi-monocoque construction is divided into five main compartments: nose, nose wheel, flight deck, center section, and rear compartment.

d. The empennage includes a full-cantilever type stabilizer. Twin fins and rudders are at each outboard end of the stabilizer.

e. Four Pratt and Whitney air-cooled radial engines (Type R-1830-43) power the aircraft.

f. The propellers are Hamilton Standard full feathering, hydromatic, three-blade type.

g. The tricycle landing gear is retractable and is hydraulically operated. The main landing gear is equipped with individually controllable dual brakes.

2. DIMENSIONS AND LEADING PARTICULARS.

a. AIRPLANE — GENERAL.

Fuselage Height	10 ft. 5 in.
Over-all Span	110 ft.
Over-all Length Airplanes prior to serial No. AF 41-11605	65 ft. 10-1/2 in.
Airplanes serial No. AF 41-11605 and on	68 ft. 5-3/8 in.
Over-all Height	17 ft. 11 in.
Height, Inboard Propeller Hub	8 ft. 8 in.
Height, Outboard Propeller Hub	9 ft. 1 in.
Clearance, Inboard Propeller Tip to Ground	3 ft. 7 in.
Clearance, Outboard propeller Tip to Ground	4 ft.
Clearance, Propeller Tip to Fuselage	2 ft. 5-1/2 in.

Clearance, Inboard to Outboard Propeller Tips   3 ft.

Clearance, Propeller to
Wing Leading Edge   6 ft. 2-1/16 in.

Clearance, Bottom of
Fuselage to Ground   1 ft. 8 in.

Paddle blade propellers.
Old type propellers have
6 inches less clearance

b. WINGS.

Airfoil Section at Root   CVAC 22 percent

Airfoil Section at Tip   CVAC 9.3 percent

Root Chord   14 ft.

Dihedral on Upper 30
percent Chord Line   3 degrees 26 minutes

Incidence   3 degrees

Sweep-Back-Leading
Edge   3 degrees 30 minutes

Total Wing Area (includ-
ing ailerons and Fowler
flap extended)   1192.00 sq. ft.

Total Wing Area
(less ailerons)   964.84 sq. ft.

c. AILERONS.

Area Aft of Hinge   (total) 64.3 sq. ft.

Area of Balance   18.86 sq. ft.

Percent of Balance   22.7 percent

Total Area   83.16 sq. ft.

Movement of Aileron UP   20 degrees

Movement of Aileron
DOWN   20 degrees

Area of Aileron Tab
(right aileron)   .2.5 sq. ft.

Movement of Tab UP   10 degrees

Movement of Tab
DOWN   10 degrees

d. FLAPS.

Area (total)   114 sq. ft.

Chord (maximum)   2 ft. 7-7/16 in.

Movement of Flaps
(maximum down)   40 degrees

e. EMPENNAGE.

(1) GENERAL.

Stabilizers Area (in-
cluding elevators)   192.00 sq. ft.

Fins Area (total)   122.98 sq. ft.

(2) HORIZONTAL STABILIZER.

Airfoil Section—Sym-
metrical Thickness   13 percent total chord

Over-all Span
(fin to fin)   26 ft.

Total Area (to elevator
hinge)   124.94 sq. ft.

(3) ELEVATORS.

Area (including tab)   67.06 sq. ft.

Area of Balance (total)   15.6 sq. ft.

Percent of Balance   23 percent

Total Area   67.06 sq. ft.

Movement of Elevator
—UP   30 degrees

Movement of Elevator
—DOWN   20 degrees

Area of Elevator Tab
(both)   2.4 sq. ft.

Movement of Tab—UP   10 degrees

Movement of Tab—
DOWN   10 degrees

Movement of Tab
Servo with 20 degree
Elevator—UP   5 degrees

Movement of Tab
Servo with 20 degree
Elevator—DOWN   7-1/2 degrees

(4) VERTICAL FINS.

Airfoil Section—Sym-
metrical Thickness   7 percent total chord

Area (both to rudder
hinge)   122.98 sq. ft.

(5) RUDDERS.

Area Aft of Hinge (in-
cluding tab, both)   48.84 sq. ft.

Area of Balance (total)   16.16 sq. ft.

Percent of Balance   24.87 percent

Total Area (both, including tabs)   64.50 sq. ft.

Movement (to each side)   20 degrees

Area of Rudder Tabs (both)   1.9 sq. ft.

Movement of Tab—Controlled   10 degrees (each side)

Movement of Tab—Servo with 20 degrees rudder   10 degrees (each side)

f. LANDING GEAR.

Tread   25 ft. 7-1/2 in.

Wheel Base (fore and aft)   16 ft.

(1) JACK PAD HEIGHTS ABOVE GROUND LEVEL.

(a) OLEO EXTENDED, FULL TIRE, PLUS 3-INCH CLEARANCE ABOVE GROUND.

Outboard Wing Jack Pad   125-3/8 in.

Inboard Wing Jack Pad   118-1/2 in.

Fuselage Nose Jack Pad   94-3/4 in.

(b) OLEO COMPRESSED, FLAT TIRE.

Outboard Wing Jack Pad   96-3/8 in.

Inboard Wing Jack Pad   89-1/2 in.

Fuselage Nose Jack Pad   69-1/2 in.

g. ENGINE.

(1) MODEL R-1830-43.

Type   radial aircooled

Number of Cylinders   14

Bore   5-1/2 in.

Stroke   5-1/2 in.

Piston Displacement in Cubic Inches   1830

Compression Ratio   6.70:1

Diameter of Impeller   11 in.

Diameter of Mounting Bolt Circle   27 in.

Number of Mounting Bolts   8

Normal Brake HP at Rated Altitude   1100

Rated Altitude   6200 ft. 25,000 ft.

Altitude Speed   2550 rpm

Propeller Reduction Gear Ratio   .5625:1 (16:9) (Decoupled)

Governor Drive Speed   .958:1

Blower Gear Ratio   7.15:1

Spark Advance   25 degrees

Propeller Hub Spline   50

Average Weight of Engine   1445 lbs.

Over-all Length of Engine   63-17/32 in.

Position of Center of Gravity:
  Vertical   9/32 inch above crankshaft centerline

  Horizontal   10-3/16 inch forward of rear face of mounting bosses.

(2) IGNITION.

Magneto Speed in Multiples of Crankshaft Speed   .875:1

Direction of Magneto Drive Rotation*   Clockwise

Spark Plug Gap   .012 in.—.015 in.

(3) VALVES AND TIMING.

Intake Opens, in Degrees before Top Center   20 degrees early

Intake Closes, in degrees after Bottom Center   76 degrees late

Exhaust Opens, in Degrees before Bottom Center   76 degrees early

Exhaust Closes, in Degrees after Top Center	20 degrees late
Intake Remains Open, in Crankshaft Degrees	276 degrees
Exhaust Remains Open, in Crankshaft Degrees	276 degrees
Cold Clearance	.010 in.
Timing Clearance	.060 in.
Valve Lift	9/16 in.

(4) ACCESSORY DRIVES AND INSTRUMENT CONNECTIONS.

Oil Pump Speed, in Multiples of Crankshaft Speed	875:1
Oil Pressure (thread)	1/8 in. pipe
Oil Tank Vent (thread)	3/4 in. pipe
Fuel Pump Flange and Drive	In accordance with installation drawing
Fuel Pump Speed, in Multiples of Crankshaft Speed	875:1
Fuel Pump Drive, Direction of Rotation	Counterclockwise
Starter Flange and Drive	Standard
Starter Shaft Speed, in Multiples of Crankshaft Speed	1:1
Starter Drive, Direction of Rotation	Clockwise
General Flange and Drive	In accordance with installation drawing
Generator Speed, in Multiples of Crankshaft Speed	1.4:1
Generator Drive, Direction of Rotation	Clockwise
Auxiliary Accessory Flange	In accordance with installation drawing
Auxiliary Accessory Speed	1:1

Auxiliary Accessory Direction of Rotation	Clockwise
Tachometer Drive Shaft	In accordance with installation drawing
Tachometer Drive Speed, in multiples of Crankshaft Speed	5:1
Tachometer Drive, Direction of Rotation	RH Clockwise, LH Counterclockwise
Vacuum Pump Flange and Drive	In accordance with installation drawing
Vacuum Speed, in Multiples of Crankshaft Speed	1.4:1
Vacuum Pump Drive, Direction of Rotation	Clockwise

NOTE

Direction of rotation is referred to as viewed from the rear of the engine.

(5) ENGINE ACCESSORIES.

Carburetor	Type PD12F-5
Magneto	Bosch SF14LU-7 and SF14LC-7
Spark Plugs	Bendix 6S9
Generator	Type P-1
Starter	Type F2 and G6
Fuel Pump	Army Type G9, AN Specification No. 4101
Hydraulic Pump	Vickers PF2-713-25BCE
Vacuum Pump	Type B-8
Turbo Supercharger	Type B-2
Supercharger Regulator	Type A-13
Oil Temperature Regulator	U.A.P. No. U-6012-08 or Airesearch No. 16230 with D-8 Thermostatic valve.

1. Propeller
2. Main Landing Gear
3. Nose Landing Gear
4. Nose Door
5. Pitot Tube
6. Upper Nose Section
7. Forward Section R. H.
8. Forward Section L. H.
9. Hand Rail
10. Nose Section Bottom Panel
11. Nose Landing Gear Doors
12. Power Plant Installation
13. Pilot's Floor
14. Radio Operator's Floor
15. Engine Mount Support
16. Engine Mount
17. L R Outboard Nacelle to Wing Leading Edge Fairing Outboard
18. L R Outboard Nacelle to Wing Leading Edge Fairing Inboard
19. L R Inboard Nacelle to

Wing Leading Edge Fairing Outboard
20. L/R Inboard Nacelle to Wing Leading Edge Fairing Inboard
21. Pilot's Enclosure
22. Front Spar of Wing
23. L/R Wing Center Section Leading Edge Attaching Panel
24. L/R Wing Center Section Leading Edge
25. L/R Wing Center Sec. tion Leading Edge (Between Nacelles)
26. L/R Wing Outer Panel Leading Edge
27. L/R Wing Outer Panel
28. L/R Wing Tip
29. L/R Aileron
30. L/R Wing Outer Panel Trailing Edge
31. L/R Flap
32. L/R Wing Center Section Trailing Edge

33. Wing Center Section
34. Bottom Panel Fuselage (Station 2.0 to 4.0)
35. L/R Side Panel Fuselage with Windows
36. L/R Side Panel Fuselage with Window
37. Truss-Fuselage to Wing (Station 4.1 to 4.2)
38. Truss-Bulkhead Station 4.1
39. Pilot's Escape Hatch
40. Navigator's Astrodome
41. Fuselage Nose Section Upper Rear Deck
42. Life Raft Hatch
43. Fuselage Section Top Panel
44. Segment Bulkhead at Station 4.0
45. Cargo Doors
46. Escape Hatch Right Side of Fuselage
47. Tail Section Fuselage
48. Tail Door

49. Horizontal Stabilizer
50. L/R Vertical Stabilizer
51. L/R Rudder
52. Elevator
53. Elevator Tabs
54. L/R Auxiliary Fuel Cells at Outboard Nacelles in Wing Center Section
55. Main Fuel Cells Wing Center Section

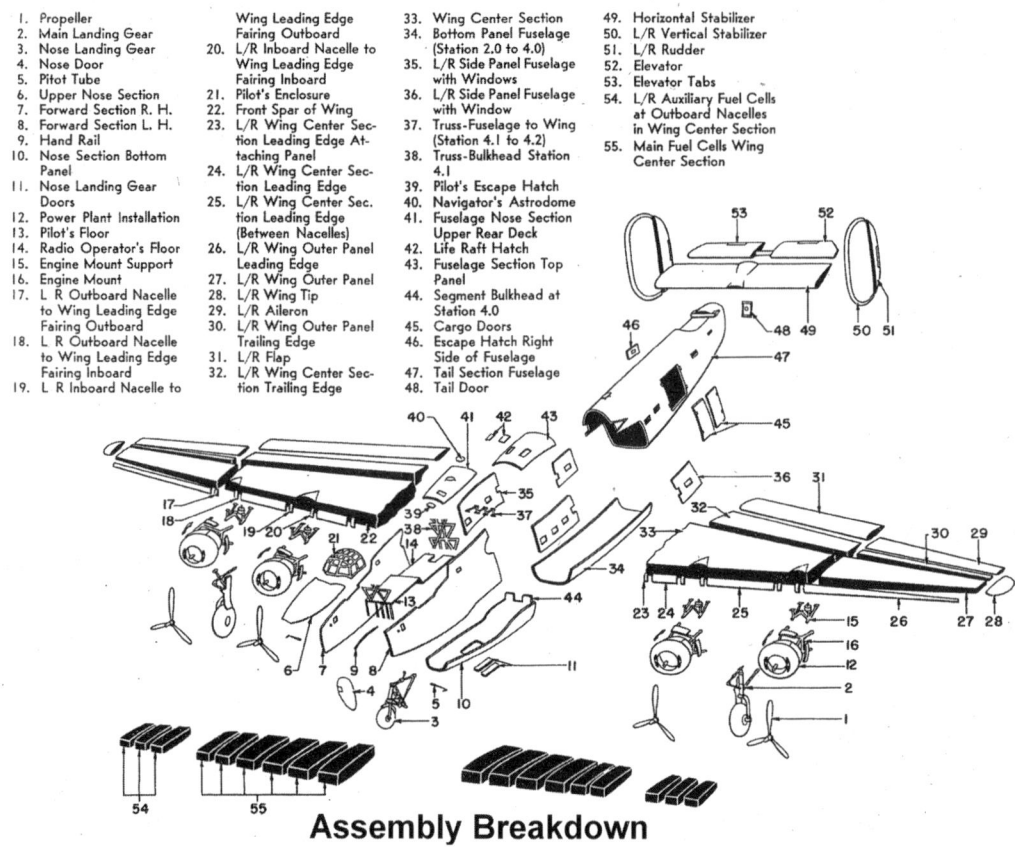

Assembly Breakdown

C-87 Contracts

All 287 C-87s were built at Consolidated/Fort Worth and were delivered between 2 September 1942 and 10 August 1944, with peak production achieved during March 1944, when 21 were delivered. The C-87s were not assigned production block numbers but there were six different versions of the C-87 that were built that incorporated several specific changes. The first 73 C-87s were procured under Supplemental Agreement #3 to Contract W-535-AC-18723, as conversions from B-24Ds at Consolidated's Fort Worth plant by adding C-87 features to previous bomber B-24 airframes. An additional 107 were to be built as dedicated transports on the Fort Worth assembly line under Supplemental Agreement No. 7 to fixed-price contract W535-AC-26992, which was later increased to 169 C-87s. Consolidated was to make 'every effort' to deliver C-87s at the rate of 25 per month, however, production was 'not to interfere with regular production of the B-24'. Consolidated was authorized to use Ford-manufactured components of the B-24E model in the production of the 107 C-87s if possible, and in addition was 'to manufacture such other parts as might be needed'. (Ford components were not used in the manufacture of C-87s.) After these initial contracts, there is confusion when trying to sort and clarify the remaining available contract records.

On 21 March 1944 contract W33-038-AC-811 covering 111 C-87s and spare parts became effective between the government and Consolidated. Due to early difficulties and confusion in production, it was necessary to build the C-87s from B-24 parts furnished by Consolidated and modified as required for this transport version. C-87s and B-24s ran on the same Fort Worth production line, however, it was necessary to partially hand-build the C-87, thereby, increasing the cost approximately 11 per cent over the B-24.

Fairfield Air Depot, part of Wright AFB, Dayton, Ohio, had previously modified 62 B-24s to the anti-submarine role that were assigned primarily to the 479th and 480th Anti-Submarine Groups of the 8AF. Once their ASW role was assumed by the Navy, these B-24s were reassigned with a number assigned to Navy units taking over the ASW function. However, most of these ASW modified B-24s were eventually converted into C-87s.

During 1944 at least six of the LB-30s operating in Panama were reported to have been returned to Consolidated's Nashville, Tennessee Modification Center for conversion to C-87 Liberator Express transports with their early circular engine cowlings preserved.

C-87 Conversion and Production

The AAF's need for transport aircraft was so urgent that the first few C-87s off the line were virtually hand-built as there was no time to wait while jigs were built and sub-assemblies tooled up together with the wait for dies, form blocks, and jigs for the cargo doors, belly covering, and the hundreds of other changes. Nevertheless, the first of these hand-built C-87s came off the line more than 30 days ahead of schedule, presenting the AAF with a transport that could carry over 6 tons of cargo over more than 3,000 miles at speeds more than 300mph, which was a specification unequaled by any transport aircraft, including the celebrated Douglas C-47.

Basic Exterior Changes

While the aircraft's exterior experienced relatively little change; the conversion did require the ingenuity of Consolidated's design engineers and assembly line specialists to complete the substantial amount of engineering and tooling procedures so that both the bomber and the transport versions could be constructed simultaneously on the same Fort Worth production line. The B-24D/C-87 conversion included the removal of all the bombing equipment and defensive armament. The B-24D nose glazing in the bombardier's compartment was replaced by a sheet metal nose with a door hinged to the right. The new nose was approximately the same shape but was a foot and half longer than the bomber greenhouse it replaced. Since its nose grew in the process of becoming a C-87, the former salvaged Arizona wreck/prototype C-87 was dubbed *Pinocchio*. The navigator's station was relocated from just aft of the cockpit to the rear of the flight deck and the astrodome was relocated in the center of the faired-over section where the dorsal turret had been. Semi-permanent flooring was installed over the bomb bays and into the waist compartment. Seven rectangular passenger windows extended on each side of the fuselage, from just under the wing along the length of the aircraft toward the cargo door. These windows were kept a uniform height from the floor, explaining their non-linear configuration towards the rear of the fuselage. Each window had a hole in the center that had an adjustable mechanism to provide a somewhat rudimentary method of individual ventilation control, which was easily closed with its Plexiglas stopper. The C-87 Erection and Maintenance Manual contained an interesting statement: 'Each window in the troop or main compartment is equipped with a port to permit defensive fire by troops with rifles or sub-machine guns (!)' A 6ft × 6ft, double-door cargo hatch was cut into the port side of the rear fuselage. After the first 42 models the tail gun turret was restructured by adding a ventral door through which long aircraft parts, such as wing flaps, ailerons, and stringers, could be placed into the aircraft endwise. The lower remainder of the turret was faired over with a large Plexiglas area left for observation.

Pinocchio

B-24D (42-40355) had an interesting career as after its Arizona crash. It was rebuilt and reconfigured with a longer *Pinocchio* nose like the C-87 prototype, during which it was sometimes unofficially referred to as the 'XC-87B'. The C-87 prototype was flown to Bolling Field, District of Columbia, by a crew of four – pilot, co-pilot, navigator, and radio operator – whereby Gen. Arnold evaluated the conversion and upon his approval the aircraft was ordered into production as the C-87 Liberator Express. The prototype

The longer-nosed *Pinocchio* C-87 prototype at Bolling Field after its conversion from a B-24D (42-40355). (*CAC/AAF*)

After its C-87 prototype duty, *Pinocchio* had LB-30 engine packages installed and served as one of Consolidated's three company Liberators. (*CAC/AAF*)

Pinocchio in its final, single-tail RY-3 configuration. (*CAC/AAF*)

was then flown to Fort Worth in May 1942 to be used as a sample for the conversion of B-24Ds into the first batch of C-87s. After its prototype duty it had LB-30 engines installed to serve as one of Consolidated's three company Liberators along with AM927 and AL610. Later it had a single tail assembly installed into a RY-3 configuration.

Basic Interior Fuselage Compartment Changes and Contents

Among the interior changes and similarities in converting the B-24D bomber to a C-87 transport were:

1) The new nose compartment contained baggage stowage space or an extra 'troop seat' could be placed there.
2) The nose wheel compartment, aft of the nose compartment, contained the nose wheel and its mechanism, anti-icer tank and pump, engine fire extinguisher, CO_2 cylinder, toilet, and other miscellaneous equipment.
3) The flight deck, above the nose wheel compartment, contained the pilot's and co-pilot's seats, instrument panels, and electrical switchboards in the forward area.
4) The area aft of the flight deck contained the radio operator's section on the right, the navigator's section on the left side, a crew member's seat behind the navigator's section, and a navigator's dome on the fuselage top center line.
5) The main cargo/passenger compartment was designed to carry cargo, personnel, or both.
   a) In the C-87 (Navy RY-2), and C-87B
      The passenger compartment provided 20 easily removable passenger seats for day travel. Tie down fittings were installed in the floor and at the sides of the compartment to adapt this space for cargo transport.
   b) In the C-87A (Navy RY-1)
      The passenger compartment provided single and Pullman-type upholstered seats for 16–20 passengers for day travel and provided five complete berths and four single seats that accommodated nine passengers for travel by night.
   c) A Tappan galley in the aft portion of the passenger compartment was equipped with food and water containers, cooking, and eating utensils.
   d) Stowage for two extra life rafts was provided in the rear right wall of the passenger compartment to supplement the two stowed on the forward ceiling of this compartment.
   e) Coat hooks were provided in the lavatory and both sides of the fuselage at Station 3.2.
6) The rear compartment, aft of the main cargo/passenger compartment, contained a toilet and lavatory basin closed off by a draw curtain, a tail jack, and entrance ladder stowage. Long narrow objects, such as flaps, ailerons, extrusions, and drawn sections, could be loaded through the tail at Station 10 in the cargo version.

7) The first 42 C-87s had provisions for the mounting of one .50 caliber machine gun in the tail with a flexible mount and bungee cord provided for quick mounting. When not in use the gun was stowed on the left fuselage wall, just forward of the tail window. Six ammunition boxes were mounted on the right fuselage wall opposite the gun stowage. A removable port in the tail window permitted firing when the tail window was closed.

The Conversion Process

By pre-war standards, the assignment of bringing their new Liberator bomber from the drawing board to volume production in only three years was a significant accomplishment for Consolidated. However, this would not be without disadvantages in the future as the B-24 design had not been engineered for true mass production or future conversion because much of the original engineering data was incomplete or non-existent. The Liberator probably incurred more engineering changes than any other Second World War aircraft; with the San Diego product alone having 1,820 major changes or an average of one change for every 2.6 aircraft delivered (7,020). Over the years, Consolidated had minimized engineering costs by utilizing existing data whenever available. Thus, even in 1944, when the Navy RY-3 transport was contracted, only a basic set of master drawings for the B-24 existed. This same set of master drawings, less the armament installations and certain structural parts, plus a few new drawings and engineering change notices, would comprise the only (and incomplete) drawings for the C-87. In its C-87 conversion, Consolidated saved months of tooling time by not changing the existing complex B-24 jigs in which bulkheads and stringers and sheets of aluminum skin became the nose and tail fuselage sections. Once out of the jigs, these sections could become either a bomber or a transport, depending on AAF requirements. Since the C-87 conversion changes were relatively minor concerning variations in both structure and installation, Consolidated found it to be more feasible to make these changes along the final assembly line. Because of the inordinate length of the Liberator assembly line, those changes could be more easily be divided and be completed at hundreds of assembly line stations, permitting a group of the workers; a few at each station, to make their installations without interruption and crowding by other workmen as would have been the case on a shorter assembly line. Using this method each potential C-87 spent less time at each station, increasing production rates.

To understand the C-87 transport conversion the standard Liberator bomber production procedure needs to be described. In the bomber version the center section of the 110ft wing was the major sub-assembly; moving from the wing bucks to the bomb bay mating jigs where the bomb bay catwalk, side panels, and bomb racks were riveted together. Farther down the line, this center structure was placed into the fuselage mating fixture, where the nose and tail fuselage sections were joined. The bomber was lifted from the mating fixture to the final assembly line and conveyors that transported it through station after station while workmen added inside installations, outer wing panels, engines, propellers; and everything else required for a completed B-24 bomber.

Numerous design problems were overcome by the flexibility of producing B-24 bombers and C-87 transports on the same line. One was the substitution of the prefabricated C-87 belly section fairing called the 'canoe' as had been used on the LB-30 transport conversion. This belly fairing canoe section was fabricated on separate jigs as one unit of 17 bulkheads and 19 stringers and skinned in aluminum. The canoe replaced the standard bomb bay doors, bomb racks, and catwalk jigged sections intended for the B-24 bomber on the line to create a C-87 transport. Once positioned, the overlapping skin and belt frame of the canoe section were cut to the proper alignment and riveted in position. The splice plates were riveted and bolted, and the C-87 was mated and ready to be lifted out of the mating fixture. When this assembly arrived at the fuselage mating fixture, massive jacks supported the wing center section, and the nose and tail fuselage sections were transported by an overhead crane to wheeled cradles that placed them into the mating fixture. In the mating fixture, a locating bar jig and stretcher bar that extended from the nose to the tail fuselage sections were inserted for alignment. This bar jig substituted for the catwalk, which performed a similar purpose in the mating of the bomber components. The nose and tail were then riveted to the wing center section and the locating jig and stretcher bar were removed. A wooden stand was placed under the aft end of the tail for support and the wheeled cradle was rolled rearward out of the way to allow clearance for the insertion of the belly fairing.

The structural changes necessary for the C-87 to be able to carry heavy loads were mostly made in the tail fuselage section. Bulkheads were reinforced and bell frames and flooring supports were added. But the major conversion changes involved the placing of the 6ft square cargo door, which was to be large enough to allow the loading of complete aircraft engines and large packing crates. To withstand most of the load at the aircraft's aft end, belly fairing tie-in strengthening sections were added to a reinforced bulkhead on the empennage side of the cargo door. A longeron was inserted in place of stringers at the top and bottom of the door and a heavier reinforcing skin was riveted on all sides of the opening and extended underneath the fuselage. Sills, hinges, and finishing strips completed the opening and readied it for the door, which was added along the final assembly line.

While the C-87 was in the fuselage mating jig, the windows were located and cut. All seven windows extending from just under the wing along the length of the aircraft toward the cargo door on each side were about 12in high and 18in wide, and were located about 2ft apart. Three of the seven windows on each side were included in the side panel that was attached to the wing center section in the bomb bay mating fixture and had been cut before the assembly reached the fuselage tie-in operation. The other four windows were cut out somewhat before the addition of the belly.

The placement of the windows necessitated the complete rerouting of the surface control cables as well as changes in the intercommunication and electrical wiring. Most of these cables were lowered and ran under the window level but placing them there put them into the cargo area, necessitating using a compressed fiber wood paneling protective covering. Since this protective paneling extended only up to the window levels, in places where the cables had to be routed higher (i.e., above the cargo door opening) special Dural guard plates and covering were installed.

Cabin heating was a requirement when the C-87 operated as a passenger transport. Ducts from the heater ran along the fuselage sides at floor level, which made it necessary to shorten the seat legs on the outboard sides. For the C-87 to serve as a cargo transport, the seats needed to be quickly removable, and the installation of cargo tie-down brackets required the reinforcement of the bulkheads at those stations. So that it would not occupy valuable cargo space, the C-87's hydraulic reservoir, which operated wing flaps and landing gear, had to be relocated from the bomb bay area, where it had been in the Liberator bomber, to the flight deck compartment. Additional cargo space or an extra seat or bench was achieved by re-fairing the bombardier's compartment and replacing its glass-paneled nose with an 18in fuselage extension and a cup-shaped cargo door. Bulkheads and floor supports were also strengthened in the nose, and protective paneling and insulating trim installed. Other changes in the C-87 involved relocating the navigator and his table from what had been the bombardier's nose compartment up to the flight deck, which then caused a relocation of the radio operator's position to the aft of the flight deck on the right. The astrodome, which had been above the navigator in the nose, was moved aft to the center of the faired-over section where the dorsal turret had been. Oxygen tank racks were relocated, and their lines ran to outlets at each seat. Canvas and Kapok soundproofing lined the interior of the fuselage, which was finishing trim held in place by lift-a-dot fasteners and studs that could be easily removed.

Early C-87 from B-24D Conversion Gallery

The first 73 C-87s were conversions at Consolidated's Fort Worth plant by adding C-87 transport features to existing bomber B-24 airframes. The bomb bay 'canoe' bomb bay replacement is seen on the ground at the left. (*CAC/AAF*)

A standard B-24 is stripped of engines and landing gear and supported on jacks. (*CAC/AAF*)

The converted bombers had their wing fuel tanks removed and 12 main self-sealing fuel cells installed, six on each side of the center line. (*CAC/AAF*)

A 'canoe' belly fairing with 17 bulkheads and 19 stringers, skinned in aluminum, was fabricated to replace the bomb bay doors, bulkheads, and catwalk keel. (*CAC/AAF*)

Fuselage side aluminum sheeting removed for window addition and bomb bay enclosure. (*CAC/AAF*)

'Canoe' in place and fuselage interior stripped of bomb racks for cargo/passenger compartment set-up. (*CAC/AAF*)

Former bomb bay area with floor laid. (*CAC/AAF*)

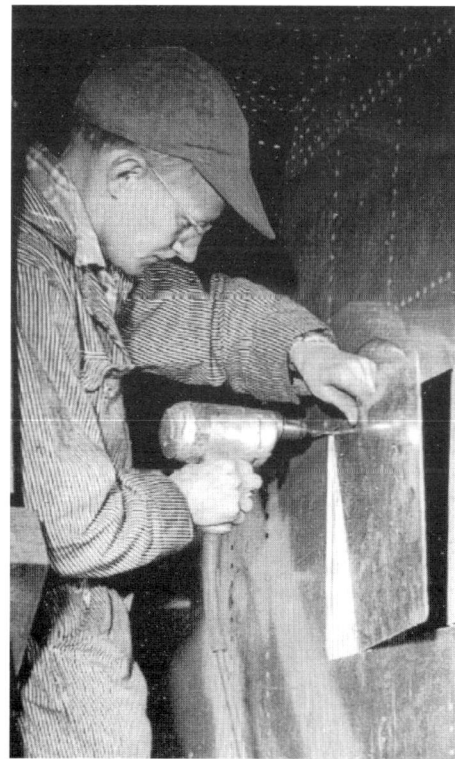

Window placement. (*CAC/AAF*)

Later C-87 Production Line Assembly Gallery

This C-87 was one of first 73 converted from existing B-24 airframes; the remainder were built on the Fort Worth assembly line as dedicated transports. (*CAC/AAF*)

The first production line C-87s were hand-built from scratch at Consolidated Fort Worth, awaiting engines, landing gear, bomb bay 'canoe' (bomb bay area has been removed), and empennage installation. (*CAC/AAF*)

Production line C-87 with engines, nose and fuselage cargo doors, and empennage installed. (*CAC/AAF*)

'Canoe' ready to be placed and windows cut out. (*CAC/AAF*)

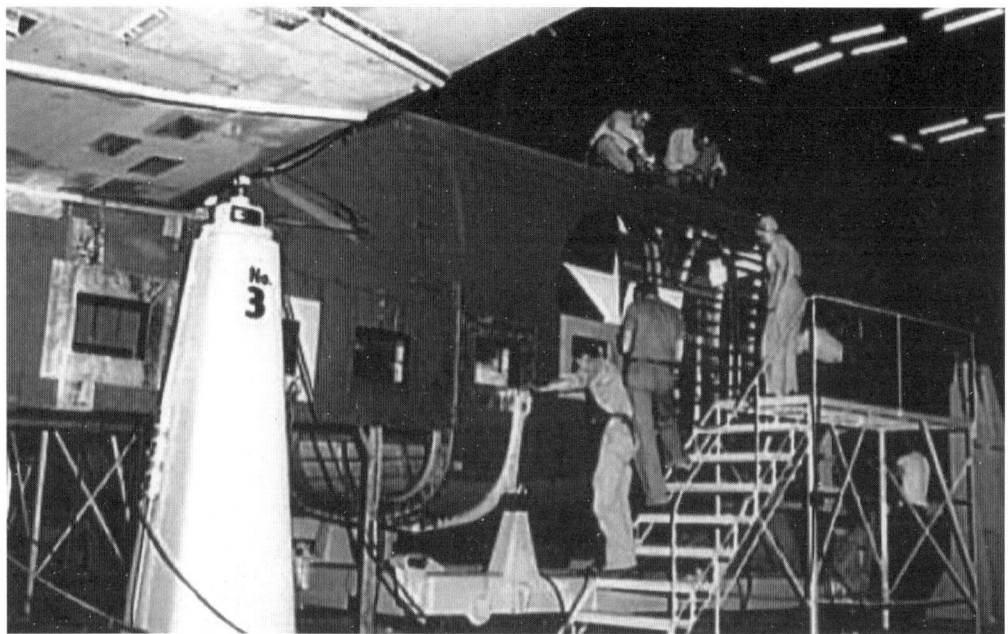

'Canoe' in jig, ready to be installed. (*CAC/AAF*)

Installation of interior components. (*CAC/AAF*)

Nose cargo door installation. (*CAC/AAF*)

Main gear installation. (*CAC/AAF*)

Troop seat installation. (*CAC/AAF*)

Celebrating the final C-87, 44-52987, to come off the Consolidated Fort Worth production line. (*CAC/AAF*)

44-52987, the last of the Consolidated Liberator C-87s in the air. (*CAC/AAF*)

C-87 General Description

Fuselage

The Liberator fuselage was of a semi-monocoque-type constructed of smooth light alloy stressed sheet metal skin, reinforced with channel-section formers and longitudinal Z-section stringers that were fastened with raised-head rivets. Sheet and drawn or rolled materials, except for tubing, were of Alclad-type aluminum alloys. Stiffeners reinforced the fuselage structure around the wing and extended continuously through the fuselage. There were three main transverse bulkheads positioned aft of the flight deck; but the bulkheads located mid-way in the bomb bay compartment and the one aft of the bomb bay compartment in the B-24 bomber configuration were deleted in the C-87 canoe configuration.

The Liberator fuselage was designed around its modified Davis Wing. The four-sided elliptical fuselage had a beam connecting the wing and empennage, which gave a deeper, stronger structure that provided the maximum space for bomb bays, crew quarters, armament, and operational equipment. By building the fuselage around the wing juncture, weight was saved through the elimination of heavy fittings and bolts at the wing attachment points, and fuselage torsional stiffness was improved. This method joined the wing and fuselage by a continuous, riveted, and bolted attachment around the periphery of the box structure of the wing formed by the upper and lower surfaces and the front and rear spars.

Although the fuselage was built in a number of sub-assemblies, it was an integral unit upon completion and could not be disassembled afterward. Construction consisted of 36 vertical pressed flange channel frames and one canted frame to which the nose wheel trunnions were attached. Longitudinal stringers were of the Z-extruded section and, unlike the wing ribs, were mounted in cutouts in the frames provided for that purpose. There are five main frames with heavy stiffeners and doublers located:

1) Aft of the bombardier,
2) Aft of the pilot,
3) At the front wing spar,
4) At the rear wing spar and
5) Aft of the cargo/passenger compartment

The complete fuselage structure weighed only 3,334lb with no equipment installed.

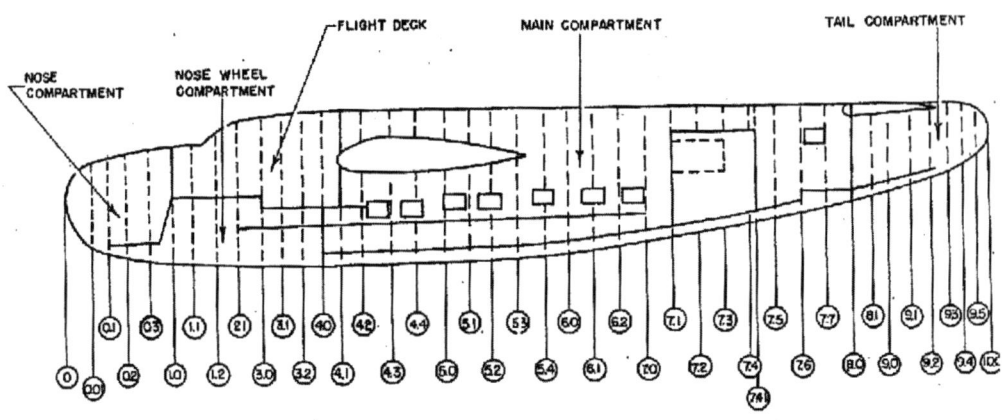

Figure 65 — Fuselage Stations

A—Nose compartment
B—Flight deck
C—Radio operator and navigator's stations

D—Nose wheel compartment
E—Main cargo compartment
F—Tail compartment

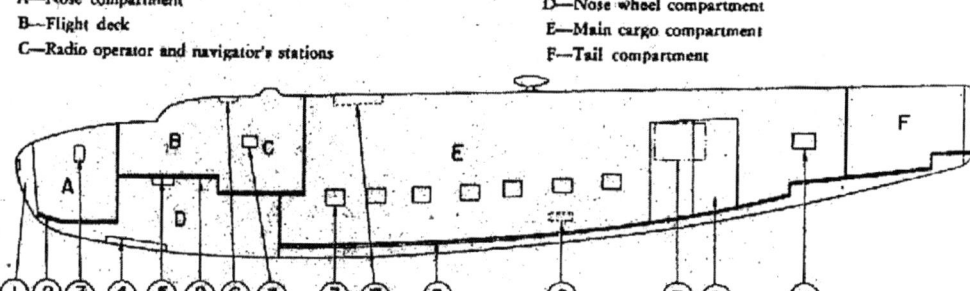

1. Nose door
2. Floors
3. Windows
4. Nose wheel doors

5. External fire extinguisher (L.H. side)
6. Escape hatch
7. Life raft
8. External fire extinguisher (R.H. side)

9. Cargo doors

Compartments

GENERAL DIMENSIONS OF COMPARTMENTS

COMPARTMENT	Length	Width	Height	Total Cu. Ft.	Floor Area Square Feet	Maximum Structural Capacity
A—Station 0.1 to 1.0	6.0	4.0	4.5	108.00	18.2	1600
C—Station 4.1 to 4.4	6.75	6.0	4.67	209.39	30.4	4460
D—Station 4.4 to 5.3						
Under Wing	2.85	6.0	4.67	79.85	12.1	
Aft of Wing	3.15	6.0	7.25	134.71	13.9	3500
E—Station 5.3 to 6.1	6.5	6.0	7.25	282.75	26.5	3000
F—Station 6.1 to 7.2	6.25	5.5	7.0	240.63	23.5	1500
G—Station 7.2 to 7.6	7.33	4.0	6.0	175.92	20.4	1000
H & I—Station 7.6 to 9.2	6.0	3.0	4.0	72.00	(I) 14.6	400
I—Station 9.2 to 9.4	5.5	2.0	3.0	33.00		
TOTAL				1336.25	159.6	

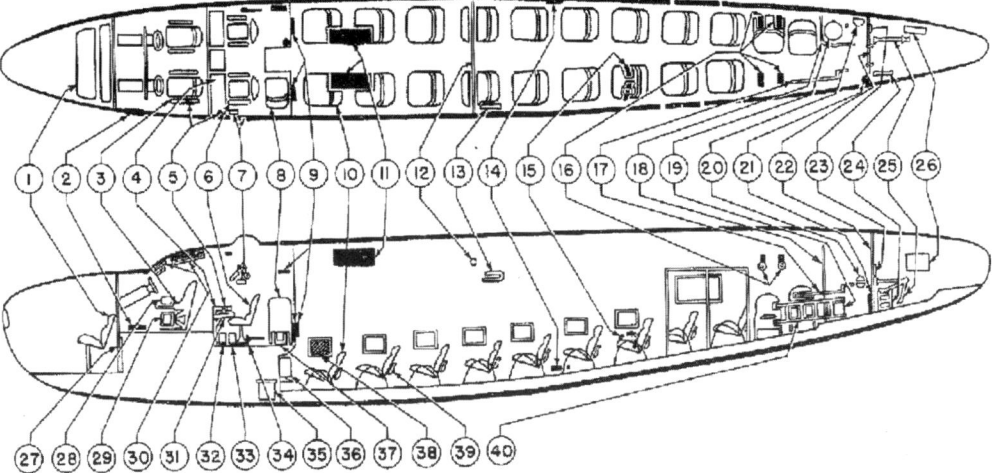

Cutaway: Fuselage Equipment Location

1. Extra Troop Seat*
2. Hand Fire Extinguisher (CCL4 Type)
3. Pilot's and Co-pilot's Seats
4. Navigator's Tables
5. Ash Receptacles
6. Radio Operator's and Navigator's Seats
7. Very Pistol & Pyrotechnic Equipment
8. Commanding Officer's Seat*
9. First Aid Kits
10. Troop Seats
11. Life Rafts
12. Coat Rack
13. Fuel Transfer Hose*
14. Hand Fire Extinguisher (CCL4 Type)
15. Safety Belts (1 Per Seat)
16. Stowage For Two Extra Rafts
17. Hand Starter Crank
18. Lavatory Draw Curtain
19. Toilet
20. Lavatory Basin
21. Portable Fire Extinguisher (CO_2 Type)
22. Tail Compartment Door*
23. Stowage For Summer Plugs*
24. Extra Ladder
25. Tail Jack
26. Water Supply Tank For Lavatory
27. Nose Compartment Door
28. Data Case
29. Flight Report Stowage and Map Case
30. Sun Visors and Glare Curtains
31. Navigators Map Container
32. Night Flying Curtains
33. Blind Flying Curtains*
34. Fire Axe
35. Toilet*
36. Thermos Jug
37. Navigator's Stool*
38. Black Out Curtains
39. Oxygen Mask Stowage
40. Fuel Access Ladder

*Deleted on Later Ships

■Denotes Emergency Equipment

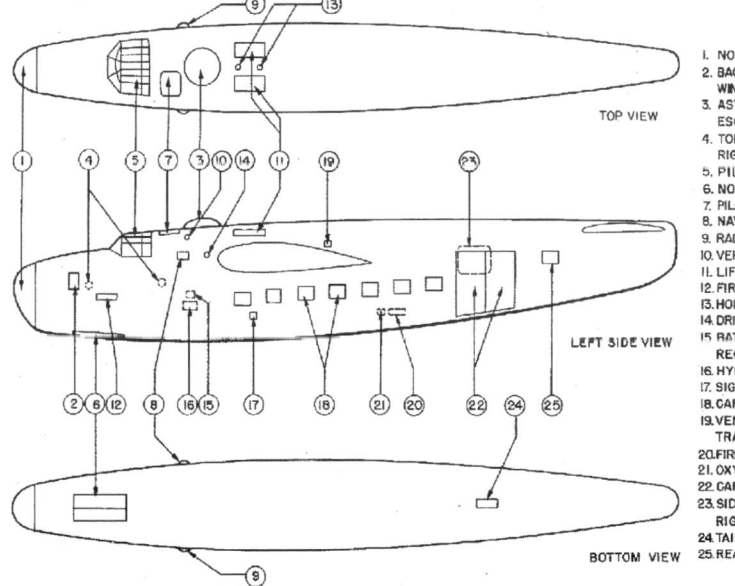

TOP VIEW

LEFT SIDE VIEW

BOTTOM VIEW

1. NOSE DOOR.
2. BAGGAGE COMPARTMENT SIDE WINDOWS.
3. ASTRODOME AND NAVIGATOR'S ESCAPE HATCH.
4. TORQUE TUBE OPENING RIGHT HAND SIDE.
5. PILOTS' ENCLOSURE
6. NOSE WHEEL DOORS.
7. PILOT'S ESCAPE HATCH.
8. NAVIGATOR'S SIDE WINDOW.
9. RADIO OPERATOR'S SIDE WINDOW.
10. VERY PISTOL MOUNT OPENING.
11. LIFE RAFT HATCHES.
12. FIRE EXTINGUISHER ON LEFT SIDE.
13. HOIST FITTING COVER PLATES.
14. DRIFT RECORDER OPENING.
15. BATTERY CART CONNECTION RECEPTACLE.
16. HYDRAULIC TEST CONNECTION.
17. SIGHT GUAGE DRAIN LINE.
18. CARGO COMPARTMENT WINDOWS.
19. VENTILATOR ABOVE TRAILING EDGE.
20. FIRE EXTINGUISHER RIGHT HAND SID.
21. OXYGEN FILLER VALVE RECESS.
22. CARGO DOORS.
23. SIDE ESCAPE PANEL ON RIGHT HAND SIDE.
24. TAIL SKID.
25. REAR COMPARTMENT SIDE WINDOW.

Fuselage Access Doors & Plates

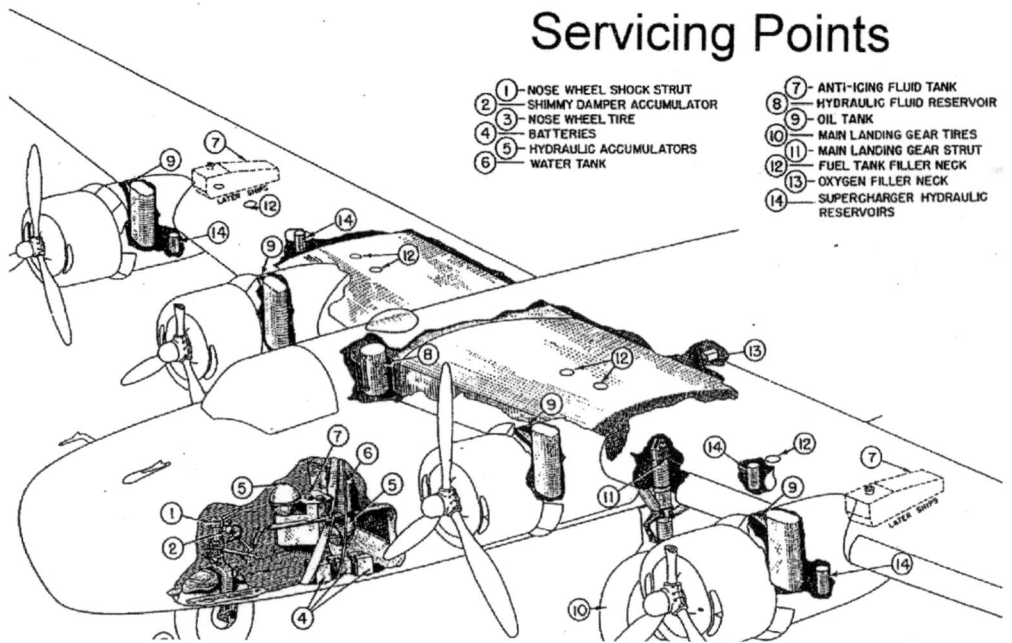

Servicing Points

(1) - NOSE WHEEL SHOCK STRUT
(2) - SHIMMY DAMPER ACCUMULATOR
(3) - NOSE WHEEL TIRE
(4) - BATTERIES
(5) - HYDRAULIC ACCUMULATORS
(6) - WATER TANK

(7) - ANTI-ICING FLUID TANK
(8) - HYDRAULIC FLUID RESERVOIR
(9) - OIL TANK
(10) - MAIN LANDING GEAR TIRES
(11) - MAIN LANDING GEAR STRUT
(12) - FUEL TANK FILLER NECK
(13) - OXYGEN FILLER NECK
(14) - SUPERCHARGER HYDRAULIC RESERVOIRS

Donald Davis and the Development of the Davis Wing

B-24 was characterized by its slab-sided fuselage and the twin tail, but it was the Davis Wing that differentiated the B-24 from its contemporaries and greatly influenced its performance. Aircraft wing design of the 1930s generally positioned the thickest portion of the wing within the first 10 to 15 per cent of the wing chord (distance from the leading to trailing edges) and the National Advisory Committee on Aeronautics (NACA) and aerodynamicist Donald Davis were both looking for wing designs that provided the maximum lift and minimum drag. NACA studies had shown that there was a direct relationship between turbulent air flow and friction drag; determining that rivets, lap joints, and even paint diminished aircraft horsepower simply due to the drag these created. These conclusions by NACA were to have substantial consequences on future aircraft design.

In summer 1937, Davis held US Patent No. 1942688 (filed 25 May 1931 and issued 9 January 1934), which concerned mathematical formulae relating to the development of a group of wing sections that he claimed gave substantially better performance and were much more efficient than any other existing airfoil. Thus, the so-called Davis Wing, which Davis called the 'Fluid Foil', was not a specific physical wing but a mathematical formula for creating high-aspect, low-drag airfoils; one of the first laminar flow wings. Generally, a laminar flow wing delays the turbulence created by the wing passing through the air by placing the thickest part of the wing as far as possible from the leading edge consistent with maintaining lift. The Davis 'Fluid Foil' was a wing design in reverse, starting with a basic low-drag teardrop shape and then modified as required to provide lift. In comparison to existing designs, the Davis design was relatively thick but had a short chord and a high aspect ratio (the length of wings to their width). Davis maintained that his new wing would offer much lower drag than designs then in use and would offer considerable lift even at a small angle of attack (angle between the wing chord line and the flight path). The Davis Wing's ability to generate lift at low angles of attack made it particularly appealing for use in (Consolidated's) flying boats as it would reduce the need to pull up the nose for take-off and landing, which was often limited in flying boats due to the way they floated on the water. Additionally, the thickness of the wing would allow for increased fuel storage, or even the use of embedded engines, which were then a fashionable aircraft design trend.

Already rejected by one major US aircraft company, Davis was granted an interview with Fleet and Laddon, who met Davis' proposal with skepticism as NACA had recently completed a comprehensive wind tunnel study on airfoil shapes. However, the NACA airfoil study did not include a wing like the Davis Wing as existing wind tunnels were too turbulent to test laminar wing theories. However, in 1938 a new wind tunnel was built at the California Institute of Technology's (Cal Tech/CIT) Guggenheim Aeronautical Laboratory. The new Guggenheim wind tunnel created smooth enough air flow to finally test concepts like the Davis Fluid Foil and Laddon reconsidered that Davis could be right. Reuben Fleet agreed to pay for a model and wind tunnel tests costing $40,000, a huge amount at the time.

The initial Guggenheim wind tunnel results were unsatisfactory as the test instruments did not 'return significant readings' to support Davis' estimates. Although allegedly among the most advanced wind tunnel of the time, Davis determined that the wind tunnel instruments were not sufficiently sensitive to record accurate performance measurements. Once the tunnel instruments were re-calibrated, the results of the test showed significantly improved readings but were considered too good to be true. Cal Tech again checked the calibrations of their wind tunnel and ran the tests twice more. When they sent their report to Consolidated it indicated that the wing appeared to deliver everything Davis claimed; that the 'remarkably high value for the Davis Wing is probably associated with a peculiar variation of boundary layer thickness with angle of attack but no real explanation for it has yet appeared'. The report also suggested the good results could be a wind tunnel 'idiosyncrasy' that could only occur in the wind tunnel, or else it could be a ground-breaking concept.

While Davis and the Consolidated engineers now knew that their airfoil had very low drag in the wind tunnel, they did not realize that it was what would become known as a 'laminar flow airfoil'. It was only later that the explanation for the Davis Wing's exceptional performance became apparent. The wing shape, discovered largely by chance, was able to maintain laminar flow over a wider area of its leading edge, to about 20 or 30 per cent of chord. In comparison, most airfoil sections of the day were more typically 5 to 20 per cent. Although later designs were able to greatly improve on this, maintaining laminar flow to upwards of 60 per cent of chord, the Davis Wing represented a great improvement at the time; its cross section showing a distinct likeness to the famous NACA 6-Series Laminar Flow Airfoils used to great advantage in the P-51 Mustang wing design.

After considerable deliberation, Fleet and Laddon decided that they would use the Davis Wing on Consolidated's new twin-engine Model 31 commercial flying boat, which was to be a private venture planned to be both a commercial transport and a possible successor to the PBY Catalina. Then, if the Davis Wing was successful, it was to be considered for use on a projected land-based bomber for which Consolidated had several design studies under way.

On 9 February 1938 Davis and Consolidated entered into a license agreement from which Davis would receive $2,500 for each prototype and a royalty on each subsequent aircraft using his airfoil, based on a sliding scale beginning at ½ of 1 per cent of the selling price of the aircraft (less engines, propellers, other items of Government Furnished Equipment (GFE) and spares) and decreasing to ⅛ of 1 per cent when and if orders reached $10 million. In addition, when total royalty payments reached $50,000, the rate was to be reduced to ¹⁄₁₆ of 1 per cent.

Donald Davis, the Man

Donald Davis had an interesting career in aviation. In spring 1920, Davis, then a millionaire sportsman and aviation enthusiast, wanted to build an aircraft to fly non-stop, coast-to-coast, and contacted Donald Douglas, the president of a fledgling aircraft company. Douglas, though disappointed with the small order of one aircraft, realized that designing and building an aircraft that could fly non-stop across America would lead to other more lucrative projects. With $40,000 from Davis, and borrowing family money, Douglas built the Cloudster, which was the first aircraft in history to airlift a useful load exceeding its own weight. The aircraft showed promise when it broke the Pacific coast altitude record of 19,160ft on 29 March 1921. The first American cross-country flight was attempted by Davis and former Martin Chief Test Pilot Eric Springer on 27 June 1921 but was cut short when their Liberty engine quit over El Paso, Texas. Before a second attempt could be made, two Army pilots, Lieutenants Oakley Kelly and John Macready, flew a Fokker T-2 monoplane from Roosevelt Field, Long Island, to Rockwell Field, San Diego:

Donald Davis (L) and Donald Douglas in 1921, when Douglas built Davis' Cloudster aircraft, which was intended to be the first to cross the US non-stop but lost out to two Army lieutenants flying a Fokker T-2. Afterwards, Davis disappeared from the aviation scene until he approached Reuben Fleet with his Davis Fluid Foil. (*CAC/AAF*)

2,500 miles in 28 hours 50 minutes. With the record broken, Davis sold the Cloudster, which was ultimately purchased in 1925 by T. Claude Ryan, who had established his aircraft company and airline in San Diego. Later, Davis developed a variable-pitch propeller for Bendix, but the 1929 Stock Market Crash ended the Bendix project and ruined Davis financially.

The Davis Wing

Wing Construction

The Liberator wing was a heavily built, all-metal (except for the ailerons), full-cantilever framework of aluminum alloy beam-bulkhead. Despite this type of heavy construction, the Liberator's wing often flexed, as could be easily seen on many photographs of the bomber in flight. It was shoulder-mounted for maximum fuselage stowage and easy aircraft loading. The wing was of the internally braced, stressed skin-type, built in three major sections, the center, outer panel, and tip; with the center section rigidly and permanently riveted to the fuselage at four points. The outer panels and wing tips were removable, as were the leading and trailing edges, however, the trailing edges of the outer panels were not. Heavy reinforcement of the wing was used as required, particularly around the center section bomb bay joints, the landing gear fittings, and the engine nacelles. The main wing was built up on two relatively large main spars, which the Davis Wing section allowed to be located close to the leading and trailing edges. The wing's rigid structure provided the maximum internal volume for fuel storage. On aircraft prior to 41-23640 the space between spars on each side of the center line was arranged to accommodate 12 self-sealing removable fuel cells. On aircraft thereafter nine sections on each side of the wing's center line were filled with Duprene sealant and could be filled with fuel; being the first, so-called 'wet wing' installed on a US military aircraft. This area contained an access panel on the under surface of the wing on either side of the center line to facilitate fuel cell installation and removal and also accommodated the large main gear wheel wells. The entire wing contained 61 ribs, the forming elements of the wing structure, which were formed from pressed Dural sheet in the center section and were mainly of built-up construction in the outer sections.

General Description and Data

The Liberator's wing was probably its most distinctive design feature, and certainly its high aspect ratio was responsible for its long-range capability and what limited aesthetic attributes the slab-sided B-24 offered. With an overall span of 110ft, the wing chord tapered from 14ft at the root to 5ft 2¹³⁄₃₂in at the edge of the detachable wing tip sections, providing a mean aerodynamic chord of 123.72in. The aspect ratio was 11.55, the leading edge was swept back at an angle of 3 degrees 30 minutes; wing incidence was 3 degrees and the no-load dihedral angle 3 degrees 26 minutes. A Consolidated Aircraft Corps

Davis Wing. (*AAF*)

(CAC) 22 per cent section used at the wing root uniformly reduced to a CAC 3 per cent section at the tip, making it a slightly modified Davis high-lift section. Wing incidence was 3 degrees, and dihedral on the upper 30 per cent of the chord line was 1.5 degrees. Each outer panel was 55ft long and spliced on the outer edge of the outboard nacelle. These structures were large, with the center section weighing 4,715lb and the outer panel 1,178lb, and each tip 20lb, for a total of more than 3.5 tons in wing weight alone! Flush, retractable, tie-down points were provided on the wing undersurface.

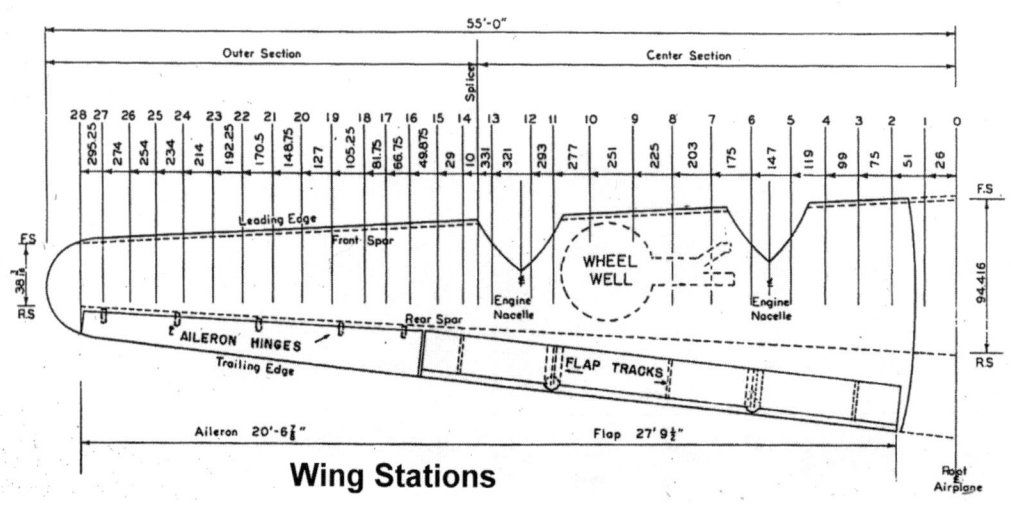

Wing Stations

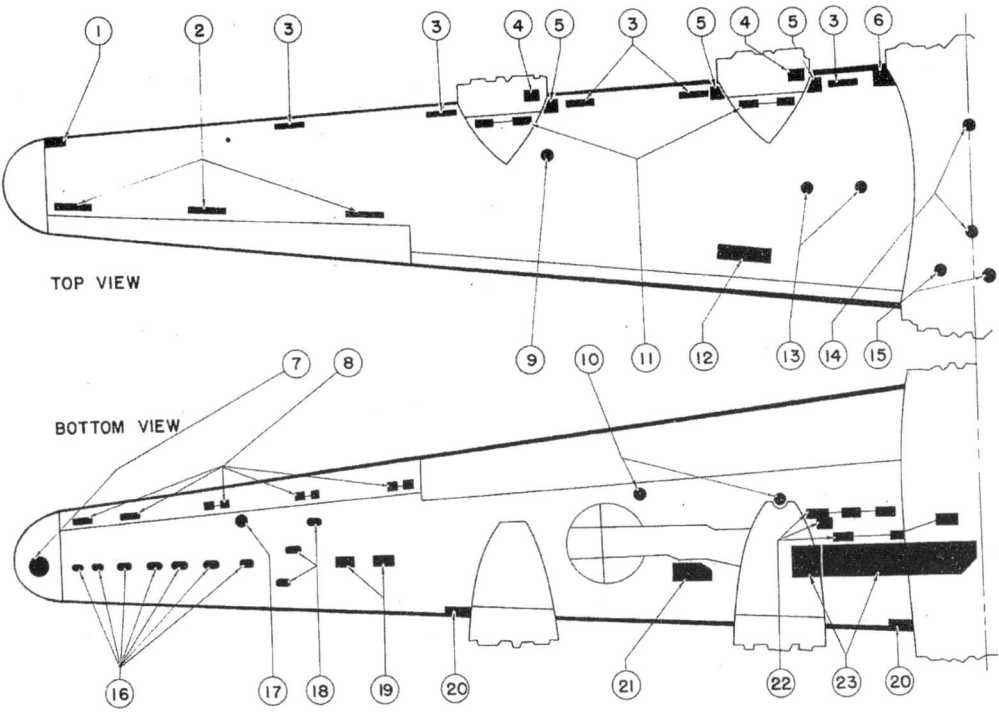

TOP VIEW

BOTTOM VIEW

Wing Access Doors & Plates

1. Wing tip wiring and splice access, under De-Icer shoe.
2. Aileron gear box access (middle access for cable adjustment).
3. De-Icer lines access under shoe.
4. Oil filler neck.
5. Wiring access.
6. De-Icer, heater, fuel, carburetor vent lines and wiring access.
7. Wing tip wiring access.
8. Aileron hinge access.
9. Auxiliary fuel filler access plates on early models. Anti-Icer fluid filler neck access on later models.
10. Jack pad access.
11. Nacelle inspection access plates.
12. Wing flap turnbuckle and flap jack access.
13. Fuel cell filler neck access plates. Two installed on airplanes equipped with fuel cells. One access plate on airplanes equipped with integral tanks.
14. Hoisting section.
15. Fuel vents.
16. Wing structure access plates.
17. Mooring ring.
18. Wing structure access plates.
19. Wing structure access plates.
20. De-Icer lines access under shoe.
21. Wing inspection door.
22. Fuel cell manifold access (airplanes with fuel cells installed).
23. Fuel access doors.

Later, the Liberator bomber and particularly the C-87 transport revealed that its high-aspect ratio Davis Wing, although meeting its promise of lift and speed, caused instability in flight when it was required to carry heavier loads. The Liberator then became difficult to fly, especially at high altitude and in poor weather (notably over the Himalayan Hump) and was also very sensitive to ice formation that distorted the airfoil section, causing lift. The wings were initially equipped with de-icer boots on their leading edges, with later aircraft being equipped with heat anti-icing and having a double-skin construction to replace the de-icer boots.

The Liberator wing consisted of five sub-assemblies as follows:

1) The wing center section was secured permanently to the fuselage and was comprised of the four engine/nacelle assemblies, landing gear, wing flaps, the main system fuel cells, units of the de-icer system, and the passing and landing lights.
2) The right wing's outer panel, which was bolted to the wing center section, was removable; and was comprised of units of the de-icer system, the right aileron, and aileron tab.
3) The left wing's outer panel was bolted to the wing center section and was removable; it and was comprised of units of the de-icer system and the left aileron, and aileron tab.
4) The right wing's tip was detachable from the outboard end of the right outer wing panel by bolts, machine screws, and rivnuts. The green navigation light was mounted on the right wing's tip.
5) The left wing's tip was detachable from the outboard end of the left outer wing panel by bolts, screws, and rivnuts. The red navigation light was mounted on the left wing's tip.

Wing Flaps

The 125lb Liberator flap assembly was of all-metal construction Fowler type, extending from fuselage to aileron. A Fowler flap is one that slides aft and down on tracks, thereby increasing the wing camber, as do other flaps, but giving an advantageous additional increase in wing area in the extended position. With a total area of 144 sq ft, these flaps gave an approximate 10 per cent increase in wing area, which produced a 10 per cent decrease in wing loading, thereby lowering the landing speed a proportionate amount. The Fowler-type flaps were fabricated of aluminum alloy and Alclad sheet and moved rearward on rollers over five steel tracks attached to lugs on the rear spar. Tracks were steel I-beams bolted to a tubular two-dimensional truss. Five carriages located along the leading edge of each flap were riveted to the flap. One single roller and three pairs of rollers were fitted in each flap carriage. One single roller and four pairs were installed in center carriage. These rollers rode on five separate, removable stainless steel flap tracks. Rubber stops, installed in the tracks, fore-and-aft, limited the amount of flap travel.

Extension and retraction of each flap was via two pairs of cables anchored to the actuating piston and attached to the flaps at Wing Stations 6 and 11 and were connected to a single hydraulic jack that was mounted on the rear spar of the left wing between Wing Stations 3 and 5. The wing flap actuating cylinder control was located on the top of the pilot's right side control pedestal and energized the flaps by pressure from the main hydraulic system. To extend the flaps, the actuating control handle was moved to the rear and to retract the flaps the handle was moved forward. When fully extended or retracted or placed at the desired flap setting, the valve operating handle was returned to the neutral position. The automatic hydraulic return-type flap operating valve was located on the right side of the control pedestal, and excessive flap loads caused the hydraulic relief valve to open and allow the flaps to retract. The relief valve was an automatic safety device and was not to be used or tested in flight.

Take-off was normally made at about 20 degrees flap and landings at the maximum extension of 40 degrees down, with any desired intermediate angular setting as required by the aircraft's loading. Maximum extension gave a 55 per cent increase in lift and a 70 per cent increase in drag. At the position of 20 degrees down the lift increased 24 per cent and the drag increased 30 per cent. The Selsyn indicator on the instrument panel always showed the flap position. The maximum airspeed at which flaps were to be lowered was set at an indicated airspeed of 155mph. The landing gear and flap operating gear were not to be operated simultaneously. In an emergency the flaps could be lowered manually by using the hand pump through an independent hydraulic line. The front emergency valve was wired open so that the hand pump was always turned ON to the main system while the flap emergency valve was wired closed. In an emergency, the safety wire was to be removed and the emergency flap valve (the rear valve of a dual unit located to the right of co-pilot's seat) was to be opened with the forward valve to the main system to be closed. The flap lever was to be placed in the DOWN position as failure to do this created a hydraulic lock, causing the flaps not to lower. Operation of the hand pump initially opened the shuttle valve to EMERGENCY and closed off the main system, then operated the flap piston. To raise the flaps, the forward emergency valve was opened while the rear valve was still open to permit the shuttle valve to return to its normal position. The Davis Wing was tapered in planform (contour) and cross section, which resulted in a warped lower surface, making it necessary that the flap also have a warped contour to ensure a continuous fit with the underside of the wing. Later, landing vibration problems necessitated reinforcement of the flap structure so that warping by cable tension was impossible and a revised inboard stop was provided to reduce the amount of warping required. This caused the inboard trailing edge of the flap to retract to a point slightly aft of its normal position, resulting in a small break in the original uniform taper of the trailing edge of the Liberator wing.

On B-24C aircraft and B-24Ds up to, but excluding, number 2350, warping the flaps was accomplished by creating differing rigging tensions between the inboard and outboard operating cables. According to the B-24 *Erection and Maintenance Manual*, 'This differential ranges up to 130lb, depending on each individual flap and airplane.'

On B-24Ds numbers 40-2350 up to, but excluding, 41-11754 (including the first 25 C-87s), the flaps were built with greater reinforcement, making warping via differential rigging tension not always feasible. For these Liberators, the *Erection and Maintenance Manual* noted: '… a larger inboard forward stop is provided and should be used, if necessary, to reduce the amount of warping required. The trailing edge of the flap will trail aft of its normal position at the inboard end on installations using the longer stops.'

Beginning with B-24D number 11754 onward and all other C-87 and C-87As, the wing flaps were constructed with the chord plane already warped 1.5 degrees to fit the wing contour. This eliminated the need for extreme rigging tension differential, although a moderate differential might still be needed to ensure a snug fit.

Ailerons

The aileron structure was of an aluminum-alloy torque box and rib construction and was fabric covered with the leading edge reinforced with Alclad sheet. Each aileron was attached to the wing outer panel at five points with pre-lubricated bearing hinges. Each had a total area of 41.55 sq ft and an effective area of 31.6 sq ft. The right aileron had an irreversible trailing edge tab.

The ailerons were direct operating with no differential ratio and were aerodynamically dynamically and statically balanced. They had a 20 degrees movement up or down and a lateral control moment arm of approximately 40 minutes. They were actuated by four anti-backlash gear boxes (two on each side), mounted on the rear spar. Three kinds of aileron gear boxes were used. Two types, having the characteristic flat top, differ in number of teeth and diameter of sprocket. The third type was rounded on top.

Aileron control cables traveled from the control unit sprockets outboard to the pulleys on left side of the fuselage at Station 1.0, aft over guide pulleys at Station 3.1 through fairleads to Station 5.1; then upward to the center section rear spar, where they wrapped around a spiral grooved drum. Cables from the aileron right and left inboard gear box sprockets also wrapped around this drum. The inboard gear box on each side was connected to a second outboard gear box by a chain and cable assembly. The four worm and pinion gear boxes operated lever arms and links that actuated the ailerons.

Aileron Trim Tab

The one trim tab, installed near the inboard edge in the right aileron, was controlled by a wheel on the aft side of the pilot's control pedestal, through two cables to a push-pull mechanism at tab station in right wing. Turning the wheel to the right moved the right wing down and turning left lowered the left wing. The flexible steel aileron trim control cables traveled from a drum (operated by the hand wheel) to pulleys under the flight deck, then aft to Station 5.1 and up to the wing rear spar. From there the cables ran outboard along the right rear spar to a sprocket on a torque tube. The torque tube operated a push-pull tube through a screw mechanism similar to the other tab mechanisms.

Wing Tip

The 20lb wing tip was attached to the wing outer panel with countersunk screws and clastic stop nuts.

Empennage

General Description

The horizontal and vertical stabilizers/fins were of a riveted, all-metal Alclad aluminum alloy, stressed skin-type construction, built up on 'U' channel spars with pressed flange ribs and spanwise stiffeners. They were initially equipped with de-icer boots on their leading edges with later aircraft being equipped with heat anti-icing and with a double-skin construction that replaced the de-icer boots. The stabilizer, constructed as a separate assembly, had a smooth sheet metal skin, and was attached to the fuselage with only four fittings to facilitate replacement. Rudder and elevator control surfaces were fabric covered on an aluminum alloy torque box and rib construction, with leading edges of sheet Alclad, and were statically and dynamically balanced. An ingenious balance system was employed on the rudders, with the leading edge slots being opposite, above and below the elevator. Rudders and elevator trim tabs, controllable from the cockpit, were either of formed Alclad sheets internally braced or of molded plastic construction. The entire Liberator tail assembly was attached to the fuselage with four (later eight) bolts and was mounted just enough forward of the tail gunner's compartment so that the trailing edge did not obscure the gunner's vision. Some landing vibration damage was discovered in early aircraft since no major structural changes had accompanied an increase in span from 24 to 26ft. However, the assembly was rugged and was eventually stressed to withstand landing load forces of 25Gs. Later, a new, single-tail assembly, designed at the request of the AAF, required relatively few changes in the original aft fuselage structures. The new stabilizer was designed to attach to the previous twin-tail fittings, with the dorsal and fin attaching to the new structure.

Horizontal Tail

The horizontal tail surfaces of the original twin-rudder assembly design were a NACA section No. 0015 aerofoil and comprised 192 sq ft including the elevator's 51 sq ft, and the span was 26ft, increased from an earlier 24ft. The maximum chord was 7ft 8³⁄₁₆in. Distance from the design gross weight CG, assumed at 25 per cent MAC (Mean Aerodynamic Chord: the average length of the chord) to the one-third maximum chord point, was 33.40ft, which was approximately 3.5 times MAC. Stabilizer area, including elevator balance, was 140.5 sq ft. The horizontal stabilizer was of the non-adjustable type; its setting relative to the normal longitudinal axis of the aircraft was 2.5 degrees.

The surface of the horizontal stabilizer was composed of one section that was to be rigidly attached to the fuselage via four aluminum alloy forgings. These forgings were riveted to the horizontal stabilizer spars and were fastened by eight bolts to similar fittings on the fuselage that would support the entire weight of the entire empennage assembly.

Elevators

The elevators had an effective area (aft of the hinge center line) of 51.46 sq ft and an area of balance of 15.60 sq ft, for a total area of 67.06 sq ft. The elevators were attached to the horizontal stabilizer, each of which could be moved 30 degrees up or 20 degrees down; they were aerodynamically, dynamically, and statically balanced; and in the trailing edge of each was a trim tab with irreversible controls. The elevators were attached to the horizontal stabilizer by five aluminum alloy (built-up) hinge brackets riveted or bolted to the horizontal stabilizer rear spar. These five hinged points were: one hinge bearing bolted to the outboard side of each elevator, a hinge bearing at each elevator cut-out (the bracket was permanently riveted to the stabilizer), and a fifth hinge at the aircraft center line where the torque tubes of both elevators joined. The elevator torque tubes were bolted together through the control lock fitting and operated the elevators as one surface.

The torque tubes of the two surfaces were bolted together through the controls lock fitting mounted on the stabilizer at the center line of the airframe and operated as one surface. The elevators were operated by two sets of control cables through two bell cranks (changes motion through an angle), two push-pull tubes, and two single end horns (torque arms) on torque shaft. When the pilot pulled back on the control column, the elevator moved up, pulling the tail down causing the nose to rise. When the pilot pushed forward on the controls, the elevator moved down, pulling the tail up and causing the nose to go down. Trim tabs were in the trailing edge of each surface. The amount of elevator movement was limited by stops in the hinge bracket at the center line of the airplane. The elevators were not interchangeable. These hinge bearings were pre-lubricated, factory-sealed, and thus, required no lubrication in service.

Elevator Tabs

The elevators had tabs on their trailing edge that had a total angular movement of ±10 degrees. The tabs were of two types: formed Alclad sheet internally braced and riveted or of molded plastic construction.

Vertical Tail (Fin)

The vertical fins used an NACA 0007 flat-sided aerofoil and had a combined area of 122.84 sq ft. Each fin was fixed with a normal setting of zero. Each vertical fin surface was rigidly attached by four bolts to the end of the horizontal stabilizer.

Rudders

The rudders had a total area of 65 sq ft, comprised of 48.84 sq ft aft of the hinge center line and the balance forward of this point. Right or left movement was 20 degrees; 10 degrees right and left of center. Like the ailerons and elevators, rudders had aerodynamic,

dynamic, and static balance; and in the trailing edge of each rudder was an irreversible control-operated trim tab. Spanwise elements were statically balanced about the hinge line. The rudder hinges were composed of a hinge support (aluminum alloy sheet), a hinge (aluminum alloy forging), and a bearing, and were riveted to the vertical stabilizers. The hinge support that attached to the fin was a built-up fitting constructed of an aluminum alloy sheet. The hinge bolted to the rudder was an aluminum alloy forging. The rudder was operated by a bellcrank whose pivot point was the rudder hinge. A cable connected the pilot's rudder pedal to one side of the bellcrank and when the pilot pushed on the rudder pedal, the rudder rotated on its hinge. The opposite rudder pedal was connected to the other end of the bellcrank to rotate the rudder in the opposite direction. Right and left rudders also were interchangeable by reversing the attaching horns.

Rudder Tabs

The twin rudder tabs, attached to each rudder trailing edge, had total area of 19.2 sq ft but this was increased to 31 sq ft beginning with 42-40753 on CO B-24 bomber and C-87 Liberators and 42-63926 on CF Liberators. Rudder tabs were of two types, formed Alclad sheet internally braced and riveted, or of molded phenolic plastic. These tabs could be set up to 10 degrees right or left, with the amount of rudder movement limited by stops in the elevator at the rudder bell cranks. The tabs were actuated by a wheel mounted on the top of the pilot's control pedestal. Rotating the wheel clockwise turned the bomber to the right and counter-clockwise to the left. A vertical torque tube inside the pedestal connected the hand wheel through a pair of gears and torque tube to the cable drum. The cables ran aft to a torque tube aft of the rear spar of the horizontal stabilizer. The torque tube connected into a gear box in the fins, which operated a screw mechanism actuating the tabs. The tab operating cables were 7 × 19 extra flexible steel. All tab screw mechanisms were lubricated at assembly and at each overhaul of the airplane.

Empennage Component Interchangeability

Vertical stabilizers were interchangeable by the transfer of the installed running light to the opposite side. Rudder horns were left or right and had to be shifted for the interchange of rudders. Left and right elevators were not interchangeable. Left and right elevator and rudder tabs were not interchangeable, but the metal tabs were interchangeable with plastic tabs without modification.

Empennage

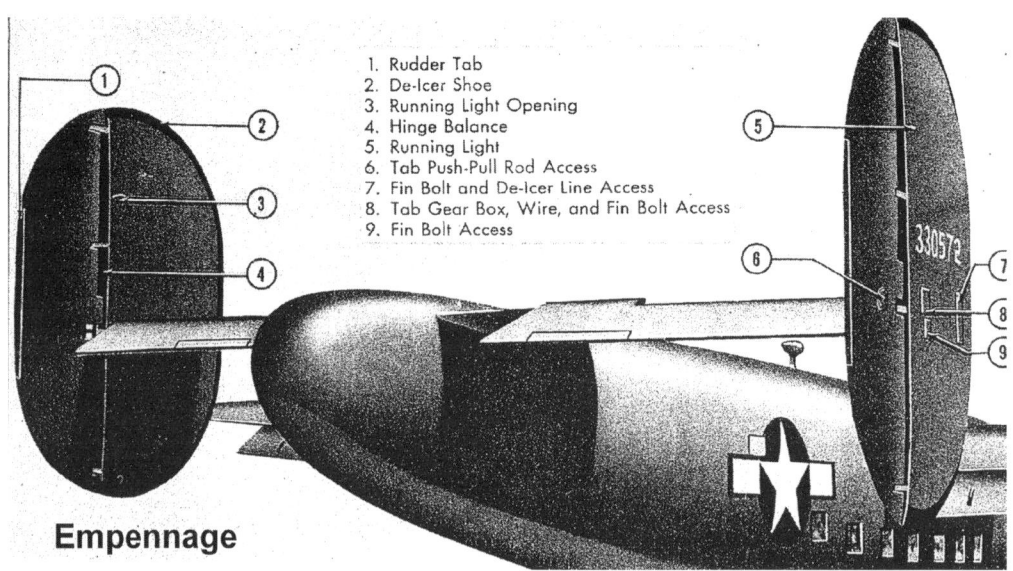

1. Rudder Tab
2. De-Icer Shoe
3. Running Light Opening
4. Hinge Balance
5. Running Light
6. Tab Push-Pull Rod Access
7. Fin Bolt and De-Icer Line Access
8. Tab Gear Box, Wire, and Fin Bolt Access
9. Fin Bolt Access

Empennage

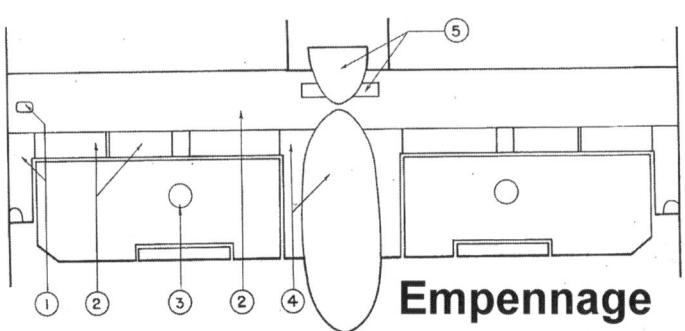

Empennage

1. RUDDER CONTROL ACCESS
2. ACCESS TO ELEVATOR HINGE, TAB CONTROLS, RUDDER CONTROLS & WIRING
3. TAB CONTROL ACCESS
4. ACCESS TO STABILIZER BOLTS, ELEVATOR TORQUE TUBE, TAB CONTROLS, RUDDER CONTROLS, & CONTROL LOCKS
5. ACCESS TO STABILIZER BOLTS, DE-ICER LINES, & SURFACE CONTROLS
6. COVER PLATE FOR RUNNING LIGHT OPENING
7. RUDDER TAB GEAR BOX, WIRES, & FIN BOLT ACCESS
8. RUDDER TAB CONTROL ACCESS
9. FIN BOLTS ACCESS HOLE
10. FIN BOLTS & DE-ICER TUBES ACCESS

NOTE:
LEFT & RIGHT
RUDDERS ARE
INTERCHANGEABLE

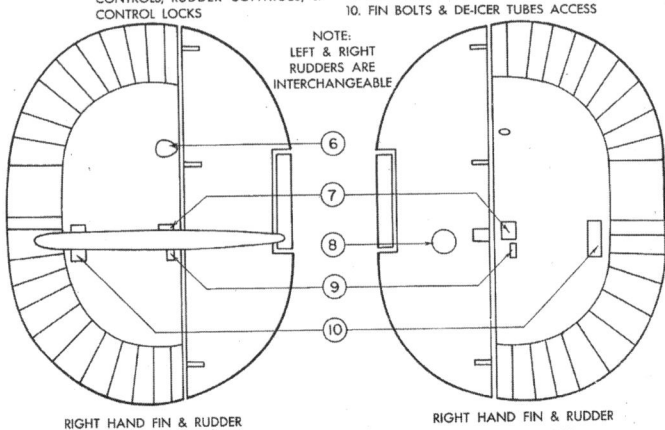

RIGHT HAND FIN & RUDDER
INBOARD SIDE

RIGHT HAND FIN & RUDDER
OUTBOARD SIDE

Surface Controls

Flight was controlled by two ailerons, two elevators, two rudders, and two hydraulically operated wing flaps that extended along the trailing edge of the wings from the fuselage to the inboard end of each aileron. Trim tabs were provided on the elevators, rudders, and on the right aileron.

Control Wheels and Columns

Two control wheels and columns, one for the pilot and the other for the co-pilot extended from the flight deck instrument panel.

Rudder Control

Dual sets of rudder pedals were located on the floor of the flight deck forward of both pilots' feet. The pedal distance from each seat was adjustable to accommodate the individual pilot. The pedals were unlocked by kicking the lever on the left side of each pedal, moving the pedal to the desired position, then jiggling the pedal until the locking pin dropped into place, locking the pedal in position.

Trim Tab Control

The aileron trim tab was controlled by a wheel at the rear of the control pedestal. The rudder trim tabs were controlled by a wheel knob on top of the pedestal, and the elevator trim tabs by a wheel mounted on the left of the pedestal. On the pedestal adjacent to the trim tab controls were scales divided and marked to indicate where the trim tab controls were set so that a glance showed previous settings if the aircraft became out of trim, enabling the pilots to always judge flight conditions.

Wing Flap Control

The wing flap control was on the lower right side of the engine control pedestal. An electric flap position indicator was located on the co-pilot's side of the instrument panel. The maximum flap deflection was 40 degrees, at which position the wing lift increase was 55 per cent and the drag increase was 70 per cent. At the 20 degrees DOWN position, the lift increase was 24 per cent, and the drag increase was 30 per cent. Flaps were never to be lowered when the indicated air speed exceeded 155mph, as excessive flap loads would cause the hydraulic relief valve to open and allow the flaps to retract. The landing gear and the flaps were not to be operated simultaneously.

Control Surface Locking

Control surfaces were locked by a lever at the rear of the pilots' control pedestal. The surfaces were locked by neutralizing the controls and slowly pulling up on the lever, slowly moving the controls to assist engagement of the lockpins. When not in use the locking lever was secured by a strap that was stowed against the ceiling, over the engine control pedestal.

Landing Gear

The Liberator was characterized by its low-slung tricycle landing gear consisting of two main wheels and a nose wheel, all mounted on the air-oil shock struts. The tricycle landing gear on the B-24D/C-87 had a tread of 25.5ft, while the distance between nose and main gear axles (center line measurement) was 16ft. Bendix pneumatic air-oil shock struts were used on the main and nose gears. The main gear uniquely retracted outward and upward into wells in the undersurface of the center wings, while the nose wheel retracted upward and slightly aft into a well just forward of the pilot's cockpit floor. The gear could be retracted in 22 seconds under pressure of 1,000 psi and lowered and locked in 44 seconds under 800 psi. There were four methods to lower the landing gear: hydraulic, an electric motor to drive a pump, a hand-operated pump, and an emergency gear box. Both gears were equipped with emergency release and retraction mechanisms.

Nose Gear

The Nose Wheel Well (Stations 1.0 to 4.0) extended from below the flight deck and radio operator's compartment. The nose wheel retracting mechanism, nose wheel and nose wheel doors were located at the forward end of this compartment and the aft end contained the auxiliary power unit (APU), fixed engine fire extinguisher cylinders (early aircraft only), liaison antenna reel, amplidyne units (on aircraft equipped with electric nose turrets), storage battery, AC power inverter, voltage regulators, hydraulic system accumulators, and various other items. The nose wheel was free to swivel 30 degrees each way and was dampened against shimmying.

   The 354lb nose landing gear was mounted in the forward part of the fuselage beneath the flight deck in the nose wheel well. It was mounted on a support shaped roughly like a reverse numeral '4' with the nose wheel axle at the bottom and the main trunnion at the apex of the horizontal angle. The actuating link was attached to the top and by moving this point aft the gear rotated forward, upward and into the fuselage. Double 'V' strut fittings, or support arms, supported the gear pivot in fittings near the bottom of Station 2.0. The drag link, with its up and down lock, pivoted from fittings under the flight compartment floor and broke near its center to allow the gear either to extend or retract, locking rigidly to hold the gear in either position. A floating hydraulic jack between the lower 'V' strut and the drag links retracted or extended the gear.

As the Liberator left the ground, two lugs on the nose wheel moved about a worm gear arrangement that placed it in a fore and aft position as the weight of the wheel moved it down; making it ready for automatic retraction. When under load on the ground the nose wheel was free to rotate. A shimmy damper mounted on the rear of the nose gear shock strut permitted slow turning movements of the nose wheel but damped out the rapid oscillating movements known as 'shimmy'. A scissors assembly transmitted torque or turning forces of the nose wheel to a shimmy damper. Until B-24D-CO 42-40392 and D-CF 42-63832, a rather complicated emergency nose gear release was standard. This was then abandoned, and the following instructions substituted: 'In all subsequent airplanes, nose gear is lowered in an emergency by kicking it out and is independent of the main gear emergency system.'

Nose Gear. (*AAF*)

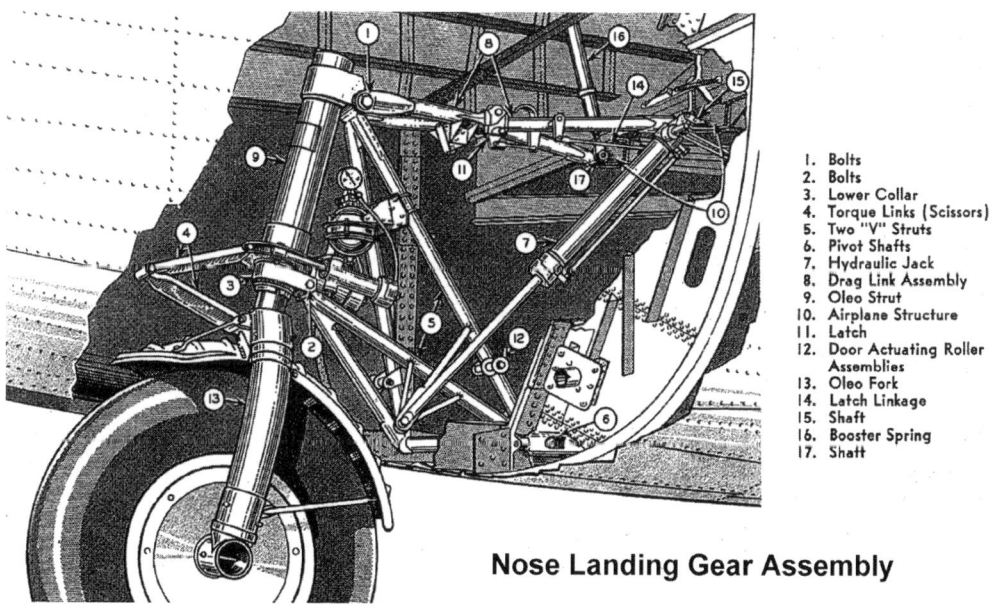

1. Bolts
2. Bolts
3. Lower Collar
4. Torque Links (Scissors)
5. Two "V" Struts
6. Pivot Shafts
7. Hydraulic Jack
8. Drag Link Assembly
9. Oleo Strut
10. Airplane Structure
11. Latch
12. Door Actuating Roller
    Assemblies
13. Oleo Fork
14. Latch Linkage
15. Shaft
16. Booster Spring
17. Shaft

Nose Landing Gear Assembly

Main Gear

The 2,562lb Liberator main landing gear assembly with a tread width of 26ft 7in was mounted in the wing center section, aft of engines No. 2 and No. 3. Each gear was supported by pivot shafts mounted in auxiliary spars located just outboard of the inboard engine cowling, between the front and rear spars. The shock strut hinged on a shaft mounted between two auxiliary wing spars outboard of Station 6. A jointed side brace was connected between the wing and the lower end of the shock strut cylinder. A free-floating hydraulic jack (i.e., attached only to the gear itself) connected between an arm on the main pivot shaft and the side brace pivot shaft, was used to extend and retract the gear. As it began to extend, the lateral strut, having less resistance, was displaced first, following which the strut action was concentrated on the main gear leg. A scissors joint was connected between the lower end of the shock absorber cylinder and the shock absorber piston to transmit wheel torque. A rigid drag strut was attached to the lower end of the shock strut cylinder and pivoted on the front shaft of the main pivot shaft when the gear was retracted. Latches were used to hold the gear rigid in the retracted and extended positions. The main landing gear units were interchangeable, left and right. Large, fixed fairings on the lower side of the wing streamlined the wheel in the retracted position, it being too wide to be fully enclosed within the wing panel.

Main Gear. (*AAF*)

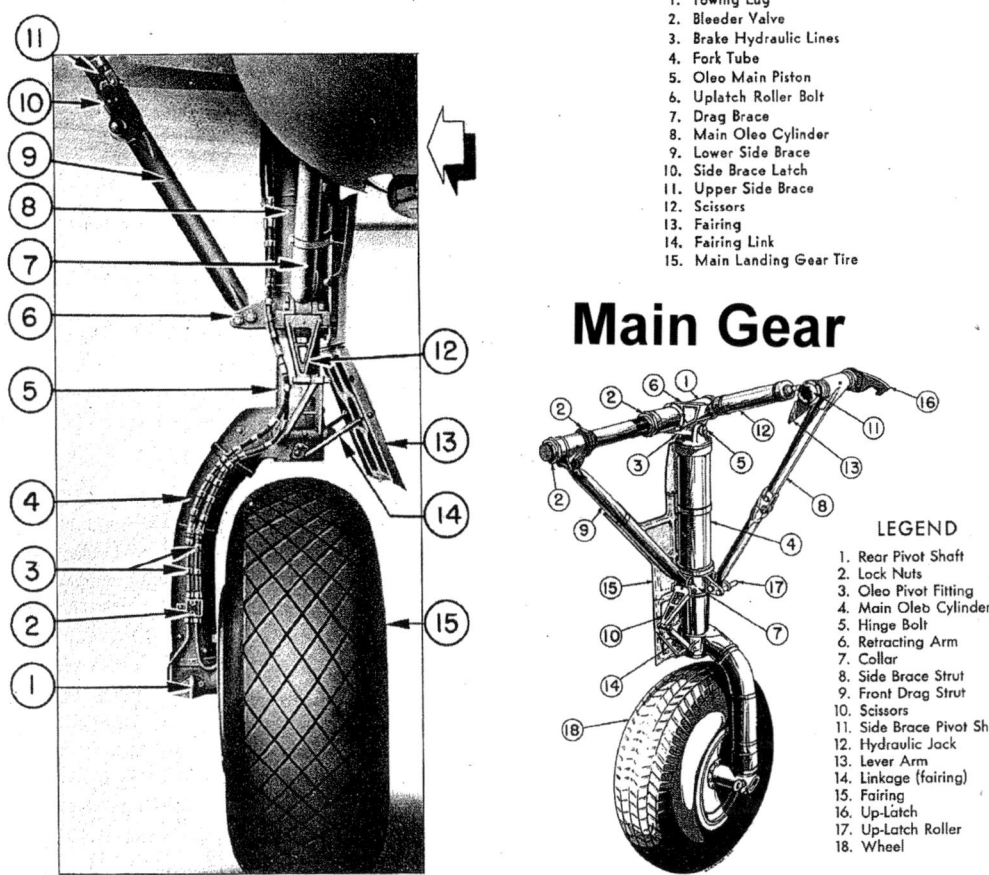

1. Towing Lug
2. Bleeder Valve
3. Brake Hydraulic Lines
4. Fork Tube
5. Oleo Main Piston
6. Uplatch Roller Bolt
7. Drag Brace
8. Main Oleo Cylinder
9. Lower Side Brace
10. Side Brace Latch
11. Upper Side Brace
12. Scissors
13. Fairing
14. Fairing Link
15. Main Landing Gear Tire

Main Gear

LEGEND

1. Rear Pivot Shaft
2. Lock Nuts
3. Oleo Pivot Fitting
4. Main Oleo Cylinder
5. Hinge Bolt
6. Retracting Arm
7. Collar
8. Side Brace Strut
9. Front Drag Strut
10. Scissors
11. Side Brace Pivot Sh(
12. Hydraulic Jack
13. Lever Arm
14. Linkage (fairing)
15. Fairing
16. Up-Latch
17. Up-Latch Roller
18. Wheel

Tail Bumper

The final component of the landing gear was the tail bumper under the rear fuselage at Station 7.2. This auxiliary tail bumper/wheel/skid was not intended as an aid to normal landing but was to protect the aft fuselage if the aircraft landed with its tail low, if it tipped backward when on the ground, or to afford a support point for the tail stand when the Liberator was being loaded or when parked. Heavy loads on the tailskid were always to be avoided. Care was to be taken that any time the aircraft was being towed backward that the tailskid never touched the ground. Very early Liberators, LB-30s, and B-24As, used an actual 75 psi, fixed-type tail wheel, permanently mounted with approximately half of its diameter remaining outside the aircraft. On early D models and a few early C-87s this was changed to a fixed, non-retractable, hard rubber bumper type consisting of twelve streamlined rubber pads extending vertically downward from the fuselage at Station 7.2.

Tail Bumper. (*AAF*)

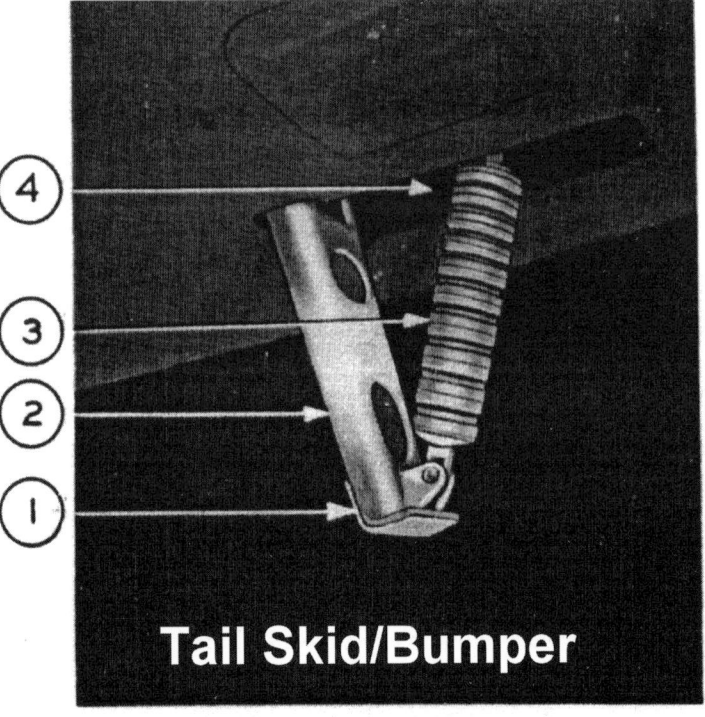

1. Skid Plate   3. Shock Strut
2. Skid Plate Brace   4. Tail Skid Retracting Opening

Tail Support Assembly

A tail support assembly, consisting of a hydraulic jack mounted on a tripod, was stowed on the right side of the rear compartment, aft of Station 8. It attached to the fuselage at Station 7.4 with two bolts that were part of the assembly. It was important on the C-87 that the tail support would always be installed when the aircraft was being loaded or unloaded, or to prevent tipping if sudden shifts of weight should occur.

Tail Support Assembly. (*AAF*)

Landing Gear Operation

All three units of the tricycle landing gear were simultaneously extended hydraulically when the landing gear control lever on the lower left-hand side of the central control pedestal was placed in the DOWN position and simultaneously retracted when the control lever was placed in the UP position. The handle returned to neutral following completion of each cycle. The landing gear warning signal was a light on the pilot's instrument panel that glowed when the landing gear was DOWN and locked. The landing gear could be raised or lowered manually in case of hydraulic system failure. A solenoid-operated locking pin on the pilot's pedestal prevented the landing gear operating handle from being pushed forward accidentally while the aircraft was on the ground. The solenoid was energized, and the locking pin released by pressing the button in the top of the landing gear operating lever.

Brakes

The Liberator brakes were a portion of the Hayes wheel and brake assembly that included an outboard brake and inboard brake. The two main landing gear wheels were equipped with hydraulically operated brakes, individually controlled by auxiliary pedals located at the tips of each rudder pedal and operated independently of the rudder control pedals. The left brake pedal operated the brake for the left main landing gear wheel, while the right brake pedal operated the right main landing gear brake. Inboard and outboard pressure gauges were on the auxiliary instrument panel to the left of the pilot's control column. The pistons of the brake hydraulic operating valves were actuated by the brake pedals through a system of push-pull rods and torque shafts. The landing gear brakes were intended for emergency use and to be used judiciously when using the flaps when slowing during a landing or stopping or manipulating the aircraft on the ground since multi-engine aircraft could be controlled by proper use of the engines.

Since braking was more important for the C-87 transport pilot who had to land with heavy cargo than the B-24 bomber pilot who had dropped his bomb load; the following policies outlined in the *C-87's Pilot's Flight Manual* were to be observed to prevent brake failure and to reduce brake maintenance:

1) Avoid continuous use of the brakes during taxiing as much as possible.
2) Allow ample time for cooling during times when it is necessary to use the brakes to such an extent that they overheat.
3) Except in an 'extreme emergency' the aircraft is not to be landed with the brakes on.
4) Never park the aircraft with the brakes set until they have been permitted to cool.
5) To protect the nose wheel, whenever practicable, turn the aircraft by other means than pivoting it on one wheel with the brakes set.
6) When operating the aircraft at high gross weights, extra care should be taken to not to overheat the brakes.
7) Brake so that the nose gear is aligned with the fuselage whenever the aircraft is brought to a stop as taxiing from this stopped position will be begun from a straight-ahead position.

The brakes were set for parking the aircraft by fully depressing both brake pedals as far as possible and pulling up on the parking brake lever located near the lower left side of the aft part of the control pedestal. When the lever reached the locking position the brake pedals were to be released; holding the aircraft with the brakes securely locked. The parking brakes were released by fully depressing the brake pedals; dropping the parking lever to disengage the brakes.

Tires and Wheels

Tires

Both main and nose wheel tires were of smooth-contour (no tread) design on early B-24D and C-87 aircraft, but later models of both were supplied with an overall diamond tread design. No-tread and non-skid-tread tires were to be used only in like pairs because of the difference in traction when brakes were applied. All dual inner tubes were designed to support 27,000lb and the set of three landing gear tires supported over 200,000lb. Tire condition and inflation was particularly important on the B-24 hauler versions and were to be to thoroughly checked before each flight because of the variation of conditions.

Main Gear Tires and Wheels

The main landing gear was equipped with Hayes 56in one-piece cast smooth contour aluminum alloy or magnesium alloy wheels, dual heavy-duty duplex expander tube brake assemblies, and tires and inner tubes. For easy tire and tube removal the wheel had a cast aluminum alloy removable rim flange mounting held in place by a tubular snap ring. The 56in diameter, 16-ply, natural rubber sidewalls and synthetic tread tires had a ground contact area of 345 sq in and mounted on an oleo-pneumatic shock-absorbing strut. The main gear tire weighed 250lb and its natural rubber tube weighed 37lb, and the weight of the complete main wheel assembly weighed 562lb. Main gear tire inflation was 56 psi for hard surface operation and 55 psi for soft surface operation.

Nose Wheel Tire and Wheel

The nose gear was equipped with Hayes 36in cast aluminum alloy or magnesium alloy wheels. The 36in diameter, 10-ply, natural rubber sidewalls and synthetic tread tires had a natural rubber tube and was mounted on an oleo-pneumatic shock-absorbing strut whose assembly included a shimmy damper. Nose wheel tire inflation was 38 psi for hard surface operation and 35 psi for soft surface operation.

Flight Deck and Pilot's Instruments and Controls

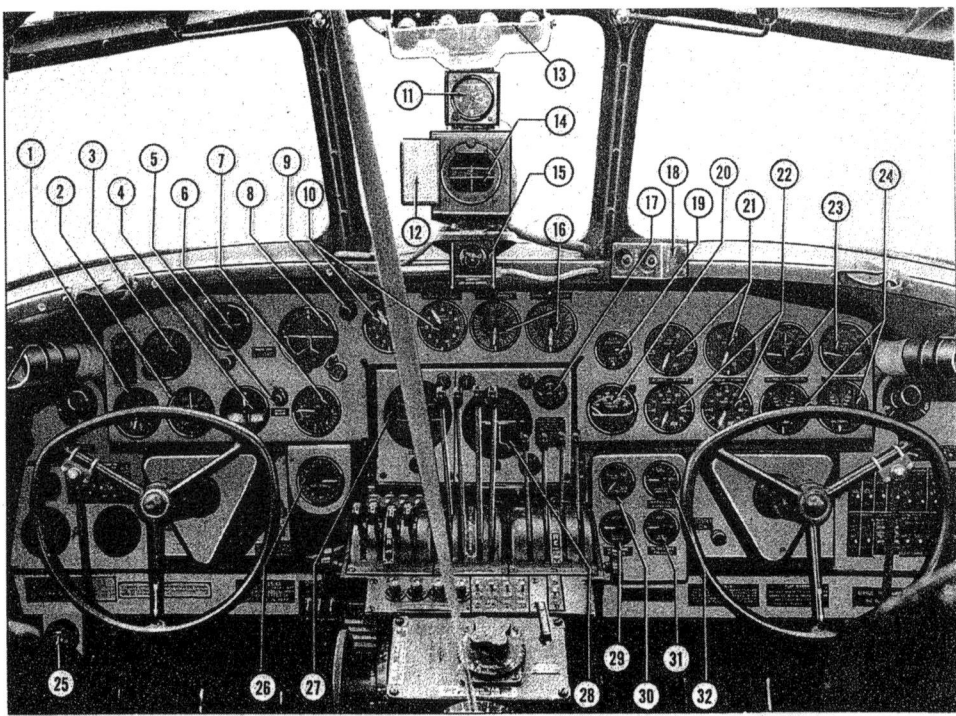

1. Altimeter
2. Air Speed Indicator
3. Accelerometer
4. Bank and Turn Indicator
5. Marker Beacon
6. Turn Indicator
7. Rate of Climb Indicator
8. Flight Indicator
9. Wheels Locked Down Light
10. Manifold Pressure Gages
11. Clock
12. Compass Card
13. Propeller Feathering
    Switches
14. Magnetic Compass
15. Compass Light Rheostat
16. Tachometers
17. Vacuum Gage
18. Radio Detonator Switches
19. Flap Position Indicator
20. Free Air Thermometer
21. Fuel Pressure Gages
22. Oil Pressure Gages
23. Cylinder Head Tempera-
    ture Gages
24. Oil Temperature Gages
25. Oxygen Regulator and
    Indicator
26. Radio Compass Indicator
27. Directional Gyro
28. Bank and Climb Gyro
29. Inboard Brake Pressure
    Gage
30. Automatic Pilot Pressure
    Gage
31. Outboard Brake Pressure
    Gage
32. Hydraulic Pressure Gage

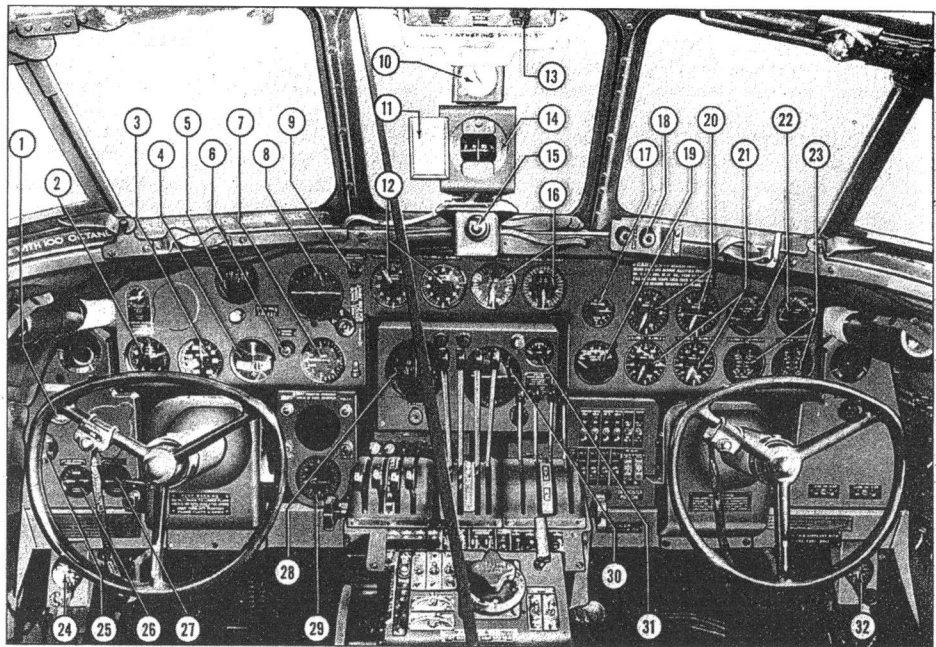

1. Hydraulic Pressure Gage
2. Altimeter
3. Air Speed Indicator
4. Bank and Turn Indicator
5. Turn Indicator
6. Marker Beacon
7. Rate of Climb Indicator
8. Flight Indicator
9. Wheels Locked Down Light
10. Clock

11. Compass Card
12. Manifold Pressure Gages
13. Propeller Feathering
    Switches
14. Magnetic Compass
15. Compass Light Rheostat
16. Tachometers
17. Flap Position Indicator
18. Radio Detonator Switches
19. Free Air Thermometer

20. Fuel Pressure Gages
21. Oil Pressure Gages
22. Cylinder Head Tempera-
    ture Gages
23. Oil Temperature Gages
24. Oxygen Regulator and
    Indicator
25. Automatic Pilot Pressure
    Gage

26. Inboard Brake Pressure
    Gage
27. Outboard Brake Pressure
    Gage
28. Directional Gyro
29. Radio Compass Indicator
30. Bank and Climb Gyro
31. Vacuum Gage
32. Oxygen Regulator and
    Indicator

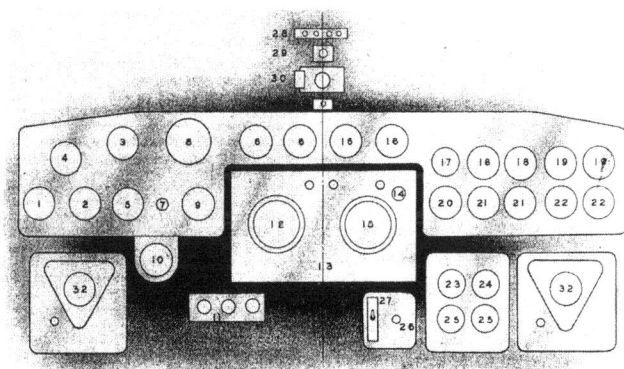

Instrument Panel Diagram

1. Altimeter
2. Air-speed indicator
3. Accelerometer
4. Turn indicator
5. Turn and bank indicator
6. Manifold pressure gage
7. Marker beacon
8. Flight indicator
9. Rate of climb indicator
10. Radio compass
11. Speed control knobs
12. Directional gyro unit
13. Automatic pilot
14. Vacuum gage
15. Bank and climb gyro unit
16. Tachometer

17. Flap indicator
18. Fuel pressure gage
19. Engine cylinder temperature gage
20. Air temperature gage
21. Oil pressure gage
22. Oil temperature gage
23. Automatic pilot oil pressure gage
24. Hydraulic pressure gage
25. Brake pressure gage
26. Pitot heater
27. Anti-icer pressure gage
28. Propeller fast feathering swisches
29. Clock
30. Magnetic compass
31. Compass light rheostat
32. Control column

INSTRUMENTS MOUNTED FOR PILOT'S VISION

Instrument	Type	Manufacturer	Part No.
Altimeter	C-12	Kollsman	671K-03
Turn Indicator	A-5 or	General Motors	
	AN5735-1	Corporation or Sperry	T95090
Flight Indicator	C-7 or	General Motors	
	AN5736-1	Corporation or Sperry	646040
Rate of Climb Indicator	C-2	Kollsman	639K-03
Turn and Bank Indicator	A-8	Pioneer	1718-25-A2
Airspeed Indicator	D-7	Kollsman	586K-028
Manifold Pressure Gages	D-8 or D-8A	Pioneer	6007-50A-14-A
Hydraulic Pressure Gage	E-4	United States Gage Co.	AW-1-7/8-17-CD
Inboard Brake Pressure Gage	E-4	United States Gage Co.	AW-1-7/8-17-CD
Outboard Brake Pressure Gage	E-4	United States Gage Co.	AW-1-7/8-17-CD
Gyro Oil Pressure Gage	H-2	Electric Auto Lite Co.	10185-A
Radio Compass Indicator	1-81-A	Pioneer	6566-NY-41
Clock	A-11	Elgin National Watch Co.	1776
Magnetic Compass	B-16	Pioneer	1818-1-a
A-3A Automatic Pilot			
Directional Gyro Control	A-3A	Jack and Heintz	JH 5000
Bank and Climb Indicator	A-3A	Jack and Heintz	JH 6000
Vacuum Suction Gage	A-3A	Jack and Heintz	

(3) INSTRUMENTS MOUNTED FOR THE COPILOT'S VISION.

Instrument	Type	Manufacturer	Part No.
Tachometers	E-10	Pioneer	6007-28C-14-A
Flap Position Indicator	DJ-11	General Electric	IN102-80
Fuel Pressure Gages	C-14 or C-14A	Pioneer	6007-14E-14-A
Engine Cyl. Temp. Gages	B-11	Western	102319
		Dejur Amsco Corp.	Z-22.22
Air Temp. Gage	C-8	Weston Electric Co.	IN79
Oil Pressure Gages	B-9 or B-9A	Pioneer	6007-4H-14-A
Oil Temp. Gages	A-24	Hickok	60012 or 60017
		Sutton Horsley Co.	2213-7
Carburetor Air Temp. Indicator	AN5795-6	Thomas A. Edison, Inc.	33205

(4) INSTRUMENTS AT NAVIGATOR'S STATION.

Instrument	Type	Manufacturer	Part No.
Drift Meter	B-5	Eastman	49258
Clock	A-11	Elgin Watch Company	1776
Compass (Magnetic)	D-12	Pioneer	1801-A-1
Compass Indicator (Radio)	1-82-A	Pioneer	162-WFSCPD-42

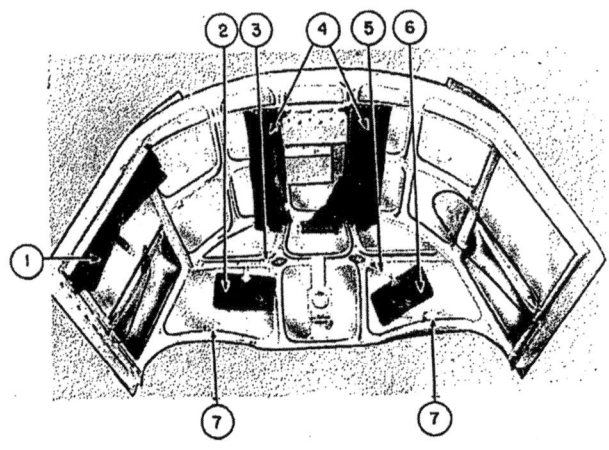

1. Pilot's Side Glare Curtain
2. Pilot's Sun Shade
3. Pilot's Sun Shade Swivel Arm
4. Pilots' Upper Glare Curtain
5. Co-Pilot's Sun Shade Swivel Arm
6. Co-Pilot's Sun Shade
7. Windshield Spot Defroster Bracket

Pilot's Glare Shields & Curtains

Control Panel Middle & Forward Position

1. Supercharger control levers
2. Propeller governor switches
3. Intercooler shutter switches
4. Throttle control levers
5. Pitot heater switch
6. Cowl flap switches
7. Fuel mixture control levers
8. Elevator trim tab control
9. Landing gear warning button
10. Passing lights and tail and wing running light switche
11. A. C. power switch
12. Fluorescent light switch
13. Aileron trim tab control
14. Rudder trim tab control
15. Landing lights
16. Automatic pilot "ON-OFF" control

1. Fluorescent light
2. Interphone jack box
3. Filter switchbox
4. Microphone disconnector cord
5. Fuse box
6. Ash tray
7. Aircraft data case
8. Power receptacle
9. Emergency hydraulic pump handle

Pilot's Compartment Right Side

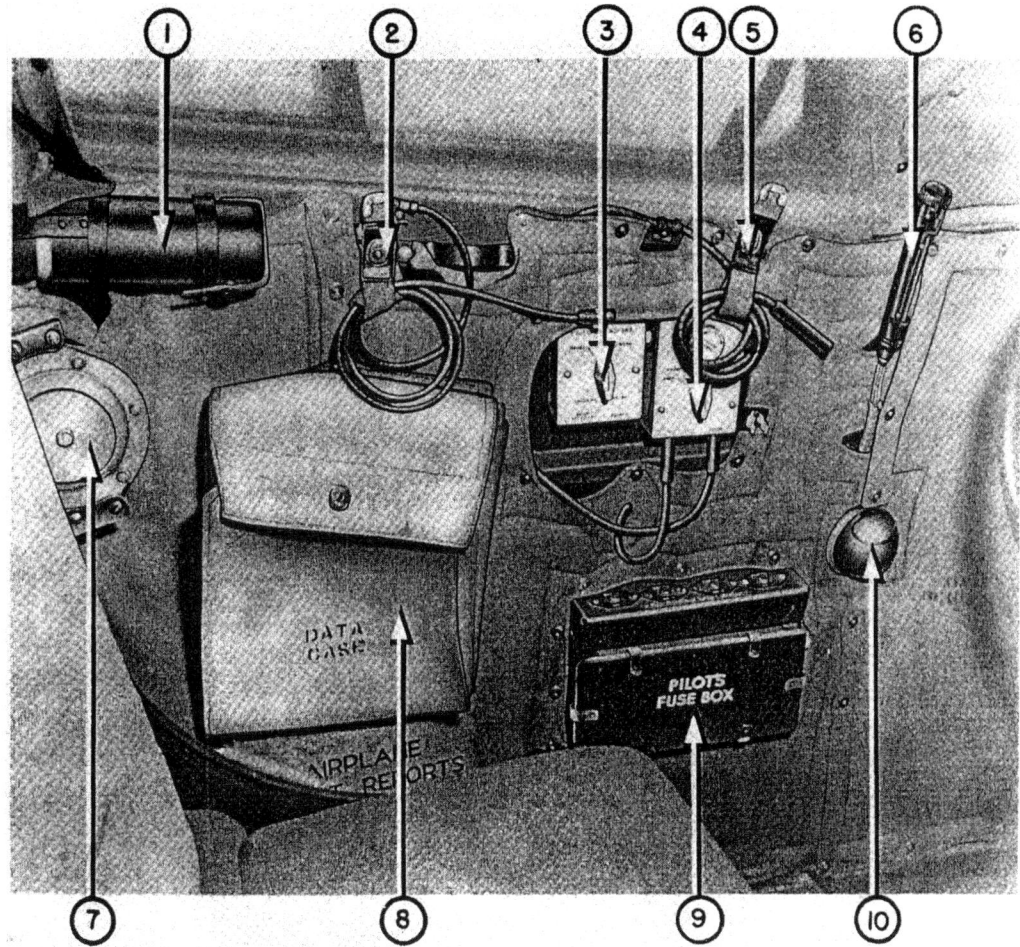

1. Defroster
2. Microphone disconnector cord
3. Filter switchbox
4. Interphone jackbox
5. Headset disconnector cord

6. Fluorescent light
7. Warning horn
8. Aircraft data case
9. Fuse box
10. Ash tray

Pilot's Compartment Left Side

Flight Engineer's Station

Navigator's Station

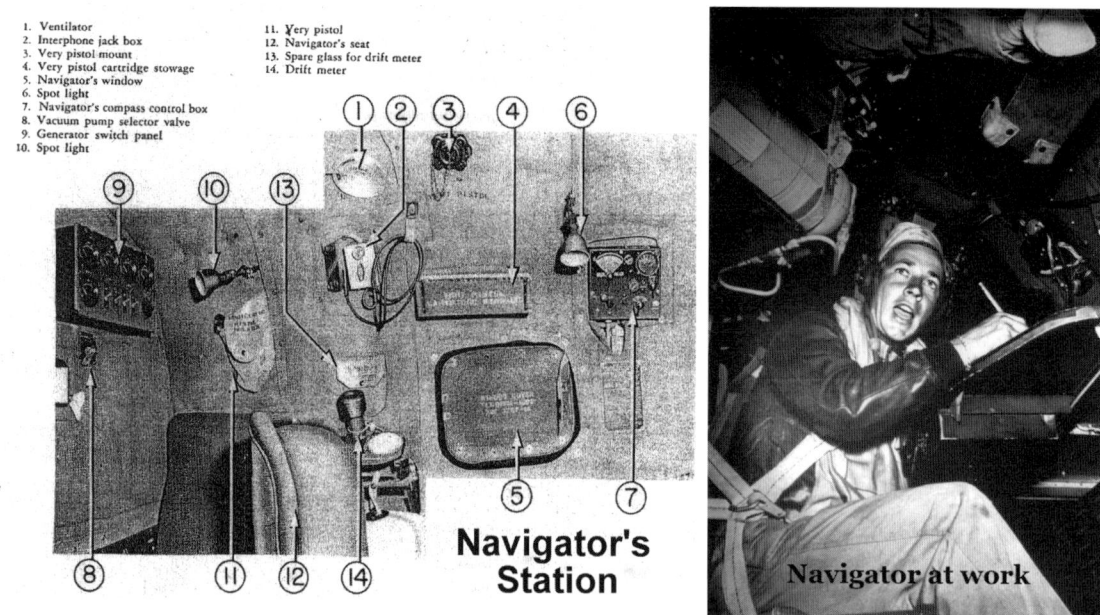

1. Ventilator
2. Interphone jack box
3. Very pistol mount
4. Very pistol cartridge stowage
5. Navigator's window
6. Spot light
7. Navigator's compass control box
8. Vacuum pump selector valve
9. Generator switch panel
10. Spot light

11. Very pistol
12. Navigator's seat
13. Spare glass for drift meter
14. Drift meter

Navigator's Station

Navigator at work

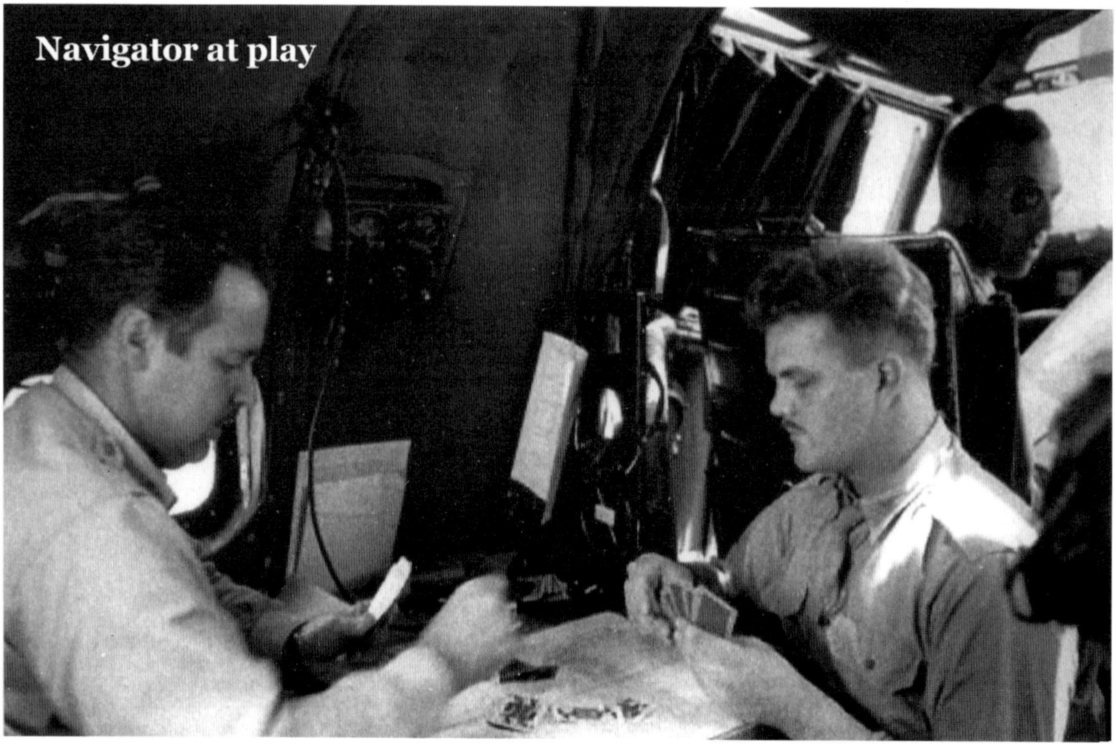

Navigator at play

Radio Operator's Station

Radio Operator's Station

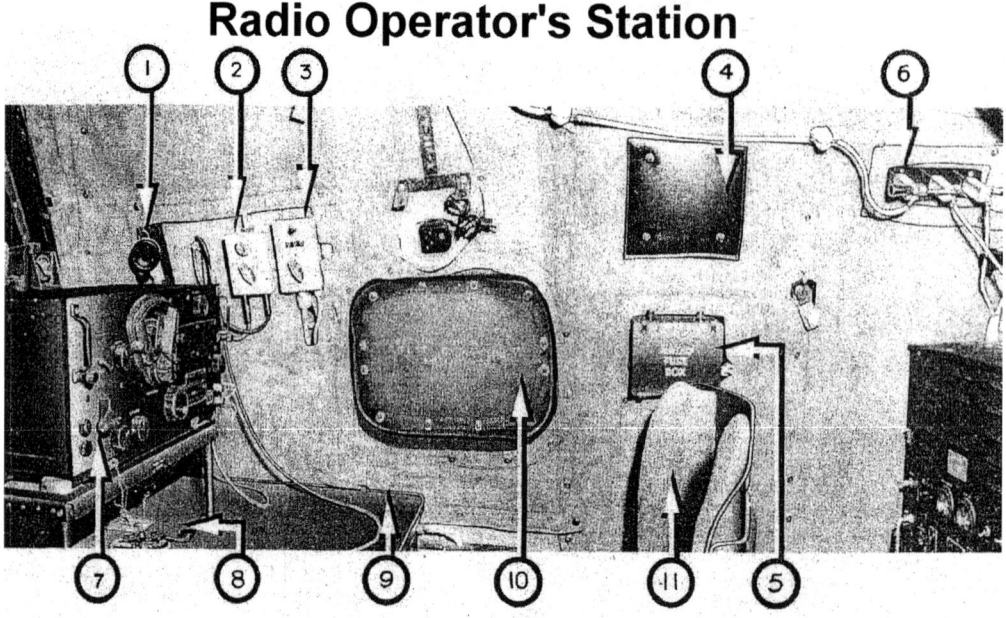

1. Microphone
2. Interphone jackbox
3. Antenna reel control box
4. First aid kit stowage

5. Radio fuse box
6. Antenna switch
7. Liaison receiver
8. Radio operator's key

9. Radio operator's table
10. Radio operator s window
11. Radio operator's seat

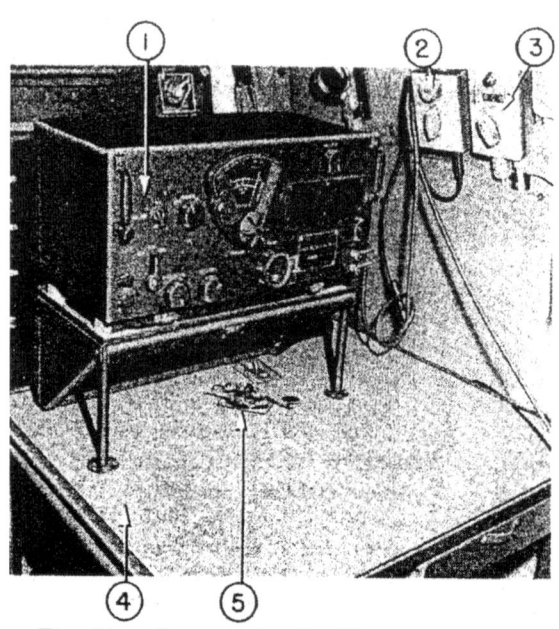

Radio Operator's Equpment

1. Liaison receiver
2. Interphone jackbox
3. Antenna reel control box
4. Table
5. Transmitting key

Pratt & Whitney R-1830-43 Power Plant and Engine Controls

The C-87 was equipped with four reliable Pratt & Whitney R-1830-43 radial, air-cooled engines, having a 16:9 propeller gear ratio. Each engine was equipped with a single-stage, single-speed, engine-driven supercharger having 7:15:1 gear ratio.

Engine Throttle Controls

The four engine throttle control levers, located in the central quadrant on the upper part of the control pedestal, were linked by cables to the operating levers on the carburetors. The automatic throttle controls were spring-loaded so that they moved to approximately 65 per cent power, with the carburetor butterfly valve opening in the event of a disruption in the control system.

Turbo-Superchargers

A General Electric Type B-2 Turbo-supercharger was installed behind each engine mount support below the lower surface of the wing. An Eclipse Regulator, installed on the aft end of each supercharger, controlled the waste gates. The turbo-superchargers were regulated by four control levers, one for each engine, located on the left quadrant on the upper part of the control pedestal. These four control levers operated the hydraulic waste-gate operating valves on the four engines.

Carburetor Air Mixture Control

The four mixture control levers in the right-hand quadrant on the pedestal were linked by cables to the operating levers on the carburetors, and each lever had four positions: IDLE CUT-OFF, AUTO-LEAN, AUTO- RICH, and FULL RICH. These positions were notched on the quadrant so that the lever could be set by the 'click and feel' method.

Intercooler Shutter Controls

The temperature of the air entering the carburetors could be controlled by four switches; each switch controlled the shutters for one engine. On early C-87s these controls were located on the co-pilot's auxiliary panel, while on C-87s 41-23669 and subsequent these switches were on the top center of the engine control pedestal. Each shutter switch had two positions: OPEN (the normal position) and CLOSED.

Engine Primers

Two double-throw toggle switches on the co-pilot's switch panel operated the engine primers. One switch operated the primers for the No. 1 and No. 2 engines: the second switch was for the No. 3 and No. 4 engines.

Ignition Switches

Four ignition switches to select one or both magnetos were located on the co-pilot's auxiliary panel on the right of the co-pilot's seat with a Plexiglas cover guard preventing the accidental operation of the switches. In an emergency the ignition switch bar, located just above the ignition switches under the Plexiglas guard, was used to instantly shut off the magnetos for all engines.

Starter Switches

An electric inertia starter was mounted on each engine. Early C-87 models were equipped with AAF Type F-2 starters with four double-throw switches, one for each engine, mounted on the co-pilot's switch panel. With this type of starter, the starter switch for the engine selected to be started was placed in the START position and held there from 10 to 15 seconds (18 seconds maximum) and then moved to the MESH position.

Later C-87s were equipped with AAF Type G-6 starters operated by four switches: two marked ACCEL that controlled the acceleration of the starter motors for the No. 1 and No. 2 engines, and the other controls the acceleration for the No. 3 and No. 4 engines. The other two switches were marked CRANK or MESH in both positions and controlled the cranking or meshing for the engines selected. With this starter system, the ACCEL switch was placed to the engine selected to start and held in that position from 10 to 12 seconds (18 seconds maximum). Then, with the ACCEL switch still ON, the CRANK or MESH switch was thrown ON.

Cowl Flaps

Engine cooling was regulated by adjustable cowl flaps designed to regulate engine temperatures. The cowl flaps were controlled for the Nos 1, 2, 3, and 4 engines by four electrical switches mounted on the co-pilot's panel; on C-87s 41-23669 and subsequent, the switches were relocated to the top of the engine control pedestal. The range of their operation was from 2 plus or minus ½ degree to plus 22 degrees. For take-off the cowl flaps were to be one-quarter to one-half open and for cruising the cowl flap setting was to be such that the engine temperatures were below these maximum allowable values:

450°F (232°C): For continuous operation
500°F (260°C): For full-power climb (for one hour only)
500°F (260°C): For high-speed (for one hour only)

Pratt & Whitney R-1830-43

The C-87 was equipped with four reliable Pratt & Whitney R-1830-43 radial, air-cooled engines. Engine cooling was regulated by adjustable cowl flaps (seen open) designed to regulate engine temperatures. (*AAF*)

The Twin Wasp seen here contained in the Liberator's characteristic oval nacelles enjoyed record-high production volume for an aircraft piston engine: 173,618 units from 1931 to 1951, which was mainly due to the enormous production of the B-24 and DC-3/C-47. (*Author*)

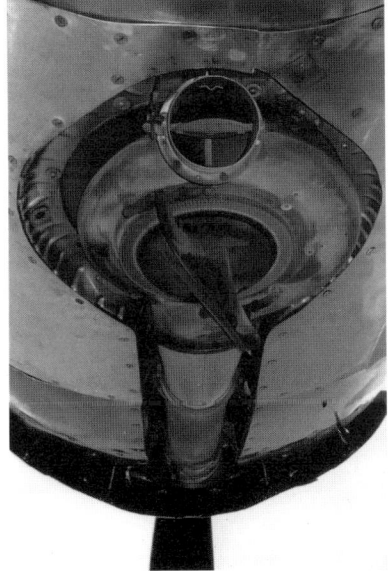

Pratt & Whitney R-1830 Twin Wasp

A General Electric Type B-2 Turbo-supercharger was installed behind each engine mount support below the lower surface of the wing. (*AAF*)

The layout of the Pratt & Whitney R-1830 (Twin Wasp) consisted of seven major sections: front, crankcase, cylinders, blower, intermediate rear, rear, and supercharger sections. The crankcase and cylinders were often referred to as the 'power sections'. (*Pratt & Whitney*)

Propellers and Propeller Controls

The Liberator Express was equipped with Hamilton Standard Hydromatic quick-feathering, three-bladed, 11ft 7in propellers controlled by toggle switches on the pilot's control pedestal. The rpm was increased by pushing the switches forward and decreased by pulling them aft. When released, the switches returned to the inoperative position. Four propeller governor signal light indicators, one for each propeller, were mounted on the radio compass panel on the pilot's instrument panel and operated when each governor reached its extreme limit of travel in either direction. Four quick-feathering push-button switches, one for each propeller, were located above the compass at the top center of the windshield. The quick-feathering switches were the master switches for the propeller circuits and overrode the propeller switches on the engine control pedestal in case of an emergency. Each propeller was feathered individually by one of the four push-button switches, which started an electric pump in the nacelle that supplied hydraulic power for the feathering operation. When the propeller was fully feathered the push button released automatically, stopping the pump. To stop the operation before feathering was completed, the switch button was pulled out manually.

The C-87/C-109 was propelled by four Hamilton Standard Hydromatic quick-feathering, three-bladed, 11ft 7in propellers. The Hamilton Standard Hydromatic propeller introduced in the 1930s was a significant advance in design and the company became the primary propeller manufacturer (530,135 units) for the Allies during the war, with virtually all bomber, fighter, and transport aircraft, as well as a significant majority of RAF aircraft, being powered by them. (*CAC/AAF*)

The distinctive oval red and black Hamilton Standard logo easily identified that company's propellers on photographs. (*Author*)

Fuel System

The first 75 C-87s, 41-11608 through 42-107250, had 12 main self-sealing fuel cells installed in the wings, six on each side of the center line. Alternate tanks on each side of the center line were manifolded together (1, 3, 5) and (2, 4, 6), with each set supplying a separate engine. Each engine was provided with an electrically driven centrifugal fuel booster pump, located at the bottom of the inboard cell of each manifold set, a strainer, and an engine-driven fuel pump. The electrical engine primer control and electrically driven fuel booster pump switches were mounted on the co-pilot's side of the instrument panel and two sight gauges were located on the forward side of Bulkhead 4.1. The fuel transfer unit was mounted overhead just aft of Station 5.1 above the rear wing spar. Six auxiliary fuel cells were contained in the outer wing panels, three on each side of the center line. The cells in each outer wing panel were manifolded together and fuel transfer from these cells was only possible by the fuel transfer system. The main fuel tank selector valves, two on the right side, and two on the left, were located between the front spar and station 4.1. A cross-feed system between the main fuel cells permitted the operation of any or all engines on the fuel in any set of main fuel cells. It also provided an auxiliary transferring of fuel from one set of cells to the other.

The fuel system for C-87s 42-107251 through 43-30557 differed from the above system in the following respects: in place of self-sealing cells, non-self-sealing bladder type cells were installed with the following capacities:

Main Cells

Tank 1:	637 gallons
Tank 2:	579 gallons
Tank 3:	579 gallons
Tank 4:	637 gallons
Total:	2,432 gallons

Auxiliary Cells

LH Tank:	239 gallons
RH Tank:	239 gallons
Total:	478 gallons
Total Capacity:	2,910 gallons

The fuel transfer system was located above the rear wingspan. Four main selector valves were located on the left side of the flight deck above the heater duct just aft of the navigator's table.

On C-87s 43-30557 and subsequent the fuel system differed in the following respects: the fuel cells were replaced by two integral wing tanks that extended from the center line to wing Station 4. No fuel transfer system was installed as a Cross Feed Manifold system was provided with four engine selector valves located on the forward face of Bulkhead 4.1.

Fuel System

The C-87's four main fuel cells held 2,432 gallons, while the two auxiliary cells contained 478 gallons for a total fuel capacity of 2,910 gallons. (*AAF*)

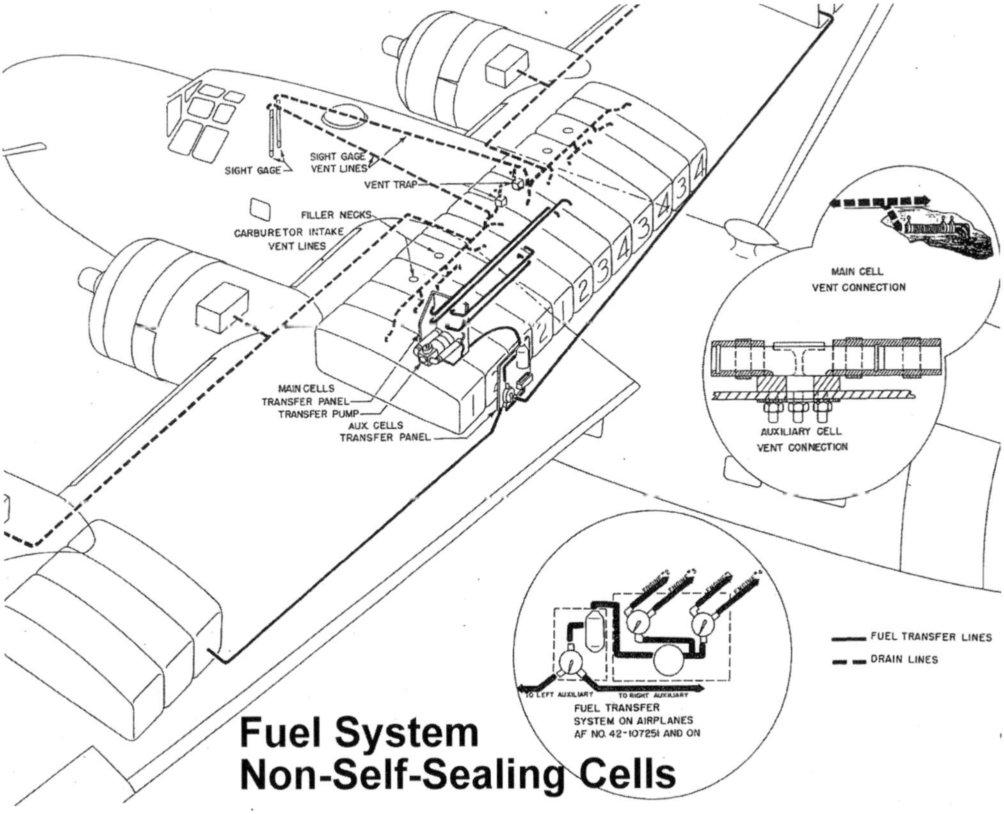

SIGHT GAGE
SIGHT GAGE VENT LINES
VENT TRAP
FILLER NECKS
CARBURETOR INTAKE
VENT LINES
MAIN CELLS
TRANSFER PANEL
TRANSFER PUMP
AUX. CELLS
TRANSFER PANEL

MAIN CELL
VENT CONNECTION

AUXILIARY CELL
VENT CONNECTION

TO LEFT AUXILIARY   TO RIGHT AUXILIARY
FUEL TRANSFER
SYSTEM ON AIRPLANES
AF NO. 42-107251 AND ON

FUEL TRANSFER LINES
DRAIN LINES

Fuel System
Non-Self-Sealing Cells

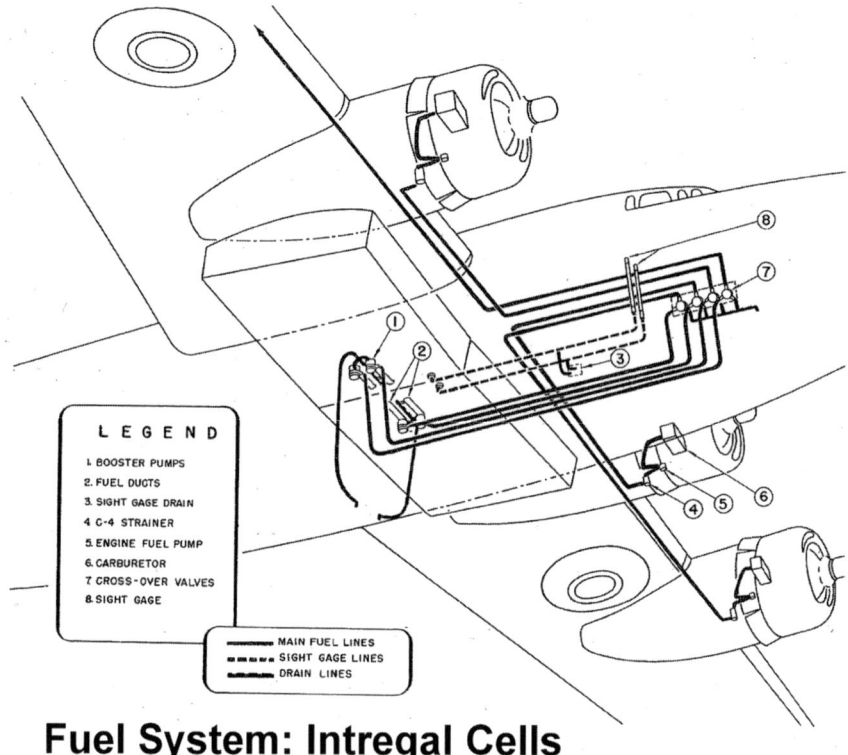

LEGEND

1. BOOSTER PUMPS
2. FUEL DUCTS
3. SIGHT GAGE DRAIN
4. C-4 STRAINER
5. ENGINE FUEL PUMP
6. CARBURETOR
7. CROSS-OVER VALVES
8. SIGHT GAGE

MAIN FUEL LINES
SIGHT GAGE LINES
DRAIN LINES

Fuel System: Intregal Cells

Oil System

Each of the four engines had an independent oil system and a supply tank with a maximum capacity of 39 gallons for a total of 156 gallons for all four tanks required for maximum fuel load with all fuel tanks full. The engine oil tanks were to be filled with oil, Grade 1120 for normal operations and Grade 1100A for cold weather. The propeller feathering pump received its oil supply from the IN line. Oil for operating the supercharger regulators was supplied from the engine oil systems on early model aircraft but on aircraft 41-11908 and subsequent an independent supercharger regulator oil system was installed with a one-gallon supply tank, located in each main landing gear wheel well. Each engine oil system was equipped with an oil temperature regulator that was connected in the OUT line. Operation of the oil cooler shutters was fully automatic and therefore no oil-cooler controls were provided in the pilots' compartment. To accelerate the warming of the engine oil, each tank was equipped with a hopper or accelerating well, and, in operation, warm oil from the engine was discharged into the top of the hopper while oil for the engine was drawn off at the bottom. Therefore, only a small volume of oil was actually circulated through the oil system, thereby permitting a more rapid engine warm-up. An oil dilution system was provided for diluting the engine oil with gasoline at the end of each engine run to afford easier starting. Two double-throw switches mounted on the co-pilot's switch panel controlled the oil dilution.

Oil System

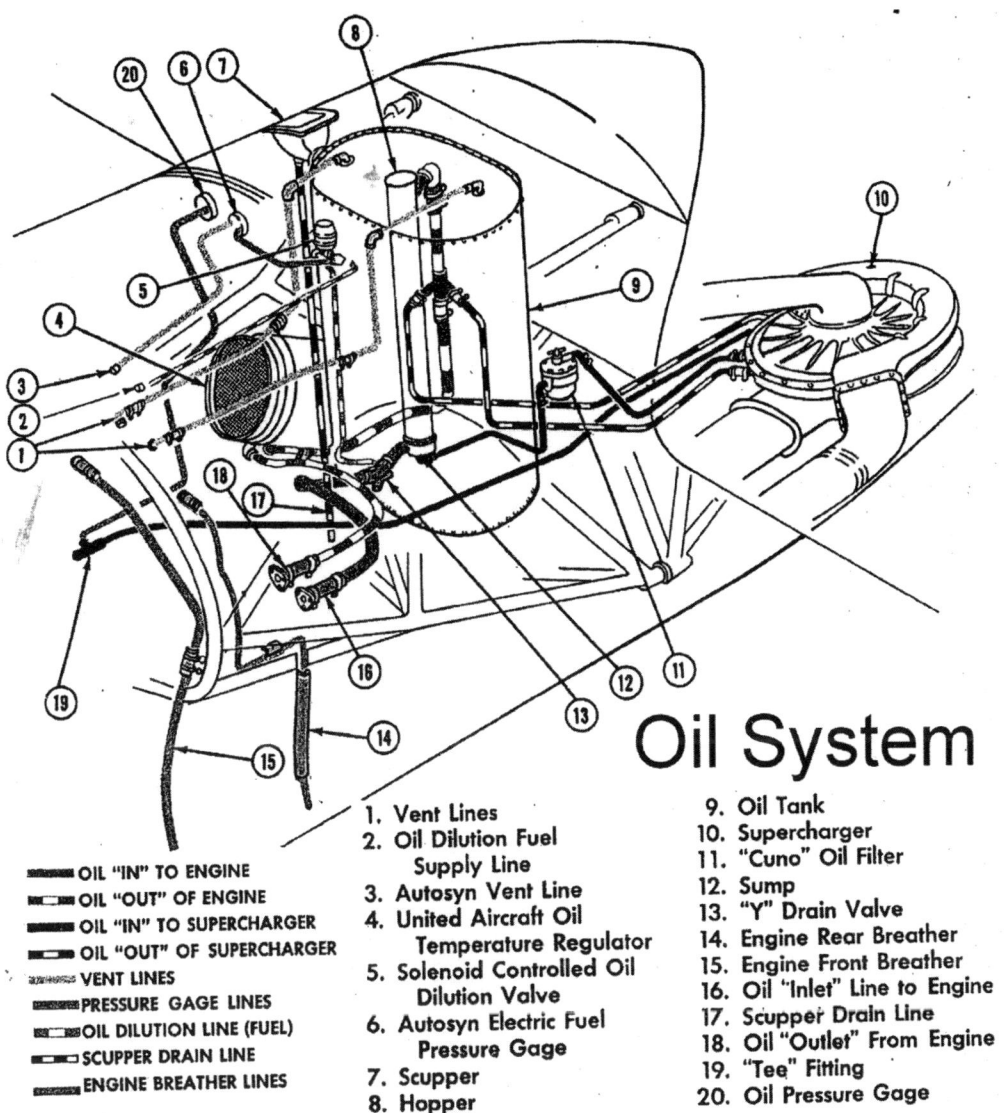

Oil System

1. Vent Lines
2. Oil Dilution Fuel
   Supply Line
3. Autosyn Vent Line
4. United Aircraft Oil
   Temperature Regulator
5. Solenoid Controlled Oil
   Dilution Valve
6. Autosyn Electric Fuel
   Pressure Gage
7. Scupper
8. Hopper

9. Oil Tank
10. Supercharger
11. "Cuno" Oil Filter
12. Sump
13. "Y" Drain Valve
14. Engine Rear Breather
15. Engine Front Breather
16. Oil "Inlet" Line to Engine
17. Scupper Drain Line
18. Oil "Outlet" From Engine
19. "Tee" Fitting
20. Oil Pressure Gage

OIL "IN" TO ENGINE
OIL "OUT" OF ENGINE
OIL "IN" TO SUPERCHARGER
OIL "OUT" OF SUPERCHARGER
VENT LINES
PRESSURE GAGE LINES
OIL DILUTION LINE (FUEL)
SCUPPER DRAIN LINE
ENGINE BREATHER LINES

Communications System

The C-87 was equipped with a radio and interphone system, providing communications between crew members within the aircraft; between the aircraft and ground stations or other aircraft; and in the reception of range and marker beacon signals and ground identification.

The system consisted of the following circuits:

Command Radio: SCR-274-N
Liaison Radio: SCR-287-H
Interphone: RC-36
Radio Compass: SCR-269-G
Marker Beacon: RC-43-A

Component units including the type and location of each unit:

Command Set: SCR-274-N
Transmitters: There were two transmitters, a Type BC-458-A, having a
                   frequency of 5,300–7,000 kilocycles (kc) and a Type BC-
                   459-A, with a frequency of 7,000–9,100 kc. These units were
                   mounted in the wing tank on the right side.
Receivers: The three receivers were Type BC-453-A (190–550 kc), Type
                   BC-454-A (3,000–6,000 kc), and Type BC-455-A (6,000–
                   9,100 kc). These units were mounted in the wing tank on
                   the right side. Controls: The controls consist of the Antenna
                   Switching Relay (Type BC-442-A), the Receiver Control Box
                   (Type BC-450-A), and the Transmitter Control Box (Type
                   BC-451-A). The Antenna Switching Relay was installed on
                   the right side in the wing tank, the Receiver Control Box, on
                   the flight deck ceiling, and the Transmitter Control Box on
                   the pedestal.

Dynamotors:
Receiver Dynamotor DM-32-A was located on the flight deck floor aft of the
    radio operator.
Transmitter Dynamotor DM-33-A was located on the floor aft of radio operator.
Transmitter Modulator BC-456-A was located on the wing tank, right side.

Liaison Set SCR-287-H.
Transmitter BC-375-E was mounted on the right side of the flight deck at Bulkhead 4.1.
Receiver BC-348 was located on the radio operator's table.
Telegraph Key J-37 was located on the radio operator's table.
Dynamotor PE-73-C was located under the transmitter at Bulkhead 4.1 on the flight deck.
Frequency Meter BC-221 was located on the flight deck floor.
Antenna Tuning Unit BC-306-A was located under the transmitter at Bulkhead 4.1 on
    the flight deck.
Tuning Units: There were seven, two under the navigator's table, two on the right aft side
    of the bulkhead, two on the left aft side of Bulkhead 4.0, and one in the transmitter.
Radio Compass SCR-269-G.
Receiver BC-433-G was located at Station 5.0 on the right side above the wing.

Remote Control Boxes BC-434:

One mounted on the fuselage top center line above the pilots' stations.

One mounted on the fuselage wall, left of the navigator's table.

Pilot's Indicator 1-81-A was located on the pilot's instrument panel.

Navigator's Indicator 1-82-A was located on the front of navigator's table.

Switching Relay BK-22-E or BK-22-A was located on the wing tank (right side), aft of
the receiver.

Marker Beacon RC-43-A.

Receiver BC-357 was located on the left side of the wing tank.

Signal Light was located on the pilot's instrument panel.

Communications System

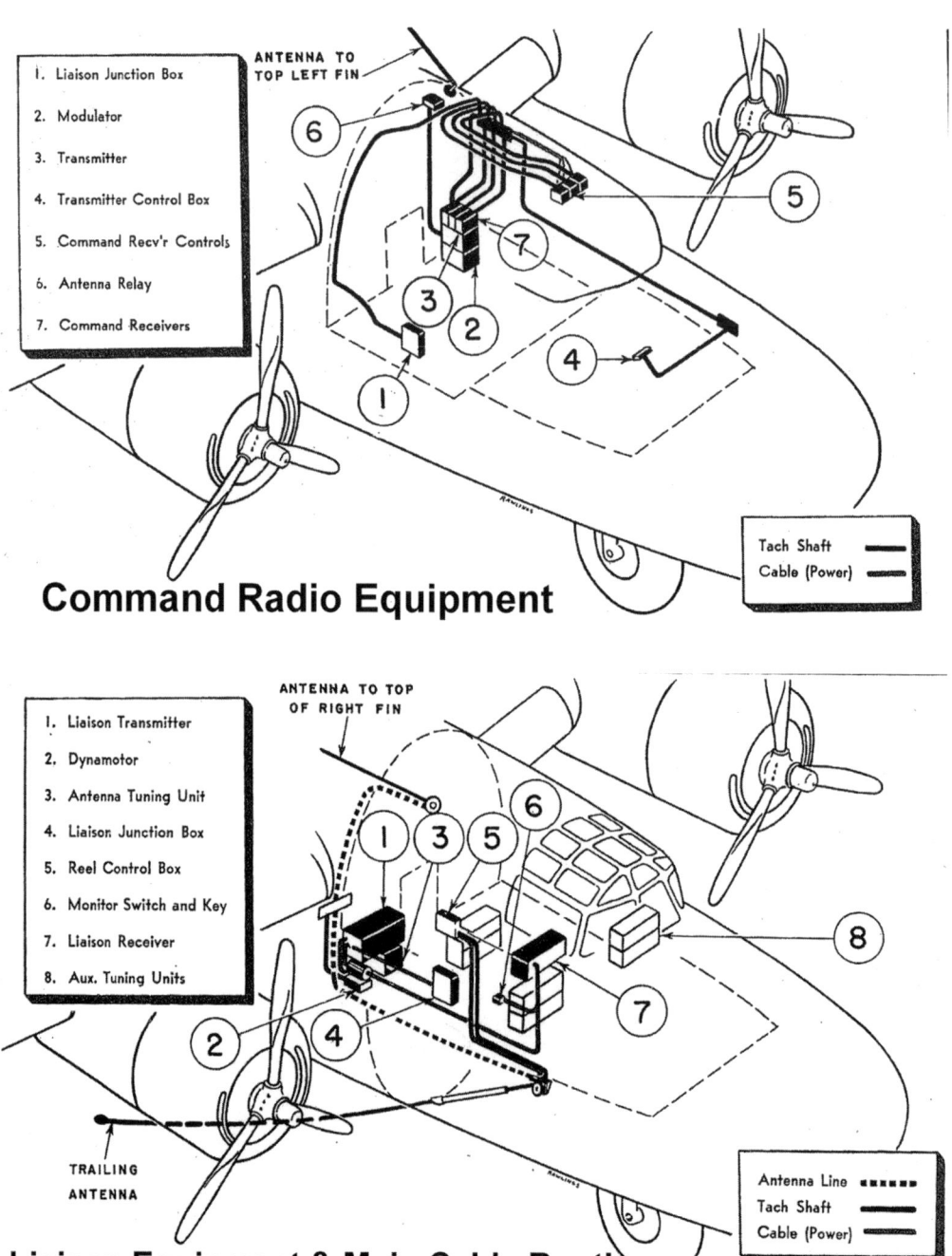

Command Radio Equipment

1. Liaison Junction Box
2. Modulator
3. Transmitter
4. Transmitter Control Box
5. Command Recv'r Controls
6. Antenna Relay
7. Command Receivers

ANTENNA TO
TOP LEFT FIN

Tach Shaft
Cable (Power)

Liaison Equipment & Main Cable Routing

1. Liaison Transmitter
2. Dynamotor
3. Antenna Tuning Unit
4. Liaison Junction Box
5. Reel Control Box
6. Monitor Switch and Key
7. Liaison Receiver
8. Aux. Tuning Units

ANTENNA TO TOP
OF RIGHT FIN

TRAILING
ANTENNA

Antenna Line
Tach Shaft
Cable (Power)

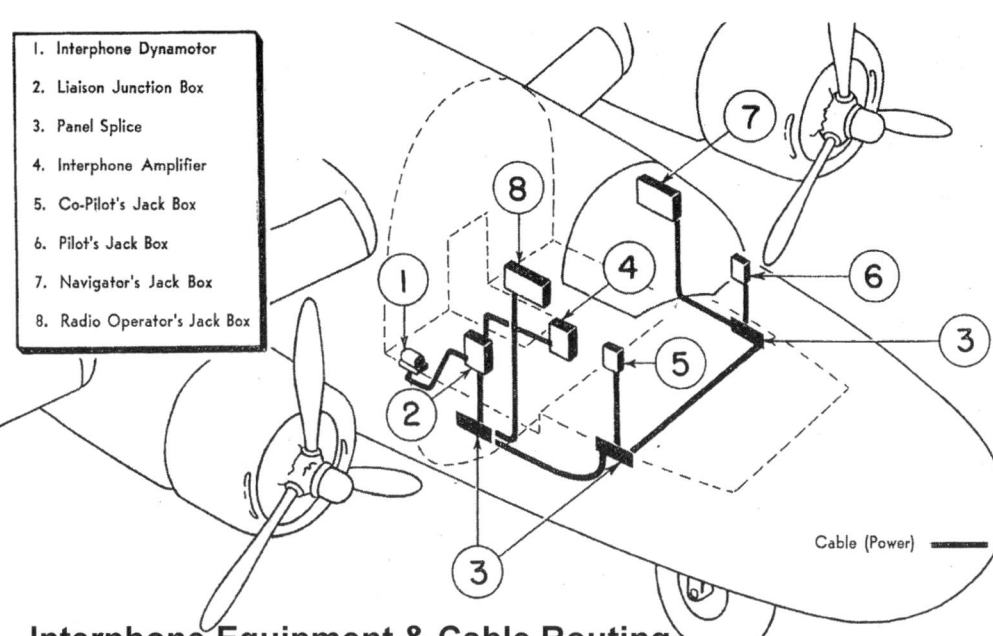

1. Interphone Dynamotor
2. Liaison Junction Box
3. Panel Splice
4. Interphone Amplifier
5. Co-Pilot's Jack Box
6. Pilot's Jack Box
7. Navigator's Jack Box
8. Radio Operator's Jack Box

Cable (Power) ▬▬▬

Interphone Equipment & Cable Routing

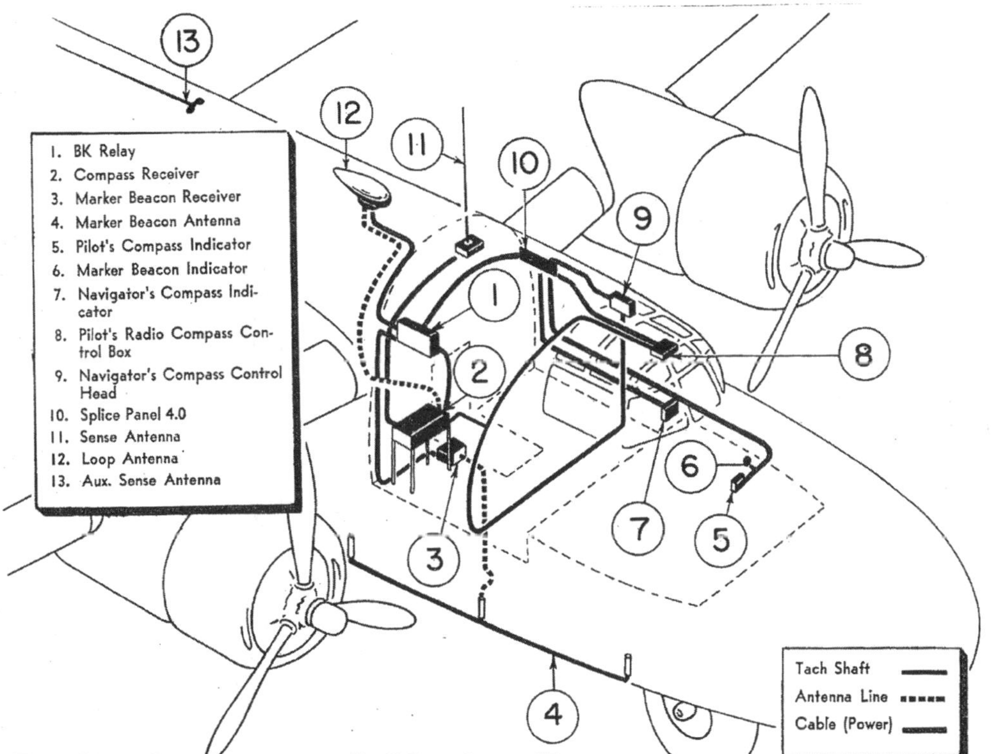

1. BK Relay
2. Compass Receiver
3. Marker Beacon Receiver
4. Marker Beacon Antenna
5. Pilot's Compass Indicator
6. Marker Beacon Indicator
7. Navigator's Compass Indicator
8. Pilot's Radio Compass Control Box
9. Navigator's Compass Control Head
10. Splice Panel 4.0
11. Sense Antenna
12. Loop Antenna
13. Aux. Sense Antenna

Tach Shaft ▬▬▬
Antenna Line ▪▪▪▪▪
Cable (Power) ▬ ▬ ▬

Radio Compass & Marker Beacon

Electrical System

Power Supply

The C-87 was equipped with a direct current single-wire electrical system. When the engines were operating, power was supplied by four 24-volt, 200 ampere generators, one mounted on each engine, with a total capacity of 22.4 kilowatts.

Generators and Power Supply Controls

The generator power control panel was located on the forward face of the bulkhead at Station 4.1, on the left side of the flight deck. There were four generator switches on this panel, one to cut each one of the four generators in and out of the main electrical system; one voltmeter with a multipoint selector switch to indicate the voltage of each generator or main bus, and four ammeters, to show the current flow of each of the four generators. Four voltage regulators, two on each side of the bulkhead at Station 4.1, under the flight deck, provided for generator voltage adjustment as dangerous overheating could result if the output of the generators exceeded 125 amperes.

Batteries

Standby power was supplied from three 24-volt, 34 ampere-hour batteries mounted in the fuselage to the left of the nose wheel door opening. Three battery control switches, one for each battery, were located on the co-pilot's switch panel on early model C-87s. On later models, these three switches were located on the co-pilot's auxiliary panel, to the right of the co-pilot's seat. A master battery switch was located on the left side of the fuselage, just aft of the batteries, in the nose wheel compartment. This switch was provided to cut out the batteries in case the voltage regulators jammed, or other abnormal load conditions developed.

Auxiliary Power Cart Adapter

For ground operation, a plug was installed on the right side of the fuselage for an external auxiliary power cart electrical power connection. A battery cart was always to be used, when available, to start the engines. The aircraft's battery control switches were always to be OFF when using an external source of power for starting.

Interior Lighting

Interior lights with easily accessible switches were located throughout the aircraft. Fluorescent lighting from lamps in the instrument panel areas was provided in the pilots' compartment on the flight deck. The refurbished rear compartment for passengers was furnished with dome lights.

Exterior Lighting

There were two retractable landing lights, one in the lower surface of each wing; each light was controlled by a switch on the lower right side of the control pedestal. One red passing light, in the leading edge of the left wing, was controlled by a double-throw switch on the lower left of the engine control pedestal.

Six running lights, one on each wing tip, top and bottom, and one on each vertical fin, were controlled by two double-throw switches on the top lower left of the control pedestal.

One white recognition light, on the top of the fuselage over the center of the wing, and three recognition lights (red, green, and amber) under the catwalk, were controlled by four switches located on the top lower right side of the control pedestal.

Electrical System and Lighting

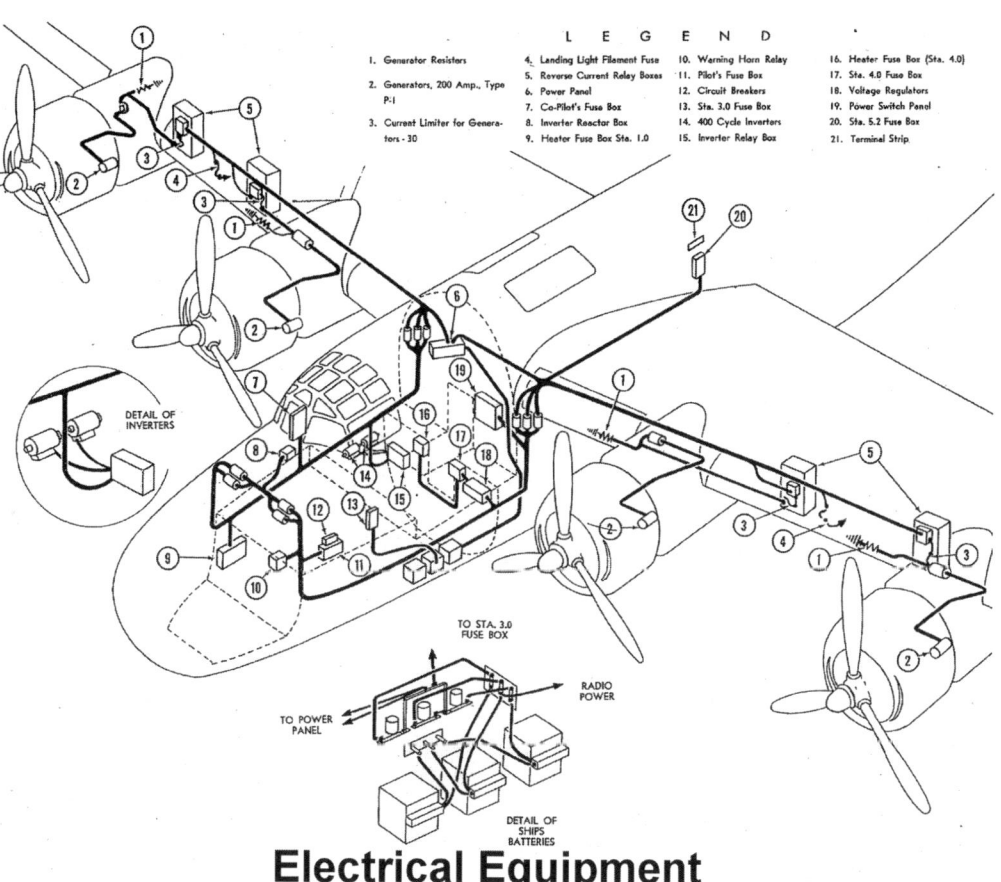

L E G E N D

1. Generator Resistors
2. Generators, 200 Amp., Type P-1
3. Current Limiter for Generators - 30
4. Landing Light Filament Fuse
5. Reverse Current Relay Boxes
6. Power Panel
7. Co-Pilot's Fuse Box
8. Inverter Reactor Box
9. Heater Fuse Box Sta. 1.0
10. Warning Horn Relay
11. Pilot's Fuse Box
12. Circuit Breakers
13. Sta. 3.0 Fuse Box
14. 400 Cycle Inverters
15. Inverter Relay Box
16. Heater Fuse Box (Sta. 4.0)
17. Sta. 4.0 Fuse Box
18. Voltage Regulators
19. Power Switch Panel
20. Sta. 5.2 Fuse Box
21. Terminal Strip

DETAIL OF INVERTERS

TO STA. 3.0 FUSE BOX

RADIO POWER

TO POWER PANEL

DETAIL OF SHIPS BATTERIES

Electrical Equipment

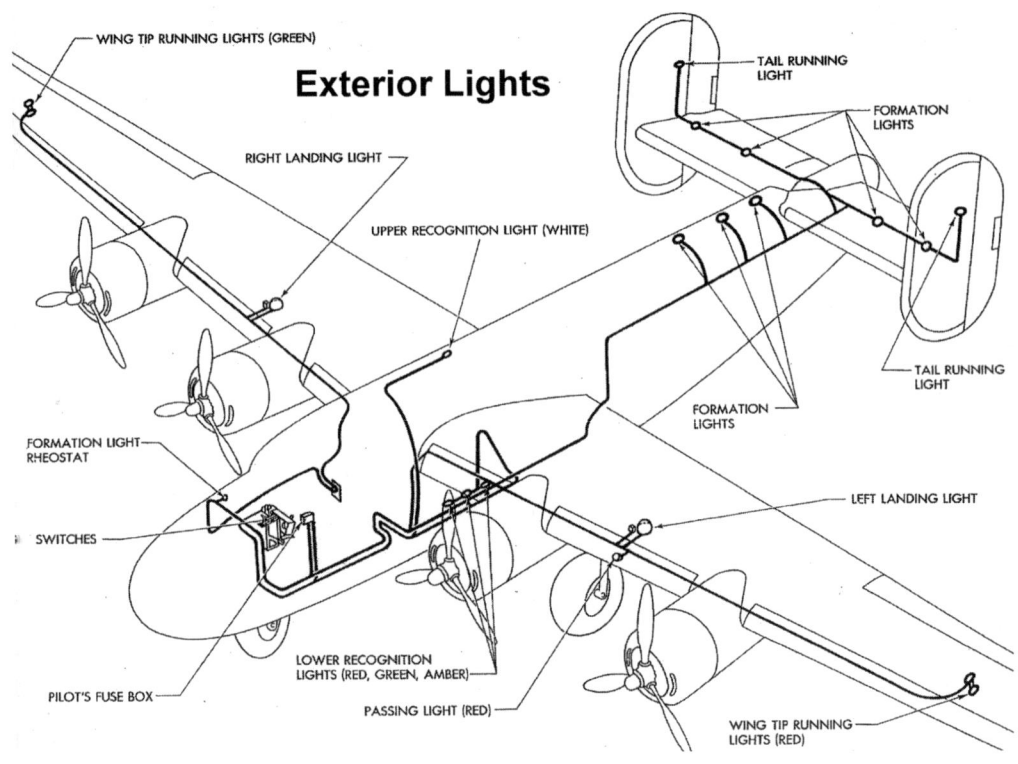

Exterior Lights

WING TIP RUNNING LIGHTS (GREEN)

TAIL RUNNING LIGHT

FORMATION LIGHTS

RIGHT LANDING LIGHT

UPPER RECOGNITION LIGHT (WHITE)

TAIL RUNNING LIGHT

FORMATION LIGHT RHEOSTAT

FORMATION LIGHTS

SWITCHES

LEFT LANDING LIGHT

LOWER RECOGNITION LIGHTS (RED, GREEN, AMBER)

PILOT'S FUSE BOX

PASSING LIGHT (RED)

WING TIP RUNNING LIGHTS (RED)

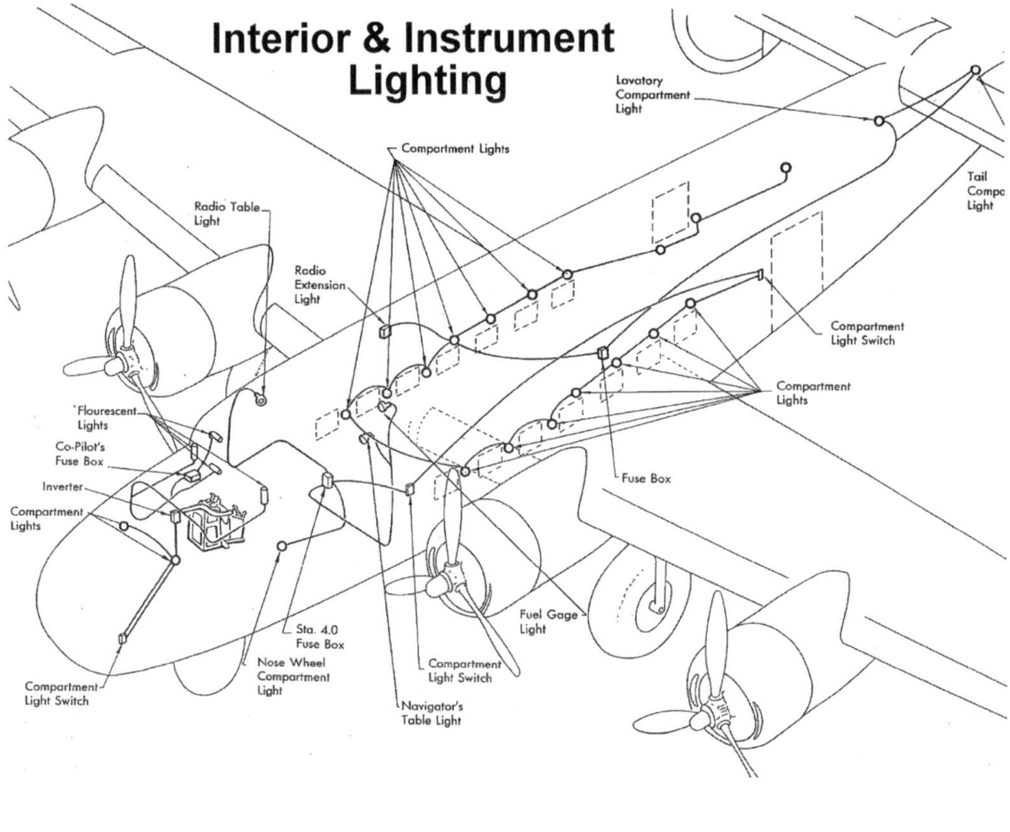

Interior & Instrument Lighting

Lavatory Compartment Light

Compartment Lights

Radio Table Light

Tail Compa Light

Radio Extension Light

Compartment Light Switch

Compartment Lights

Flourescent Lights

Co-Pilot's Fuse Box

Fuse Box

Inverter

Compartment Lights

Sta. 4.0 Fuse Box

Fuel Gage Light

Nose Wheel Compartment Light

Compartment Light Switch

Compartment Light Switch

Navigator's Table Light

Hydraulic System

The open center type main hydraulic operated the landing gear and the wing flaps by fluid under pressure from the engine-driven pump or auxiliary, electrically driven, hydraulic pump, which was mounted on the right side of the fuselage under the radio floor just forward of Bulkhead 4.0. Pressure built up in two direct-pressure type accumulators operated the brakes and the automatic pilot. Gauges on the co-pilot's panel indicated the pressure in the brake accumulator as well as in the circulating system. The hydraulic landing gear and flap-retracting systems were not designed to be operated simultaneously and were always to be operated separately. If the engine-driven pump failed, the auxiliary electric hydraulic pump would supply pressure for all services when a shut-off valve to the right of the radio operator was turned ON. Normally, with this valve OFF, the electrically driven pump operated through a pressure switch to keep the accumulators charged.

The main system and accumulator system were isolated by check valves, so that either could operate independently if the other failed. A hand pump for emergency hydraulic pressure was located on the floor at the right of the co-pilot. The hydraulic system reservoir was mounted on the forward side of Bulkhead 4.1 near the top of the aircraft and was to be filled with hydraulic fluid, Specification No. AN-VV-O-366.

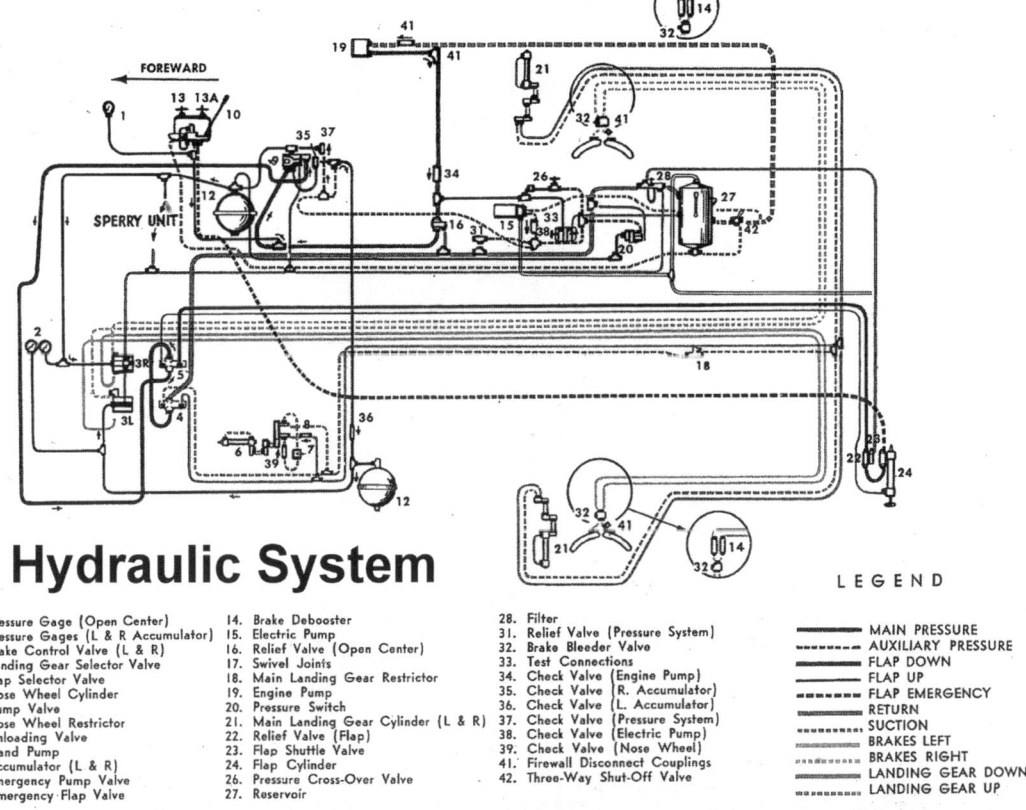

Hydraulic System

.1. Pressure Gage (Open Center)	14. Brake Debooster	28. Filter	
2. Pressure Gages (L & R Accumulator)	15. Electric Pump	31. Relief Valve (Pressure System)	
3. Brake Control Valve (L & R)	16. Relief Valve (Open Center)	32. Brake Bleeder Valve	
4. Landing Gear Selector Valve	17. Swivel Joints	33. Test Connections	
5. Flap Selector Valve	18. Main Landing Gear Restrictor	34. Check Valve (Engine Pump)	
6. Nose Wheel Cylinder	19. Engine Pump	35. Check Valve (R. Accumulator)	
7. Dump Valve	20. Pressure Switch	36. Check Valve (L. Accumulator)	
8. Nose Wheel Restrictor	21. Main Landing Gear Cylinder (L & R)	37. Check Valve (Pressure System)	
9. Unloading Valve	22. Relief Valve (Flap)	38. Check Valve (Electric Pump)	
10. Hand Pump	23. Flap Shuttle Valve	39. Check Valve (Nose Wheel)	
12. Accumulator (L & R)	24. Flap Cylinder	41. Firewall Disconnect Couplings	
13. Emergency Pump Valve	26. Pressure Cross-Over Valve	42. Three-Way Shut-Off Valve	
13A. Emergency Flap Valve	27. Reservoir		

LEGEND

———— MAIN PRESSURE
– – – –▲ AUXILIARY PRESSURE
———— FLAP DOWN
———— FLAP UP
– ▪ – ▪ – ▪ FLAP EMERGENCY
▬▬▬▬ RETURN
▪▪▪▪▪▪ SUCTION
▪▪▬▪▪▬▪ BRAKES LEFT
▪▪▬▪▪▬▪ BRAKES RIGHT
▬▬▬▬ LANDING GEAR DOWN
▪▪▬▪▪▪▪ LANDING GEAR UP

Ice Elimination Systems

Anti-Icer System

On aircraft prior to 41-23669 a 6-gallon anti-icing fluid supply tank was located in the nose wheel well compartment just forward of Bulkhead 4.0. Two Eclipse, Type 744, metering pumps for supplying the fluid to the slinger rings on the propeller hub were found immediately below the tank. One pump supplied both inboard engines, while the other supplied both outboard engines.

Beginning with C-87s 41-23669 through 43-30556, the tank capacity was increased to 53 gallons and was relocated on the right side of the nose wheel compartment and provided fluid for each pilot's windshield and for each engine carburetor scoop and propeller slinger ring. Two pumps, located on the port side, forward of Bulkhead 4.0, were added to supply fluid to each of the carburetors, one pump supplying both inboard engines and the other supplied both outboard engines. The reinstallation of fuel cells on aircraft 43-30556 and subsequent resulted in the installation of a 16-gallon anti-icing tank mounted in each wing, behind the front spar and inboard of the wheel well with their two pumps mounted outboard of each tank.

The 53-gallon fluid reservoir was accessible for filling from the cargo compartment or by a hose through the nose wheel well opening to the reservoir filling spout. The wing reservoirs were filled through the top of each wing inboard of No. 1 and No. 4 engines. A shut-off valve was located on each outlet of the reservoir to facilitate repairs, without draining the reservoir. The anti-icing fluid was Specification No. AN-F-13.

The anti-icer system was operated by starting the propeller anti-icer motors and turning the rheostat to the extreme right, causing the pumps to run at maximum output. The system was to be left in this position for about two minutes to fill tubing and begin the flow of the anti-icing liquid on the propellers. The rheostats were then to be adjusted to provide the minimum amount of fluid necessary to keep the propellers free from ice. If ice were already present, as indicated by rough engine performance, the rheostat was to be left at the full ON position until the ice was removed.

To start the motors for the carburetor anti-icing, the two switches were to be placed in the ON position.

On windshield anti-icer on aircraft prior to 41-23669, the pilot's and co-pilot's windshields had windshield sprays supplied with anti-icing fluid from a one-quart container located at Station 1.0 on the right-hand side under the flight deck. The fluid was transferred to the pilot's and co-pilot's windows by a hand-operated primer pump located at the co-pilot's right side. By turning the pump handle a selector valve operated a pump that directed the fluid to either the pilot's or co-pilot's side of the windshield, where a needle valve created the spray. Beginning with aircraft 41-23669 through 43-30556', the fluid for all windshield anti-icing was supplied by the 53-gallon tank of the propeller anti-icer system. Beginning with 43-30557, the windshield anti-icing system was deleted and hot air from the heaters carried through ducts was used to defrost the windows. These ducts were flexible cloth-covered tubing that carried hot air from the nearest heater to the spot where defrosting action was required.

De-Icer System

The wing and tail de-icer system employed fabric-reinforced rubber shoes, containing longitudinal inflatable cells, fastened to the leading edges of the wing, stabilizer, and fins. Two engine-driven vacuum pumps on engines Nos 1 and 2 supplied pressure for inflating the shoes. To ensure complete deflation, the vacuum side of one vacuum pump was connected with the shoes by a four-way valve. A distributor valve controlled the flow of the air to the shoe cells, inflating and deflating each cell every 40 seconds. When the system was not in operation the control valve bypassed the pressurized air overboard.

The de-icer shoes consisted of inflatable tubes bordered by elastic zones, the outer margins of which were attached to the wing and tail leading edges. On the wing, the inflatable tubes were from 1¾in to 3in wide in the deflated condition. The tubes were tapered from their inboard to their outboard ends to fit the contour of the wing. These tubes, which were alternately inflated and deflated in a sequence, were automatically controlled by the distributor valves. Any de-icer shoe was in the completely deflated condition at least 50 per cent of the operating cycle. The tube on the leading edge was inflated first, and as it deflated, the tubes immediately beside it were inflated together. Thus, the total effect was a distortion and stretch of the shoe which cracked and peeled the ice from the surface. The tail de-icer shoes made use of a 'sine-curved tube', which was two separate tubes manifolded together and separated by a scallop or 'sine-curve'.

Ice Elimination System

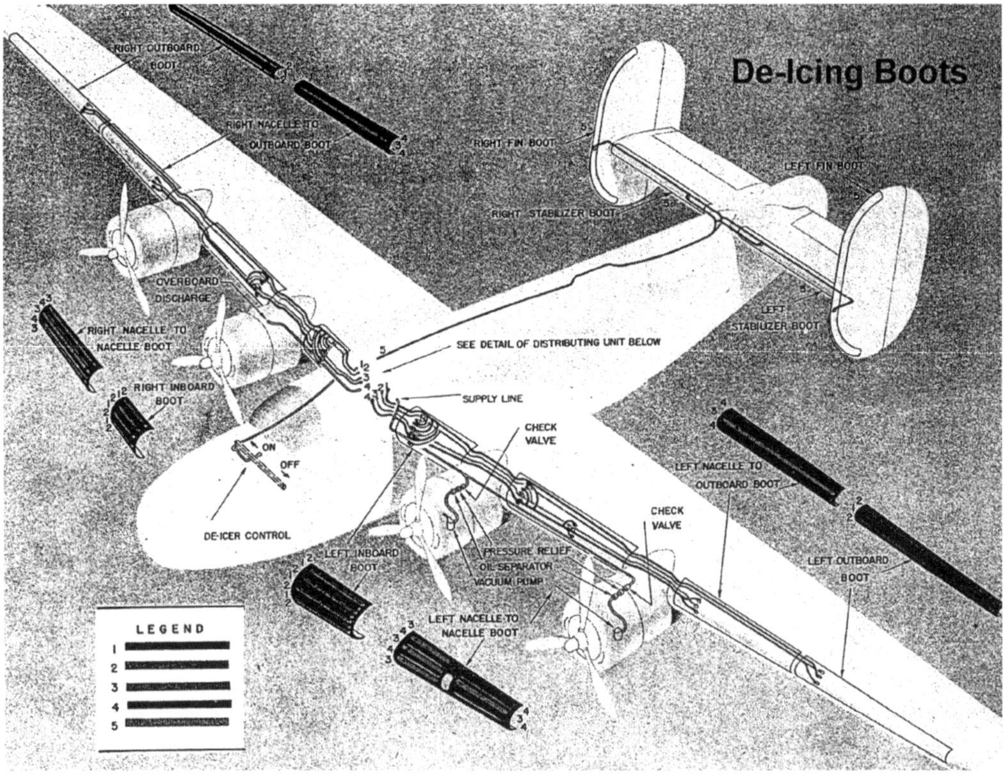

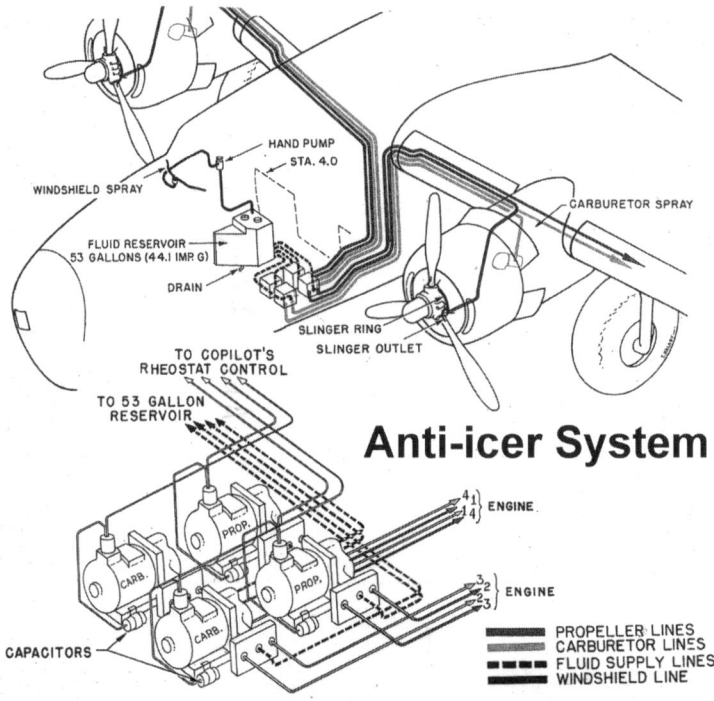

De-Icing Boots

RIGHT OUTBOARD BOOT

RIGHT NACELLE TO OUTBOARD BOOT

RIGHT FIN BOOT

LEFT FIN BOOT

LEFT STABILIZER BOOT

RIGHT STABILIZER BOOT

OVERBOARD DISCHARGE

RIGHT NACELLE TO NACELLE BOOT

SEE DETAIL OF DISTRIBUTING UNIT BELOW

RIGHT INBOARD BOOT

SUPPLY LINE

CHECK VALVE

ON
OFF

DE-ICER CONTROL

LEFT INBOARD BOOT

LEFT NACELLE TO NACELLE BOOT

PRESSURE RELIEF
OIL SEPARATOR
VACUUM PUMP

CHECK VALVE

LEFT NACELLE TO OUTBOARD BOOT

LEFT OUTBOARD BOOT

LEGEND
1
2
3
4
5

HAND PUMP
STA. 4.0

WINDSHIELD SPRAY

CARBURETOR SPRAY

FLUID RESERVOIR
53 GALLONS (44.1 IMP. G)

DRAIN

SLINGER RING
SLINGER OUTLET

TO COPILOT'S
RHEOSTAT CONTROL

TO 53 GALLON
RESERVOIR

Anti-icer System

4
1   ENGINE
1
4

PROP.

3
2   ENGINE
2
3

CARB.
PROP.

CAPACITORS

CARB.

PROPELLER LINES
CARBURETOR LINES
FLUID SUPPLY LINES
WINDSHIELD LINE

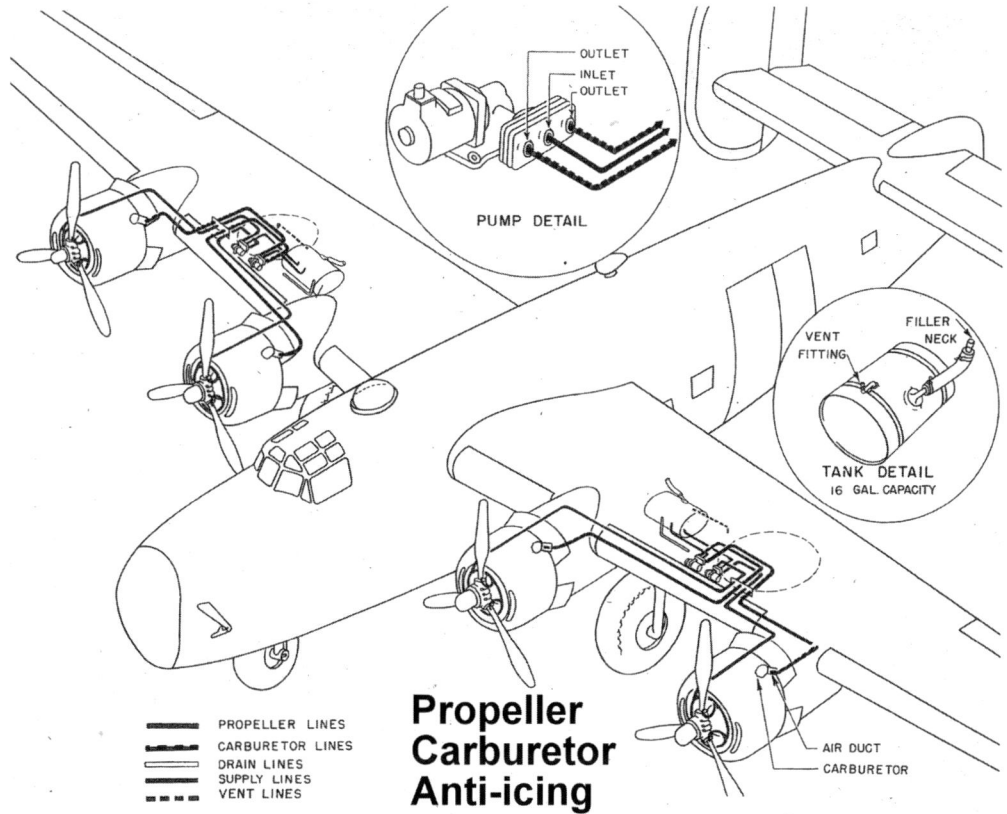

OUTLET
INLET
OUTLET

PUMP DETAIL

FILLER NECK
VENT FITTING

TANK DETAIL
16 GAL. CAPACITY

Propeller Carburetor Anti-icing

PROPELLER LINES
CARBURETOR LINES
DRAIN LINES
SUPPLY LINES
VENT LINES

AIR DUCT
CARBURETOR

Heating System

General

The first 35 C-87s were equipped with four heaters on the flight deck as follows: two heaters for pilot and co-pilot on Bulkhead 1.0, one just aft of the co-pilot at the inboard edge of the radio table, and one at Bulkhead 4.0. Seven Stewart-Warner fuel-air mixture spot heaters delivered heat from the top side of the blower cases of the inboard engines to the flight compartment. Two Stewart-Warner fuel-air mixture space heaters delivered heat from the left side of the blower cases of the inboard engines to the main compartment. On aircraft 41-11800 through 41-23791 inclusive the fuel mixture for the main compartment was delivered from the outboard engines. Electrically operated solenoid valves, mounted in front of the firewall at the engines, controlled the flow of fuel-air mixture to the heater groups. Individual magnetic valves were installed separately in the intake line of each heater.

Spot Heaters: Beginning with aircraft 41-11908, all seven spot heaters were Type 789-AC. Pilot and ccco-pilot: Center, under the instrument panel between stations 1.0 and 1.1 (two Type 789-G).

Navigator: Left side behind the navigator (one Type 789-F installed on 41-11908 and subsequent).

Radio Operator: Right side of the fuselage, aft of the operator (one Type 789-F).

Astrodome: Right of the hydraulic reservoir (one Type 789-F).

Pilot and co-pilot: One each behind the pilot and co-pilot; used to defrost side windows in pilots' enclosure and for general heating (two Type 789-G installed on 41-11908 and subsequent).

Space Heaters: Two heaters, one on each side, were installed on the floor of the cargo compartment just aft of the flight deck partition (two Type 791-D). On aircraft prior to 41-11800 one Type 782-D (located aft of Station 8.0 right side) was used for heating the cargo compartment, after which there were two 40,000 BTU per hour heaters just aft of Bulkhead 4.0. To serve as a passenger transport, cabin heating was a requirement. Ducts from the heater ran along the fuselage sides at floor level, which made it necessary to shorten the seat legs on the outboard sides.

Defroster Tubes

There were flexible defroster ducts for all heaters except for the radio operator and navigator. These heaters had deflector plates that, when opened, allowed warm air to flow to the crew, and when closed, deflected air upward through the flexure ducts for defrosting. Two defroster knobs, one on the pilot's control column and one on the co-pilot's auxiliary panel, controlled the deflector plates on the pilot's and co-pilot's heaters. The deflector plates of the other heaters were controlled manually at the heaters.

Flying Suit Receptacles

On aircraft after 43-30557 the outlets for flying suit heaters are listed in the table below. Two receptacles were provided at each location, one connected directly to the 24-volt DC system; the other was connected by a heavy-duty rheostat that adjusted the heat from warm to hot.

Heating System

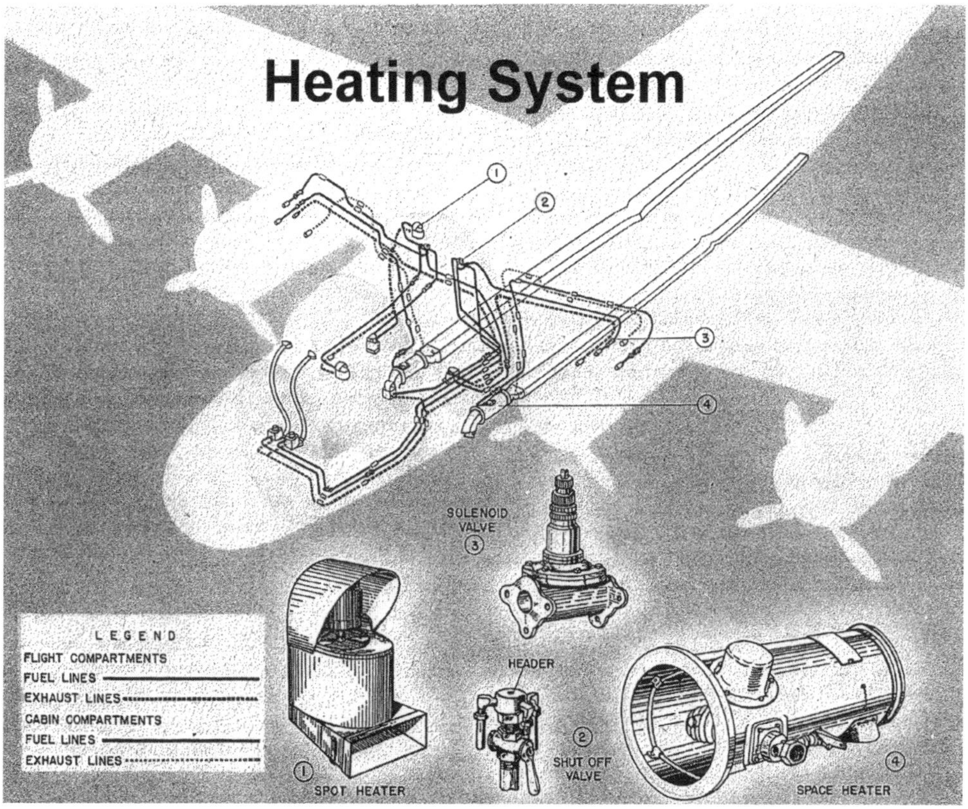

Space Heater

1. Exhaust Line
2. Idler Solenoid Valve
3. Fuel-Air Line
4. Butterfly Valve
5. Heat Outlet
6. Distribution Duct
7. Heater Unit
8. Saddle Strap
9. Air Scoop
10. Scoop Control Lever

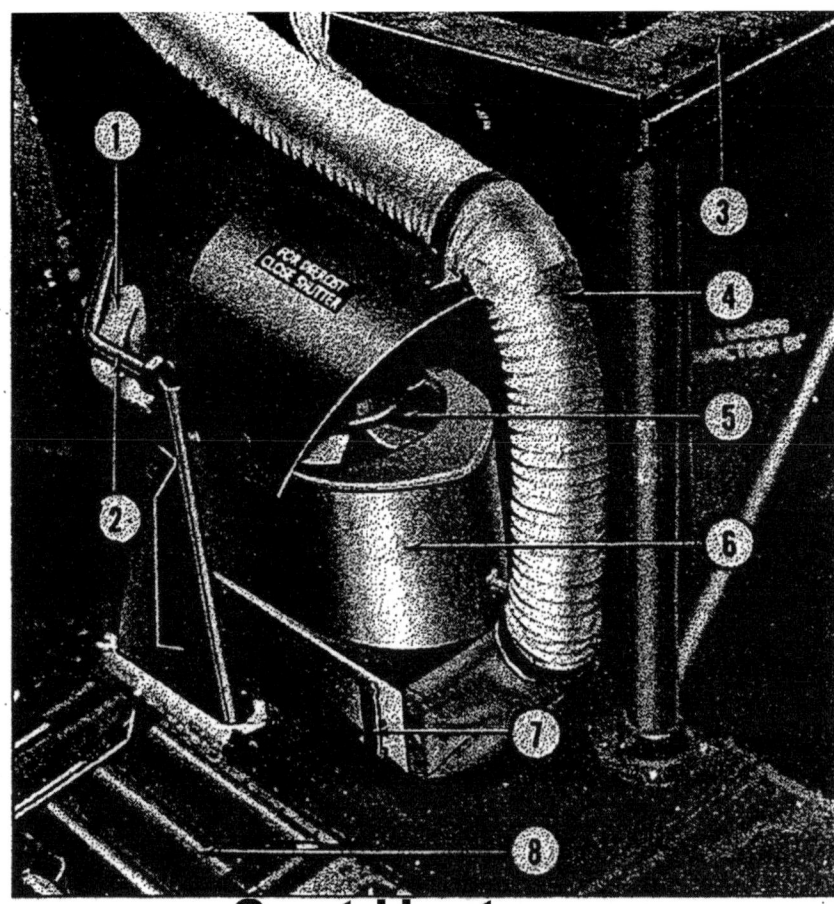

Spot Heater

1. Fuel-Air Line
2. Exhaust Line
3. Radio Operator's Table
4. Defroster Tube
5. Fan
6. Heater Unit
7. Defroster Control
8. Co-Pilot's Platform

FLYING SUIT AND MISCELLANEOUS HEATER DATA

Description	Location	Data
Pilot's Suit Heater Outlet	Left side of pilot's compartment	Outlet with rheostat—20-amp. fuse—station 3.0 fuse box
Copilot's Suit Heater Outlet	Right side of pilot's compartment	Outlet with rheostat—20-amp. fuse—copilot's fuse box
Navigator's Suit Heater Outlet	Left side of flight deck	Outlet with rheostat—20-amp. fuse—station 3.0 fuse box
Radio Operator's Suit Heater Outlet	Right side of flight deck	Outlet with rheostat—20-amp. fuse—station 3.0 fuse box
Commanding Officer's Suit Heater Outlet	Left side of flight deck, aft of navigator	Outlet with rheostat—20-amp fuse—station 3.0 fuse box
Pitot Heater	In Pitot mast	Switch on pilot's pedstal—15-amp. fuse—copilot's fuse box

Ventilating System

Flight Deck, Forward Area

Fresh air for the pilot and co-pilot was obtained from cut-outs in the left and right pitot static tubes. The ventilators at the outboard ends of the instrument panel were the ball-and-socket type, rotating the ball opening or closing them.

Flight Deck, Aft Area

An intake duct in the leading edge of the right wing supplied fresh air to the aft part of the flight deck. A Y-duct supplied both ventilators, one on the left and one on the right side at Station 3.2. A control at each ventilator allowed adjustment from the OPEN to the CLOSED position.

Main Cargo Compartment

Scoops on the right and left sides of the fuselage supplied fresh air via a duct extending along each side with outlets above the windows. The telescoping outlets could be locked closed by turning clockwise to engage a notched stop.

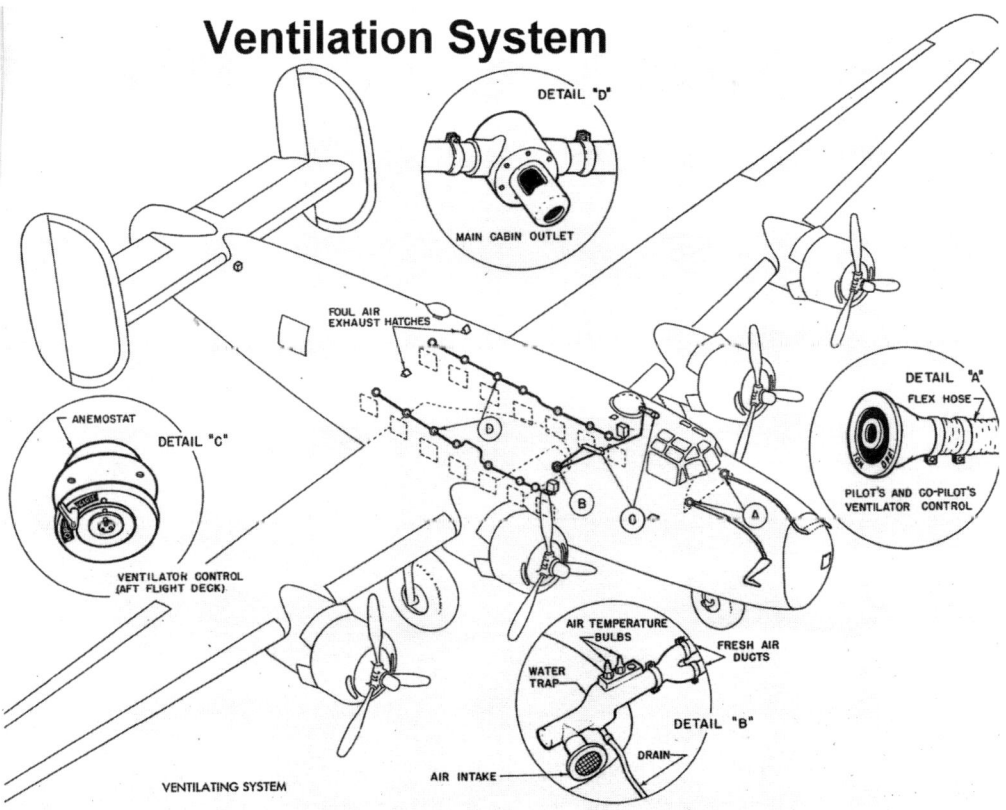

Oxygen System

General

Oxygen breathing equipment was stored in 24 Type G-1 cylinders and was distributed to two oxygen systems: a crew system supplied by seven oxygen cylinders, and a troop oxygen system that was supplied by 17 oxygen cylinders. In some C-87s there were 20 G-1 oxygen cylinders, four of which supplied oxygen to the crew and 16 of which supplied oxygen to troops in the rear. Later aircraft were equipped with removable Type J-1 oxygen cylinders supplying the troop oxygen system. The two sections of the oxygen system were separated by a line valve that could be opened to provide the flight crew with more oxygen when there were no troops on board. Type-12 demand regulators and visible indicating instruments were located at each crew position. Earlier aircraft were equipped with constant flow Type A-9A regulators. The troop oxygen system was equipped with two automatic continuous flow regulators that controlled the oxygen supplied to the troop oxygen outlets.

Constant Flow Type

Aircraft prior to 43-30557 were equipped with the constant flow type system, the oxygen being stored under 400 psi 24 Type G-1 fixed cylinders located at fuselage ceiling. The bottles were connected in groups of one, two, or three with 14 bottles serving the main cabin and 10 the flight deck. Check valves were located at each manifold outlet to prevent loss of pressure from the entire system in the event of a ruptured bottle or line. Lines from the manifolds led to three selector valves, mounted on the flight deck at left of the hydraulic reservoir. The top selector valve permitted the flow of oxygen from system to main cabin outlets; the bottom valve permitted oxygen flow to the crew outlets, while the center valve connected both systems. The valves were to be either fully open or fully closed.

   An A-9A oxygen regulator that was to reduce system pressure to the low pressure required by the oxygen masks was installed at each outlet. The upper half of the dial showed that if the correct rate of flow was being received for the indicated altitude, the lower half showed the oxygen system pressure. Filler valves for both sets of bottles were contained in a closed metal box behind a hinged access door on the right side of the fuselage, below the wing trailing edge. Two valve adapters for use when charging the system with British equipment were also contained in the box. Relief valves were installed on early aircraft to relieve the system pressure when more than 450 psi.

Demand Type

Beginning with 43-30557 onward, the oxygen installation was replaced by a demand-type; the supply being divided into two groups of cylinders. One group of 17 G-1 bottles were mounted on the fuselage ceiling from the rear wing spar to Station 7.0 to supply the main cargo compartment. Another group of seven bottles was mounted on the ceiling of the nose compartment to supply the crew. The bottles were connected through aluminum alloy tubing to oxygen regulators. An outlet fitted with an automatic coupling was provided at each passenger seat in the main compartment to which an oxygen mask hose could be attached. Regulator outlets in the flight deck were equipped with flexible hoses to which masks could be attached. At each crewman's station in the flight deck, panels were provided on which were mounted his demand regulator, a flow indicator, a pressure gauge, and an indicator lamp that blinked a warning when the supply was becoming low. Portable bottles were furnished for each crew member at his individual station and could be replenished by connecting the portable recharger to the main line of his group or, in emergency, to any group.

Two pressure gauges were mounted separately in the main compartment with accompanying warning lights. Three troop-type oxygen regulators were provided in the cargo compartment and were all mounted together on a bracket above the wing center section to the left of the center line.

The system filler valve was mounted externally behind the access door on the fuselage right side below the wing trailing edge. A line valve was installed inside the fuselage at Station 6.0 on the right wall that allowed the bottles in the nose compartment (supplying crew) to be filled without replenishing those in the main compartment.

Regulators

A-12 Type: The Pioneer A-12 demand oxygen regulator was developed for use in high-altitude flying and automatically delivered the system pressure. Filler valves for both sets of bottles were housed in a closed metal box behind a hinged access door on the right side of the fuselage, below the wing trailing edge. Two valve adapters used when charging the system with British equipment were also contained in the box. Relief valves were installed on early aircraft to relieve the system pressure when more than 450 psi.

A-11 Troop Type: Three Type A-11 oxygen regulators mounted on a bracket were installed on the left side of the fuselage above the wing center section provided automatic regulation of oxygen.

Pressure Gauges

Type K-1 pressure gages, indicating available oxygen pressure, were located as follows: two in the main cabin, one to the right of the flight deck door, and one on the fuselage ceiling center line at Station 6.0; four on the flight deck, one at each crew member's station. Warning lights mounted with each pressure gauge informed personnel when the system pressure dropped below 95 psi.

Portable Walk-Around Cylinder

Crew members were supplied with low-pressure portable oxygen units that could be recharged at recharging valves throughout the aircraft. This portable unit consisted of a small A-4 oxygen bottle that contained 6 to 12 minutes supply of oxygen per charging. It was fitted with a Type A-13 demand regulator to which was attached a recharging valve with a pressure gauge and a mask hose connection. Troop passengers were supplied with high-pressure portable units that could not be recharged on the aircraft.

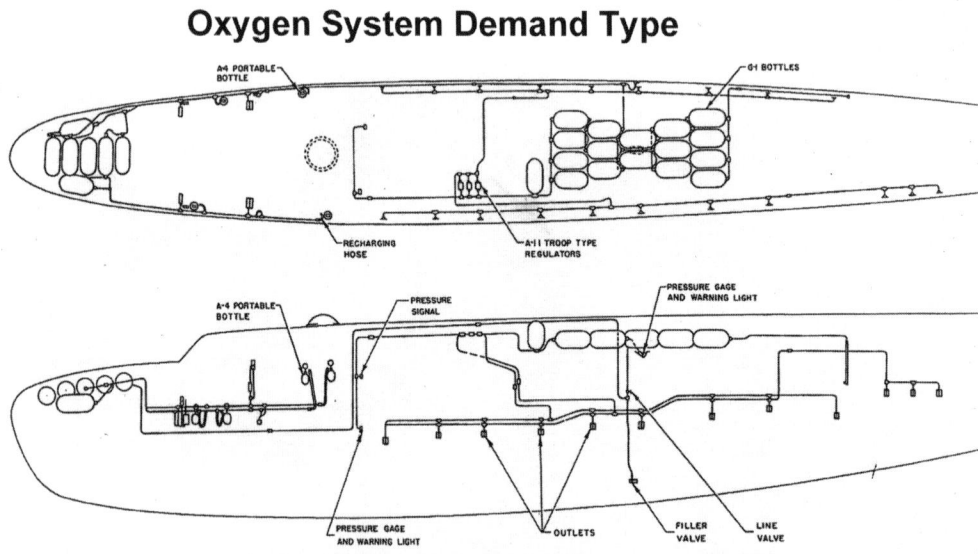

Oxygen System Demand Type

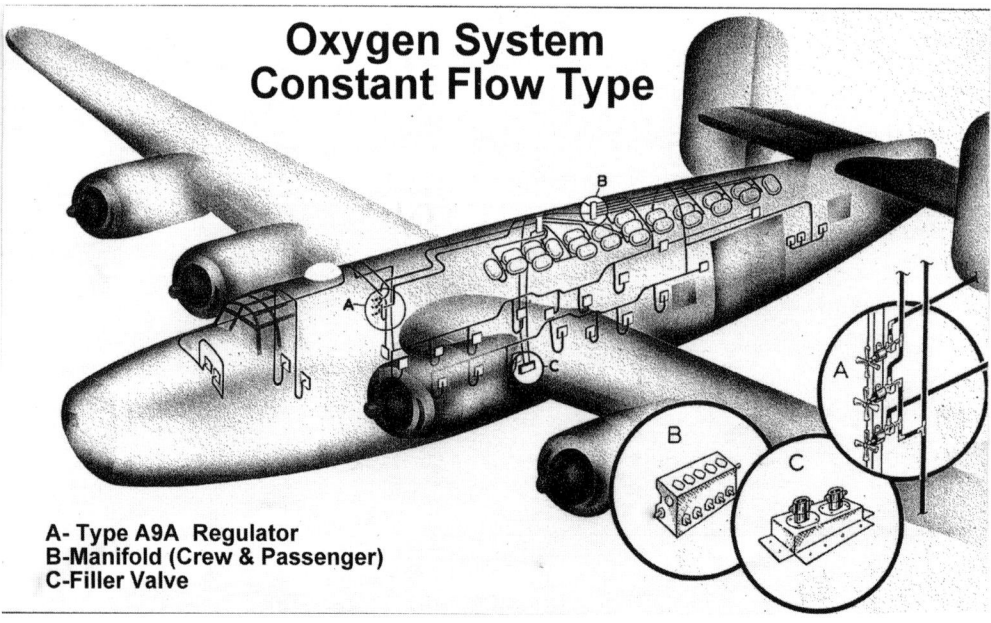

Oxygen System Constant Flow Type

A- Type A9A Regulator
B-Manifold (Crew & Passenger)
C-Filler Valve

TROOP TYPE OXYGEN REGULATOR

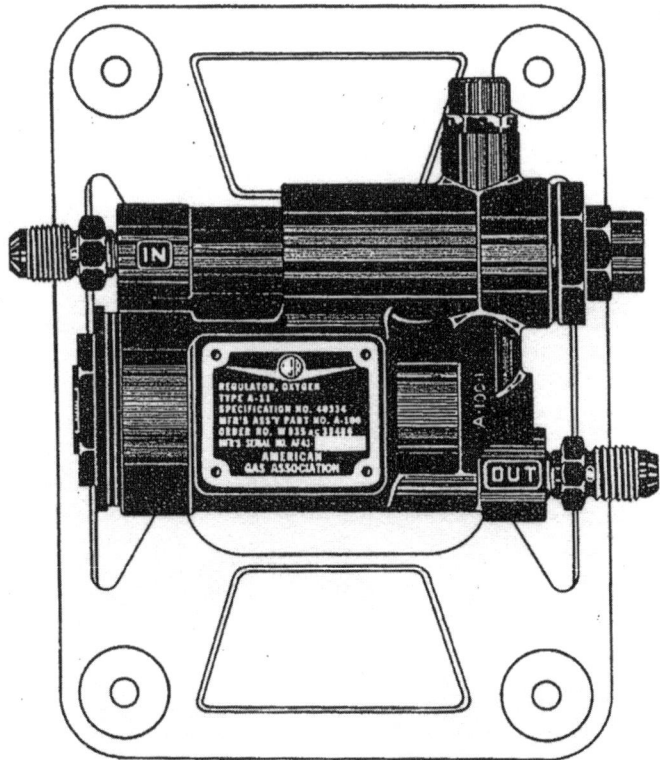

Seats

The pilot's and co-pilot's seats were installed side-by-side in the forward area of the flight deck. Fore-and-aft adjustment was via by a foot lever under the seat, while vertical adjustments were made by manipulation of a lever on the outboard side of each seat. The tilt of the seat back was controlled by a lever above the seat level on the outboard side. The compression springs in each chair leg could be adjusted to the degree of stiffness desired. The radio operator's seat, on the right side of the aft portion of the flight deck, was on a pedestal and was of the swivel type, turning 90 degrees. The navigator's seat, on the left side of the aft portion of the flight deck, was like that of the radio operator. A navigator's stool was stowed under the additional crew member's seat in the aft section of the flight deck.

Miscellaneous Equipment

On cargo C-87 versions a toilet was installed on the right side of the fuselage forward of Station 8.0 and another forward of Station 4.0 underneath the flight deck. The pilot's relief tube was on the left side of the airplane aft of the pilot's seat.

A drinking water cooler was installed on the right aft side wall of Bulkhead 4.

Blind flying curtains were provided for all windows in the pilots' and main cargo compartment and, in addition, a partition curtain for the pilot and co-pilot was provided.

Cases, Folders, and Bags: The flight report holder was installed on the left side of the fuselage beside the pilot's seat. The map container was mounted underneath the navigator's table on the left side. The data case hung on the left fuselage wall, aft of the pilot's seat. The tool bag was stowed on the right side of the nose-wheel compartment, just forward of Bulkhead 4.0.

The starter hand crank was stowed forward of Station 8.0 on the left side.

A Very pistol and holster were stowed on the fuselage.

Emergency Exits and Life Rafts

Main Cargo Door: This door, located in the main cargo compartment on the left side of the fuselage, was hinged at Stations 7.1 and 7.4. By pulling the emergency release the hinge pins were removed and the forward half of the door fell free. This door was generally used by all crew for entering and leaving.

Dedicated Emergency Exit: An emergency exit on the starboard fuselage, opposite the main cargo door, swung in and up by pulling the door handles inward.

Flight Deck Emergency Exit: The flight deck emergency exit was in the fuselage ceiling just aft of the pilot and provided an escape if the aircraft was on the ground or after a crash landing and NOT while in flight due to the danger of contact with the tail surfaces when bailing out. The latch was released by pulling the handles outboard and the door opened inward.

Nose Wheel Door: This exit was via a door under the pilot's seat and then through the nose wheel door. There were two red emergency levers at the top rear of the navigator's compartment and both levers had to be pulled their full travel, with sufficient force to break the safety wiring.

Crew members and passengers used seat-type parachutes.

Two Type A-2, five-man life rafts were installed in cradles in the top of the fuselage, over the wing, while four Type A-3, five-man life rafts were stowed in cradles farther aft in the top of the main cargo compartment. These rafts connected with a cable linkage to their respective CO_2 filler bottles and their cradle covers, so that a pull on any of the six raft release handles would release the cradle covers and open the release valves on the CO_2 bottles. Inflation of the rafts caused them to eject themselves from the aircraft. One life raft release handle for the two forward rafts was located on the flight deck, in the top of the radioman-navigator's compartment. One life raft release handle for the two rafts aft of the wing was in the top of the main cargo compartment on the port side, about even with the second window forward of the rear cargo door. The other four release handles were located on the outside top of the fuselage, two aft of each pair of life raft covers. Two Type E-2 seven-man rafts were stowed on the main cargo door and two more were stowed on the side of the fuselage aft of the main cargo door.

Emergency Equipment and Exits

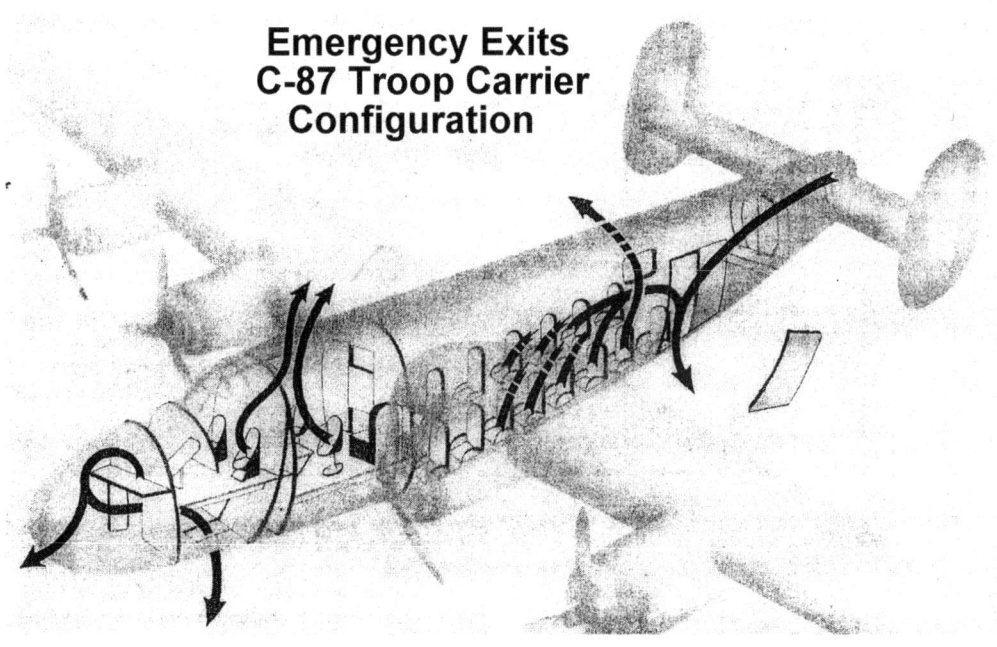

**Emergency Exits
C-87 Troop Carrier
Configuration**

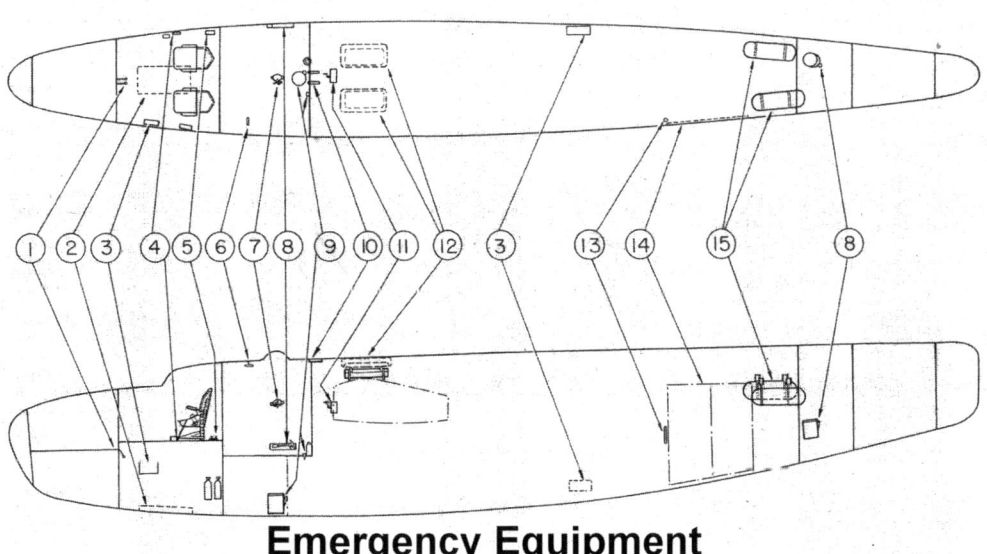

Emergency Equipment

1. Nose wheel doors—emergency release.
2. Nose wheel doors.
3. Fire extinguisher (A-2)—accessible from outside only.
4. Emergency lowering of flap control.
5. Engine pressure fire extinguisher and control.
6. Life raft release (inside).
7. Emergency hydraulic valve.
8. Fire axe.
9. Toilet and relief tube.
10. Life raft release (outside).
11. Emergency landing gear lowering.
12. Life rafts (outside).
13. Cargo door emergency release.
14. Cargo door.
15. Auxiliary life raft.

The C-87: The True Liberator Hauler

C-87 Cargo and Troop-Carrying Provisions

Useful Load	Max. Fuel* (3,100 gal)	Max. Cargo** (1,556 gal)	Max. Troop (max 25)
Crew (4)	720lb	720lb	720lb
Fuel	14,400lb	9,333lb	14,400lb
Oil	960lb	960lb	960lb
Cargo	7,633lb	12,700lb	xxxx
Troops/Equipment	xxxx	xxxx	4,375**/3,278lb*
Total Useful Load	23,713lb	23,713lb	23,713lb
Weight Empty	32,287lb	32,287lb	32,287lb
Total Gross Weight	58,000lb	58,000lb	58,000lb

*3,550 miles **1,732 miles

C-87 Troop-Carrying Provisions

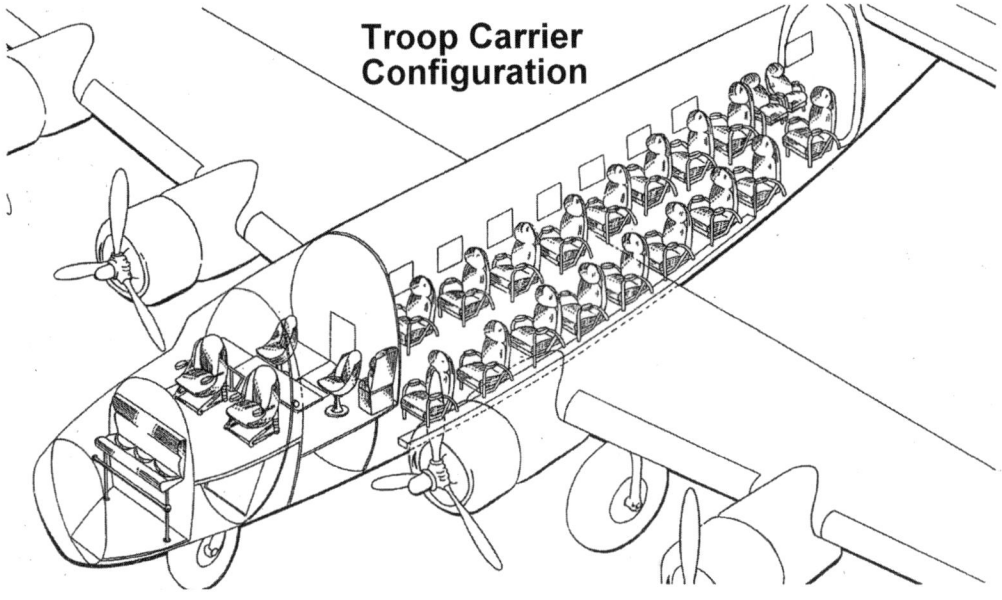

Troop Carrier Configuration

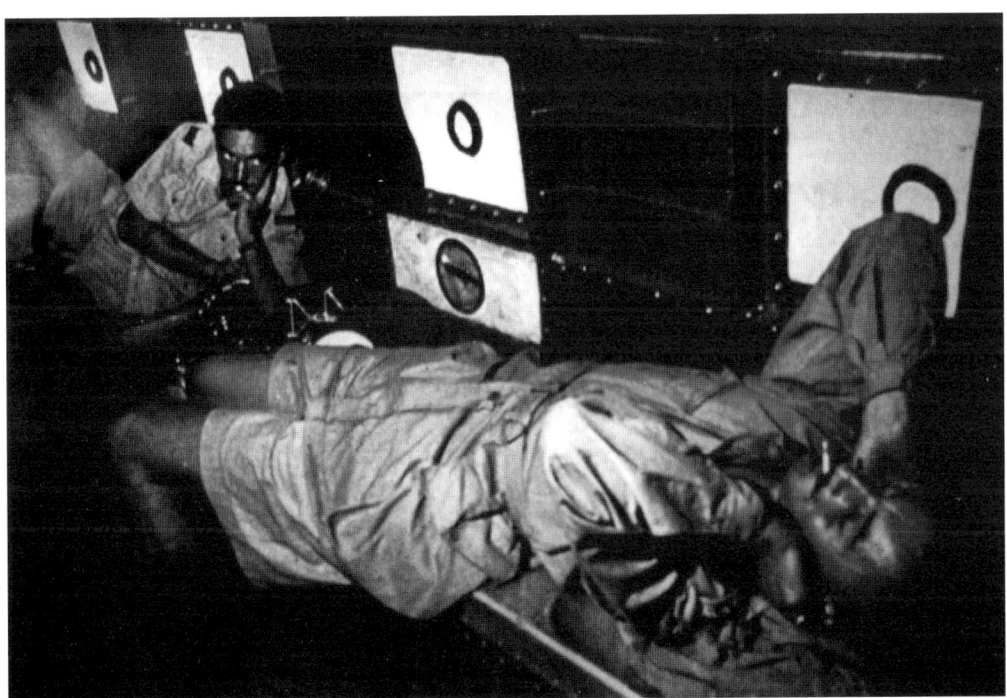

Bench seating on early C-87s. Note window with portal in center for troop use in fending off enemy air attacks! (*AAF*)

Jam-packed C-87 troop and cargo accommodations. (*AAF*)

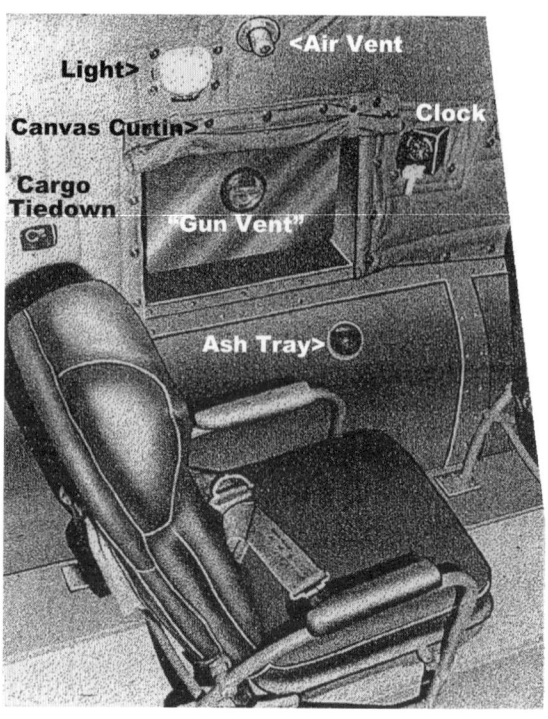

A flight manual drawing of the dedicated passenger seat, ventilating nozzle and dome light can be seen above the curtained window. (*AAF*)

Double-row seating looking forward towards the wing interruption on the ceiling. (*AAF*)

Forward passenger compartment looking into the flight deck entrance and stairs. (*AAF*)

Three-row seating looking aft. (*AAF*)

Passenger amenities. (*AAF*)

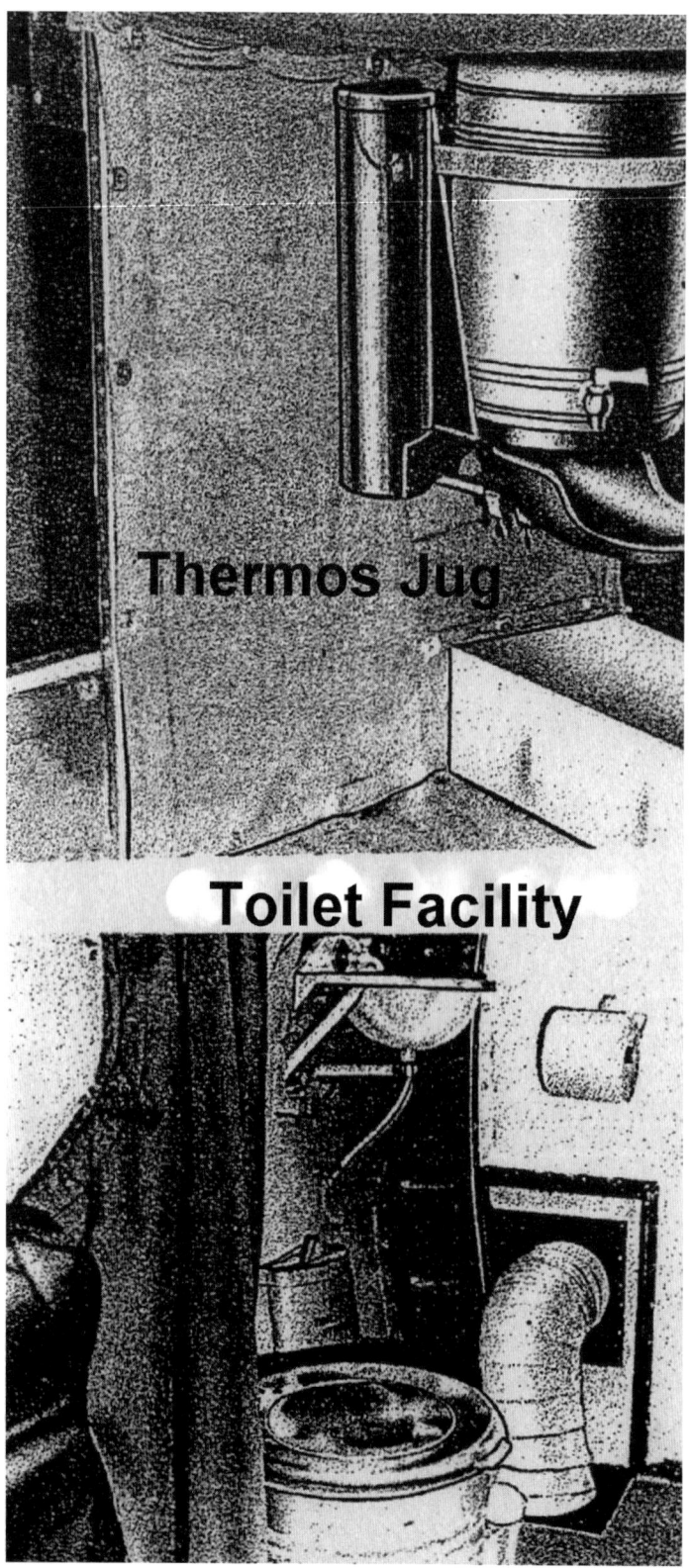

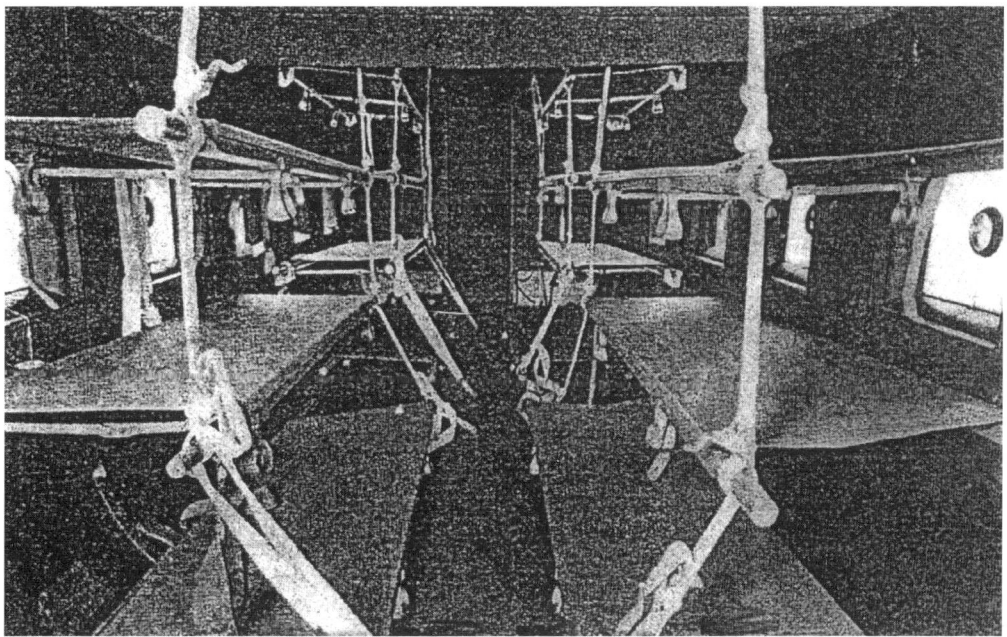

The C-87 could carry as many as 25 passengers. (*AAF*)

The C-87 could carry up to 16 tiered litters. (*AAF*)

C-87 Cargo-Carrying Provisions

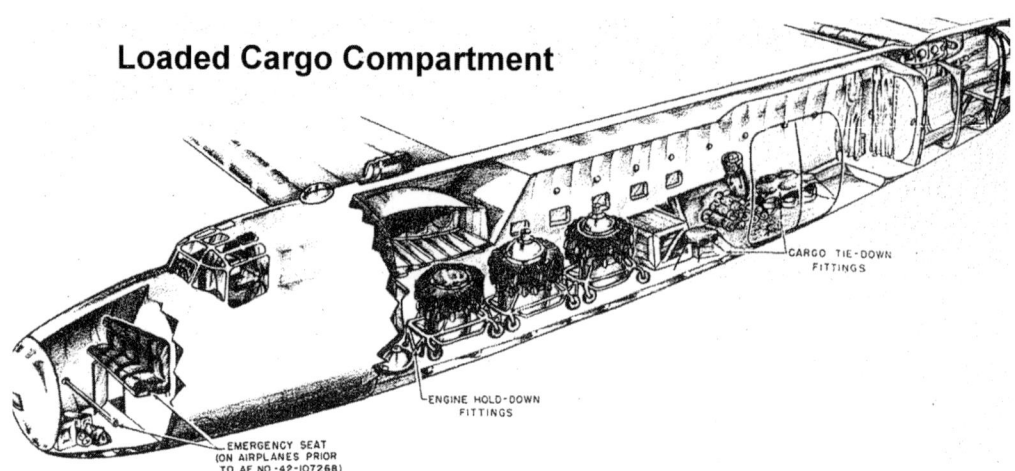

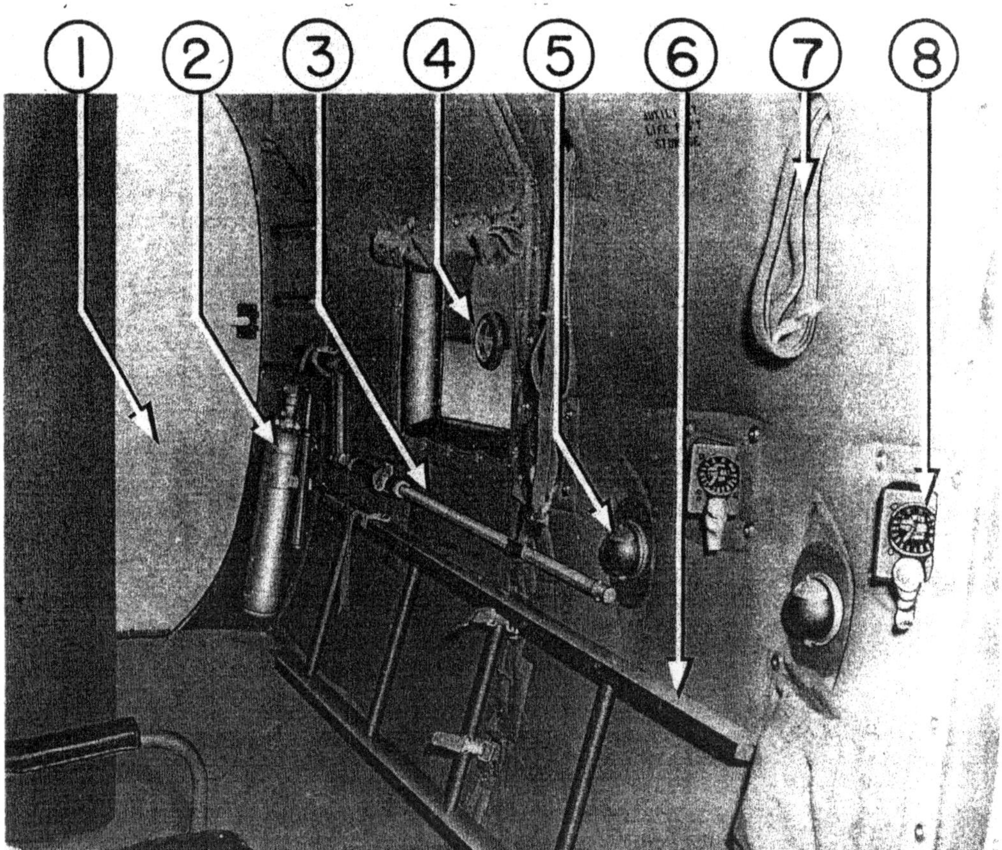

Loaded Cargo Compartment
CARGO TIE-DOWN FITTINGS
ENGINE HOLD-DOWN FITTINGS
EMERGENCY SEAT (ON AIRPLANES PRIOR TO AF NO.-42-107268)

1
2
3
4
5
6
7
8

Main Cargo Compartment

1. Door at bulkhead
2. Fire extinguisher
3. Engine hand crank
4. Fuselage window
5. Ash tray
6. Ladder
7. Auxiliary life raft stowage strap
8. A-9A oxygen regulator and outlet

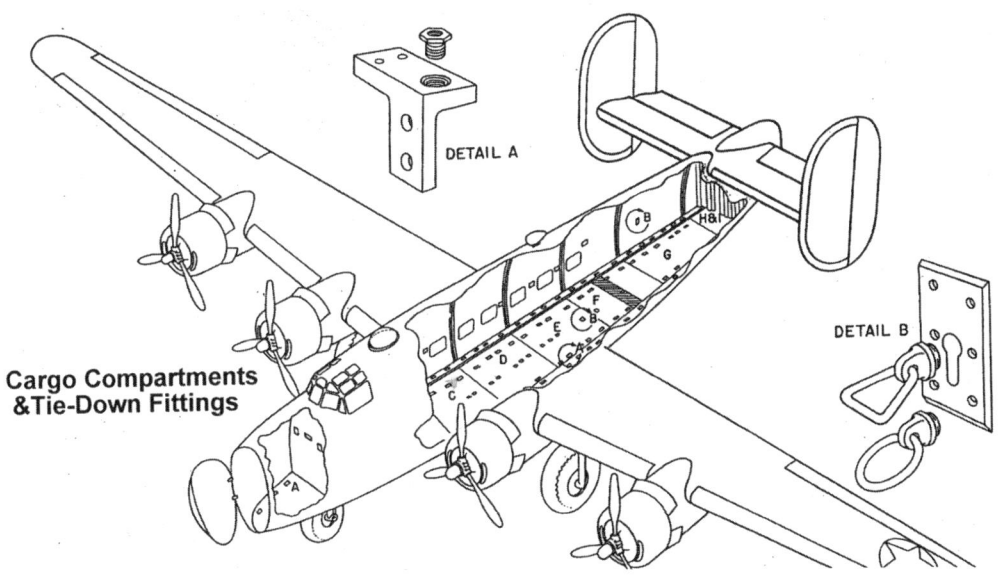

DETAIL A

DETAIL B

**Cargo Compartments
&Tie-Down Fittings**

C-87 Nose Cargo Door and Compartment

Nose cargo in open position. (*AAF*)

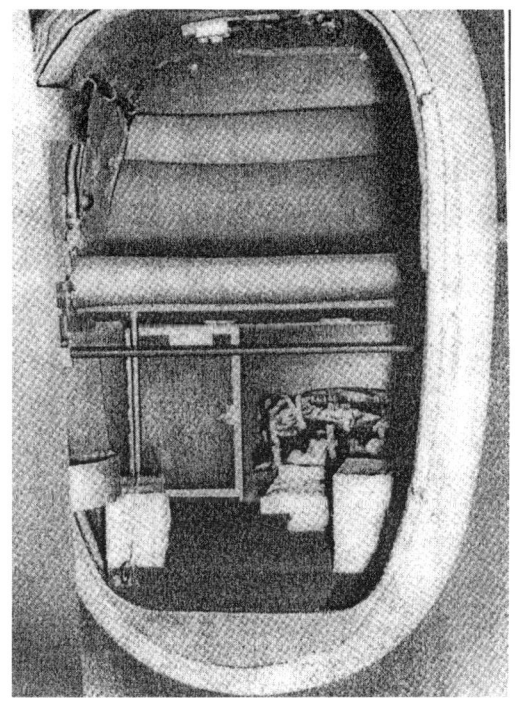

The interior of the nose cargo compartment could be used for cargo or have a straight bench or five individual upholstered seats on the back wall. (*AAF*)

Loading and unloading the nose cargo compartment was easy as it was at the level of the standard truck bed. (*AAF*)

A view of entrance of the nose compartment from the flight deck. (*AAF*)

C-87 Side Cargo Doors and Tail Fairings and Compartment

Loading through the starboard waist gun window before a standard cargo door was cut and installed in the fuselage side. (*AAF*)

C-87 passenger door. (*AAF*)

Cargo Doors

1. Aft Door Securing Bolts
2. Bolt Access Flaps
3. Bolt Access Plates
4. Forward Door Emergency Release Cable

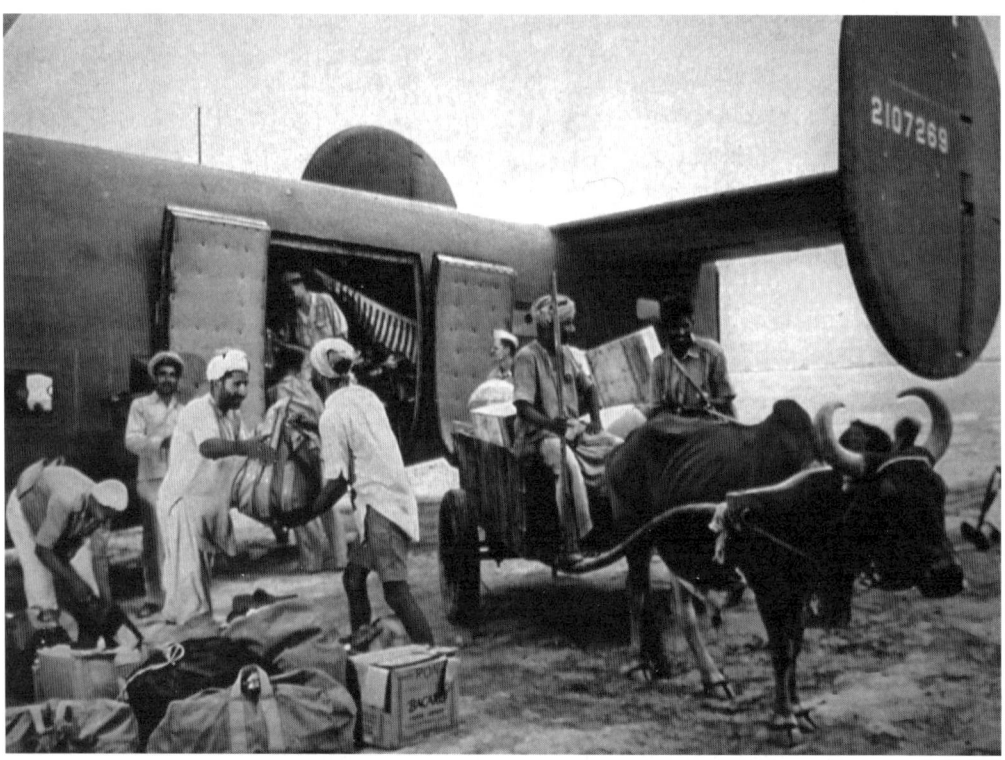

Primitive loading through a double cargo door on an Indian airbase. (*AAF*)

The low-slung Liberator fuselage and its tricycle landing gear configuration made for a level floor and easier loading than the tail-dragging C-47. (*AAF*)

Cargo doors closed with the area around the door giving space for last-minute baggage or cargo. (*AAF*)

After some heavy maneuvering the C-87 hold could accommodate three or four aircraft engines. (*AAF*)

Tail Machine Gun Provisions
1) Gun Suspension Cord
2) Gun Mount
3) Ammo Boxes
4) Gun Stowage

For early C-87 conversions the tail armament was removed but could be replaced if needed. (*AAF*)

C-87 navigator taking a navigational fix through tail machine gun glass. (*AAF*)

Some early 1942 Ferry Command versions retained their LB-30 tail .50 caliber machine gun position. (*AAF*)

An exterior view of former tail machine gun position faired over with a translucent cap. (*AAF*)

On later C-87s the machine gun tail was replaced with a prefabricated aluminum fairing with two small windows. (*AAF*)

Another prefabricated aluminum tail fairing version was of a more aerodynamic cone-shaped type. (*AAF*)

C-87A Liberator Express

The C-87A was touted by Consolidated as a 16-seat 'VIP' version of the basic C-87 utilitarian passenger transport that had essentially been a 'no-frills' transport, with little attention being paid to passenger comfort. For night flying, the C-87A could be equipped

The C-87A was touted by Consolidated as a 16-seat 'VIP' version of the basic C-87 utilitarian passenger transport. (*AAF*)

with Pullman-type upholstered seats that were convertible into five berths. Because of the seating arrangement, the window layout was different to the C-87. The C-87As were procured under Supplemental Agreement #3 to Contract W-535-AC-18723, as amended by Change Order #5, dated 15 October 1942. Six were built, three each for the AAF and USN. The three AAF C-87As were christened *Gulliver I* (41-11680), *Gulliver II* (41-23863?), and *Gulliver III* (41-24159). The other three C-87As were former AAF C-87A VIP transports outfitted for 16 passengers that were assigned to the Navy under the designation RY-1 and given the BuNos 67797/67799.

Famous C-87A Passengers

Wendell Willkie

The best-known C-87A was *Gulliver I* (41-11608), which carried Wendell Willkie as President Roosevelt's 'One World Ambassador', on a 28,487-mile trip during August 1942. The aircraft, assigned from the 10th Ferry Squadron, was flown by American Airlines pilot Maj. Richard Kight with co-pilot Alexis Klotz during the 51-day diplomatic mission. Willkie was accompanied by *Look Magazine* publisher Gardner 'Mike' Cowles, *New York Herald Tribune* foreign correspondent Joseph Barnes, US Navy Captain Paul Pihl, and US Army Major Grant Mason. In August 1942, Roosevelt asked Willkie, his 1940 Republican opponent for the Presidency, to make an around-the-world flight as his 'special emissary and fact finder' to persuade world leaders that although America was engaged in an energetic isolationist political debate at the time, the country was united against fascism. The flight involved stopovers at Cairo, Palestine, Baghdad, Tehran, Moscow, and China, and then a return to the United States via a route across the Pacific. Several firsts were made on this flight: the first flight from the Soviet Union into China, from China to Alaska, and from China to the United States across the Pacific. Willkie later recounted his world travels on the *Gulliver* in his 1943 best-selling book, *One World*. This highly influential book made a well-supported appeal for post-war international cooperation and solidified Willkie's role as a major force in American politics, but he died of a heart attack in October 1944 at the relatively young age of 52. Willkie's pilot, Maj. Richard Kight, was transferred to the CBI (China–Burma–India) wing of the Air Transport Command in December 1942, where he served as Chief of Staff and Director of Operations for 'Hump' operations between Burma, India and China. After a distinguished 30-year, career Kight retired as a brigadier general in 1963.

After completing the Willkie around-the-world trip during August 1942, the ex-*Gulliver I*, now a B-24D-CO, served in the Caribbean and then was refurbished at Olmstead Field, Middletown, Pennsylvania, during June 1944, after which it received a new serial number, 41-39600, and was assigned to the ATC/Pacific Wing flown by American Airlines. The Liberator was scrapped by RFC at Bush Field 19 November 1945.

Itinerary of *Gulliver*'s One World Flight

Departed New York City, New York (26 August 1942)
West Palm Beach, Florida
Puerto Rico (Note A)
Brazil: Belem, Natal
Ascension Island (Note B)
Accra, Ghana
Kano, Nigeria
Khartoum, Sudan (Note C)
Egypt: Cairo, El Alamein, Alexandria
Ankara, Turkey (Note D)
Beirut, Lebanon (Note E)
Jerusalem, Palestine* (Lydda)
Iraq: Habbaniyah, Baghdad
Tehran, Iran
Soviet Union: Kuybyshev, Moscow, Tashkent
China: Urumchi, Lanchow, Chengtu, Chungking, Sian
Soviet Union: Chita, Yakutsk, Seimchan
Fairbanks, Alaska
Edmonton, Alberta, Canada
Arrived Minneapolis, Minnesota (14 October 1942)

Notes:
A) While in Puerto Rico, Willkie visited his son, Philip, who was stationed with the US Navy there.
B) *Gulliver* landed on Ascension Island in the Atlantic Ocean. This stopover is not referred to in *One World* because the island concealed a secret US military base.
C) *Gulliver* flew from Kano via Khartoum to Cairo.
D) To maintain its wartime neutrality, Turkey would not allow *Gulliver* to enter Turkish airspace, so Willkie flew to Ankara on a Pan American flight.
E) Willkie's stop in Beirut, Lebanon, was to meet with French General Charles de Gaulle.

The best-known C-87A was *Gulliver* I (41-11608), which carried Wendell Willkie as President Roosevelt's 'One World Ambassador', on a 28,487-mile trip during August 1942. Pilot Maj. Richard Kight is seen in the cockpit hatch. (*ATC*)

Willkie arriving at Cairo and descending through a half-open padded cargo door. There is a good view of the Air Transport Command insignia. (*ATC*)

Another view of Willkie and his entourage being greeted at Cairo by British and American military and Egyptian officials. (*ATC*)

Eddie Rickenbacker

After his rescue from a 22-day ordeal of being stranded on a life raft after a crash in in the Pacific during October 1942, Eddie Rickenbacker was sent on an inspection tour to the Soviet Union. His 55,000-mile round trip (his mileage estimate) during the spring and summer of 1943 first took him along the South Atlantic air route and then via American bases in Africa to Cairo flying on a C-54. From Cairo he traveled to India by a C-87 piloted by ex-Northwest Airlines pilot William Richmond and a crew of three to the large base at Abadan, Iran, that had been built to assemble Lend-Lease aircraft meant for Russia. In his 1967 autobiography, Rickenbacker describes the C-87 as a 'new, four-motor luxury plane', Since the Cairo C-87 was unarmed, the trip over the Hump was flown in a required armed C-87. Once in China he met Chiang Kai-shek and toured bases in China in a C-47. On his return over the Hump, he again boarded the armed C-87 and on the trip: 'I went back to the .50 caliber machine gun in the tail of the plane and shot down on one of the fields (Japanese airfields).' In India he again boarded his original unarmed C-87 and flew from New Delhi to Tehran and on to Russia, landing at Kuybyshev, which had served as the Russian capital while Moscow was under siege. He headed for Moscow by road and continued his inspection tour, that included helping the Soviets with their American-built Lend-Lease aircraft and to assess their military capabilities. He was permitted a rare view of Russian ground and air equipment and returned with valuable intelligence information, but is mostly remembered for his error in informing the Soviets of the secret B-29 Superfortress project. On his return trip, the

During October 1942, Eddie Rickenbacker (L) (with pilot William Richmond) was sent on an inspection tour to the Soviet Union. Note the 'Hat-in-the-Ring' logo of Rickenbacker's First World War 94th Aero Squadron on the nose of the C-87. (*ATC*)

C-87 flew to England via Tehran, Marrakech, and well off the Portuguese coast to avoid Luftwaffe fighters that had shot down several aircraft (including an aircraft in which English actor Leslie Howard was a passenger several weeks before). After meeting Prime Minister Churchill, Rickenbacker returned to the US via Reykjavik, Iceland, but had to make a weather-diverted landing in Greenland for two days before landing at LaGuardia in New York via Gander, Newfoundland. For his trip, Rickenbacker received the Medal for Merit from the United States government.

FDR

Roosevelt was the first President to fly on official business. The first aircraft specifically used for presidential travel was a Douglas Dolphin, a US Navy RD-2 amphibian delivered in 1933 and based at the Naval base at Anacostia, Washington DC. The four-passenger Dolphin was modified with luxury upholstery and a small separate sleeping compartment. Although there are no records confirming that the President flew in the aircraft, it remained in the inventory as a presidential transport from 1933 until 1939. The ideal VIP transatlantic transport during the first years of the war was air travel as the Secret Service felt that overseas travel by ship was not only too time-consuming but too dangerous due to Kriegsmarine U-boats. During January 1943, Roosevelt traveled 5,500 miles (in three legs over 42 hours) on the *Dixie Clipper*, a Pan Am-crewed Boeing 314 flying boat, to secretly meet Churchill at the Casablanca Conference in Morocco. However, AAF leaders, concerned about relying upon commercial airlines for presidential transport, ordered the conversion of a military aircraft to accommodate the Commander-in-Chief, who also had special needs, not only for his tall 6ft 2in frame but also for his challenges as a polio victim at 39 years old. When traveling by aircraft he was unable to move about in his wheelchair or on crutches as he was able to on a train or ship. Also, loading him and his wheelchair were a concern.

Wartime VIP travel accommodation began during July 1942 when the ATC at Gravely Point, Washington DC, assigned the 10th Ferry Squadron to provide air transport support for the War Department to fly government officials. Until four-engine transport became available in late 1943 and early 1944, the ATC used C-47s for longer trips and C-60As (Lockheed Lodestars) for short trips to fly officials out of Washington National Airport.

Maj. Gen. Harold George, head of the new ATC, needed a staff pilot for his command plane, a Douglas C-84 (former TWA DC-3B), and chose an aide, Maj. Henry Myers who was stationed with the nearby 10th Ferry Squadron. Myers had logged 12,000 hours flying time and was experienced in flying Commercial DC-3s and would fly Gen. George for the remainder of his command.

1Lt Elmer Smith, a January 1942 graduate of single engine flying school with less than 1,000 hours flight time when selected as Myer's co-pilot. Although disappointed not to be selected to fly glamorous fighter aircraft, Smith decided that as Myer's co-pilot this posting would be the best experience for a post-war position as a commercial airlines pilot. For a VIP passenger aircraft, a navigator was added as on other flights the AAF required that the navigation responsibility be that of the pilots. Capt. Theodore Boselli had joined the AAC in 1940 as one of the first to be chosen for the new navigator school. He became a very experienced long-distance navigator, flying on the September 1941 Harriman Moscow flight. The remainder of the C-84 crew consisted of Radio Operator T/Sgt Charles Horton and Crew Chief T/Sgt Frederick Winslow.

During their time flying the C-84 on VIP missions, the crew was always on 24/7 call. Among their flights were flying Poland's Prime Minister General Sikorski, Czech President Edvard Benes, and Gen. Joseph Stilwell when he returned from Burma.

The first dedicated aircraft proposed for presidential VIP transport use was C-87A 41-24159, the former *Gulliver III*, which was modified in 1943. *Gulliver III* was one of three AAF *Gulliver* C-87As: *Gulliver I* (41-11680), *Gulliver II* (41-23863?), and *III* (41-24159), that was delivered on 6 June 1943 to Washington National. Three other C-87s were converted as former AAF C-87A VIP transports outfitted for 16 passengers that were assigned to the Navy under the designation RY-1. The C-87B remained in its olive drab with a light grey underside paint scheme. It was converted to commercial airline comfort standards and could sleep seven to nine and carry 20 passengers with enough head room provided by its boxy rectangular fuselage. The aircraft had four Pullman Compartments, 1, 2, 3 and 4, which had two double facing seats separated by a removable table on the right side for daytime use. Separated by an aisle, the aircraft's left side contained a three-person bench-type seat opposite the four seats and table. Compartments 2, 3, and 4 could be made into upper and lower berths using Pullman curtains. Compartment 1 was under the wing and did not have an upper berth. The two lavatories between Compartments 2 and 3 could be isolated from the rest of the aircraft by a curtain. A Tappan-type kitchen galley with an electric range and oven was located between Compartments 3 and 4. There was a closet and linen storage cubicle in the extreme tail. Compartments 1, 2, and 3 had two windows on each side, while Compartment 4 had one on each side, The lavatories and rear closet/storage had no windows. The aircraft was also equipped with upgraded radio and navigational equipment, additional oxygen supply, and a removable ramp for FDR's wheelchair.

After the *Gulliver III*'s modifications the new presidential aircraft was to be named *Sudden Notion* but it was renamed, tongue in cheek, as the *Guess Where II* (*II* meaning 'to', as in where to?) by pilot Maj. Henry Myers, who also the nicknamed the unit the 'Brass Hat Squadron'. *Guess Where II* was briefly painted on the nose but soon painted over for security purposes.

The *Guess Where II* crew remained the same as the *Gulliver III* except that a cabin steward (Cpl Preyden) was added. During November 1942 Myers and Smith were given B-24 pilot training at Tarrant Field Fort Worth (now Carswell) in anticipation of flying the C-87 as a possible presidential aircraft.

After the usual shakedown flights, *Guess Where II*'s first long-distance mission was a two-month globetrotting flight beginning on 25 July 1943 transporting four Senators of the Truman Committee: Richard Russell, Ralph Brewer, Henry Cabot Lodge, and Richard Mead, who represented the US Senate on a fact-finding tour to observe and report on the progress of the war, the delivery of supplies, and Lend-Lease. The mission would cover 36,798 air miles, the longest leg being from Columbo, Ceylon, to Western Australia, a flight of 3,200 miles, which made it the first land-based passenger-carrying aircraft flight over that route until that time (PBY Catalinas had made mail flights previously). The next *Guess Where II* mission was to transport Treasury Secretary Henry Morgenthau across the Atlantic to England, then return via Africa, crossing the South Atlantic to Brazil, and then returning to Washington DC.

The next months were spent waiting and preparing for the long-anticipated consecutive presidential trips to the Cairo (22–26 November 1943), Tehran (27 November–2 December), Second Cairo (2–7 December) Conferences to meet with Prime Minister Winston Churchill and Premier Joseph Stalin. After meticulous planning, the *Guess Where II* crew left Washington National for French Morocco to wait for instructions to support FDR, who had crossed the Atlantic on the battleship USS *Iowa*. While waiting the crew was informed that FDR would be flown by contract commercial airline C-54s (despite their high fuselage loading doors to accommodate the President's wheelchair) to the conferences instead of by the ATC, which had the supposed official responsibility.

However, after a review of the C-87's highly controversial in-service safety record, its proclivity to fires, and its appearance to enemy fighter aircraft, as well as to those in friendly foreign destinations, to its derivative B-24 bomber warplane, the Secret Service categorically refused to approve the *Guess Where II* for presidential transport. FDR would be transported via a TWA Douglas C-54 Skymaster. Had *Guess Where II* been accepted, it would have been the first dedicated aircraft to be used in presidential service, in effect the first Air Force One.

Apparently, while not considered presidentially safe, the aircraft was safe enough to transport senior members of the Roosevelt Administration on various trips, including the First Lady. In March 1944, it transported Eleanor Roosevelt on a goodwill tour of several Latin American countries. The *Guess Where II* continued to carry VIPs until its final flight on 30 October 1945, after which it was scrapped in 1945 at Walnut Ridge, Arkansas.

Myers served as the presidential pilot from June 1944 (Franklin Roosevelt) to January 1948 (Harry Truman), flying the only Douglas VC-54C Skymaster, which was the first

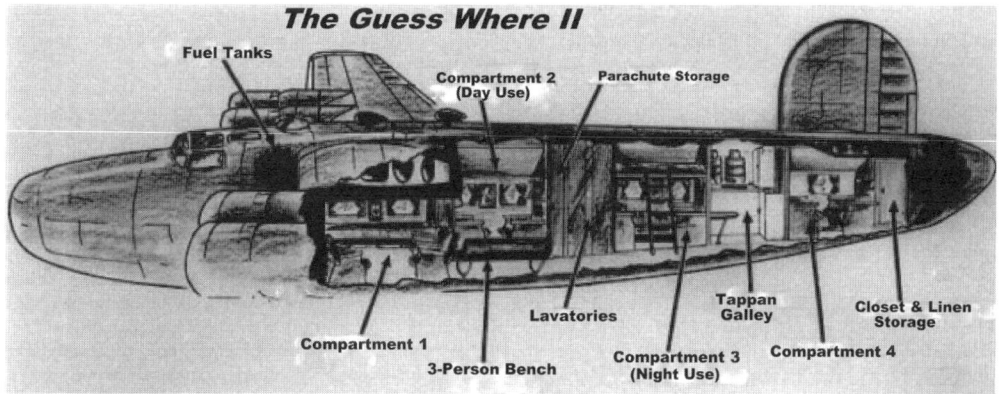

President Franklin Roosevelt's C-87 *Guess Where II*? was never used by him as a transport as the C-87's accident record deemed it as too dangerous. However, it was not considered too dangerous for wife Eleanor to use for her 1944 Latin American goodwill inspection tour of American and Allies bases. (*Newsreel still*)

aircraft purpose-built to fly an American President. Carrying the staff transport 'VC' designation, the aircraft was officially named *The Flying White House*. However, the aircraft became better known by its unofficial nickname, *Sacred Cow*, referring to the high security surrounding the aircraft and its special status. The unpressurized cabin included an executive conference room with a large desk and a rectangular bulletproof window and radio telephone. A private lavatory was installed next to the President's seat, and a fold-down bed was concealed behind the sofa. The galley had an electric refrigerator and stove, an uncommon luxury for 1945. A battery-powered retractable elevator was installed at the rear of the aircraft, which allowed President Roosevelt to board the aircraft easily while in his wheelchair. The aircraft was used only once by Roosevelt before his death, on his trip to the Yalta Conference in February 1945.

Later C-87 Special Missions

On 26 July 1943 a flight of ten P-47 fighters, intended to augment various units in the UK, were supported on their delivery flight by two B-24s and one C-87 to aid navigation. The 27th Ferry Squadron pilots flew their Thunderbolt fighters, equipped with auxiliary fuel tanks, from Presque Isle, Maine, to Prestwick, Scotland, with stops at Goose Bay, Labrador, Greenland, and Reykjavik, Iceland. The C-87 carried life rafts along with search and rescue and survival gear to be dropped to the crew of any aircraft making a forced landing. Eight P-47s landed in the UK on 11 August; two had developed mechanical problems and were left at airfields along the route. These pilots made the first

AAF captain and future Arizona Senator/presidential candidate Barry Goldwater takes off from Presque Isle, Maine, to lead a flight of ten P-47s during August 1943. Aided by a navigational C-87, the P-47s landed at Prestwick, Scotland, achieving the first, last, and only flight of single-engine fighters across the Atlantic in the Second World War. (*AAF*)

and only flight of single-engine fighters across the Atlantic in the Second World War. The flight leader was Capt. Barry Goldwater, who became a Senator from Arizona and later ran for President in 1964. Goldwater was awarded an Air Medal for this mission: 'This officer volunteered to act as pilot of a P-47 with the full realization that engine failure on this route would result in almost certain death in the freezing waters of the North Atlantic. Captain Goldwater completed this mission in such a manner as to reflect highest credit upon himself and the military forces of the United States.'

After *Operation Tidal Wave*, the 1943 8AF and 9AF B-24 low-level bombing mission against the Ploiești oil refineries, a special C-87 airlift brought a supply of Pratt & Whitney engines to Benghazi to replace those that had been damaged or worn out during the spectacular mission. C-87s flew other emergency airlifts that transported nearly anything that suddenly became in short supply and could not wait for the long shipboard ocean voyage to the combat zones.

C-87B

The C-87B was a proposed armed version but was not put into production. Preliminary specifications included two nose guns and the standard Martin dorsal turret, in addition to a single tunnel and tail guns. In late 1942, Col Edward Alexander of the AAF India-China Wing recommended the replacement of unarmed C-87s serving with this wing with fully armed aircraft of the same type in support of Gen. Chennault's proposed offensive, in which armed C-87s were to deliver supplies 'where active hostile air action could be expected daily'. He recommended that after November 1943, the end of monsoon season, all C-87s in his wing should be armed with one .50 caliber machine gun in the tail, two fixed caliber .50 guns in the nose, a power-driven dorsal turret mounting two .50s, and one flexible belly gun. A letter dated 27 November 1942, from Air Transport Command (ATC) Headquarters, stated that approval to arm the 12 C-87s was scheduled for the India-China Wing. However, tail guns were not mentioned. The first of these armed C-87s was to be ready by 15 December 1942 but it appears that the armed CBI C-87Bs were cancelled along with all proposed C-87Bs.

C-87C

Consolidated received a Letter of Intent in September 1943 for 125 AAF C-87C transports (44-52853/52977), which were to have the basic configuration of the PB4Y-2: stretched fuselage, single tail, non-turbo power plants, and integral fuel tanks. Subsequently, because of their similarity to the Privateer, it was decided to procure those aircraft under a Navy contract as an order for 112 RY-3s and the USAAF serials were cancelled (see RY-3).

C-87C TRANSPORT

CONSOLIDATED VULTEE AIRCRAFT CORPORATION
DEVELOPMENT ENGINEERING   SAN DIEGO, CALIF

C-87 Accidents and Problems

Because of its makeshift origin converted from B-24 bombers and the crucial need to produce it in quantity, the C-87 incorporated many compromises that reduced its potential as a transport aircraft. The C-87's inherent problems became so critical that some crews even considered refusing to fly them. During a layover at Natal, T&WA and Pan Am crews publicly deliberated the apparent problems with their C-87s in an open five-page letter outlining the aircraft's inherent defects. They were particularly anxious about the lack of action to remedy the numerous serious deficiencies, especially with the fuel system, engine area fire hazards, and cockpit accessories. They expressed their frustration with AAF and Consolidated's standard excuses for the inaction; lack of parts and no engineering orders from the AAF. Veteran pilot Ernest K. Gann, in his 1961 memoir, *Fate is the Hunter*, (Simon & Schuster) wrote the following about the C-87: 'They were an evil bastard contraption, nothing like the relatively efficient B-24 except in appearance.' Air Force, Air Transport Command and civilian airline crews flying C-87s under contract were certainly not dedicated to their Liberator cargo aircraft as during 1943 they readily exchanged their transports for the more reliable Douglas C-54 Skymasters when they became available.

Accidents

The C-87 had a distressing reputation involving accidents, with the Bureau of Aircraft Accidents Archives listing 18 crashes involving 145 fatalities, while the Aviation Safety Network lists a total of 129 accidents.

The first fatal C-87 accident occurred on 2 August 1942 when C-87 41-24027, flown by a United Air Lines crew operating under contract to the Air Transport Command, crashed just after take-off from Whenuapai, New Zealand, headed for Amberley, Australia. Of the 25 on board, three crew and 11 passengers died in the crash and another passenger died later of injuries. A group of Japanese internees who were being swapped for Allied PoWs in a secret operation were reportedly among the passengers. One of the most significant accidents occurred on 26 February 1945 when C-87A 41-24174, operated by the AAF, crashed into the Pacific Ocean without a trace during a flight from Guam to Honolulu, killing all 10 on board. On board was Lt Gen. Millard Harmon and his Chief of Staff, Brig. Gen. James Andersen. At the time Harmon had petitioned AAF Headquarters for operational control of all AAF combat operations in the Pacific Ocean Area and partial operational control of the B-29 operations against Japan, from his headquarters on Guam. He also had previously gained control of all Army and Navy land-based bombers and fighters; all of which brought him into conflict with Gen. Arnold's objective of maintaining absolute control of 20th Air Force operations

The C-87's reputation was damaged by its poor accident record. Shown is 41-23852, which was written off with no injuries after crashing off an Indian runway while taking off during a heavily overloaded Hump mission during January 1944. (*AAF*)

independent of any theater commands. The issue peaked in February 1945 when Harmon disagreed with Maj. Gen. Curtis LeMay, the new Commander of the XXI Bomber Command, over the command of five long-range fighter groups assigned to the 20AF as escorts for strategic bombers. LeMay prevailed but Harmon objected, and Harmon and Andersen were on their way to Honolulu to resolve the fighter dispute. The worst fatal C-87 accident occurred on 26 July 1944, involving C-87-CF 41-11706, operated by Consairway. The transport left Canton Island bound for Guadalcanal but while on a night-time final approach the aircraft hit a mountain slope on the Florida Island, off Guadalcanal. The wreckage was spotted two days later with 27 deceased occupants, including RAF Air Commodore Isaac John Fitch, Deputy Director of Intelligence at the Air Ministry. A Navy rescue team found Fitch's briefcase marked TOP SECRET that was carrying war plans being delivered to General MacArthur, detailing an upcoming major Pacific offensive.

The worst accident involving an AAF crew occurred on 17 January 1943 when C-87 41-11708, operated by the AAF, disappeared without a trace while flying from Ascension Island to Natal, with the loss of six crew and 20 passengers.

The worst accident involving a domestic airline crew occurred on 7 February 1943 when C-87-CF 41-23903, operated by United Airlines for the ATC, on its final night-time approach to Canton Island went out of control and crashed into the sea several hundred yards offshore, killing its 18 occupants while three others were rescued. The crash report 'deemed possible that an asymmetric flap deployment caused the accident'.

C-87 Problems and Solutions

Loading Problems and Solutions

A dedicated cargo transport was to be designed initially with a built-in contiguous cargo compartment that gave it a safety margin for fore-and-aft loading variations. It was determined that the C-87's hasty conversion from bomber to cargo transport led to longitudinal instability and with incorrectly loaded cargo there could be a shift in the center of gravity, easily making the C-87 unstable in flight. Later this problem was exacerbated by the wartime coercion to carry heavier loads and the failure of the Air Transport Command to instruct its loadmasters on the proper loading of the C-87. In the field there was no way to weigh cargo loads and the weights were guesstimated by looking at how far the landing gear struts had depressed! The C-87 was unable to climb effectively when heavily loaded, a dangerous characteristic when flying out of the unimproved, rain-soaked airfields of India and China. Several C-87s were lost after take-off as they were unable climb over nearby obstacles and terrain. In *Fate is a Hunter*, Ernest Gann recounted a near-collision with the Taj Mahal after take-off in a heavily loaded C-87, causing him to hastily deploy full flaps to gain altitude to avoid the landmark.

Landing Gear Problems and Solutions

The landing gear of the B-24 bomber version was mostly trouble-free because, after dropping its bombs, the lightened bomber usually landed on a well-maintained hard runway of permanent bases. However, the nose gear was inadequate for a heavily loaded C-87 making repeated hard landings on rough unimproved airstrips. The problem was eventually remedied by replacing the gear actuating cylinder piston rod eyebolts with solid shank eyebolts. The proper loading of the C-87 was also important as the nose wheel was not steerable and the aircraft had to be steered by a combination of brakes and throttle manipulation. If the load weight was placed too far aft, making the C-87 tail heavy; the aircraft would not move.

Fuel and Oil System Problems

The C-87's fuel system was a chronic fire and explosion threat as the fuel tanks leaked and the fuel caps didn't siphon, filling the wing with fumes. The aircraft's auxiliary long-range fuel tanks were linked by improvised and often leaky fuel lines that criss-crossed the crew compartment, exposing the flight crews to noxious gasoline fumes and creating an explosion danger. The radio transmitter in the aircraft center section had flashovers that could ignite the gasoline fumes that always lingered, which led to the installation of wing center section fuel tank vents to reduce fuel vapor concentrations. The fuel lines under the fuselage center section required protection from rupture by cargo being thrown against them in rough air. The self-sealing fuel cells, which added 2,000lb, diminished range because of decreased fuel capacity and added to maintenance problems. The use of these cells was necessary since Fort Worth was unable to engineer leak-tight integral tanks in the wings for the C-87 at this time.

Fuel and Oil System Solutions

1) Fuel transfer system revision.
2) Installation of a fuel cross-feed system to permit any tank to serve any engine.
3) Installation of electric fuel pumps with sufficient capacity to provide an engine with fuel should the engine-driven fuel pump fail.
4) Relocation of the cabin fuel valves from the cargo area to an area where they could be accessed by the crew.
5) Installation of fuel flow gauges.
6) Installation of more accurate fuel quantity gauges (that read more accurately than within 200 gallons).
7) Installation of oil tank shut-off valves and oil quantity gauges.

Lighting System Problems and Solutions

1) The fluorescent cockpit lights often failed and weren't supplied with replacement bulbs. It was recommended that some type of auxiliary lighting should be installed so that the pilots would no longer have to make many night landings with a flashlight but these seem not to have been implemented as the CBI Hump was a backwater war.
2) The retractable Grimes electric landing lights often burned out or became jammed in the intermediate position, jeopardizing safe landings. Again, there was a shortage of replacement bulbs.

Other Problems and Mostly Non-Fixes

1) Tail flutter was reported on several of the early C-87s. On 9 February C-87 41-23850 took off from Hollywood, Florida, on its way to Brazil and about 10 miles into the flight the transport experienced severe tail flutter, causing the four-man crew to bail out. The unmanned aircraft continued across the Gulf of Mexico and crashed into a mountain in Mexico.
2) Awkward flight control layout.
3) The alarming tendency to lose electrical power in the cockpit during take-off and landing.
4) Relocation of radio transmitters from the wing center section area that collected dangerous gasoline fumes.
5) Installation of a firewall aft of the engines.
6) Installation of a drip pan over the engine exhaust manifold.
7) Installation of fire bottles with sufficient capacity and with some nozzles in the oil tank compartment.
8) Installation of an air accumulator for emergency brakes.
9) The C-87 also had some dangerous icing properties that made it a very risky plane to fly over the Hump.

Serials of C-87 and C-87A Liberator Express

41-11608*	Consolidated C-87-CF Liberator Express
	Later re-serialed 41-39600
41-11639/11642	Consolidated C-87-CF Liberator Express
41-11655/11657	Consolidated C-87-CF Liberator Express
41-11674/11676	Consolidated C-87-CF Liberator Express
41-11704	Consolidated C-87-CF Liberator Express
41-11706/11709	Consolidated C-87-CF Liberator Express
41-11728/11733	Consolidated C-87-CF Liberator Express
41-11742/11747	Consolidated C-87-CF Liberator Express
41-11788/11789	Consolidated C-87-CF Liberator Express
41-11800	Consolidated C-87-CF Liberator Express

41-11837/11838	Consolidated C-87-CF Liberator Express
41-11907/11908	Consolidated C-87-CF Liberator Express
41-23669/23670	Consolidated C-87-CF Liberator Express
41-23694/23696	Consolidated C-87-CF Liberator Express
41-23791/23793	Consolidated C-87-CF Liberator Express
41-23850/23852	Consolidated C-87-CF Liberator Express
41-23859/23862	Consolidated C-87-CF Liberator Express
41-23863	Consolidated C-87A-CF Liberator Express
41-23903/23905	Consolidated C-87-CF Liberator Express
41-23959	Consolidated C-87-CF Liberator Express
41-24004/24006	Consolidated C-87-CF Liberator Express
41-24027/24029	Consolidated C-87-CF Liberator Express
41-24139/24141	Consolidated C-87-CF Liberator Express
41-24158	Consolidated C-87-CF Liberator Express
41-24159	Consolidated C-87A-CF Liberator Express
41-24160/24163	Consolidated C-87-CF Liberator Express
41-24172/24173	Consolidated C-87-CF Liberator Express
41-24174	Consolidated C-87A-CF Liberator Express
41-39600	Consolidated XC-87 Liberator Express
42-107249/107275	Consolidated C-87-CF Liberator Express
	107266 converted to AT-22
43-30548/30568	Consolidated C-87-CF Liberator Express
43-30569/30571	Consolidated C-87A-CF Liberator Express
	All to US Navy as RY-1 67797/67799
43-30572/30627	Consolidated C-87-CF Liberator Express
	30574 and 30584 converted to AT-22
44-39198/39298	Consolidated C-87-CF Liberator Express
	39198/39202 to US Navy as RY-2 39013/39017
	39219, 39248/39261 to RAF as Liberator C.VII
44-52978/52987**	Consolidated C-87 Liberator Express

* After flying the Willkie around-the-world trip during August 1942 B-24D-CO 41-11608 served in the Caribbean and was then refurbished at Olmstead Field, Middletown, Pennsylvania, during June 1944, after which it received the new serial number 41-39600 and was assigned to the ATC/Pacific Wing flown by American Airlines. What is unusual about its new serial is that for some unknown reason it is one higher than the total 1941 fiscal year range for all US aircraft.

** Ten aircraft (44-39299 through 44-39308) were given these serials on the production line, as a carry-on from the previous block of C-87s, 44-39198–39298. There was a miscommunication between the Consolidated production line and the contract office, and these serial numbers were applied in error. The official records recorded these aircraft correctly as 44-52978 through 44-52987 and they were subsequently re-serialed as 44-52978 through 44-52987.

'Official' B-24 to C-87 Conversions

Besides LB-30 conversions the only 'Official' B-24 to C-87 conversions after which individual aircraft records were altered to indicate the new designation were:

B-24D-CO serials 41-11680, 42-40355, 40499, 40503, and 40552
B-24D-CF serials 42-63779, 63780, 63783, 63785, and 63790
B-24E-FO serials 42-6976 and 6985

Navy C-87As

Three C-87A VIP transports were transferred to the Navy under the designation RY-1. Navy BuNos were 67797/67799, while five other C-87s were transferred to the Navy under the designation RY-2. The BuNos were 39013/39017 and they are discussed elsewhere.

C-87 to AT-22 Training Conversions

Five C-87s (42-107266, 43-30549, 43-30561, 42-30574 and 43-30584) were built on the Fort Worth assembly line and accepted as AT-22s. Four of these AT-22s became the only B-24s to carry 43- serials. The first, 42-107266, was accepted by the AAF on 11 June

Five C-87s were built on the Fort Worth assembly line and accepted as AT-22s, stripped of their transport provisions and used for training flight engineers. (*AAF*)

1943 for training flight engineers and was augmented by four more. These aircraft had their C-87 transport provisions removed, cargo tie-downs and passenger seating and lights. The removal of the heating and ventilation system and oxygen provisions only on the flight deck made for an austere training fuselage area that contained six stations for students seated at individual flight control panels to learn the operation of B-24 and B-32 power plants. During 1944 all five AT-22 were redesignated as TB-24Ds.

TB-24 Trainers

During the early war years, B-24 trainers augmented by already war-weary B-24s were flown well beyond their air frame flight time limits and were particularly accident prone, much to the consternation of instructors and students. By 1944, the supply of combat B-24s became adequate so that one in twelve new bombers could be allotted to Training Command as TB-24 trainers with 621 TB-24Js (crew training), 194 TB-24Ls (radar training), 111 TB-24Ms (crew training), one TB-24H (B-29 gunner training), and one RB-24L (B-29 gun crew training) being assigned.

Because of the availability of excellent flying weather, AAF flight training centers were primarily located in the southern and western US. By 1944, before crew assignment, B-24 pilots were typically receiving 105 hours of 4-engine flying time. The crew then trained together for an additional 90 days in a Replacement Training Unit (RTU) before overseas assignment.

Contemporarily, the B-24 was a relatively complex aircraft but most newly arrived pilots, having just graduated from Advanced Training School where they flew the docile twin-engined AT-10 and AT-17 trainers, discovered, rather importantly and to their relief, that a correctly loaded and properly trimmed Liberator was easy to fly under training conditions. The student pilots found the Liberator's normally heavy controls were manageable, and it exhibited integral directional stability, exceptional longitudinal stability over a wide variety of center of gravity locations, no abnormal stall characteristics, and adequate reserves of power. However, this was only if trim was established correctly! This would not be the case later in combat, when the B-24 normally became overloaded and/or improperly trimmed. The operational Liberator was known as 'strictly an instrument aircraft', and neophyte pilots were customarily advised

During 1944 all five AT-22s were redesignated as TB-24Ds and used for B-29 gunnery training. (*AAF*)

by their instructors that 'the only reason that there were windows was to see other aircraft and mountains and to see if the sun is shining'. Turns were generally restricted to 45 degrees of bank as there was a rapid increase of G-forces in tighter turns. 'Control with power' was the watchword for good landings, with the bomber to be flown on to the runway instead of being dropped onto it.

CB-24s

Later in the war, a number of Liberators were removed from combat and converted for use as either cargo or general-purpose transports or a combination, officially redesignated as CB-24s. Several were revised extensively and often had their armament, bombing equipment, and paint removed. Most of the LB-30/C-87 conversions had their paint stripped to improve both their speed and appearance. Examples of this conversion involved B-24Ds 41-23838 and 41-24168, which were well known as the *Pacific Scamp* and *Pacific Vamp*. *Vamp* started life as a B-24D-20-CO named *Valhalla* from the 867BS, 494BG, 7AF, and was used by Brig. Gen. Truman Landon of the 7AF Bomber Command as the staff transport. Other known CB-24s included: 42-63787, 42-29408, 42-7616, 42-40543 42-40939 42-63780 42-63781 42-63783 (ex C-87), 42-64175 (ex F-7A), 42-73037, 42-109946, 44-40633, and 44-40678. (via Alan Blue)

CB-24 conversion *Pacific Vamp* was used by Brig. Gen. Truman Landon of the 7AF Bomber Command as a staff transport. (*AAF*)

AAF to RAF C-87s

Under Lend-Lease 24 USAAF C-87s were transferred to the RAF for use by Transport Command as Liberator C.VIIs and assigned RAF serials EW611/EW634. Known USAAF serial numbers account for only 15 of the 24 C.VIIs. They were used by Nos 232, 246, and 511 Squadrons from mid to late 1944 until the end of the war. The RAF did not keep its Liberator C.VIIs for long, disposing of the last ones in 1946; leaving two at Chakeri Airfield, India, at the end of the war. These two were used by the Indian Air Force 102 Survey Flight for mapping and photo missions until 1956, when they were scrapped.

No. 232 Squadron reformed on 15 November 1944 at RAF Stoney Cross as a transport unit equipped with Wellington Mk.XVIs until 6 January 1945, when these aircraft were transferred to No. 242 Squadron and the ground crews were used to form two other squadrons. No. 232 Squadron was not disbanded, and it immediately received new Liberators and crews, after which it moved to India in February and immediately began transport duties throughout Southeast Asia. In July some Douglas Skymaster Mk.Is were received and these were used to fly a Ceylon–Australia service until March 1946, when the Skymasters were returned to the UK and the Liberators were retired and replaced by Lancastrians.

No. 246 Squadron was reformed on 11 October 1944 at RAF Lyneham as a transport unit flying the Liberator and Halifax transport conversions from No. 511 Squadron Flight. After moving to RAF Holmsley South in December, the squadron began to convert to the Avro York (a transport based on the Lancaster). In February 1945 the Halifax were retired and the Douglas Skymaster was introduced and gradually replaced the Liberators by November 1945. In 1945 the squadron standardized on the York and operated scheduled services to India and the Middle East until it merged with 511 Squadron on 15 October 1946.

There were 24 USAAF C-87s transferred to the RAF under Lend-Lease for use by Transport Command as Liberator C.VIIs (EW615 shown). (*RAF*)

No. 511 Squadron was formed on 14 October 1942 from No. 1425 Flight at Lyneham and the squadron continued that flight's duties, operating regular transport schedules to Gibraltar using Liberators. As the war progressed, 511 Squadron expanded its long-range transport role, and it was the first squadron to operate the York. Initially, the Liberators and Yorks were operated as separate flights, but the Liberator flight became 246 Squadron in 1944.

Canadian RCAF Liberator Transport Conversions

Initial Transport Conversions

The first ten RCAF transport Liberators, assigned serials #570 to #579, were new standard Fort Worth-built B-24Js that arrived in June and July 1944 with their turrets and painted in their USAAF insignia. No. 4 Repair Depot at Scoudouc, New Brunswick, was assigned to undertake their conversion to transport configuration. Although many sources record that these ten Liberators were to be converted to the C-87 standard, renowned RCAF historian Carl Vincent, in his book *Canada's Wings 2*, records: 'This is far from true. The conversion was familiarly known to the RCAF as "quick and dirty" (though they were probably the neatest and most attractive transport Liberators) … It seems probable that the RCAF used the plans or the assistance of Trans Canada Airlines, which was converting the Liberators for BOAC at Dorval; the conversions seem to be identical externally.' These ten aircraft received no RCAF designation and in official documents they are referred to indiscriminately as B-24Js, Liberator VIs, or Liberator C.VIs.

During their conversion the armament was removed, a new nose section installed, a new fuselage end with a door was mounted instead of the characteristic C-87 tail cone, and the bomb racks were removed but the bomb bay doors were not. The conversions of eight of these first transports were completed as such but the other two received further transformation by 168 (HT) Squadron.

The conversion #570 was assigned as the personal transport for the RCAF's Chief of Air Staff. The work on this aircraft modified only the rear fuselage aft of the bomb bay with no external alterations and it was entered from the rear fuselage. Seats, a washroom in the tail, and a wide mattress bunk over the rear bomb bay were added to the interior.

Canada's First Air Force One

On 30 June 1944, the Rockcliffe aerodrome, Ottawa, received a special B-24J (44-10583) directly from the B-24 factory at Consolidated Convair Fort Worth, Texas. Designated as #574, this Liberator was converted to be the RCAF's first VIP aircraft intended to transport Canadian Prime Minister William Lyon Mackenzie King. This conversion was more elaborate and involved major structural modifications: the rear fuselage had windows cut into its sides and the rear bomb bay doors were removed with new stringers installed and the area skinned over. Since the crew could no longer enter through the bomb bay, a new door had to be cut into the side of the fuselage. This presented problems as the control cables passed aft along the sides of the Liberator. The most obvious and uncomplicated solution was to install a door and steps in the bottom of the rear fuselage. However, this resolution was rejected as an unworthy entrance for a Prime Minister and the cutting of a side door and the arduous task of re-routing the control cables along the roof was commenced. When completed, #574 had a private compartment in the rear bomb bay, including a toilet, a bed that disappeared into the ceiling, a separate section for the PM's secretary, plus 10 seats in the rear fuselage for the PM's entourage and the press. The tail section contained a galley with a refrigerator and another toilet in the very rear. Because this conversion was non-standard, the aircraft was tested scrupulously, and the changes of weight positioning was examined meticulously as the Liberator was particularly center of gravity susceptible. The conversion was finished in a highly polished natural aluminum exterior finish with a lightning bolt flashing from its nose to tail and a newly designed roundel on the rear fuselage sides that featured a red maple leaf inside a dark blue roundel. This was to become the symbol of the RCAF from 1946–48.

The aircraft, nicknamed the *Silver Salon*, transported Prime Minister Mackenzie King to the signing of the United Nations Charter on 26 June 1945 in San Francisco. RCAF #574 continued to transport Mackenzie King and other Canadian military and government officials until he retired in 1948, when the *Silver Salon* was flown CFB Trenton, Ontario, and placed into surplus storage. It was purchased by Air Chile airline in 1951, for whom it served for four years. However, upon landing at Santiago, Chile, on 21 February it suffered a landing gear malfunction that caused it to leave the runway. The damage was surveyed and considered too expensive to repair, and after being stored for four years the aircraft was scrapped in 1959.

Final RCAF Transport Conversions

The final RCAF Liberator transport conversions consisted of one Fort Worth-built B-24J and four Ford built B-24Ms that were delivered in January 1945 and officially taken on RCAF strength during February. Unlike Liberators #570 to #579, these aircraft were to be much more extensively converted by 8 Repair Depot (8RD) at Winnipeg, Manitoba. Externally they were to duplicate C-87s, with similar side windows and tail cones. Internally, they were to be converted to near 'civilian airline standard' with passenger seats, washrooms, etc. Though the conversion began soon after delivery, it required more time and effort than expected and continued past VE Day, after which conversion slowed with the cutback of RCAF funding and the discharge of many skilled personnel to civilian life. Some 4RD personnel were posted to 8RD when 4RD was disbanded in June, but the turnover and increased cost and availability of material became a problem. The Liberator transport conversion concluded 8RD's work before disbandment and the first conversion flew on 26 September 1945, while the others left Winnipeg during February 1946.

The first ten Canadian RCAF transports were Fort Worth factory-fresh standard-built B-24Js, which arrived in June and July 1944 and assigned serials 570 to 579. Shown is 576 receiving mail into its nose compartment. (*RCAF*) The second VIP Canadian Liberator conversion, #574, was more elaborate, intended to transport Canadian Prime Minister William Lyon Mackenzie King to the signing of the United Nations Charter. (*RCAF*)

C-87s Replaced by C-54s

The peak USAAF inventory of 208 C-87s was reached in July 1944. As 1945 approached, the ATC was planning a Pacific fleet of 160 4-engine Douglas C-54 Skymaster transports and the airlines also gradually exchanged their C-87s for C-54s as they became available. Understandably, the C-87 was not very popular with its crews, who complained about its numerous problems and hazards as previously enumerated. There were no tears shed when the C-87s were withdrawn from service and replaced by more reliable, albeit two-engine, Curtiss C-46 Commandos and finally by the four-engine Douglas C-54 Skymasters, which offered similar performance combined with greater reliability and more benign flight characteristics. By the beginning of 1945, C-87s were being used only for flights within the United States and as far as Iceland and Greenland as C-54s had replaced them on transatlantic flights. Some surviving C-87 aircraft were converted into VIP transports or flight crew trainers, while several others were sold to the Royal Air Force. Five C-87s outfitted for 20 passengers were transferred to the Navy under the designation RY-2 and given the BuNos 39013–39017, while a further 15 were cancelled. The prototype was scrapped by the RFC on 12 December 1945.

Douglas C 54 Army Transport
THE LARGEST TRANSPORT IN QUANTITY PRODUCTION IN THE WORLD

Role of the Airlines in the Second World War

After the Air Mail scandal of the mid-1930s it was thought that the government would possibly nationalize the air transport industry as a national emergency as it had the railroads in the First World War. Fortunately for the airlines, on 14 January 1936 the highly regarded and accomplished Edgar Gorrell was named as President of the Air Transport Association of America (ATA), which represented the domestic carriers. Gorrell was a West Point graduate (1912); a ranking First World War military officer, rising rapidly in rank from first lieutenant to colonel; an early advocate of strategic bombing; historian (editor of the 280-volume *History of the Air Service, AEF)*; and a manufacturing entrepreneur (CEO of the Stutz Automobile Company). Gorrell became a strong advocate for the airlines as President of the ATA and would continually campaign to persuade President Roosevelt and the War Department to develop a plan for the use of civil air transport in wartime. Gorrell died on 5 March 1945 at 54 after a brief illness.

Throughout the pre-war years Gorrell had linked the purpose of the ATA to national defense. Soon after Gorrell became ATA President the War Department requested that the Aeronautical Board review the issue of the use of the airlines in wartime and prepare a policy that would be an advantage to both the airlines and the Army and the Navy. Chief of the Air Corps Maj. Gen. Oscar Westover estimated that Air Corps' air transport requirements would have a deficiency of at least 200 transport aircraft on that required during the first 120 days of wartime mobilization. When the Aeronautical Board issued its report in February 1937, it specifically recommended against a military appropriation of the airlines and recommended instead that a civilian 'Federal Coordinator' be selected to control and coordinate airline operations to eliminate any overlap, and that airline personnel be deferred from military service to continue with their carriers. Then, during May 1937, the War Department issued a revision of the existing 1922 Industrial Mobilization Plan and placed all airlines together with all other forms of transportation. In response, Gorrell, colluding with three future airline icons: Cyrus 'C.R.' Smith of American Airlines (CEO from 1934 to 1968 and from 1973 to 1974), William 'Pat' Patterson of United Airlines (President from 1934 until 1966), and William 'Jack' Frye of Transcontinental & Western Airlines (President from 1934 to 1947), prepared 'a structure of action' for the airlines. By April 1938 Gorrell had successfully convinced most leaders of both services that nationalization would be an error by showing them how the airlines could 'integrate themselves into a strategic contingency while maintaining their autonomy, by limiting competition among them during the emergency and using government contracts to support the war effort'. As a result, by the time war broke out in Europe in September 1939, comprehensive plans were made and revised monthly by the War Department, the Air Corps, and the ATA.

Once America was at war, it was found that to operate a worldwide air logistics system, maximum use would have to be made of the country's civil airlines as the Ferrying Command was hard-pressed to expand its own military transport services. Several airlines responded immediately to emergency transport requests and on 11 December Gorrell informed both AAC Chief Lt Gen. Henry Arnold and Army Chief of Staff Gen. George C. Marshall that the airlines would be performing their assignments according to the set plans. Nevertheless, on 13 December 1941, President Roosevelt issued Executive Order (EO) 8974, which authorized the Secretary of War to nationalize the airlines, although, except for a few specific emergencies in early 1942, this was not invoked. That same day, mindful that measured airline responsiveness was central to forestalling nationalization, Gorrell quickly and efficiently delivered aircraft and crews at the first request made to the ATA. The next day, Gorrell negotiated with Assistant Secretary of War for Air Robert Lovett to voluntarily submit more than half the airlines' aircraft and crews to the Ferrying Command (ACFC) on a contract basis. When, FDR's EO was not revoked, another EO was issued in an attempt to transfer the Civil Aeronautics Administration (CAA) to the AAC in order to place the Civilian Pilot Training Program under military control, which would also effectively give the AAF regulatory control of the airlines. In January 1942 Donald Connolly was recalled to active duty from his civilian position as CAA administrator and made Military Director of Civil Aviation (MDCA) with the obvious resolve of executing EO 8974 and finally nationalizing the airlines. Gorrell and a six-man ATA liaison staff joined the MDCA on an advisory basis, to establish travel priorities and organize a scheme for the mass movement of troops within the Western

Edgar Gorrell of the Air Transport Association of America. (*ATA*)

Cyrus 'C.R.' Smith of American Airlines. (*AAL*)

William 'Pat' Patterson of United Airlines. (*UAL*)

William 'Jack' Frye of T&WA. (*TWA*)

Hemisphere and to Hawaii using the airlines. Because this plan was on an 'on-demand' basis, it was found to be impracticable and before it was fully implemented Gen. Arnold ordered the ACFC Commander Maj. Gen. Robert Olds to take 'complete military control over all parts of your (airline) operation'. On 18 February 1942, all overseas airline contracts except those in the Western Hemisphere were cancelled and their associated civil operations (mostly Pan American's) were militarized. However, the civil airlines, in addition to having the available flying personnel (most of whom had previously learned to fly in the Air Corps) and the aircraft and auxiliary equipment, had the administrative competence and practical knowledge in conducting scheduled air transport operations. The AAC had no such expertise or experience in operating in an airline-like manner and engaged commercial airlines to assist in operating its transport system. Former American airlines CEO C.R. Smith, now a colonel in the AAF, was appointed second-in-command of ACFC in April and passed his comprehensive transport experience on to the deficient ACFC senior officers. In this position Smith developed a feasible long-range plan to maintain the civil status of airline operations before further militarization took place. Smith, using American Airlines crews, played a major role in opening the Great Circle route, which connected Newfoundland, Greenland, Iceland, Ireland, and Great Britain, for use by ATC transports. Once the feasibility of the Great Circle route had been proven, the ATC averaged 500 transatlantic flights a month. Lt Gen. Smith was named the Deputy Commander of the Air Transport Command and when the war ended Maj. Gen. Smith returned to American Airlines as its CEO for 25 years.

In the meantime, Secretary of War Henry Stimson opposed the attempt to incorporate the CAA into the AAF and kept Lovett's agreement with the airlines not to invoke EO 8974. In August 1942, Stimson and Secretary of the Navy Frank Knox ended the nationalization of the civil airlines subject by informing Secretary of Commerce Jesse Jones that the CAA would function as a civilian agency.

Commercial Airlines Fly the C-87

During the Second World War, in addition to transporting supplies and materials, a large requirement arose to transfer high-priority personnel, such as aircrews and VIPs, around the globe. To augment the Air Transport Command (ATC), contracts were let to civilian airlines and other companies to service global air routes. United Airlines (UAL), American Airlines (AAL), and Transcontinental & Western Airlines (T&WA) all operated the C-87 Liberator Express on such contracts, as did Consairway, Consolidated Aircraft's private airline. These contract carriers achieved an extraordinary record in the daily utilization of the aircraft assigned to them.

American Airlines (AAL)

During January 1943, American Airlines was awarded a contract by the ATC to operate C-87s over North Atlantic and South Atlantic routes. These transports flew in military insignia and markings and carried USAAF serials but were operated by five-man civilian crews: captain, first officer, navigator, radio operator, and flight engineer. The initial cadre of American Airlines crews went through transition training on the B-24/C-87 at Smyrna AAF, Georgia, during the fall of 1942.

On 27 January 1943, American Airlines was engaged to operate a pair of modified C-87s (41-11744 and 41-11788) on a trial basis, as part of the North Atlantic Wing of ATC. Each aircraft was modified to carry a pair of DC-3-type fuel cells in the cabin to give a total fuel capacity of 3,150 gallons. C-87 41-11744 would be destroyed during take-off on 4 September 1943 in China while flying for the AAF. Later, American Airlines operated C-87s for the Ferrying Command over both the North Atlantic and South Atlantic routes. The payload carried across the South Atlantic was 21,147lb, while over the North Atlantic this was reduced to 20,397lb because of the additional emergency equipment, de-icing gear, and added engine oil. The AAL crews were elated when they were ordered to trade in their unpopular C-87s for the more advanced Douglas C-54 Skymasters.

American Airlines and *Project 7A*

During 1943, there was a shortage of cargo being flown over the treacherous Hump and the AAF called upon American Airlines to assist under the secret *Project 7A*. Between August and November 1943, ten C-87s, under Capt. E.S. 'Toby' Hunt, were employed by these civilian crews to bolster the Hump transport effort. The C-87s assigned to the project had been equipped with new engines but had been otherwise been accident-salvaged B-24s converted to transports. These had to struggle to get over the Hump and AAL lost three crew in accidents. At the end of operations AAL personnel had flown 499 Hump trips, carrying over 4.2 million pounds of cargo. These brave aircrews received no formal recognition by the AAF for their efforts but ex-American Airlines pilot Ernest Gann's best-selling novel *Fate is the Hunter* and movie based on the book was loosely based on American Airlines operations under *Project 7A*.

A summary of the *Project 7A* operations is shown in the following table.

Month	Sorties	Hours	Cargo	lb	A/C	Losses
Aug	115		790:48	941,350	10	1
Sept	113		794:36	963,890	10	1
Oct	161		1,901:00	1,313,610	11	0
Nov	110		828:12	941,594	10	1
Total	499		4,314:36	4,160,444	41	3

C-87s flown by American Airlines: 41-11608 (Willkie C-87), 41-11639, 41-11657 (flew 56 Hump missions), 41-11674, 41-11675 (flew 74 Hump missions), 41-11729 (flew 57 Hump missions), 41-11731, 41-11744 (flew 25 Hump missions), 41-11745 (flew 17 Hump missions), 41-11746, 41-11788 (flew 60 Hump missions), 41-23695, 41-23859,

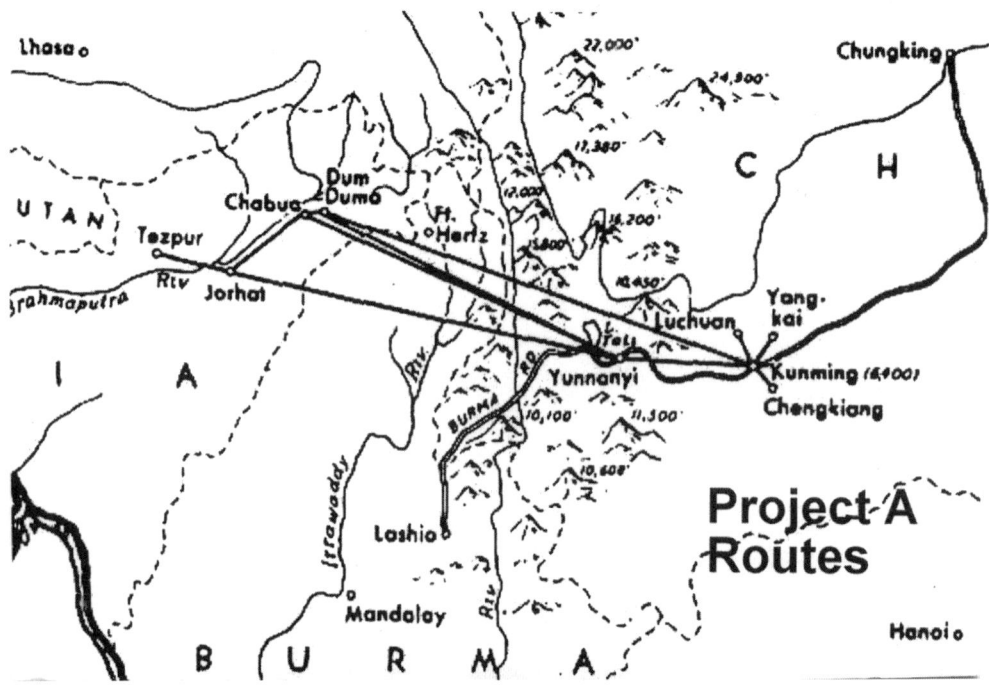

(*Author's Library*)

41-23792 (flew 25 Hump missions), 41-23959 (flew 52 Hump missions), 41-24141 (flew 29 Hump missions), 41-24163 (flew 18 Hump missions), 42-107274, 43-30565.

On 10 December 1943, C-87 (43-30565), *The Ruptured Vulture*, flew the last AAL crew out of the CBI to Morrison Field, Florida, thus ending the airline's Hump operations. By 1944, AAL had become the second largest international carrier in the world, only behind Pan Am.

United Airlines (UAL)

United Airlines was awarded a contract by the ATC to fly trans-Pacific routes and to fly intra-theater leave shuttles ferrying armed forces personnel back and forth between the front and leave ports in Australia and New Zealand. During July 1942, Gen. Harold George, Commander of ATC, proposed *Operations Pacific* to create logistics routes in the Pacific, and UA President W.A. Patterson established an entirely new 8,269-mile trans-Pacific route within 40 days. A total of 25 new pilots, co-pilots, flight engineers, navigators, and radio operators were assembled for the operation and checked out at the Boeing School in Oakland, California. *Operations Pacific* routes were as follows:

Hamilton Field, CA–Hickam AB, HI:	2,446 miles
Hickam AB, Hl–Canton:	1,908 miles
Canton–Nandi:	1,250 miles
Nandi–New Caledonia:	865 miles
New Caledonia–Amberley Field, Brisbane:	1,800 miles

Between 5 September and December 1942, United Airlines operated five C-87s within the Pacific Sector of ATC's South Pacific Wing, with a sixth aircraft added on 10 October 1942. The inaugural flight was a debacle as just three hours into the flight the fuel pressure gauges read zero. Capt. Jack O'Brien returned to San Francisco, only to find that there was an ample fuel supply as malfunctioning gauges were to blame and these would continue to malfunction throughout the C-87's career.

United would operate a fleet of as many as nine C-87s on the Hamilton Field–Brisbane route during the first half of 1943. A total of 125 round trips would be flown by the United C-87s during this time. These were:

Jan	Feb	Mar	Apr	May	Jun
23	23	18	19	24	28

UAL C-87s suffered several accidents that lowered crew morale and confidence in the C-87. Of UAL's more than 7,000 flights in all transport types, there were 3 fatal accidents, all involving C-87s, while a disproportionate number of C-87s suffered other problems that put them out of service. United voiced its difficulties with the C-87s with the ATC and in November 1942 three of its aircraft were transferred to the India-China

United Airlines (UAL) was awarded an ATC contract to fly trans-Pacific routes and to fly intra-theater leave shuttles. (*UAL*)

Wing of ATC. In exchange UAL received three Naval Air Transport Service Douglas C-54 Skymasters, marking the beginning of the C-87 phase out. United Airlines would be authorized a maximum of 20 C-54s and be reassigned to the India-China Wing.

C-87s operated by United Airlines included 41-24005, 41-24027, 41-24028, 41-24160, 41-24252,* 41-24253,* 41-11608, 41-11640, 41-11642, 41-11642, 41-11655, 41-11656, 41-11789, and 41-11861.

* Modified with integral fuel cells at Fort Worth.

Transcontinental & Western Airlines (T&WA)

Transcontinental & Western Airlines (T&WA), later to become Trans World Airlines (TWA), operated Liberators for training and in support of AAF Ferrying Command. In late 1942, T&WA's new Intercontinental Division was assigned three C-87s (s/ns unknown) to fly the South Atlantic route between the US and the Middle East.

In June 1941, T&WA began supporting the AAC by providing training for the RAF at their Eagle Nest Flight Training Center in Albuquerque, New Mexico, under Col Robert Olds from the AAC Ferrying Command and Chief Air Marshal Sir Frederick Bowhill. The program was delayed when permission to utilize US Navy Reserve officers for this mission was postponed until July. Training for RAF and RCAF crews was conducted until late December 1941 and then T&WA trained AAF Liberator crews at the Eagle Nest until June 1942. A single LB-30 (AM927), painted in standard RAF camouflage with RAF roundels, was employed initially by T&WA for this training. This aircraft encountered a main and nose gear collapse on 24 July 1941 and was out of service for repairs for six months. T&WA negotiated a new training contract with the AAF Ferrying Command for instructing pilots, co-pilots, navigators, flight engineers, and radio operators for long-range flights. The curriculum provided for 24 hours of instruction for each crew position, including one long cross-country leg and one over 20,000ft to ensure training in the use of oxygen equipment. The school operated a mixture of LB-30, B-24A, and B-24D Liberators and at its peak had 15 assigned aircraft.

On 24 December 1942, T&WA President Jack Frye signed Contract DAW 535-AC-1062 with the War Department, which authorized T&WA 'to hire and train all personnel, procure necessary facilities, materials and supplies, and to secure necessary certificates of convenience and necessity, licenses, and permits essential to providing air service on a worldwide basis for the United States Army'. On the same day that Frye signed the contract, which designated T&WA as Contract Carrier No. 16, he established T&WA's Intercontinental Division (ICD).

By 1 November 1942, T&WA was assigned three C-87s, bringing its Intercontinental Division (ICD) fleet to 24 aircraft of all types, which it operated mainly over the South Atlantic and Africa. During one transport support mission, three B-25 Mitchell medium bomber groups that had been flying endless devastating missions against Rommel's

TWA C-54 Skymaster being loaded in the foreground with one of the three TWA C-87s being loaded in the distance. (*TWA*)

Afrika Korps' Panzers were in urgent need of spare parts. Three C-87s from the ICD were dispatched to fly in a loose formation from Palm Beach, Florida, and delivered the necessary parts. After delivering their cargo, these C-87s were based out of Accra, Ghana, where they supplemented five Boeing C-75s (307 Stratoliner) on the South Atlantic shuttle operation.

Bomber Transport Conversion Addenda

Addenda 1: Consolidated LC-7 Model 33 Commercial Passenger Version

Consideration of a LC-7 commercial passenger version of the B-24 occurred during March 1940 shortly after the first flight of the XB-24 (29 December 1939) and before that of the C-87 military transport version (October 1941). Consolidated 'officially' introduced the proposed LC-7 design on 25 March 1941 via a company promotional brochure. The concept aircraft was an obvious conversion of the Model 32 (B-24) airframe, duplicating its fuselage that accommodated five crew, 18 passengers seated in

**Model 32 (LC-7)
Commercial Concept Aircraft**

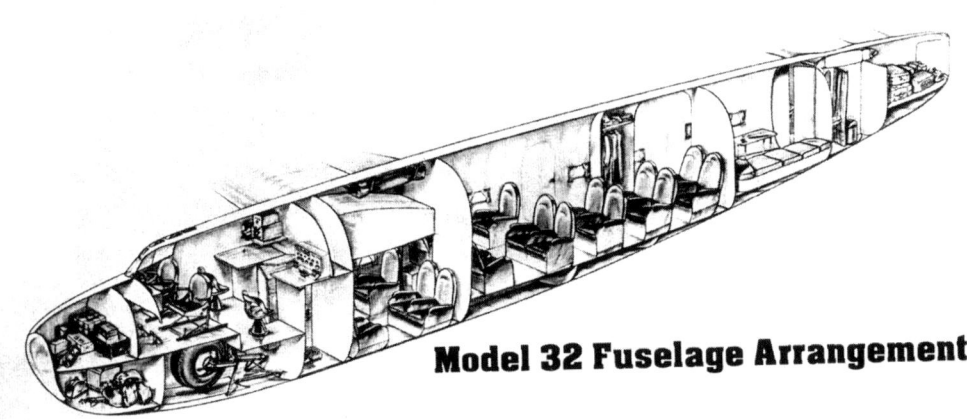

Model 32 Fuselage Arrangement

comfortable reclining seats six in a cabin under the wing and 12 in a cabin behind that. Four passengers were seated on bench seats in a rear lounge with a lavatory behind the lounge (see drawing). The aircraft weighed 45,000lb, had a maximum speed of 295mph, and cruised over a range of 1,650 miles at cruising speed of 220mph powered by four P&W R-1850 engines. Further development was postponed by the war.

Addenda 2: The B-17 C-108/C-17 Transport

In the eternal B-24 vs. B-17 'which was best' debate, it seems as though the B-24 transports undoubtedly win based on numbers, utility, and operational use. The designation XC-108 was assigned to a B-17E (41-2593) that was converted as a special transport for

The XC-108A was a B-17E (41-2595) converted as a cargo aircraft as part of an experimental program to test the feasibility of converting obsolescent bombers into cargo transports. (*AAF*)

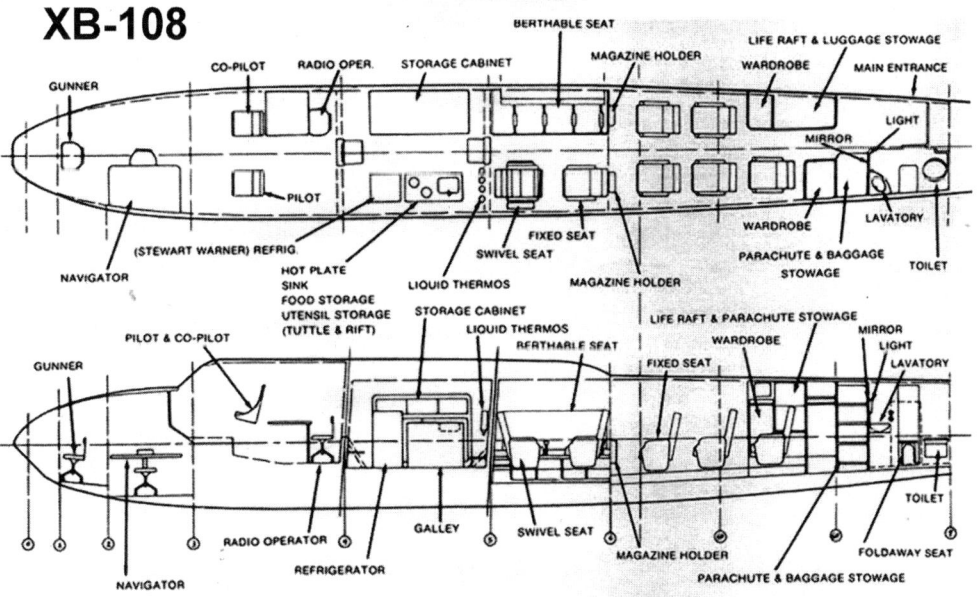

The C-108 had provisions for cargo or troop transport installed in both the former bomb bay and the aft fuselage. (*AAF*)

Gen. Douglas MacArthur in 1943. All armor and armament except the nose and tail guns were deleted. A drop-down entry door with built-in steps was cut into the rear fuselage, extra windows were installed, and the interior was furnished as a flying office, complete with living and cooking facilities. The designation YC-108 was assigned to B-17F-40-VE (42-6036) that was converted into VIP transport aircraft like MacArthur's aircraft.

The XC-108A was a B-17E (41-2595) converted at Patterson Field, Ohio, between August 1943 and March 1944 as a cargo aircraft to be part of an experimental program to test the feasibility of turning obsolescent bombers into cargo transports. All armament and military equipment was removed, and a large cargo door was cut into the rear fuselage. The interior arrangement was

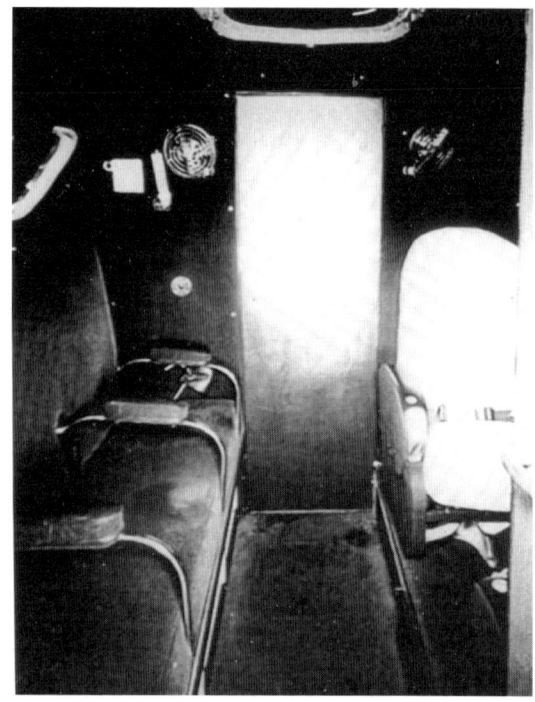

The B-17's narrow fuselage area made for very cramped seating and cargo space, and was unsuitable as a conversion. (*AAF*)

revised, and the radio operator and navigator positions were relocated behind the pilots where the dorsal turret had originally been located. The nose compartment was renovated to provide space for cargo or personnel, with access via the crawlway under the cockpit or by a solid, hinged nose piece that replaced the transparent nose of the standard B-17E. The bomb bay doors were sealed and the bulkhead between the bomb bay and the radio compartment was removed, as was the bulkhead between the radio compartment and the waist area. Provisions for cargo or troop transport were installed in both the former bomb bay and the aft fuselage. The XC-108A was based in India and used for transportation of materials into China over the Hump. Chronic engine problems and its proven unfeasibility as a cargo transport limited its success and no further conversions were made. The XC-108A returned to the States in October 1944 and after the war it was consigned to a Maine scrapyard. The XC-108B was a B-17F (42-30190) converted as a fuel transport aircraft with all armor and armament removed and extra fuel tanks installed in the fuselage to test the feasibility of converting bombers into tankers for use in ferrying fuel over the Hump from Burma to China. Like the XC-108A, the XC-108B also proved to be unsuccessful.

Two other cargo transport and VIP transport versions were converted from the B-17: the CB-17G troop transport version capable of carrying up to 64 troops, of which 25 were built, and the VB-17G, the VIP transport version for high-level staff officers, of which eight were built.

Chapter 3

C-109 Fuel Transport

C-109 Concept, Contracts, Testing, and Acceptance

The C-109 concept came into fruition because of an early AAF air plan that required 20th Air Force B-29 groups to bomb Japan by October 1944 from newly constructed bases in China, which, at the time was the closest point in range of Japan for these new heavy bombers. The ten B-29 groups were to be supported by no fewer than 2,000 dedicated C-109 fuel tankers, which would fly aviation gasoline over the Himalayan Hump from India, with both the B-29 group and C-109 figures to be doubled by May 1945. However, the objectives of this original plan were reduced considerably when B-29 operations were relocated from China to newly captured and refurbished bases in the Mariana Islands, from where they could be much better supported by Navy tanker vessels. The much fewer than 2,000 C-109s (208 were built in total) were then transferred to the Air Transport Command. On 8 September 1943 the Air Materiel Command ordered the conversion of one B-24E-20-FO (42-7221) into an 'Aerial Tanker XC-109' configuration by Ford. The XC-108B, a B-17F (42-30190), was also to be converted simultaneously for comparison. Unlike the 74th onward C-87 cargo/passenger transport, the C-109 fuel tankers were not new, dedicated aircraft but were to be conversions of existing B-24J and B-24L bombers.

After testing, the Ford B-24E-20-FO Liberator-based (42-7221) XC-109 prototype was considered to be superior to the B-17-based XC-108B and a large-scale conversion program was embarked on with 207 more Liberators modified to C-109 tanker specifications.

After the first XC-109 was converted by Ford, nine C-109s were converted by Douglas-Tulsa:

41-51368 and 41-51390 from B-24J-5-DTs
41-51411/420/424/425/426/427/442 from B-24L-10-DTs

Ford then modified 198 B-24Js and Ls into C-109s. There are some reports that the Glenn L. Martin Company modified a few Liberators for use in the ETO by using collapsible Mareng fuel cells that reduced the fuel load to about 1,200 gallons from about 3,150 gallons. C-109s converted were as follows: one B-24E-20-FO, two J-5-DTs; seven J-10-DTs; 29 J-10-FOs; 36 J-15-FOs; 18 J-20-FOs; 56 L-1-FOs; 47 L-5-FOs; and 13 L-10-FOs.

C-109 Conversion

For the C-109 conversion a standard B-24J/B-24L bomber was stripped of all armament (some turrets were retained on a few C-109s) and bombing provisions, including armor plate, turrets, bomb shackles, bombing instruments, and associated wiring. Additionally, all non-essential items such as flooring, unnecessary brackets, upholstering, and curtains were also removed. A series of radio and oxygen modifications, and other structural modifications were also made. The C-109 provisions mainly consisted of a series of eight metal cargo fuel tanks distributed throughout the aircraft. The average basic weight of the stripped aircraft, without C-109 requirements and without aircraft gasoline and oil,

The C-109 was essentially a standard B-24 bomber that was stripped of all armament and bombing provisions, including armor plate, turrets, bomb shackles, bombing instruments and most other all non-essential items to become a flying fuel tank. (*ATC*)

The C-109 provisions mainly consisted of a series of eight aluminum cargo fuel tanks distributed throughout the aircraft. The C-109 had an advantage over the C-46 in transporting fuel as it carried it in its large internal tanks, whereas the C-46 carried fuel in 55-gallon drums and the weight and size of the steel drums decreased payload. (*ATC*)

A C-109's eight fuel-carrying tanks being filled with as much as 2,900 gallons of gasoline for over the Hump delivery between India and China as part of the massive attempt to support B-29 operations from bases in China. (*ATC*)

was approximately 32,500lb; thus, providing increased fuel-carrying capacity. The basic weight with C-109 provisions (i.e., cargo tanks and provisions installed, and all other structural provisions including radio installations, but without gasoline and oil) averaged approximately 35,500lb. The C-109s carried such names as *Big Gas Bird*, *Gas Laden Lady*, *Gasoline Alley*, and *Petrol Packin' Mama*.

Modifications for Fuel Transport

Nose Modifications

The forward electrically operated nose turret was removed, and the area covered with a specially constructed spherical nose fairing, conforming to the approximate shape and size of the Plexiglas turret housing, which had been removed. These C-109 conversions used a solid nose, whereas the sole XC-109 that resulted from the conversion of a B-24E retained its nose glazing.

Bombardier's Compartment

Everything armament related in the bombardier's compartment was removed, along with the drift meter and astro-compass installations. A cradle was installed to hold the barrel-shaped 100-gallon-capacity fuel tank. To completely seal gasoline vapors in the nose section from the flight deck, a heavy two-piece canvas curtain was installed at Station 3.0 with lift the dot fasteners. Access to the nose tank was through a double-sided zipper opening in the lower curtain at a position convenient to the passageway under the flight deck. To provide additional ventilation for the nose compartment the original factory-installed ventilation louvers intended for the nose turrets were left open and an additional exhaust scoop was installed on each side of the nose.

Flight Deck

As part of weight reduction, the flight deck was stripped of all unnecessary articles such as flak curtains, navigator's table and chair, and bombing instruments. Also, various

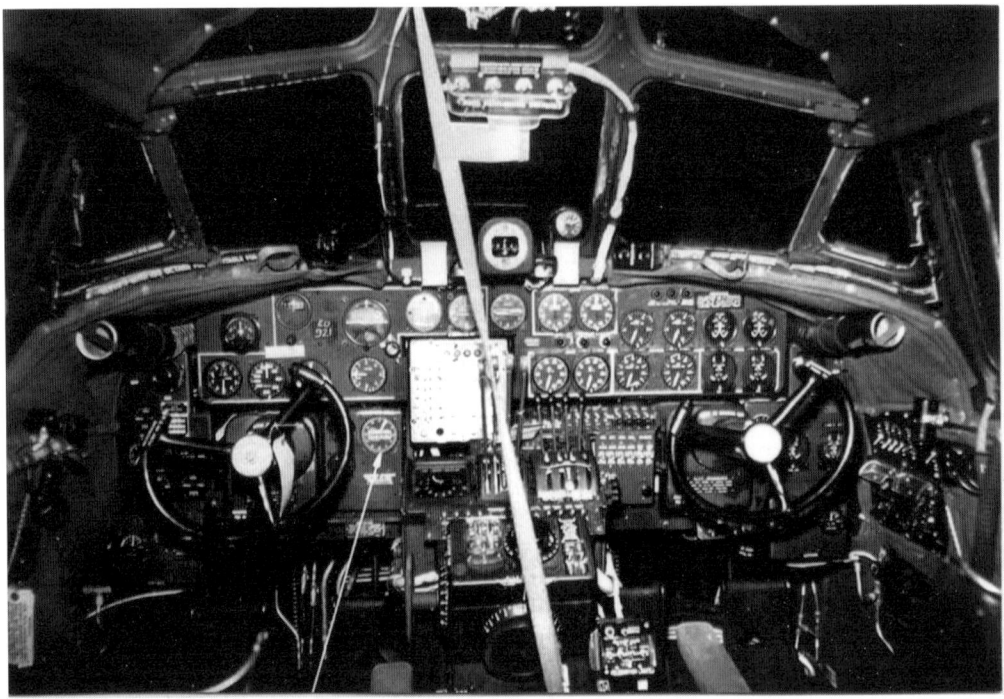

C-109 pilot's instruments and controls. (*Ford/ATC*)

C-109 radio operator's station.
(*Ford/ATC*)

pieces of radio equipment had to be relocated from other areas of the aircraft. The Martin dorsal turret was removed, and the hole left by its removal was plugged with a reinforced circular plate riveted in place. The bottom of this plate was then upholstered to conform with the rest of the upholstering on the flight deck. The auxiliary power unit was removed from under the flight deck and in its place a rack holding four CO_2 tanks and the four pressure-reducing valves for the purging system were installed. Four 0.25in CO_2 pressure lines ran from the bottles on this rack for each cargo tank with the cables from the release valves running directly overhead, through the flight deck floor, to the pull handles.

Forward Bomb Bay

The forward bomb bay was stripped of all bomb shackles, electric bomb release devices, and associated wiring and replaced by two 400-gallon aluminum cargo fuel tanks held by straps and cradles furnished as a kit originally delivered with the aircraft from the factory. A tank was installed on either side of the catwalk against the bomb rails. The tanks were droppable through the bomb bay, with all fuel and vent connections having breakaway coupling.

Aft Bomb Bay

The aft bomb bay was also stripped of the bomb shackles, electric bomb release devices, and associated wiring and were replaced by two 425-gallon aluminum cargo fuel tanks. These tanks were also droppable and were installed in straps and cradles similar to the forward bomb bay tanks except that the release mechanism differed in details. The hole in the Plexiglas waist windows due to the removal of the waist guns was left open for ventilation reasons. However, a fabricated Plexiglas patch to plug this opening was stowed in a canvas bag.

Tail Section

The tail section was stripped of all armament and armament provisions, including the tail turret, ammunition tracks and boxes, and the corrugated flooring. All electrical harnesses and applications, brackets, etc., not affecting

View looking aft at the tail section's prefabricated fairing. (*Ford/ATC*)

aircraft operation were also removed. The space left due to the removal of the tail turret was capped and riveted in place with a reinforced fairing of similar size and shape to the removed turret. The housing for the bombing formation lights located immediately under the tail fairing was removed and the resulting hole was repaired with an aluminum alloy plate riveted in place.

Tests and Flight Characteristics

Since the C-109 was intended as a dedicated fuel carrier, tests completed at Wright Field during October 1943 concerned its fuel-carrying capacity vs. flight characteristics. The tests established the following using the original XC-109 weighted at the different actual weights without crew, using different fuel capacities and various fuel tanks located in various areas of the aircraft. Army Air Forces Material Command Engineering Division Report Service No. ENG-51-524-2-2, dated 28 October 1943 reports the following:

The first test flight was made at 54,000lb gross weight. The gasoline was carried as follows: 2,360 gallons in main wing tanks, 471 gallons in deck tanks, 320 gallons in one rear bomb bay tank. The balance, with the crew, at this weight was 30.5 per cent MAC. The crew reported that the airplane handled satisfactorily with no unfavorable flying characteristics. A crew of two was carried.

The second test flight was made at 58,000lb gross weight. The gasoline was carried as followed: 2,360 gallons in main wing tanks, 471 gallons in deck tanks, 320 gallons in rear bomb bay. The balance with the crew was 28.7 per cent MAC. The report of the crew was the same as that of the 54,000-pound test. A crew of two was carried.

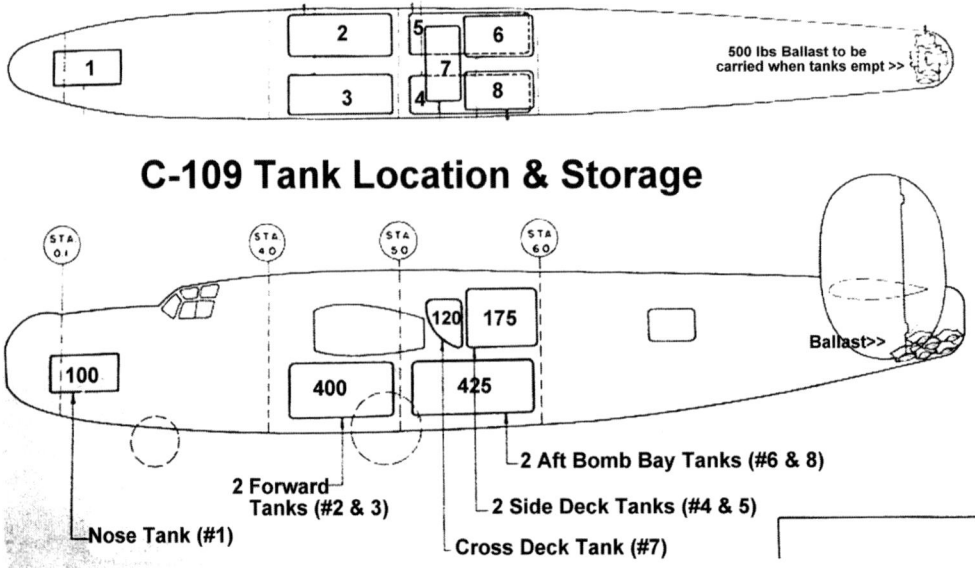

C-109 Tank Location & Storage

Fuel System

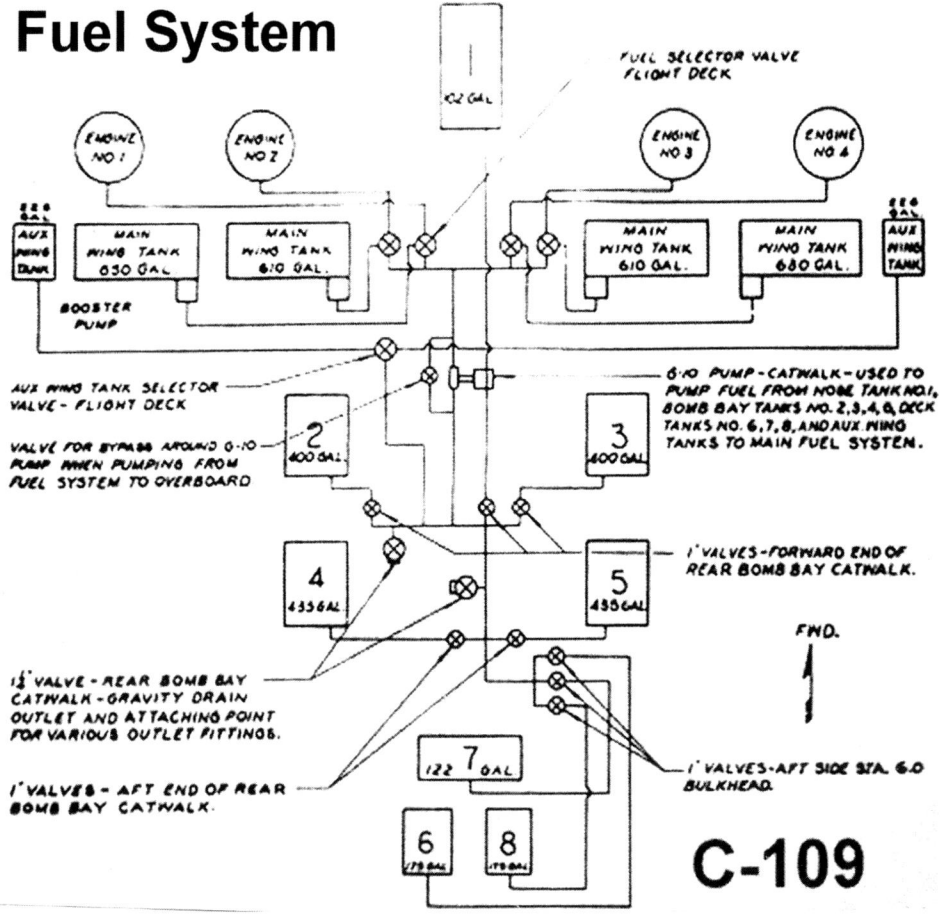

The third test flight was made at 64,500lb gross weight. The airplane took off and remained in the air until 900 gallons of gasoline had been consumed. It then landed at approximately 59,000lb gross weight. The gasoline was carried as follows: full main wing tanks (2,360 gallons), full auxiliary wing tanks (465 gallons), full deck tanks (472 gallons), full front bomb bay tanks (800 gallons), full nose tanks (103 gallons), and 670 gallons in rear bomb bay. (Due to inaccuracies of the gauges on the gasoline trucks, these figures may vary, but it was estimated that approximately 4,850 gallons can be carried at this gross weight.) The balance with crew was 31.35 per cent MAC. The take-off was made crosswind on a concrete runway. The airplane left the ground after approximately a 4,000ft run. The report by the crew was the same as that of the 54,000lb and 58,000lb tests.

It must be noted here, however, that when the airplane is empty, that is, when no fuel is carried in the cargo tanks, 500lb of ballast must be carried in the tail cap. When all cargo tanks are filled, as noted above, the airplane is tail heavy, and the 100-gallon cargo tank in the nose is used to counteract this condition.

Fuel-Carrying Tanks

The cargo system of the C-109 consisted of a series of aluminum alloy fuel tanks distributed as follows:

Tank No.	Location	Capacity
1	Nose Compartment	100 gallons
2 & 3	Fwd. Bomb Bay	400 gallons each
4 & 5	Aft Bomb Bay	425 gallons each
7	Fwd. Command Deck	120 gallons
6 & 8	Side Command Deck	180 gallons each

* Total Cargo Capacity   2,230 gallons

* Not including outboard auxiliary fuel cells in wings, which may also be used to transport fuel.

The C-109 had an advantage over the C-46 in transporting fuel as it carried it in its large internal tanks, whereas the Curtiss aircraft carried it in 55-gallon steel drums and the weight and size of these decreased payload.

The tanks were interconnected by a system of piping that terminated at defueling manifolds located on the catwalk in the aft bomb bay. It was possible to transfer gasoline in the cargo fuel tanks into the aircraft's main fuel system via a 'T' connection into an electric fuel transfer pump, located on the catwalk in the forward bomb bay, thus making this extra gasoline available to the C-109 while in flight. A defueling unit consisting of a stowed portable gasoline-driven defueling pump and 30ft of hose were used to pump stored fuel out of the cargo tanks by connecting it to the outlet fittings provided on each of the two defueling manifolds. Selector valves on each manifold, accessible from outside the aircraft by opening the rear bomb bay doors, allowed individual tanks to be emptied. The fuel was transferred in one hour by the standard fuel transfer system for loading and unloading through a single hose union located on the side of the fuselage. Inert CO_2 gas was injected into the tanks as fuel was pumped out to eliminate the danger of explosion. Internal pumping provisions allowed the C-109 to be able to use all the 4,850 gallons of its own fuel cargo, vastly increasing its range. In operations, the tank in the forward fuselage was left empty, apparently for aircraft longitudinal stability considerations. Initially, the on-board electric auxiliary power unit (APU) was used to power the refueling/defueling system. However, it was soon realized that this procedure using electricity was not safe in the fuel fume-laden environment. To reduce the possibility of an explosion, external pumping systems were employed. If flights were made to remote stations, a portable A-6 refueling unit could be carried on the aircraft.

Individual Tank installations

Nose Tank (Cargo Tank #1)

This non-droppable tank, located in the bombardier's compartment, had a capacity of 100 gallons (not including expansion space) and was attached rigidly to the aircraft structure. It was installed in a felt-lined wooden cradle by felt-lined metal straps using turnbuckles for adjustment. The filler cap was located on the top aft end of the tank and was accessible for filling through the nose wheel opening. A 0.75in vent connection on the forward end of the tank was connected to a vent flange, riveted to the upper skin of the nose, by a 0.75in rubber hose. A welded 'Y' fitting in the vent line adjacent to the tank connected to the CO_2 purging line. The outlet or defueling connection consisted of a 1.0in (OD) tube running from a flange on the bottom of the tank directly to the forward defueling

The original XC-109 nose-mounted fuel tank. (*Ford/ATC*)

Interior view of the nose tank of a later solid-nosed C-109. (*Ford/ATC*)

manifold on the catwalk in the aft bomb bay. Due to poor longitudinal stability during flight with a full nose fuel tank and the added weight on the Liberator's notoriously weak nose gear, this tank was most often not filled.

Forward Bomb Bay Tanks (Cargo Tanks #2, #3)

These droppable 400-gallon tanks were located in the forward bomb bay on each side of the catwalk and were installed in felt-lined straps suspended from the bomb rails. An installation kit was furnished by the factory as loose equipment. Both the vent and outlet connections on these tanks ran through Hallett-type quick disconnect fittings with check valves for dropping purposes. The vent was connected to the top skin of the C-109 by a 0.75in rubber tube. The outlet connections consisted of 1.0in (OD) tubing running to selector valves on the forward defueling manifold on the catwalk in the aft bomb bay. The filler caps were located on the top aft inboard end of each tank and were accessible from the ground when the forward bomb bays were opened.

View looking aft along the catwalk at forward bomb bay at the bomb bay tank supporting provisions. (*Ford/ATC*)

Aft Bomb Bay Tanks (Cargo Tanks #4, and #5)

The installation of the aft 425-gallon bomb bay tanks was essentially the same as the forward bomb bay installation except that the droppable mechanism differed in detail. The outlet and vent connections were the same and the filler caps were also located on the top aft inboard and of each tank and were also accessible for filling from the ground when the rear bomb bay doors were opened.

Deck Tanks (Cargo Tanks #6, #7, and #8)

These tanks were located on the command deck and were installed in felt-lined wooden cradles thar were fastened rigidly to the aircraft structure. The #7 tank (120 gallon) was located crosswise on the command deck and adjacent to the rear spar of the wing center section. Tanks #6 and #8 (180 gallons each) were left-hand and right-hand tanks located lengthwise on either side of the command deck. They were all held in the cradles with felt-lined metal straps using turnbuckles for adjustment. The outlet or defueling lines ran from a fitting on the bottom of each tank to a header clamped to the bulkhead at Station 6.0. The three outlet lines joined at this point and a single 1.25in line runs from this header to the manifold located on the catwalk in the aft end of the rear bomb bay. A 0.75in rubber hose vent line that ran from the top of each tank to individual fittings was riveted to the fuselage top skin. A filler cap was located on top of each tank and to fill these tanks it was necessary to bring a filler hose in through the rear bomb bay or through the waist windows.

Command deck fuel tank cradles. (*Ford/ATC*)

Command deck tanks looking forward from the waist area. (*Ford/ATC*)

Command deck tanks at Station 6.0 (note oxygen tanks overhead and the plywood floor covering the previous Sperry ball turret area). (*Ford/ATC*)

Vapor Dilution System

Because the C-109 was a flying fuel tank and gasoline vapors were a constant ignition hazard, especially after the fuel cargo tanks were emptied, a CO_2 system was devised to purge these vapors from the empty tanks. A bottle rack containing four CO_2 bottles was installed under the flight deck between Stations 3.0 and 3.2 on the left-hand side. These bottles were tubed to discharge through four discharge ports installed between Stations 3.0 and 3.1, left-hand side. The release handles for the CO_2 bottles were installed just aft of Station 3.0 on the flight deck floor, left-hand side. The release handles were connected to the bottles via a series of cables and corner poles. The 1.4lb cylinder was connected through a series of 0.3125in tubing to the nose tank. The 5lb cylinder was connected through 0.3125in tubing to the three tanks on the command deck. One 9.5lb cylinder was connected through 0.3125in tubing to both forward bomb bay tanks. Each bottle had a pressure regulator installed between the bottles and respective tanks. Generally, the CO_2 system was only operated when the cargo tanks were empty; usually on the return trip after dispensing the fuel. The system was a 'one-time' system, as the complete contents of a bottle were used with one pull of the release handle. It was recommended that once the empty cargo tanks were filled with CO_2 vapors, the C-109 was flown at a constant altitude, which minimized the 'breathing' of the tanks and ensured the maximum effectiveness of the system.

A bottle rack containing four CO_2 bottles was installed under the flight deck to purge fuel vapors from the empty tanks. (*Ford/ATC*)

Oxygen System

All but ten of the G-1 oxygen bottles were removed, with three of these remaining in the Sperry ball turret well; three remained on the stringers overhead of the turret while the remaining four bottles were left installed in and around the waist gunner's compartment. All but four of the oxygen outlet stations were deleted, with the pilot, co-pilot, left-hand radio, and right-hand radio compartments outlet stations remaining. The pilot and co-pilot were allotted approximately three bottles apiece, while the left and right-hand radio stations were allotted approximately two bottles apiece. The system was filled through a filler valve in the Sperry ball turret well at approximately Station 6.2. There were no shut-off valves or single line check valves installed in this system.

Automatic Direction Finder (ADF)

To aid navigation during their long-range flights, most C-109s were equipped with a dual Automatic Direction Finder (ADF) system, as was denoted by the presence of two football-shaped antennae on top of the fuselage. The ADF determined the direction or bearing to a Non-Directional Beacon (NDB) radio transmitter at a known location relative to the aircraft by using a combination of directional and non-directional antennae to sense the direction in which the combined signal was strongest.

The Typical C-109 Flight

The typical C-109 route was one of the most difficult anywhere, leaving bases in Assam in the morning and flying over trackless Burmese jungles and then the rugged, uncharted Himalayas to bases in China. Many flights were relatively uneventful but could encounter storms, turbulence, and winds well over 100mph with no turning back. Regardless of the weather, a pilot was expected to fly through it. The only redeeming element was the tailwind flying over the Hump fully loaded. The flights usually took five hours and consumed 1,100 gallons of fuel. The aircraft could be very difficult to control when landing at full load, especially with a runway length of less than 6,000ft (1,800m). After the fuel was onloaded, the C-109 was readied for the mid-afternoon return flight. Using a stick to measure the gasoline remaining in the C-109's tanks, the flight engineer estimated if there would be adequate fuel (1,700 gallons) for the return trip. One positive attribute of the C-109 was that range and the Himalayan altitude proved to be no problem after take-off as the four reliable Pratt & Whitney engines and their turbos allowed the aircraft to fly nearly any Assam to China route.

Like the C-87s, the C-109s soon earned a poor reputation among their crews for being accident prone. (*Ford/ATC*)

C-109 Problems

Like the C-87s, the C-109s soon earned a poor reputation among their crews. The C-109 suffered 21 total accidents, with seven involving 30 total fatalities (all crew, no passengers) and the worst involving five fatalities (the maximum crew). The XC-109 prototype was lost over the Hump on 31 August 1944. These fully loaded tankers were especially difficult to land on airfields that were located above 6,000ft. After consuming fuel and dropping their bombs, standard B-24 bombers normally returned to base to land considerably lighter than when they took off, However, the overloaded C-109s took off and landed on short, rough fields carrying 2,900 gallons of fuel to be delivered, which led to type being given the death-defying name 'C-one-oh-nine BOOM'. After the ATC realized the tanker's problems, it began an intensive training program in the CBI for each new arriving crew, which often included a very experienced pilot completing the training course before flying an operational mission.

Conversions of B-24s to C-109s

42-7172/7229	Ford B-24E-20-FO Liberator
	7221 converted to XC-109
42-51293/51395	Douglas-Tulsa B-24J-5-DT Liberator
	51368 converted to C-109
	51390 converted to C-109
42-51396/51430	Douglas-Tulsa B-24J-10-DT Liberator
	51411 converted to C-109
	51420 converted to C-109
	51424/51427 converted to C-109
	51429 converted to C-109
42-51611/51825	Ford B-24J-10-FO Liberator
	51615 converted to C-109
	51647 converted to C-109
	51659 converted to C-109
	51676 converted to C-109
	51684 converted to C-109
	51697 converted to C-109
	51706 converted to C-109
	51712 converted to C-109
	51716 converted to C-109
	51721 converted to C-109
	51727 converted to C-109
	51730 converted to C-109
	51734 converted to C-109
	51740 converted to C-109
	51748 converted to C-109
	51756 converted to C-109
	51758 converted to C-109
	51766 converted to C-109
	51774 converted to C-109
	51782 converted to C-109
	51784 converted to C-109
	51786 converted to C-109

51788 converted to C-109
51792/51793 converted to C-109
51809/51810 converted to C-109
51817 converted to C-109
51825 converted to C-109

42-51826/52075   Ford B-24J-15-FO Liberator
51826 converted to C-109
51830 converted to C-109
51839 converted to C-109
51844 converted to C-109
51846/51847 converted to C-109
51849/51850 converted to C-109
51854 converted to C-109
51857 converted to C-109
51860 converted to C-109
51862 converted to C-109
51876/51877 converted to C-109
51883 converted to C-109
51887 converted to C-109
51890 converted to C-109
51893 converted to C-109
51901 converted to C-109
51904 converted to C-109
51921 converted to C-109
51930 converted to C-109
51962 converted to C-109
51982/51983 converted to C-109
52000/52001 converted to C-109
52005/52006 converted to C-109
52012 converted to C-109
52014 converted to C-109
52020/52021 converted to C-109
52023 converted to C-109
52033 converted to C-109
52042 converted to C-109
52049 converted to C-109

44-48754/49001   Ford B-24J-20-FO Liberator
48755 converted to C-109
48792 converted to C-109
48877 converted to C-109
48879 converted to C-109
48882/48883 converted to C-109

48888 converted to C-109
48890/48892 converted to C-109
48948 converted to C-109
48968 converted to C-109
48974 converted to C-109
48979 converted to C-109
48984 converted to C-109
48995/48996 converted to C-109
49001 converted to C-109

44-49002/49251   Ford B-24L-1-FO Liberator

49007/49009 converted to C-109
49011/49020 converted to C-109
49022/49023 converted to C-109
49025 converted to C-109
49030/49031 converted to C-109
49034/49035 converted to C-109
49037 converted to C-109
49040 converted to C-109
49045/49046 converted to C-109
49050/49051 converted to C-109
49057 converted to C-109
49059/49060 converted to C-109
49062/49063 converted to C-109
49065 converted to C-109
49067 converted to C-109
49071 converted to C-109
49075 converted to C-109
49077 converted to C-109
49079 converted to C-109
49184 converted to C-109
49191 converted to C-109
49197 converted to C-109
49204 converted to C-109
49208 converted to C-109
49219 converted to C-109
49222 converted to C-109
49230 converted to C-109
49234/49236 converted to C-109
49238 converted to C-109
49240 converted to C-109
49245/49249 converted to C-109
49251 converted to C-109

44-49252/49501	Ford B-24L-5-FO Liberator
	49253 converted to C-109
	49255/49258 converted to C-109
	49265 converted to C-109
	49267 converted to C-109
	49269/49272 converted to C-109
	49274/49277 converted to C-109
	49280/49281 converted to C-109
	49283/49285 converted to C-109
	49288/49290 converted to C-109
	49292 converted to C-109
	49295 converted to C-109
	49299 converted to C-109
	49302/49303 converted to C-109
	49305 converted to C-109
	49313 converted to C-109
	49317 converted to C-109
	49319 converted to C-109
	49326 converted to C-109
	49330 converted to C-109
	49333 converted to C-109
	49337 converted to C-109
	49344 converted to C-109
	49348 converted to C-109
	49351/49354 converted to C-109
	49358/49359 converted to C-109
	49445 converted to C-109
	49466 converted to C-109
	49490 converted to C-109
44-49502/49751	Ford B-24L-10-FO Liberator
	49510 converted to C-109
	49615 converted to C-109
	49621 converted to C-109
	49628 converted to C-109
	49660 converted to C-109
	49662 converted to C-109
	49684 converted to C-109
	49691 converted to C-109
	49704 converted to C-109
	49715 converted to C-109
	49720 converted to C-109
	49723 converted to C-109
	49728 converted to C-109

Chapter 4

Navy RY Liberator Hauler Series

Τ he Consolidated RY Liberator was the US Navy designation for transport
aircraft based on the C-87 and covered three variants; the first two identical to
the AAF aircraft and the other being custom-built for the Navy.

RY-1/RY-2

The RY-1 and RY-2 were the Navy versions of the C-87A VIP transport aircraft and
C-87 Liberator Express transport. Only eight aircraft received these designations:

1) Three RY-1 C-87A VIP transports assigned BuNos 67797/67799 transfers
   from C-87 (43-30569/30571).
2) Five RY-2 C-87s assigned BuNos 39013/39017 transfers from C-87A
   (44-39198/39202) with 15 additional conversions cancelled.

RY-3 Privateer Express (C-87C/C.IX Consolidated Model 101)

General

The US Navy Consolidated San Diego Model 101 RY-3 was a four-engine land-based
cargo and passenger transport version of the Navy Consolidated PB4Y-2 Privateer that
was externally like the Liberator except the fuselage was longer to accommodate a flight

engineer's station and it had a tall single vertical stabilizer rather than the B-24's twin-tail configuration. The tricycle-type landing gear was retractable and hydraulically actuated. The single tail assembly had a single rudder and vertical stabilizer. Fuselage and wing structures were of aluminum alloy.

RY-3/C-87C/C.IX Consolidated Model 101 Described

Nose Compartment

The main door to this compartment also formed the nose of the fuselage and was hinged to open the entire front of the compartment when loading cargo. Access to the compartment from the interior was via a passageway through the battery compartment and the nose wheel well. The maximum cargo capacity of the nose compartment was 1,600lb (vs. 400lb for the C-87) but, essentially, the amount of cargo that could be loaded, within the 1,600lb limit, depended upon the center of gravity location for a particular load.

Flight Deck

This compartment was aft of the nose compartment at a higher level and provided the aircraft's crew operating stations. The flight deck provided crew stations for the pilot, co-pilot, radio operator, and navigator.

It was divided into two areas:

1) The pilot's and co-pilot's stations at the forward end, housing the main instrument panel, flight controls, engine controls, pilot's and co-pilot's seats, and pilot's and co-pilot's radio and interphone controls.
2) The radio operator's and navigator's stations aft of the pilot's and co-pilot's seats. The radio operator's seat, table, and equipment were on the right side; the navigator's seat, table and equipment were on the left side of this area. The navigator's astrodome was installed in the top center of the fuselage in this area.

The door in the rear flight deck bulkhead allowed access to the cargo/passenger compartment.

Nose Wheel Compartment

The nose wheel compartment was located under the forward part of the flight deck and lodged the retracted nose landing gear. Doors linked to the nose gear closed the bottom of the compartment when the gear was retracted and automatically opened when the gear was extended.

Battery Compartment

This was a small compartment located below the flight deck aft of the nose wheel compartment and contained the batteries, battery vent jar, current limiters, and the Station 4.0 fuse box.

Main Cargo Compartment

The main cargo compartment occupied the entire fuselage from the flight deck aft to approximately the position where the horizontal stabilizer front spar passed through the fuselage. This cargo compartment became the passenger compartment when seats were installed. A side entrance door was located near the forward end of this compartment on the starboard side and could be released and jettisoned during flight in an emergency. A main cargo loading hatch was located near the aft end of the compartment on the port side. This hatch was closed by double doors, hinged at the fore and aft edges of the opening, and latched together in the middle. The forward half of the double doors also could be released and dropped during flight in case of an emergency. The total maximum load capacity of the main cargo compartment with an approximate volume of the cargo compartment was 1,588 cu ft accommodating 15,790lb.

Tail Compartment

This compartment was separated from the main cargo space by a bulkhead. The tail compartment contained the toilet, relief tube, and two Type J-1 oxygen bottles. The rear end of the main cargo or passenger compartment consisted of a 29 × 4in tail cone that

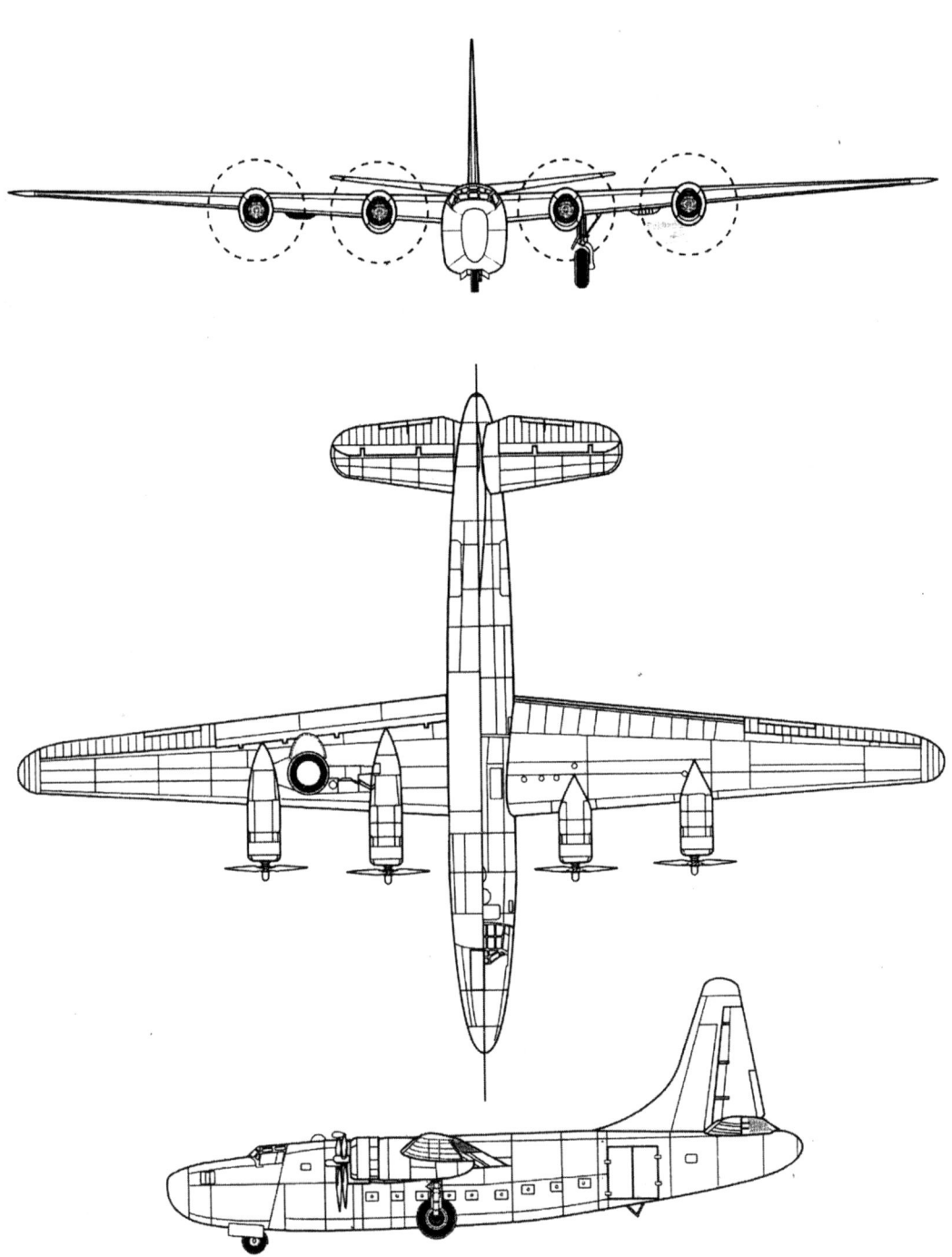

RY-3 PRODUCTION DATA

Buno.	CVAC No.	RAF serial	U.S. Service	RAF Service	RCAF Service	Disposition
90020	1		To U.S. Navy			SOC 3/31/48
90021	2	JT973		45 Group, Dorval, Canada	Rockliffe Ice Wagon	SOC 9/20/48
90022	3	JT974 (ntu) Not Taken Up	Consolidated, retained for testing			
90023	4	JT975		45 Group		
90024	5	JT976		45 Group		SOC 4/16/46
90025	6	JT977 (ntu)	Consolidated, retained for testing			SOC 1/46
90026	7	JT978		45 Group		SOC 2/28/46
90027	8	JT979		45 Group		crashed Whenaupai, New Zealand, Sept. 1, 1945
90028	9	JT980 (ntu)	To Patuxent River for flight test			SOC 2/28/46
90029	10	JT981		45 Group		SOC 4/16/46
90030	11	JT982		45 Group/231 Squadron		Lost at sea, July 4, 1945
90031	12	JT983		45 Group		SOC 4/16/46
90032	13	JT984		231 Squadron		SOC 4/16/46
90033	14	JT985		45 Group		crashed Dorset, England, June 15, 1945.
90034	15	JT986		231 Squadron		SOC 4/16/46
90035	16	JT987		231 Squadron		SOC 4/16/46
90036	17	JT988		231 Squadron		SOC 4/16/46
90037	18	JT989		231 Squadron		SOC 2/28/46
90038	19	JT990		231 Squadron		SOC 4/16/46
90039	20	JT991		231 Squadron		SOC 2/2846
90040	21	JT992		231 Squadron		SOC 4/16/46
90041	22	JT993		231 Squadron		SOC 4/16/46
90042	23	JT994		45 Group		SOC 4/16/46
90043	24	JT995 (ntu)	To U.S. Marine Corps, VMR-352			SOC 7/46
90044	25	JT996 (ntu)	To U.S. Marine Corps, VMR-352			SOC 2/46
90045	26	JT997	Pool San Diego	45 Group		SOC 4/16/46
90046	27	JT998	To U.S. Marine Corps, VMR-352, 10/46 FASRON 118			SOC 5/31/48
90047	28		Pool Clinton			SOC 2/28/46
90048	29	JV936	To U.S. Marine Corps, VMR-352			SOC 2/28/46
90049	30	JV937				SOC 2/28/46
90050	31	JV938				SOC 2/28/46
90057	32					SOC 2/28/46
90058	33		Pool Clinton			SOC 2/28/46
90059	34					SOC 2/28/46

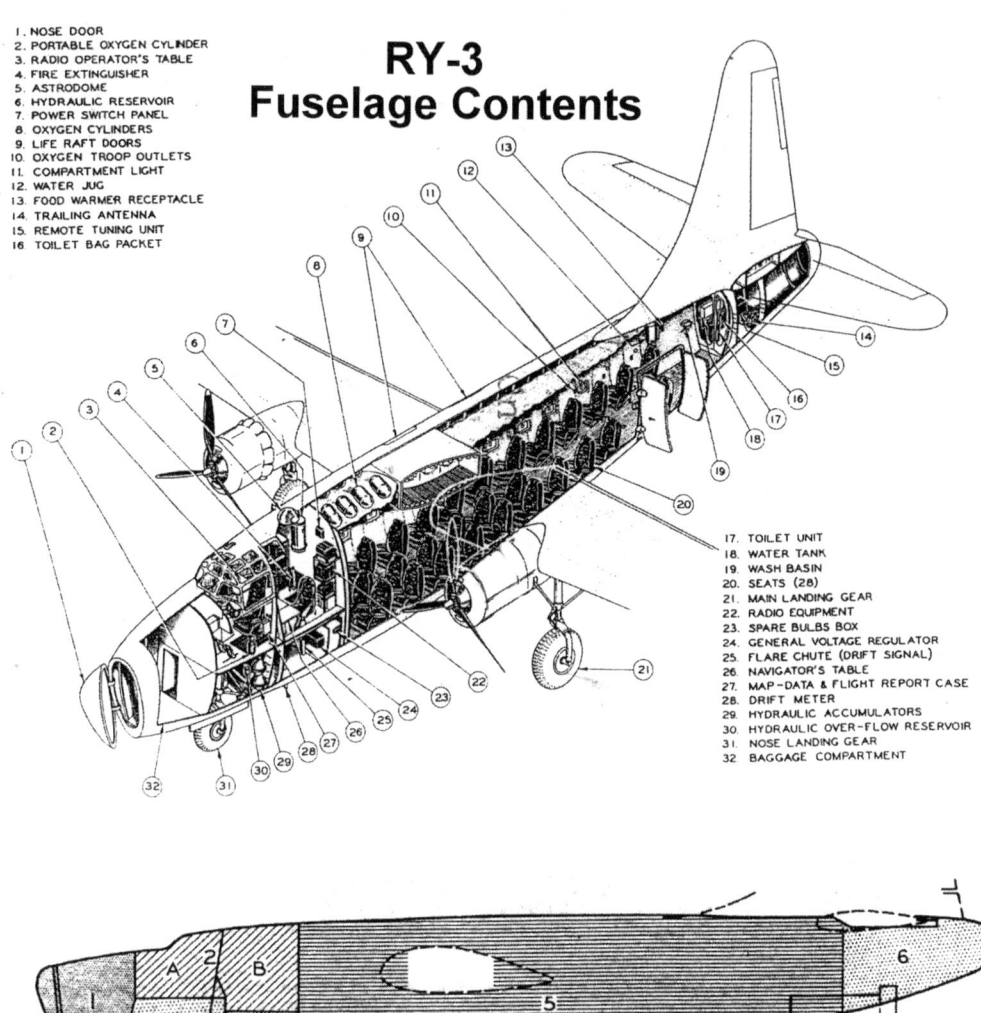

1. NOSE DOOR
2. PORTABLE OXYGEN CYLINDER
3. RADIO OPERATOR'S TABLE
4. FIRE EXTINGUISHER
5. ASTRODOME
6. HYDRAULIC RESERVOIR
7. POWER SWITCH PANEL
8. OXYGEN CYLINDERS
9. LIFE RAFT DOORS
10. OXYGEN TROOP OUTLETS
11. COMPARTMENT LIGHT
12. WATER JUG
13. FOOD WARMER RECEPTACLE
14. TRAILING ANTENNA
15. REMOTE TUNING UNIT
16. TOILET BAG PACKET

RY-3
Fuselage Contents

17. TOILET UNIT
18. WATER TANK
19. WASH BASIN
20. SEATS (28)
21. MAIN LANDING GEAR
22. RADIO EQUIPMENT
23. SPARE BULBS BOX
24. GENERAL VOLTAGE REGULATOR
25. FLARE CHUTE (DRIFT SIGNAL)
26. NAVIGATOR'S TABLE
27. MAP-DATA & FLIGHT REPORT CASE
28. DRIFT METER
29. HYDRAULIC ACCUMULATORS
30. HYDRAULIC OVER-FLOW RESERVOIR
31. NOSE LANDING GEAR
32. BAGGAGE COMPARTMENT

STATIONS 1.0   2.0 3.0 4.0 4.1   7.6 8.0 9.0 9.1

1. Nose Compartment
2. Flight Deck
   A. Pilot's and Copilot's Stations
   B. Radio Operator's and Navigator's Stations

3. Nose Wheel Compartment
4. Battery Compartment
5. Main Cargo Compartment
6. Tail Compartment

could be removed to allow the loading of long, narrow cargo. Removal of eight bolts from a belt frame aft of the rear-most oxygen bottle released the tail cone, to permit loading of long narrow objects, such as flaps, ailerons, extrusions, drawn sections, rods, tubing, etc., through the tail.

RY-3 flight deck. (*CAC*)

General Dimensions

Max. Fuselage Height	10ft 6.5in
Max. Fuselage Width	7ft 5.7in
Overall Span	110ft
Overall Length	75ft 5.4in
Overall Height	29ft 1.6in
Maximum cross section of fuselage:	
Height	10ft 5in
Width	7ft 5in
Ground Clearance Fuselage	1ft 8in
Ground Clear: Inboard Prop Tip	3ft 1in
Ground Clear: Outboard Prop Tip	3ft 6in
True Propeller Diameter	11ft 7in

Wings

Root Chord	14ft
Chord at Tip	5ft 2.5in

Chord Mean Aerodynamic	123.7in
Leading Edge Dihedral	4 degrees
Incidence at Root	3 degrees
Incidence at Construction Tip	3 degrees
Sweepback Leading Edge	3.5 degrees

Areas

Wing With Ailerons and Flaps	1,048 sq ft
Aileron Aft of Hinge Line Flaps	64.3 sq ft
Flaps	144.4 sq ft
Horizontal Tail	268.2 sq ft
Stabilizer	192.8 sq ft
Elevator	75.4 sq ft
Vertical Tail	165.0 sq ft
Fin	96.5 sq ft
Rudder	45.5 sq ft
Dorsal Fin	21.0 sq ft

Weights

Wing	6,454lb
Tail	1,033lb
Fuselage	4,693lb
Landing Gear	2,984lb
Nacelles	1,550lb
Power Plants	9,749lb
Equipment	3,896lb
Empty Weight	30,359lb
Gross Weight	56,000lb
Max Fuel (3,008 gallons)	70,231lb

Performance

Power Plants	Pratt & Whitney R-1830-94
Propellers	
Hamilton Standard: Hydromatic,	
Full-Feathering, Constant-Speed, Three-Bladed	11ft 7in
Stalling Speed	88mph
High Speed Cruise (at 13,750ft)	264mph
Max Cruising Speed (at 10,000ft)	230mph
Max Cruise Speed (at 15,000ft)	240mph
Take-Off (over 50ft obstacle)	3,100ft
Landing Distance (over 50ft obstacle)	3,200ft
Service Ceiling	21,300ft

In Service

BuOrd Serials: 90020 to 90050 and 90057 to 90059

USMC: VMR-352 operated four ex-RAF: JT995 (90043), JT996 (90044), JT998 (90046) and JV936 (90048)

RAF 45 Group operated 11 RY-3s and 231 Squadron operated 10 RY-3s as the Liberator C.IX with the serials JT973 through JT999 and JV936

RCAF: JT973 (ex-BuOrd 90021) *Rockcliffe Ice Wagon* ice research aircraft

Consolidated retained 90022 and 90025 for testing

Patuxent River Testing: 90027

Useful Load as Cargo Transport

Total Useful Load	35,642lb

Useful Load as Personnel Transport

Total Useful Load	25,641lb

Crew members had access to any part of the fuselage interior during flight and access to the aircraft from the outside by:

1) The nose cargo door
2) The nose wheel doors
3) The forward (normal) entrance door on the starboard side of the main cargo compartment
4) The double cargo doors at the rear of the main cargo compartment, on the port side

RY-3 as a Passenger Carrier

When used as a passenger carrier, 16 readily removable single and six double-type passenger seats were installed in the main cargo compartment with suitable safety belts provided. The RY-3 could accommodate 26 medial litters: four tiers of four, two tiers of three (under the wing), and one tier of four (across from the port cargo door). A 24-volt electric hot plate, galley equipment, wash basin, and 5-gallon water tank were located near the aft bulkhead of the main cargo compartment. The life raft location and configuration were similar to that of the passenger-carrying C-87.

Passenger Transport Useful Load

Crew of Four	680lb
Fuel (2,645 gallons)	15,870lb
Oil	1,343lb
Passengers (@28 maximum)	4,760lb
Baggage	1,120lb
Seats	650lb
Equipment	1,218lb
Total Load	25,641lb

Looking aft: the RY-3 could seat 28 (left: 12 in a double row, then followed by four single seats and 12 in a single row on the right). Note the overhead partition enclosing the wing. (*CAC*)

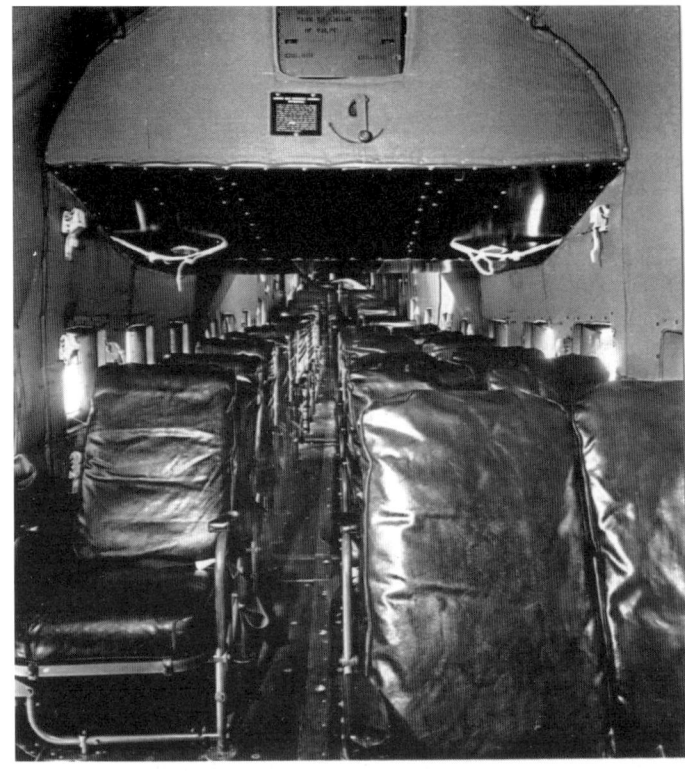

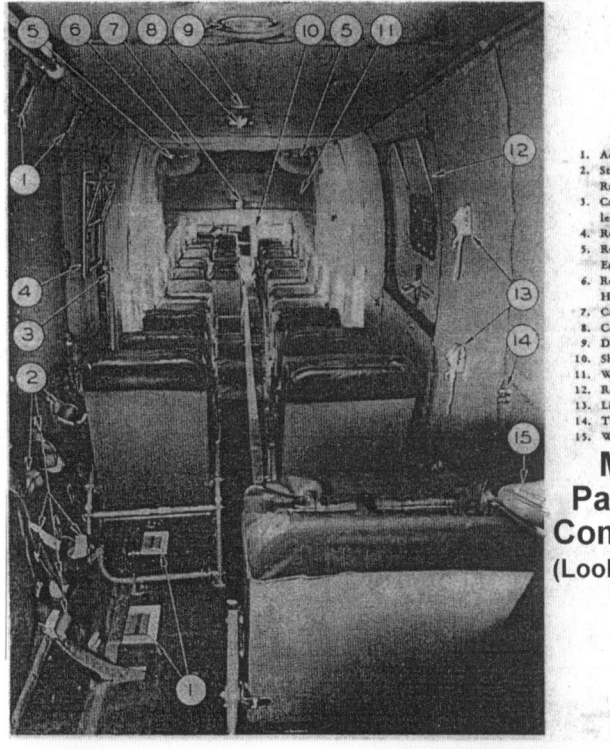

1. Access to Cargo Door Lock
2. Stowage Straps for E-2 Life Rafts
3. Cargo Door Emergency Release Lever
4. Rear Step Ladder Stowage
5. Rear Life Raft Cradles and Escape Hatches
6. Rear Life Raft Release Handle
7. Cabin Heat Thermostat
8. Cabin Ventilator
9. Dome Lights
10. Ship's Alarm Bell
11. Wing Center Section
12. Rear Escape Panel
13. Litter Support Straps
14. Troop Oxygen Outlets
15. Wash Basin

Main Passenger Compartment
(Looking Forward)

The RY-3 could accommodate 26 litters: four tiers of four, two tiers of three (under the wing), and one tier of four (across from the port cargo door). (*CAC*)

RY-3 as a Cargo Carrier

Tie-down fittings were set flush with the cargo deck, spaced conveniently for securing cargo to the deck. Evans Skyloader kits were provided according to need for securing various types of cargoes. The main cargo compartment deck was divided into four compartments by yellow lines painted at intervals along the wainscoting on both sides of the fuselage. The maximum load capacities of the areas between the yellow lines were stenciled on the wainscoting on both sides of the fuselage. Capacities of the compartments were as follows:

Compartment D: Extending from the rear bulkhead of the flight deck to a line even with the wing front spar: 4,840lb.

Compartment E: Extending from under the wing front spar to a line even with the wing trailing edge: 5,000lb.

Compartment F: Extending from under the wing trailing edge aft approximately 8ft: 3,950lb.

Compartment G: Extending from the rear boundary of compartment F aft 14.5ft: 2,000lb.

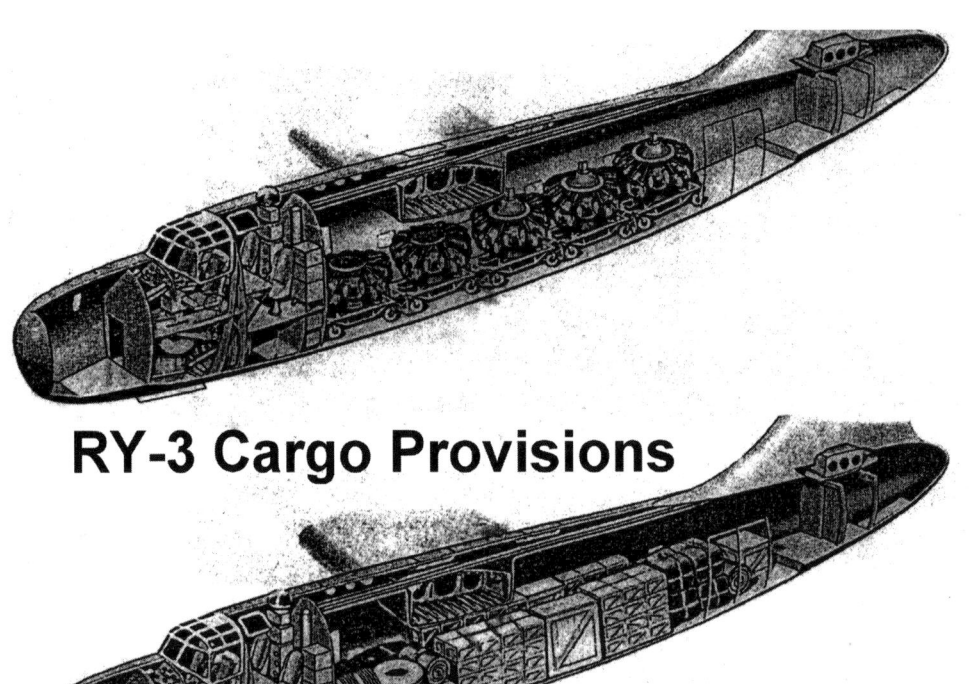

RY-3 Cargo Provisions

RY-3

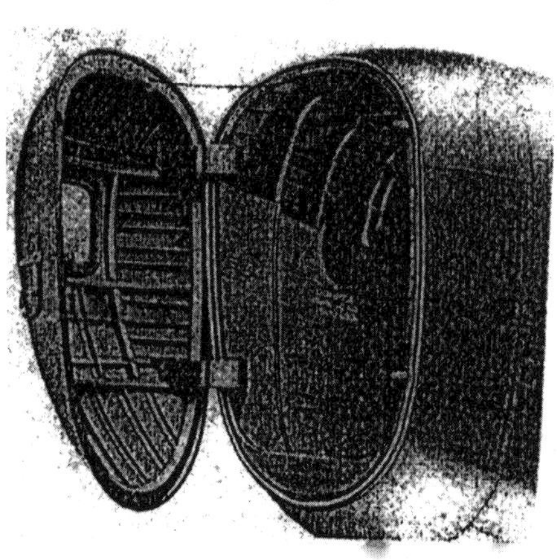

Nose Compartment

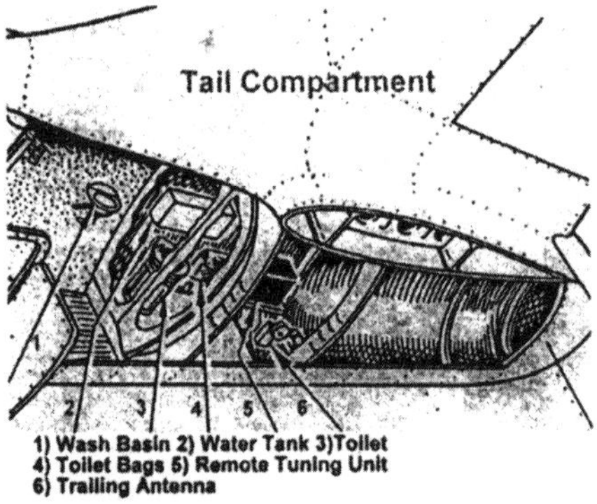

Tail Compartment

1) Wash Basin 2) Water Tank 3)Toilet
4) Toilet Bags 5) Remote Tuning Unit
6) Trailing Antenna

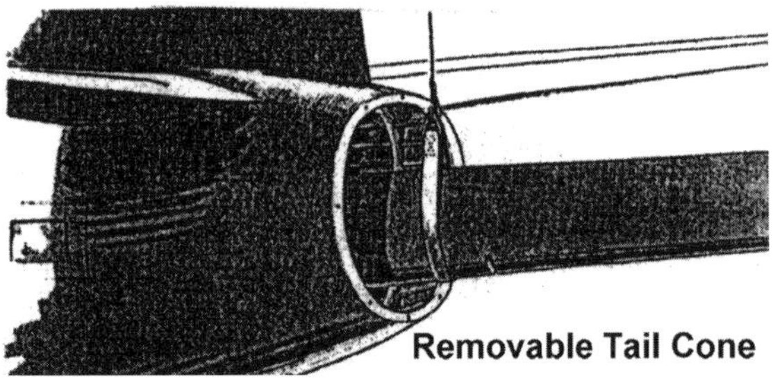

Removable Tail Cone

Cargo Transport Useful Load

Crew of Four	680lb
Fuel (2,645 gallons)	15,870lb
Oil	1,343lb
Cargo	7,239lb*
Equipment	509lb
Total Load	25,641lb

* The main cargo compartment was able to transport five R-1830 aircraft engines, with two of the engines with their nose sections removed, loaded under the wing center section.

RY-3/C-87C/C.IX/Consolidated Model 101 in Service

By late 1943 the US Navy and Marine Corps found themselves in desperate need of transport aircraft and had been relying on the passenger-carrying PB4Y-1 Privateers and PB2Y Coronado Flying Boat conversions for long-range transports. While the AAF could rely on its C-87 Liberator transport conversion until the Douglas C-54 Skymaster came into more widespread use, the USN and USMC looked to Consolidated's proposed cargo/passenger transport version (not conversion) of the PB4Y Privateer using as many parts and components of the PB4Y-1 and -2 as possible for timely delivery into service.

After extended discussions and negotiations during the fall of 1943, Consolidated tendered an official proposal to the Bureau of Aeronautics on 22 November 1943 for the C-87C (Consolidated Model 101). Consolidated's cancellation of San Diego-built PB2Y Coronado production and the transfer of San Diego PBY Catalina production to New Orleans freed production area and capacity at its San Diego plant. The change of B-24/PB4Y-1 production to B-32 Dominator production at Fort Worth allowed San Diego to build 100 PB4Y-2s per month, which was 25 more per month than required by the Navy and left 25 Privateer transport versions to be built as C-87C transports. This transport was able to carry 3,500lb more cargo than the C-87 (B-24 conversion) because of the C-87C's lesser weight due to the weight savings from using non-turbo-supercharged engines, integral fuel tanks (not individual fuel cells), and a single tail.

On 14 March 1944 Consolidated was granted contract NOa(s)-3236 for 125 company-designated Model 101 C-87Cs plus 18 per cent spare parts at $165,000 each, with the first aircraft scheduled to be delivered in June 1944 and the last during March 1945. However, shortly thereafter the Bureau of Aeronautics reduced the number of aircraft from 125 to 112 with only 15 per cent spare parts to be delivered; the contract was valued at $19,964,000, with the delivery rate set at an average of 8 aircraft per month.

Soon after the contract was approved, the Navy's Aviation Planning Division Director received a memorandum requesting the change of the C-87C's model designation to RY-3, the reason being that it was considered that there was sufficient difference between the C-87C and the new aircraft to merit the designation change. The same memorandum requested that Consolidated's Model 39, which utilized the same wing and engine group as the PB4Y-2/RY-3 but was 15ft longer, be redesignated as the R2Y-1 (the Liberator Liner) and both model designations were changed, and the cargo/passenger version of the Privateer officially became the RY-3.

The B-24/PB4Y-1 was already a proven design, so the subsequent PB4Y-2 was considered a simplified modification and its cargo version, on paper, should have been an easy conversion as supposed by Consolidated engineers to only be the removal of armament and adding seats. Even in 1944, when the RY-3 transport was contracted, only a basic set of master drawings for the B-24 still existed. This same set of master drawings, less the armament installations and certain structural parts, plus a few new drawings and engineering change notices, had comprised the only and incomplete drawings for the C-87. These same basic B-24 drawings, less specific armament, power plant, and structural items, plus new drawings, and engineering orders, had also constituted the drawings for the Navy's PB4Y-2 Privateer patrol bomber. The combination of these two sets of drawings, plus additional deletions of certain drawings relating to structures and equipment, plus additional drawings and engineering changes, would later become the working drawings for the RY-3.

Consolidated engineers modified the PB4Y-2 fuselage to carry a crew of four and 28 passengers or 26 litters. A large cargo-loading door was cut into the left rear fuselage and a hinged nose was installed to permit access to a cargo compartment in the very forward fuselage that could carry 1,600lb of freight. The main passenger and cargo compartment was located behind the flight deck, which also carried the life raft equipment stowage and a compact toilet. A special heating system for warming the cabin was installed using engine exhaust gases to heat air, which was then distributed by ducts throughout the fuselage. The aircraft was unarmed, and fairings were installed where the nose and tail turrets had been removed. A row of nine, almost square, windows were placed on both sides of the fuselage, under the wing, two forward of the wing leading edge and others extending to the loading door. In an all-freight configuration, the RY-3 had a 25,615lb cargo capacity.

While intended to be a US Navy transport, most RY-3s were to fly for the Royal Air Force as the Liberator C.IX. All the RY-3s were scheduled to be delivered in camouflage paint, however, in late spring 1944, the Navy chose to have the RY-3s delivered in natural metal finish (NMF) and with only national insignia. When the first two aircraft were painted and delivered to the RAF in NMF on 27 July 1944, the RAF objected to the finish and requested that all future RAF-allocated RY-3s be delivered in Army and Navy Standard Colors Nos 603, 609, and 613. On 11 September 1944, after further deliberation, the RAF decided to have its RY-3s delivered as NMF aircraft, with a camouflage scheme or not then contingent upon each aircraft's intended role and if it was to be flown in forward areas.

RAF RY-3/Liberator C.IXs were flown on the Return Ferry Service across the Atlantic between Dorval, Ontario, Canada, and the UK and with the South East Asia Command (SEAC) from Ceylon (Sri Lanka) to Australia; flights that could cover distances as great as 3,300 miles. RAF aircraft destined for SEAC had the word 'SNAKE' applied after their serial number during ferrying to prevent them being appropriated by other commands along the route. To fly these long distances, mostly over water, the RAF requested that Consolidated incorporate changes to the C.IX. Among these changes were the installation of AN/APN-4 Loran navigation equipment in addition to the SCS-51 blind landing system consisting of the RC-103 Localizer receiver and AN/ARN-5 Glide Path Indicator, outer wing tip tanks for greater range, fuel flow meters, and a retroactive engine synchroscopes installation (to phase unsynched the engines, which could be unbearably noisy in the cockpit in an otherwise excessively noisy aircraft). The RAD also requested the supply of retrofit windshield wipers kits and galley equipment. The RAF also found the interior of the Liberator C.IX to be excessively loud and asked the Bureau of Aeronautics to investigate the problem.

Once the RY-3 was completed and delivered it experienced structural design and manufacturing quality control problems that would plague it throughout its career. These troubles were attributed to poor workmanship, oversight, and inspection deficiencies at the Consolidated San Diego Factory. On 14 April 1945, the BuAer Consolidated representative reported that he had discovered missing parts and rivets in many sections on various RY-3s that required all delivered aircraft, nine to the RAF and six to the US Navy, to be returned to the factory for inspection and necessary repairs.

The RY-3's problems became so critical that the BuAer's representative stated, 'Current RY-3 situation is the cumulative result of hurried initial engineering, confusing drawings, inadequate tooling, inexperienced and careless production workers, insufficient and incompetent supervision, and a lack of inspection quantity and quality.'

However, it must be acknowledged the Consolidated did attempt to remedy the situation, and it was determined that most of the aircraft's aerodynamic problems were related as the aircraft's tail buffeting and the ensuing stall characteristics were linked to the ice accumulation and de-icing system. These were corrected by replacing, reducting, and adding scoops to the de-icing system.

During static tests, the RY-3 fuselage failed at 130 per cent of the design load in a high angle of attack (i.e., nose-up attitude in relation to the direction of flight) horizontal tail load pull-up condition. The fuselage failed between Stations 7.4 and 7.7, with secondary bending where the upper longeron of the rear cargo door joined Bulkhead Station 7.1. These tests determined that the doorframe and sections aft to be the weakest fuselage section.

In service, the belt frame at Station 6.1 was found to be susceptible to failure and a structural reinforcing kit was issued and installed to reinforce this area and also in the areas around Stations 4.2 and 5.1. The RY-3's major structural concern was failure of the elevator assembly as in less than six months in service, five RAF C.IXs (JT987, 988, 990, 991, and 992) had been inspected and discovered to have cracked ribs adjacent to the trim tab torque tube, along with a serious fracture at the forward end of the trim tab fairing. These cracks were due to the two ribs that supported the trim tab not having been strengthened, which caused distortion in the elevator hinge bracket attaching bolts, which then sheared off causing a loss of control.

Although the elevator inspection then became part of the pre-flight inspection, RAF Transport Command's 45 Group, 231 Squadron Liberator C.IX (JT982) was lost over the Atlantic on 4 July 1945. The aircraft was returning to the UK carrying six crew and nine VIPs from San Francisco and the United Nations Charter signing. Since JT982 was lost without a distress signal, 45 Group's Commanding Officer reported: 'Cause of accident obscure and lack of distress signals suggests sudden structural failure. Consider that the standard of workmanship and the inspection of all RY-3s supplied to the RAF are highly unsatisfactory and recommend that they all undergo a 100 per cent inspection at CVAC San Diego before being allowed to operate again.'

In November 1945, the Navy terminated the RY-3 contract after Consolidated had received $17 million for the construction completed to date. This included BuNos 90045, 90047, 90049 (to be assigned JV937), 90050 (to be assigned JV938), 90057, 90058, and 90059, which were in various stages of final assembly, either nearly completed or on the ramp having the final small parts installed. The Navy requested that these aircraft be completed only so that they could be flown from the San Diego Factory across San Diego Bay to NAS North Island; after which the Navy would decide to send them for Fleet duty or dispose of them. The RAF did not accept BuNos 90049 and 90050 and their RAF serials, JV937 and JV938, were not taken up (NTU) and both were flown to the storage pool at NAS Clinton, Oklahoma, to become part of the more than 8,000 Navy aircraft scrapped there. The War Assets Administration offered seven RY-3s as part of a sealed bid sale on 12 May 1947 assigned Lot Number 2 as part of a sale that included 23 Martin JM-1s, nine Vought OS2U-3s, one Convair RY-1, one Curtiss SOC-1, two Naval Aircraft Factory SON-1 s, and three Douglas SBD-6s; all to be scrapped.

The last Navy RY-3 was retired in 1948. Marine Corps transport units operated a few RY-3s post-war, but these quietly disappeared and were probably scrapped. The remaining Liberator C.IXs had been flying the RAF's Return Ferry Service between Canada and the UK and were flown back to Canada at the end of the war as a stipulation of the Lend-Lease agreement. There are reports that at least 11 were returned to Canadair's factory at Cartierville, outside Montreal, where all were scrapped and any low-time engines being used on post-war DC-3 conversions. One Liberator C.IX fuselage ignominiously became a walk-up 'milk bar' near Montreal. The last operating RY-3/Liberator C.IX was JT973 (90021), *Rockcliffe Ice Wagon*, which was used by Canada's National Research Council to study electro-thermal propeller de-icing and wing de-icing. Like many of the unpopular C.IXs, the Ice Wagon had spare parts and mechanical issues. It flew until January 1949, when it was replaced and scrapped on 16 November 1949.

Serials of Consolidated-Vultee RY-3 Privateer

90020/90050	Consolidated-Vultee RY-3 Privateer
90021/90047	To RAF as JT973/JT999
90048	To RAF as JV936
90049/90050	To RAF as JV937/JV938 but not delivered
90051/90056	Cancelled contract for RY-3 Privateer
	Were to have gone to RAF as JV939/JV944
90057/90059	Consolidated-Vultee RY-3 Privateer
	Were to have gone to RAF as JV945/JV947 but delivered To Navy
90060/90131	Cancelled contract for RY-3 Privateer
90060/90111	Were to have gone to RAF as JV948/JV999
90132/90384	Cancelled contract for R2Y-1

RY-3 Users

The USN originally specified all RY-3s be in camouflage but after two were delivered (seen here) all subsequent aircraft were to be delivered in natural metal finish. (*USN*)

US Navy RY-3. (*USN*)

US Marine Corps RY-3. (*USMC*)

US Coast Guard RY-3. (*USCG*)

RAF RY-3. (*RAF*)

RCAF: *Rockcliffe Ice Wagon* ice research aircraft. (*RCAF*)

R2Y-1: Liberator Liner

In early 1943, as a private venture anticipating a future post-war market for a large transport aircraft to be used by both civil and military (the Navy) operators, and building upon the C-87 Liberator Express, Consolidated had built a cargo/transport version of the Privateer known as the RY-3 (BuNos 90020–90059). However, the RY-3's fuselage cross section was thought to be too narrow for post-war airline service, so the company developed and prototyped its Model 39 Liberator Liner to meet an expected post-war demand for a large cargo/passenger aircraft.

In order to reduce the compromises always involved in converting bombers to cargo aircraft and to flip the bomber into a cargo aircraft in a short time, Consolidated made it a hybrid by grafting existing parts onto an entirely new bigger fuselage. Essentially the Liberator Liner was a stock PB4Y-2 using the Privateer's wings, newly developed R-1830-94 engines, single vertical tail, and landing gear, which was then mated to the new 89ft 9in-long fuselage, 10ft 6in in diameter, circular cross section and cigar-shaped fuselage that had a large cargo door incorporated into the port waist area and a built-in cargo handling system. The fuselage was fabricated in the Fort Worth factory when it changed from building B-24s to B-32 Dominators in late 1944 and then shipped to San Diego for the addition of its Privateer elements.

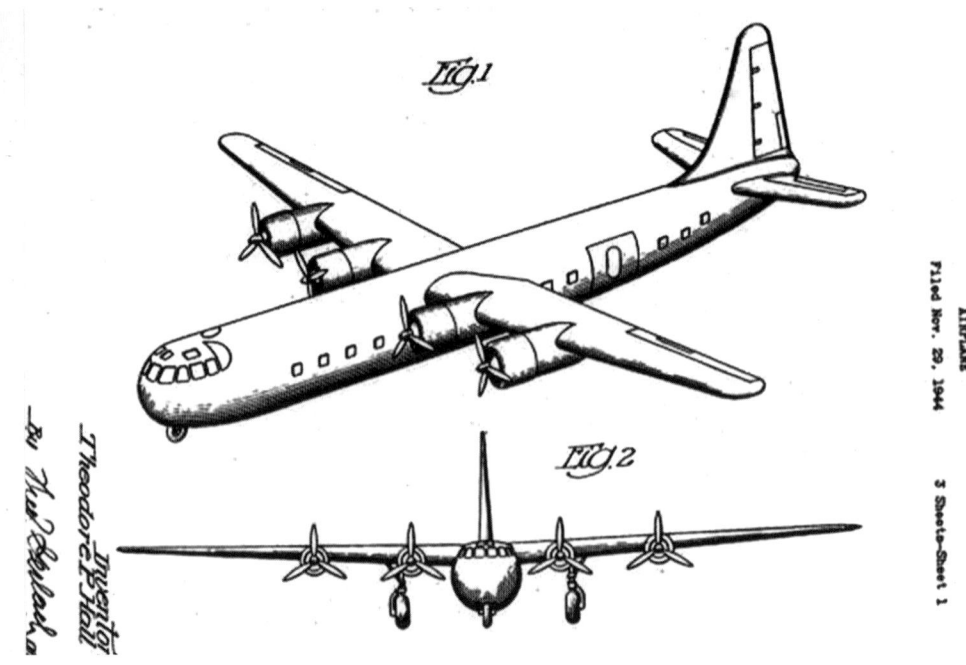

R2Y-1 wind tunnel model.

R2Y-1 Specifications
Crew: 3 normal
Length: 90ft (27.45m)
Height: 30ft (9.14m)
Wingspan: 110ft (33.55m)
Wing area: 1,048 sq ft (97.36 sq m)
Airfoil: Davis (22 per cent at root to 9.3 per cent at wingtip)
Gross weight: 56,000lb (25,000kg)
Maximum take-off weight: 64,000lb (29,000kg)
Normal take-off weight: 55,027lb (24,960kg)
Powerplant: Four Pratt & Whitney R-1830-94 radial engines, 1,350hp each

Performance
Cruise speed: 240mph (380km/h)
Maximum speed: 282mph (454km/h)
Ceiling: 26,000ft (7,925km)
Range: 4,000 miles (6,400km) at 200mph (322km/h)
Payload: 48 passengers and their baggage
12,000lb (5,500kg) of cargo (after refit) including 1,200lb (550kg) of mail

The Navy, wanting to acquire a large transport aircraft of its own on a short timetable, was attracted by the large Consolidated Liberator Liner, which could accommodate 48 passengers or 18,500lb of cargo. On 20 March 1944, as the Model 39 was reaching completion, the Navy issued a Letter of Intent to Consolidated for 253 of the aircraft, which were to be designated as R2Y-1s with BuNos 90132/90384 assigned. Simultaneously to the Navy's Letter of Intent, Consolidated approached the Canadian Aircraft Production Branch of the Department of Munitions and Supply concerning building commercial Model 39s under license. At the time, the Canadians were being courted by Douglas to build its DC-4 and later, after the Navy cancelled its Consolidated R2Y-1 order, the Canadians built their own DC-4 spin-off, the post-war, Rolls-Royce Merlin-powered, Canadair DC-4M North Star.

Under Navy Contract No. 3237 the first prototype, NX30039 (c/n 1), was to be delivered for flight testing during August 1944, with two more to follow in September. The total contract was to be completed upon delivery of 50 aircraft each during May and June 1945. The private venture Model 39 (NX3939) was not a part of this Navy contract, nor did the contract order any prototype.

R2Y-1 Second Prototype NX3939 (c/n 2)

Consolidated soon completed the R2Y-1 second mock-up for USN inspection during 10–12 April 1944, which resulted in the Navy's rejection of the transport based on these main evaluations:

1) The wing structure carried through and encroached into the cargo compartment.
2) The R2Y-1's landing weight and gross weight would be limited and unsatisfactory with its lighter bomber landing gear remaining in use.
3) The use of a wing and landing gear originally designed for an aircraft of lower gross weight potentially limited the future development of the aircraft by the usual method of installing more powerful but heavier engines.
4) The estimated length of the take-off run for a fully loaded aircraft was too long and thus limited the aircraft's military value.
5) The wing loading was too high.
6) Lack of overall potential for future modifications.

These objections led to the Navy's termination of the Liberator Liner Letter of Intent in favor of pursuing the Douglas C-54/R5D and other transport aircraft then in service. Consolidated offered to purchase the second prototype from the USN in its uncompleted condition for $120,400 and pay an additional $93,000 for the two sets of Government Furnished Equipment (GFE) installed in this aircraft and in the first prototype, NX30039. The assigned Navy BuNos were cancelled and part of the serials, 90132/90271 were then reassigned to new PB4Y-ls. The second aircraft was registered as NX3939 and Consolidated changed its Model 39 designation to Consolidated Model 104, re-engined it with standard P&W R-1830-65s (from -94) and reserved it for flight testing. Consolidated constructed a full-scale fuselage mock-up for its potential airline customers to better envision the aircraft in its passenger configuration. The aircraft itself was outfitted in its 48-passenger configuration, which was much less luxurious than the mock-up. All work was ordered to be stopped on 6 July 1944.

R2Y-1 NX3939 Second Prototype

The R2Y-1's rather spacious flight deck with pilot's instruments and controls. (*CAC*)

View forward showing wing traversing through cargo compartment. (*CAC*)

The main gear was like that of the C-87s and C-109s. (*CAC*)

The second prototype NX3939 in Navy configuration as Consolidated requested permission from the USN to fly the aircraft in military colors and markings. (*CAC*)

NX3939 probably at San Diego with an array of Consolidated aircraft surrounding it, namely British RY-3s and the tail of a standard B-24. (*CAC*)

NX3939 in a very aesthetic inflight view with its four 1,200hp Pratt & Whitney R-1830-94 radial engines giving it a cruising speed of 240mph over 4,000 miles at 200mph. (*CAC*)

R2Y-1 Liberator Liner

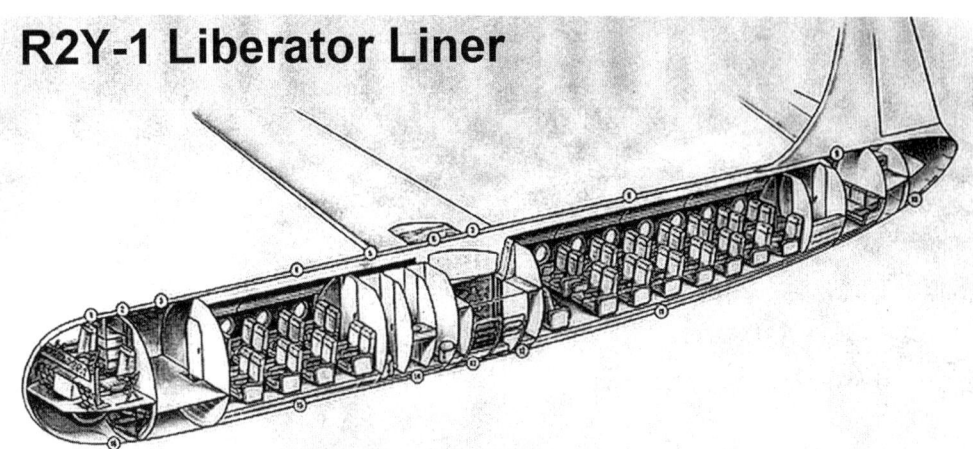

1) Pilot & Co-pilot
2) Radio
3) Cargo Compartment
4) 16 Seats
5) Galley

6) Fuel
7) Baggage
8) 32 Seats
9) Ladies Lounge
10) Tail Cargo Compartment

11) Aft Baggage
12) Clothes Closet
13) Entrance Doors
14) Men's Lavatory
15) Fwd. Baggage
16) Nose Wheel

Consolidated constructed a luxurious full-scale fuselage mock-up for its potential airline customers to better envision the aircraft in its passenger configuration. (*CAC*)

Mock-up looking toward aft from just forward of the wing junction. (*CAC*)

Not so luxurious actual seating for 48 passengers (looking aft from near the unpadded wing junction faring on early NX3939). (*CAC*)

Looking forward on a later interior of NX3939 with a padded and upgraded wing junction fairing. (*CAC*)

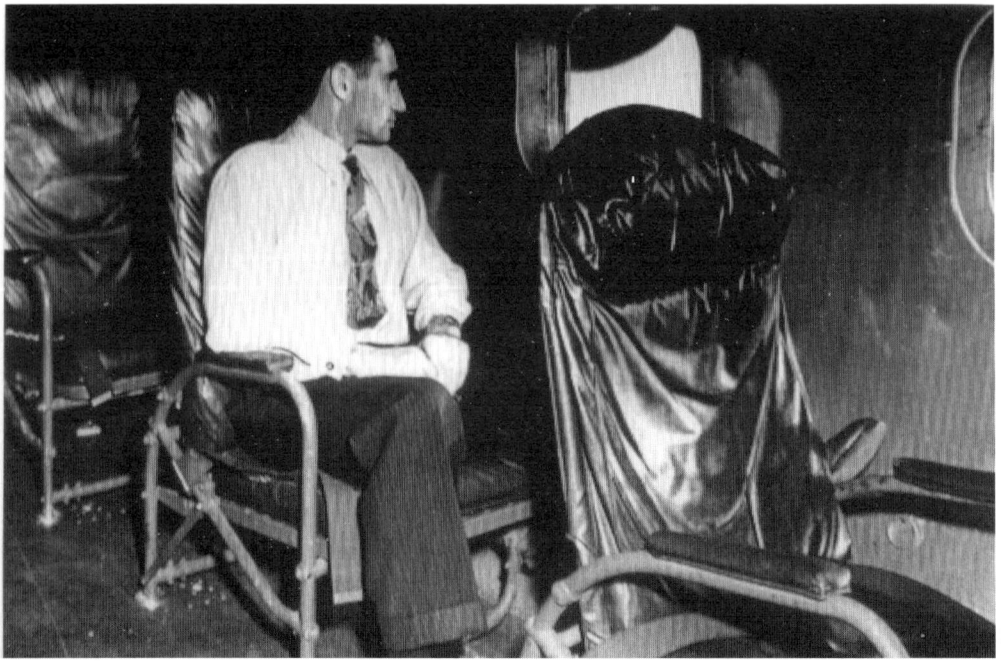

Basic removable seating for cargo carriage. (*CAC*)

Pilot's rest area behind flight deck (note the ashtray on the wall under the window). (*CAC*)

R2Y-1 First Prototype NX30039 (c/n 1)

Consolidated continued work on the first Model 39, NX30039 (c/n 1), at its own expense and as it neared completion during April 1944, the company requested that the USN assign a serial number so it could be flown prior to obtaining civil CAA certification. Consolidated also requested permission to fly the aircraft in military colors and markings so that 'test flights will not be hampered (i.e., "shot at") in coastal defense areas'. The USN pondered this request and for administrative purposes the R2Y/Model 39, was assigned Navy Bureau number 09803. On 13 April 1944 it was completed as the Consolidated XR2Y-1, initially equipped with R-1830-65 engines. Thus, the Navy had the XR2Y-1 registered and serialed even though it did not contract, did not buy, or intend to own the transport. The XR2Y-1, powered by R-1830-94 engines on loan from Pratt & Whitney, made it first flight on 29 September 1944, piloted by veteran Consolidated test pilot Philip Prophett.

Prophett had tested late model B-24 bombers, and later would have a distinguished career with Consolidated testing the CV-340 and CV-880 airliners, the giant XC-99 transport, and the B-36 and the XB-46 jet bombers. In 1954 he was named Convair's Chief of F-102/F-106 interceptor flight test at Edwards, and by 1961 he was Chief of Engineering Flight Test with over 7,000 hours of flight time. Prophett was assigned to the Atlas ICBM program in 1961 to assume the troubled base activation program. He left the Atlas program in 1966, becoming Convair's Director of International Sales, and retired in 1977.

Meanwhile, the first XR2Y-1 (NX30039), sporting a lightning bolt cheatline and the name Liberator Liner applied to its sides, was used as the sales demonstration aircraft with representatives from Transcontinental & Western Airlines (T&WA), United Air Lines, and Pennsylvania Central Airlines all testing the Model 39. As an airliner the Liberator Liner would have carried 48 seated passengers or 24 in sleeping berths and their baggage. The payload was to be 12,000lb of cargo (including 1,200lb of mail) loaded directly from flat trucks into the aircraft through large fuselage doors. Its loaded weight was 56,000lb with a maximum take-off

Philip Prophett tested the R2Y-1, after which he continued a distinguished career with Consolidated as a test pilot and a project manager. (*CAC*)

weight of 64,000lb. Its four 1,200hp Pratt & Whitney R-1830-94 radial engines gave it a cruising speed of 240mph and a range of over 4,000 miles at 200mph. The aircraft's cargo-carrying advantage was its low cargo floor that was designed to be the same height as a commercial truck bed, which eliminated the need for the expensive ground handling equipment used by the Douglas DC-4 and Lockheed Constellation. As part of its sales pitch, Consolidated engaged pioneer industrial designer Henry Dreyfuss to construct a luxurious full-scale fuselage mock-up to enable its potential airline customers to better envision the aircraft in its passenger configuration. Dreyfuss is known for designing some of the most iconic devices found in American homes and offices and had long-term relationships with AT&T, John Deere, Honeywell, Polaroid, and American Airlines.

R2Y-1 NX30039 First Prototype

First prototype Model 39, Consolidated NX30039, was a private venture to be used as the sales demonstration aircraft to be shown and flown by airline representatives. (*CAC*)

The NX30039 had the name 'Liberator Liner' added to the rear fuselage and carried the US Stars & Bars and company lightning bolt cheatline on its fuselage and the Navy serial 09803 on its tail. (*CAC*)

During June 1945, Consolidated and American Airlines began a 90-day demonstration trial, having the NX30039 hauling produce from California's Salinas Valley to cities on the east coast. This trial was intended to establish the aircraft's economic ability to carry freight while developing many post-war operating procedures. American Airlines named the aircraft *City of Salinas*, maintaining its practice of naming aircraft after destinations. Because it was experimental, NX30039 was flown by Consolidated flight crews but the NMF aircraft was flown with American Airlines logos. The aircraft carried the words 'American Flagship' on its rear fuselage and NX30039/Air Express/Air Freight on its tail. The nose had *City of Salinas* inscribed under the cockpit window, while the fuselage area behind the cockpit had two circular logos: a large American Airlines above a smaller Consolidated logo. A red cleat line flowed across the mid-fuselage from front to rear, while the nose, front engine cowlings, and rudder were also red.

The first of its 35 cross-country flights took place on 4–5 July 1945, when the City of Salinas transported 18,500lb of fresh fruit from Salinas to Cleveland. After a 13-hour overnight flight, the cargo was unloaded and delivered to the Fisher Brothers' grocery store chain in the Cleveland area. Further flights were made from El Centro and Salinas, California, to St Louis, Chicago, Detroit, and Cincinnati, flying two to three times per week.

After their flight tests, American Airlines also decided against its purchase as it reported that the two inboard engines were mounted too close to the fuselage, causing a 'disturbing rumble' inside the cabin as propeller airflow hammered against the fuselage.

The Liberator Liner failed to attract the interest of any post-war airline because it could not compete with the proven Douglas DC-6 and Lockheed Constellation in performance and reliability and was faced by an aviation market divided into customers who bought or leased surplus new and almost new C-46s/R5C, C-47s/R4Ds, and C-54/R5Ds at bargain prices or who wanted completely new, advanced commercial designs.

Fates of the XR2Y-1s

During September 1945, the company ordered the scrapping of both the first XR2Y-1 (NX30039/c/n 1) and second prototype XR2Y-1 (NX3939/c/n 2); ending any hope of Consolidated keeping its post-war production lines open manufacturing the Liberator Liner. NX3939 made its final flight on 15 September 1945 but NX30039 was reprieved and was assigned to the Consolidated Flight Research Department, where it briefly participated in tests with full-span flaps and made its last flight on 20 September. Both R2Y-1s were subsequently scrapped by Convair and sections of their fuselages were used to test sound insulation and propeller distances for the company's Model 110, which would serve as the prototype for the successful post-war Convair 240/340/440 line of medium-range airliners.

R2Y-1 American Airlines *City of Salinas*

Beginning in June 1945, Consolidated and American Airlines (AAL) tested the NX30039 with much hoopla and with attractive AAL new markings, beginning a 90-day demonstration trial hauling produce from California's Salinas Valley to cities on the east coast. (*AAL/CAC*)

AAL NX30039 port view with 'American Flagship' on its rear fuselage and the NX30039/Air Express/ Air Freight on its tail. The nose had *City of Salinas* inscribed under the cockpit window, while the fuselage area behind the cockpit had two circular logos, a large American Airlines above a smaller Consolidated logo, and a red cleat line flowed across the mid-fuselage from front to rear. (*AAL/CAC*)

How could a Jeep not be loaded without the help of pretty women? Consolidated's PR Department utilized the classic publicity ploy of the loading of a Jeep into the cargo hold. (*AAL/CAC*)

The actual loading of the Jeep was undoubtedly much more difficult than this photo makes it out to be! (*AAL/CAC*)

The loaded Jeep probably after much undocumented maneuvering. (*AAL/CAC*)

Publicity photo showing not only delicious produce cargo and pretty women, but also the American Airlines and Consolidated logos. The *City of Salinas* carried produce from California's nearby rich agricultural area to the mid-west and east. (*AAL/CAC*)

Chapter 5

XB-24B Test Bed Becomes a VIP Transport

After its maiden flight on 29 December 1939, the XB-24 (serial 39-556) prototype was delivered to the AAC for initial testing on 19 February 1940. After these tests were completed on 9 June 1940, on 26 July 1940 it was decided that it would be retained by Consolidated because its relatively slow maximum speed of 273mph did not meet the originally estimated 311mph; the AAC recommended that some changes be made to improve its performance, especially at high altitude. The first and perhaps foremost of these changes was to give the aircraft a better high-altitude performance by the introduction of turbo-superchargers to replace the mechanical two-speed superchargers of the earlier engines. Accordingly, the XB-24 was re-engined with 1,200hp Pratt & Whitney R-1830-41 (S4C4-G) radials, which were equipped with General Electric B-2 turbo-superchargers mounted on the lower surface of each engine nacelle. The oil coolers were relocated to the sides of the front cowlings and the air intakes for the turbo-superchargers were placed on the sides of the engines, which gave the redesigned nacelles a characteristic elliptical cross section that remained with the Liberator all throughout its production. The engine controls were modified so that they permitted at least 60 per cent engine power even if the controls were damaged. Electrical engine primers were added. The AAC also directed that Consolidated eliminate the 'wet' wing and install self-sealing fuel tanks in the wing. The tail span was increased by 2ft.

With all these extensive changes, the XB-24 was redesignated XB-24B and on 20 January 1941 the serial number was officially changed (corrected) to 39-680 by Engineering Order #P-2392. The first flight of the XB-24B took place on 1 February 1941 and the performance was noticeably improved with the B-2 turbo-superchargers installed. The original take-off power of 1,200hp could be maintained to well above 20,000ft; resulting in an increase in maximum speed to 310mph. These turbo-superchargers would remain an aspect of all later production Liberators. Throughout 1941 the Pratt & Whitney R-1830-41 engines encountered numerous problems and on 26 January 1941 the Materiel Command approved their replacement with the more reliable 1,200hp R-1830-43.

The XB-24B continued as a test bed at the San Diego plant over the next two years for future Liberator modifications. During March 1942 the main wheels were covered with full fairings to explore the effect of this streamlining on the aircraft's speed and rate of climb. In the study the gear was left in the down position and a non-operating dummy fairing was placed over the strut and wheel openings in the wing. The fairings comprised three parts: a fairing attached to the landing gear, the fixed aft fairing, and a hydraulically operated door hinged on the wing at the outboard side of the wheel well. The test showed that there only was a 9.5mph increase in speed at 100 per cent power at 25,000ft and future tests on a working fairing were suspended due to other commitments. The next tests on a working fairing occurred between 16 April and 21 May 1943 and showed a 2.5mph decrease in speed under similar test conditions due to the difference in pressure sealing between the dummy and actual working fairings. Nonetheless, the XB-24B's top speed in level flight with its almost enclosed gear was a more than adequate 319mph.

The XB-24B continued as a test aircraft, acquiring the nickname *Old Gran' Pappy*. Part of its test program involved the installation of full-span flaps to study their possible use on the future Consolidated B-36. Later, a gloved wing, a large panel attached to the leading wing surface to increase laminar flow, was studied to decrease the Liberator's high wing loading. During these tests pressure profiles during a dive were investigated and during one of these dives a true airspeed of 465mph was attained.

In 1944 the AAF bailed the XB-24B to Consolidated (then Convair), which would convert the aircraft into an additional executive transport. The aircraft was gutted and refurbished into the *АМЕРИКА* (*AMERICA*) powered by P&W R-1830-65 engines and a luxurious interior looking out through large windows. The interior of the aircraft was quite opulent for the time, as seen in the accompanying photos taken from a Consolidated brochure. The conversion included gutting the interior, cutting new windows, and dividing the interior into compartments with individual and bench seating, and two-tier Pullman-style sleeping berths, an in-flight galley with a sink, refrigerator, two-burner range, a small oven, and hot plates. There was a lavatory located in the rear of the aircraft with a toilet and sink plus a window. The lighting and services for the main deck were controlled by a panel over the main passenger door. The aircraft was delivered to the 6th Ferry Group in April 1945, where it flew VIPs overseas from Washington National Airport until March 1946 serving with the 503rd AAFBU. On 30 April, although a luxurious VIP aircraft (unfortunately a B-24), it was ordered to Brookley AAB, Mobile, Alabama, and was scrapped on 12 May or 20 June 1946.

AAF XB-24B Liberator VIP Transport

XB-24B prototype 39-556, shown in mid-1940, did not meet AAC specifications and was re-engined and used as a test bed. (*AAC*)

Old Gran' Pappy test aircraft at the San Diego plant. (*CAC*)

In 1944 the AAF returned the XB-24B to Consolidated, which would convert it into an additional executive transport. The aircraft is seen on the left with its wings stripped for the installation of new P&W R-1830-65 engines and on the ground is the prefabricated aft fuselage floor. (*CAC*)

The aircraft interior was completely gutted and refurbished, as seen in this photo looking aft from the wing. The prefabricated floor had been installed and large windows cut. (*CAC*)

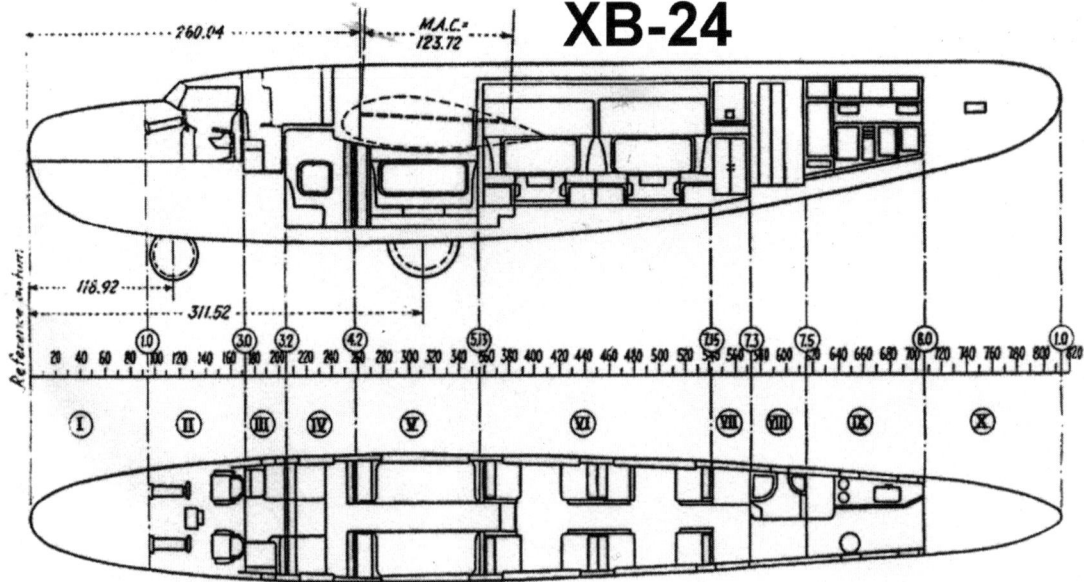

Layout drawings of the XB-24, which was redesignated XB-24B and re-serialed 39-680 after numerous changes. (*CAC*)

Starboard view with three staggered passenger windows and small forward navigator's windows. (*CAC*)

Port view with Pratt & Whitney R-1830-65 engine and a small radio operator's window forward of the large rectangular passenger windows. (*CAC*)

Close-up of what the original caption only referred to as an 'insignia', which was an eagle shield with the Russian word *АМЕРИКА*. (*CAC*)

A rather plush pilot's position for a B-24! (*CAC*)

Radio (L) and navigator's stations. (*CAC*)

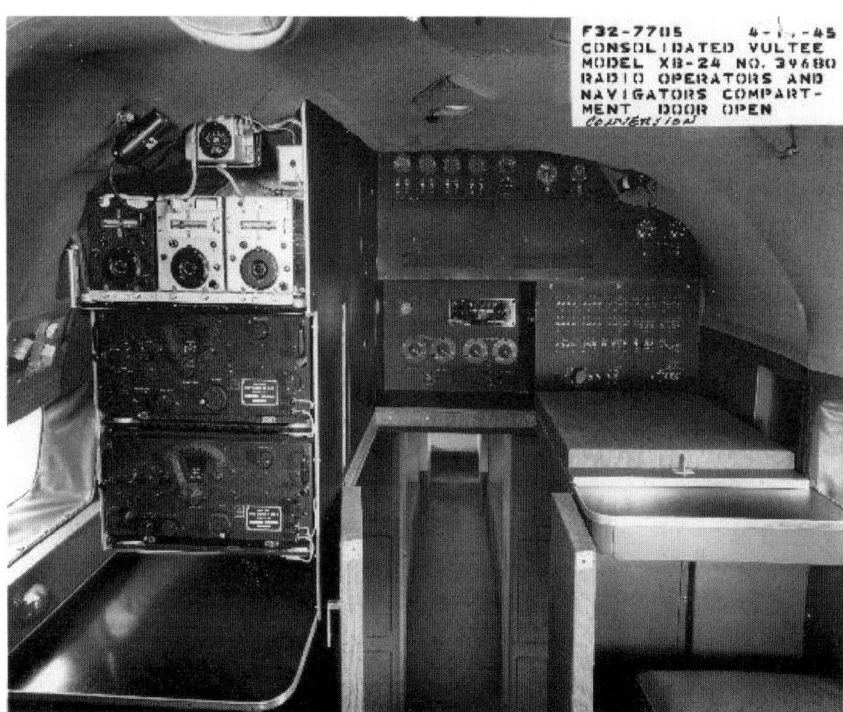

Entrance to the flight deck. (*CAC*)

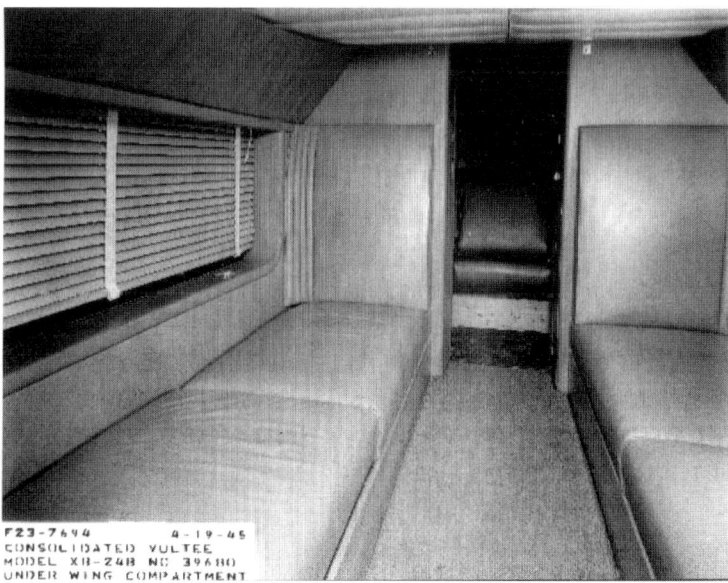

Bench seating under the wing fairing looking forward at the flight deck entrance. (*CAC*)

A passenger sitting at aft end of the bench seats looking up aft into main passenger cabin. (*CAC*)

Main passenger cabin looking forward into the bench seat area. (*CAC*)

F32-7696   4-19-45
CONSOLIDATED VULTEE
MODEL XB-24B NO 39680
PASSENGER COMPARTMENT
VIEW LOOKING FORWARD

Main passenger seating (face-to-face) looking towards the underwing bench seating and flight deck. (*CAC*)

Convertible lower berth with curtained upper berth in the main passenger cabin. (*CAC*)

F32-7709   4-19-45
CONSOLIDATED VULTEE
MODEL XB-24 NO. 39680
VIEW OF UPPER AND
LOWER BERTH

Handy drop-down desk on the bulkhead wall of the main passenger cabin (note Venetian blinds). (*CAC*)

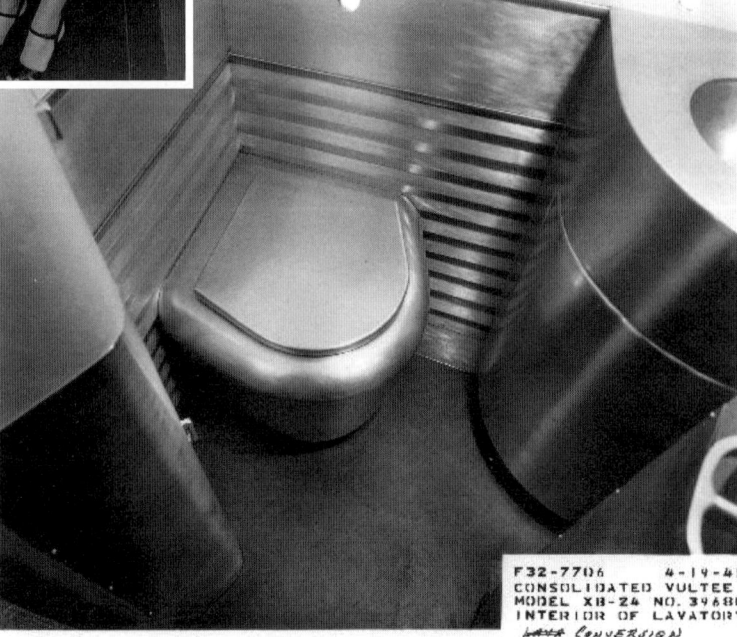

The galley equipped with a refrigerator, small oven, two-burner range, and a sink. (*CAC*)

The lavatory located in the rear of the aircraft had a toilet and sink plus a window. (*CAC*)

Chapter 6

C-87s and C-109s in Over the Hump Service

Introduction

The Japanese had been contesting China since the early 1930s and because the Japanese controlled the China Sea, supplies had to be delivered from India to the besieged country through Burma, along the 717-mile (1,154km) Burma Road, until it was captured in April 1942. With the fall of Burma, China was completely cut off except through Russia to the north, but the Soviets were besieged by the Nazis on the Eastern Front and declared themselves as a neutral nation in the Far East. Since Japanese control of the seas around the Chinese coast made seaborne supply of China impossible, to support Chiang Kai-shek's beleaguered Nationalist Chinese armies and the proposed forward air bases in China, the only viable alternative was to have an American aerial supply of fuel and supplies from India over the lofty Himalayan peaks, dubbed the 'Hump'.

So with China isolated from supply and Chiang Kai-shek clamoring for an airlift to supply 10,000 tons a month, American politicians made some rather ambitious promises that could not be delivered with the insufficient aircraft resources the US had available. The US official stated goal was 4,000 tons per month but in practice it was unable to haul more than a few hundred tons. At the time the China National Aviation Corporation (CNAC) had been successfully flying supplies since 1937 in its war against Japan and flew its first Hump flight in November 1941, after which it was headquartered in India and flew supplies from Assam into south-western China.

In his memoir *Over the Hump* (1964), Col William Tunner, Commander of the ATC's India-China Division, wrote:

It's easy to think of the Hump as just one route; actually, of course, it was many air routes, separated both laterally and vertically, from thirteen bases in India to six in China. At first, we had a narrow corridor of only fifty miles to accommodate two-way traffic. … On toward the end we had a corridor two hundred miles wide … Through this corridor, every day, were flying an average of 650 planes, one taking off every two and a quarter minutes of the day's twenty-four hours.

This was all new. No other air operation, civilian or military, had ever before even attempted to keep its fleet in continuous operation all around the clock, in all seasons, and in all weathers. No other operation had such extremes of weather and altitudes. And our cargo was varied, to say the least, from V-mail to mules to machinery. The age of air transportation was born right there on the Hump.

The Tenth Air Force was the initial combat command to be reluctantly responsible for air operations in the China–Burma–India (CBI) Theater. When the airlift was evaluated by the USAAF in October 1942, it found the attitudes of the 10AF command regarding its viability were typified as 'defeatist'. The report described the living conditions for both airlift flight crews and support personnel as 'by far the worst in the entire theater, with primitive quarters, poor sanitation, bad food and mess facilities, pervasive disease, and lack of recreation. Apathy became widespread and morale dropped to a dangerous point.'

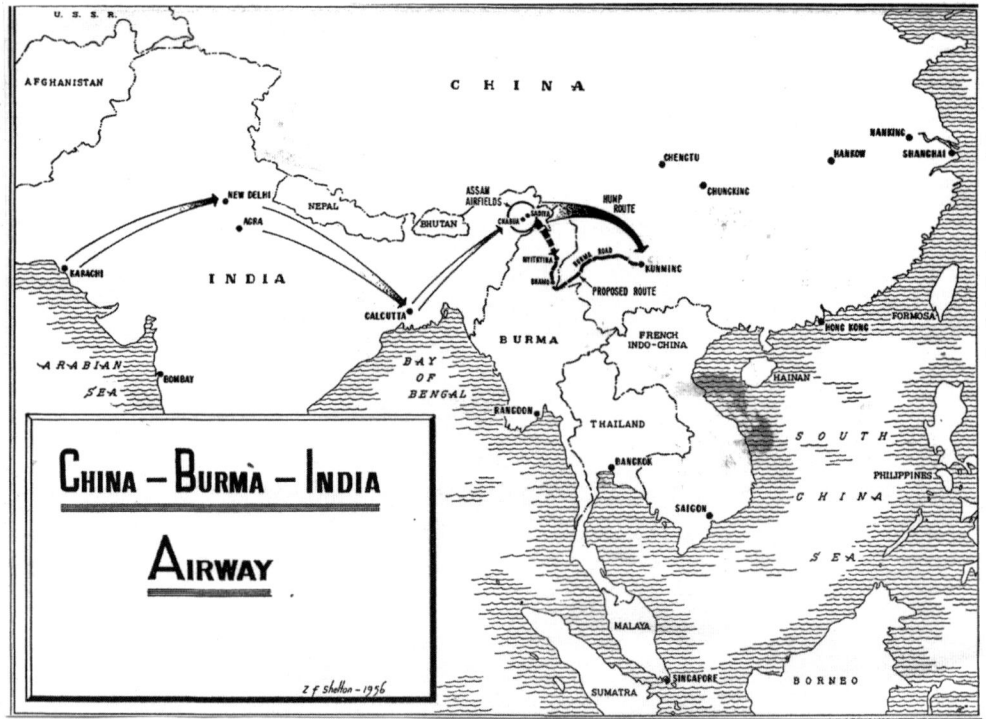

On 13 October 1942, after assessing the AAF evaluation, the India-China Wing of the Air Transport Command assumed responsibility for the operation. On 1 December 1942, the India-China Wing ATC (ICWATC), was activated and commanded by Col (later Brig. Gen.) Edward Alexander, who was air officer for Lt Gen. Joseph Stilwell, the American senior commander in the China Theater. The ATC had begun wartime service with an assortment of military and civilian aircraft and crews with the civilian resources provided on contract by US domestic airlines. During mid-1942, and for several months thereafter, the Command depended on twin-engine transports, primarily C-47s and a few converted B-24 bombers. Both the C-47 and the forthcoming Curtiss C-46 Commando were twin-engine designs, which placed them at a two-engine safety disadvantage on long flights over water or unhospitable mountain terrain. Four-engine aircraft not only offered a safety advantage but could also haul more cargo. However, there were no suitable purpose-built four-engine cargo/transport models available in late 1942, although there had been attempts to convert civilian airliners to that role.

There were only five Boeing C-75s, the militarized Model 307 Stratoliner, available. Lockheed offered the C-69 Constellation but the factory's dedication to production of the P-38 fighter restricted its delivery. Douglas's C-54, the military designation of the company's DC-4, was still under development and was not scheduled to enter service in large numbers until 1943.

The ATC India-China Wing Commander, Col Edward Alexander, complained that the C-47 Skytrains that initially equipped and were the backbone of his command were unsuitable for flying Hump operations that began in January 1943. The ATC planned to replace their C-47s with more powerful C-46 Commandos and had ordered 200 in 1940 but due to design and manufacturing problems only 2 were delivered by Pearl Harbor. However, during this time, one important change was made to the Commando as more powerful and reliable 2,000hp Pratt & Whitney R-2800 Double Wasp engines replaced the two Wright Twin Cyclones. Despite the new P&W engines, when the AAF began deliveries of the new C-46A configuration, the first 30 were sent back to the factory for 53 immediate modifications, the most important being enlarged cargo doors, a strengthened load floor, and a convertible cabin that speeded changes from carrying freight to carrying troops and vice versa. Even, by November 1943, although many were minor, 721 modifications had been made to C-46 production models, which further delayed the type's arrival.

The only available four-engine transport was the C-87 Liberator Express conversion of the versatile B-24, which began entering service in September 1942 and arrived in India in January 1943, immediately after the Air Transport Command assumed responsibility for the Hump airlift. The C-87 could transport a payload of 7,500 to 9,400lb (3,402 to 4,264kg) over a 3,250-mile (5,230km) route and its high-altitude capability enabled it to ascend over the lower mountains (16,000 to 20,000ft/4,877 to 6,096m) without resorting to flying through the hazardous mountain passes like the C-47s. Therefore, by proxy it was chosen as the four-engine transport to inaugurate the ATC's long-range Himalayan Hump transport routes from India's Assam Valley to Chungking, China. Other C-87s operated over routes from the US to Assam, flying over the southern ATC route from Miami to Natal, Brazil, then on to Africa and across Asia to India.

In early March 1943, the first 11 C-87s arrived in India to augment the ATC's 76 C-47s and at the same time the first few C-46s left the Curtiss factory for India to replace an equal number of C-47s. These were to be followed by 50 more C-87s and C-46s, which would become responsible for a large share of ATC operations until the much-anticipated four-engine Douglas C-54 Skymaster entered service in sufficient numbers. The Curtiss C-46, the largest twin-engine aircraft built to that point, would become the workhorse of the Hump airlift by fall 1943. While this was more difficult to fly than the much-loved C-47; its excellent visibility, large doors, and large cargo capacity (twice that of the C-47) compensated for its liabilities. Nonetheless, the C-46 was referred to by ATC pilots as the 'flying coffin', with at least 31 known instances of fires or explosions in flight between May 1943 and March 1945 and with many other aircraft missing and never found. When the C-87s arrived in India they were found to have several problems that much reduced their Hump airlift capability, but corrections and modifications could not be implemented due to the ATC's pressing need to keep its transport aircraft in service. The C-87 was unsuited for flying the Hump, particularly for use on the high-altitude, rough airfields then employed on the route. The higher elevations of the airfields in Assam considerably reduced its take-off performance, leading to frequent accidents. Like its bomb-carrying Liberator counterparts, despite the C-87's four engines, the aircraft climbed poorly with heavy loads, and often crashed on take-off if an engine was lost. On landing with a heavy load, the long-standing problem nose and main gear weakness caused aircraft to leave the runway. Once off the ground, with their heavy cargos these aircraft were then subjected to poor weather, strong winds, turbulence, and ice over the mountains that lay beyond their Indian bases and towards their destinations inside China. The poor cockpit illumination was inadequate for bad weather flying and especially during instrument take-offs, its electrical and hydraulic systems frequently froze at high altitude and malfunctioned, and its flight deck heating system was prone to produce either stifling heat or none at all. Despite its shortcomings, the C-87 was appreciated for the reliability of its engines, speed that enabled it to significantly reduce the effect of head and cross winds, a service ceiling that allowed it to surmount high peaks and most weather fronts, and a range that permitted its crews to seek out favorable winds and evade oncoming poor local weather.

The primary cargo was gasoline, carried in sometimes leaky 55-gallon drums and which was augmented by siphoning extra fuel from tanks of the carrying aircraft. Also carried were small arms and ammunition, artillery and mortar shells, small vehicles, heavy equipment disassembled and transported in pieces, truck and aircraft engines, bombs and aircraft ammunition, hospital equipment, critical and VIP personnel, etc. While the C-87 was essentially a B-24 that had been stripped of the elements that made it a bomber and equipped with a cargo floor, the C-109 was a dedicated fuel tanker that incorporated a system of tanks that could be filled with fuel. Both the C-87 and C-109 were designed so that ground crews could drain extra fuel from their tanks at the Chinese bases. During the last years of the war, much of the gasoline was carried by tanker aircraft and by 1945, gasoline and oil accounted for nearly 60 per cent of the tonnage flown eastward over the Hump into China.

All operations over the Hump necessitated the use of oxygen, with regulations requiring its use above 12,000ft during daytime and above 10,000ft at night. Oxygen was provided by very uncomfortable oxygen masks via a demand system that provided oxygen on inhalation. It also had a constant flow and an emergency forced flow capability.

Much of the flying over the Hump had to be flown on instruments, making for dangerous navigation over the shrouded 17,000ft plus mountain peaks along the route. Deviating off route to the north meant encountering nearby 22,000ft plus peaks, while going off route to the south placed you over Japanese-controlled Burma. Hump airlift operations were not considered very hazardous in terms of interception by enemy fighters as the Hump route was directed north away from Japanese-controlled Burma, flying north from India's Assam Valley across the lower reaches of the Himalayas, then east

The Hump airfields were primitive and poor weather conditions there would make landings and take-offs dangerous. This C-109 transport is having its fuel cargo drained after its landing gear collapsed and it departed the runway. (*AAF*)

to China. Nonetheless, unneeded fighter protection for the ATC was provided by both the 10th and 14th Air Forces. The C-87 had a hypothetical, but unattainable, loaded service ceiling of 28,000ft at 56,000lb take-off weight but carrying a heavy payload in icing conditions while on instruments could significantly reduce the ceiling and a loaded C-87 was known to fly in a nose-high attitude that exacerbated its susceptibility to icing. Because of its slim Davis Wing, it also tended to spin out of control when encountering even mild icing conditions over the mountains. Hump pilots described the C-87 as 'an evil, bastard contraption … and a ground-loving bitch (that) could not carry enough ice to chill a highball'.

The appalling weather over the Himalayan area, plus the high altitudes and poor conditions of the ATC airfields in the Assam Valley and at the destination airfields in China, caused an exceptionally high accident rate. The C-87s (and later C-109s), because of their much heavier take-off and landing weights, experienced an accident rate that was five times higher than that of C-54s and other transports in the ATC system. Being at the bottom of the supply priority list, the India-China Wing of ATC was only able to fly a meager 45 tons of the anticipated monthly 2,000 tons of freight to China during the first ten days of 1943, severely curtailing 14th Air Force operations in China. However, during that January the ATC's 76 C-47s were augmented by three Consolidated C-87 transports, which was increased to 11 in March with a projected total of 50 by the end of the summer. At the time it was determined that a C-87 transport burned three and a half tons of 100-octane gasoline flying the Hump to deliver 4 tons to the 14AF.

This necessitated that before a bombardment group could fly a single mission, a tanker had to fly the Hump four times to build up its supplies. AAF Commanding General Henry Arnold had personally observed the perils of flying the Hump in February 1943 when the *Argonaut*, the B-17 that was transporting his group following the Casablanca Conference, became lost as it approached Kunming upon crossing the Hump, although it landed safely after several anxious minutes. At Kunming, Arnold met Chiang Kai-shek, who informed him that China's cooperation with Lt Gen. Joseph Stilwell to reconquer Burma would require a 500-plane air force and delivery by the airlift of 10,000 tons of fuel and supplies a month. As deliveries had finally surpassed 2,000 tons a month, in May 1943, at the Trident Conference, President Roosevelt ordered the ATC to deliver 5,000 tons a month to China by July; 7,500 tons by August; and 10,000 tons by September 1943. With the onset of heavy monsoon rains in March 1943, the ATC was reduced to operating from the only all-weather base at Chabua but a critical shortage in flight crews prevented the ATC from even achieving its modest goal of 4,000 tons a month. This shortage of crews led Alexander to request additional personnel and *Project 7* was established by the ATC at the end of June to fly 2,000 men, 50 transports, and 120 tons of material from Florida to India. Despite this effort, July's tonnage was less than half of its goal. The airfields were nowhere near completion, nearly all the new pilots had been single-engine instructor pilots, specialized maintenance personnel and equipment were being sent by ship, and the complexities of the newly arriving C-46s had become evident. The scorching heat and torrential rains of the summer monsoon completed the undermining of the ambitious goals. The long-delayed work on existing fields resulted in an intervention by Chief of Staff Gen. George C. Marshall in which he ordered the Services of Supply to complete the work by 1 July and issued a deadline of 1 September 1943 to have three additional fields ready for operations, but airfield construction problems were not overcome for several months.

Frustration at the failure of the ICW to meet the Trident goals led Arnold to dispatch another inspection team to India in September 1943, led by ATC commander Maj. Gen. Harold George. Accompanying George was Col (later Brig. Gen.) Thomas Hardin, the assertive former Vice President of Trans World Airlines who had already served a year as head of ATC's Central African Sector. On 16 September, to revitalize India-China operations, George immediately reassigned Hardin to command the new Eastern Sector of the ICW. Alexander was replaced in command of the ICW by Brig. Gen. Earl Hoag on 15 October.

Brig. Gen. Thomas Hardin. (*AAF*)

Hardin altered operations by introducing night missions and declining to cancel scheduled flights because of adverse weather or threat of Japanese interception. Although losses to accidents and enemy action increased, and replacements for the high number of C-46s that had been lost ceased entirely for two months, the tonnage delivered rose sharply. After new C-46s loaded with much-needed C-46 spare parts began arriving in numbers, the operation finally surpassed its tonnage objective in December, with over 12,590 tons delivered to Kunming for which the unit received a Presidential Unit Citation. By the end of 1943, Hardin had 142 aircraft in operation: 93 C-46s, 24 C-87s, and 25 C-47s.

This came about as George C. Marshall and Arnold dispatched Maj. Gen. George Stratemeyer, the Chief of Air Staff, in a C-87 on a special mission to India to examine ICWATC operations and report back with recommendations. Similarly, Eddie Rickenbacker flew the Hump in a C-87 to reach China during his fact-finding mission to the Far East and the Soviet Union, and both he and Stratemeyer found ICW's performance critically inadequate. While ICW was carrying more tonnage by virtue of having nearly ten times as many aircraft as CNAC (and half of those with a larger load capacity), the Chinese carrier was far more efficient in tonnage lifted per aircraft, by a factor of 2.5 to 1. The primary cause of ATC's failure was the complete inadequacy of its airfield facilities, but other major factors were unsatisfactory performance by overwhelmed aircraft maintenance personnel that grounded a hundred ATC aircraft per day, a predominance of inexperienced pilots (particularly compared to those of CNAC), and a dearth of radio and navigation aids in ATC transports. Rickenbacker and 10AF Commanding General Clayton Bissell recommended return of the operation to theater command, but Stratemeyer disagreed, as did Maj. Gen. Howard Davidson, who was about to replace Bissell in command of 10AF and had made an inspection tour of his own in June.

Col William Tunner relieved Brig. Gen. Earl Hoag as Commander of the ATC's India-China Division, just as its size was greatly increased by the transfer of the XX Bomber Command transports to ATC. During his career Tunner was known for

Gene Autry: The famous television and movie singing cowboy was a C-109 pilot, flying missions over the Hump. Autry enlisted in the AAF in 1942 and became a tech sergeant but, holding a private pilot's license, he was determined to become a military pilot and earned his service pilot rating in June 1944, serving as a C-109 transport pilot with the rank of flight officer with the ATC. (*ATC*)

his expertise in the command of large-scale military airlift operations. Tunner expertly commanded the Hump airlift supply operation from India to China during spring 1944. He returned to the CBI to command the India-China Division (ATC) during September 1944. To increase airlift cargo tonnage and to reduce a distressingly high accident rate Tunner relied on the increasingly available four-engined C-54 Skymaster to reduce the dependence on the accident-prone cargo C-87/C-109s. Tunner also announced a second route to China called the 'Low Hump' that widened the airlift

Brig. Gen. William Tunner. (*AAF*)

corridor from 50 to 200 miles to increase efficiency. He instituted Hump maintenance and flying safety programs that reduced the accident rate to less than a quarter of what it had been when he took command, despite more than doubling the tonnage and hours flown, reaching the 12,500-ton goal in December 1943. Under Tunner's command the combination of an increased number of aircraft and shorter routes at lower altitudes from India to China understandably resulted in an increase in the amount of cargo carried in 1944 and 1945, reaching its maximum capacity in July 1945. During 1944 the China National Aviation Corporation, which had first explored routes over the Himalayas, delivered 41,000 tons of cargo to supplement the record 230,000 tons flown in by Air Transport Command.

Later, Tunner commanded the Military Air Transport Service (MATS) during the 1949–51 Berlin Airlift, in which he created a level of organization to each western Allied-controlled air corridor such that the per-day tonnage brought into Berlin by air eventually exceeded that brought in by train. Tunner's efficiency and stringent control of his subordinates, along with his unconventional solutions to problems, earned him the nickname 'Willie the Whip'. As head of the Combat Cargo Command (CCC) during the Korean War, Tunner had the initial task of providing the airlift for the Inchon invasion and subsequent airborne operations. In its four and a half months under 'Tonnage Tunner', the CCC flew 32,632 sorties; delivered 130,170 tons of cargo; carried 155,294 passengers including paratroopers; and evacuated 72,960 casualties. Tunner eventually rose to the rank of lieutenant general and commanded Air Material Command.

C-54 Arrives

In May 1944 the reduction in the threat of Japanese interception from Burma allowed ATC crews headed for China to fly a more southerly route over lower and less adverse terrain. These lower altitudes allowed the four-engine Douglas C-54 Skymaster to be integrated into the airlift. Although a proven and reliable transport with considerable payload capacity, its limited high-altitude performance had excluded it from Hump flights. The C-54 had a much better safety record than the C-87, although this was feasibly largely due to the Douglas transport being operated at lower elevations than the Consolidated aircraft. However, it was C-46s, not C-87s, that the C-54s began replacing.

C-87s and C-109s Plagued by Accidents

Even though losses to enemy air action were minimal, Hump aircraft and crews were being lost to accidents at an incredible rate. Between June and December 1943, there were 155 major accidents on the Hump route, with 168 crew fatalities. By January 1944, the AAF was losing 3 crewmen for each thousand tons of cargo reaching China, eventually costing over 1,000 lives. The route between India and China became littered with so many wrecked aircraft that it was nicknamed the 'Aluminum Trail'. However, most of the accidents actually occurred at the airfields themselves, where the combination of higher elevations and hot temperatures placed the transports at the very limits of their operational performance envelope.

Under Tunner, both the accident rate and the raw number of accidents decreased notably except for the C-87/C-109 types, which remained five times higher than for the C-54. This was no doubt due to the lack of adequate runway lengths for the altitudes involved. The AAF had established 6,000ft as the required runway length for a loaded C-87, seemingly without considering the occurrence known as 'density altitude'. Due to high temperatures, density altitude, which is the altitude that effects an aircraft's performance, was significantly higher than the actual elevation, thus considerably increasing take-off distance and significantly affecting climb performance. The loss of an engine during take-off on a hot day in high terrain was disastrous.

At least eighty C-109s were involved in major accidents between September 1944 and August 1945. Like the C-87, they were not popular with their crews since they were very difficult and dangerous to land when fully loaded with fuel, particularly at airfields such as Kunming at 6,000ft elevation that were often in poor condition. The C-109s often demonstrated unstable flight characteristics when all eight fuel cargo tanks were full. Low longitudinal stability during flight with a full fuel storage tank in the front fuselage forced the crew not to carry fuel in it, which reduced the volume of fuel transported. A crash landing of a loaded C-109 inevitably resulted in an explosion and crew fatalities.

The C-87s and C-109s Replaced

The C-87 was never entirely displaced on the air routes by the C-54 and C-46, which offered similar performance combined with greater reliability and more benign flight characteristics. Beginning in September 1944 about 70 ATC C-109s were initially planned to fly the Hump with XX Bomber Command but eventually 208 C-109 conversions served in the CBI under the ATC after B-29 *Matterhorn* operations were transferred from China back to India.

The ATC in the CBI, starting with 71 total aircraft, saw that number grow to 308 in January 1945; with the maximum aircraft strength occurring on 31 July 1945 at 640 aircraft: 230 C-46s, 167 C-47s, 132 C-54s, 67 C-87/C-109s, 33 B-25s, 10 L-5s, and 1 B-24. As late as August 1945, C-87s and C-109s still carried 15 per cent of the tonnage but with fewer accidents. This number then fell from 67 to 24 C-109s in December 1945. Tunner had asked for their replacement entirely by C-54s and plans were made to increase the Skymaster force to 272 by October 1945 and 540 by April 1946. From February 1946 on, there was but a single Liberator in the ATC inventory. With a fleet of 410 C-46s augmenting the ICW, the tonnage lift capability over the Hump was predicted to become more than 86,000 tons per month. The Hump flights were terminated before this plan could take effect but would have needed to be modified due to a shortage of C-54 engines and logistical concerns.

Hump Cargo Aircraft

Consolidated C-87 Liberator Express. (*AAF*)

Douglas C-47 Dakota. (*AAF*)

Curtiss C-46 Commando. (*AAF*)

Douglas C-54 Skymaster. (*AAF*)

Operation Matterhorn: C-87s and C-109s Fly the Hump to Supply 20AF B-29s

Operation Matterhorn was developed by Brig. Gen. Kenneth Wolfe in October 1943 and proposed that 20AF B-29s arriving in India during the spring of 1944 were to stage through forward airfields in China to bomb targets in Japan, Manchuria, and East Asia. The forward airbases in China were to be self-sustaining, supplied out of India by flying fuel and other military and personnel supplies, of which every gallon and pound had to be flown over the Hump.

In preparation to accommodate the B-29s, Advance Army Air Forces echelons arrived in India during December 1943 to organize the building of airfields in India and China. Initially, thousands of Indians constructed four permanent bases in eastern India around Kharagpur as well as constructing or adapting existing airfields in Bengal. Meanwhile, 1,000 miles (1,600km) to the northeast, across the Himalayas, about 350,000 Chinese workers continued the back-breaking labor of building four staging bases in western China near Chengtu and new airfields near Kunming. During the construction stages of the Chinese bases, the 20AF's 20 C-87 transports were assigned to ATC along with several C-109s and three C-46 bomber support squadrons. The self-proclaimed C-87 'Hump Drivers', based in the Lower Assam Valley, flew their transports loaded with cement mixers, rock crushers, and fuel, depending on inadequate weather reports, navigation aids and radio range to find the way. Once arriving at the airfields at Kunming and Chengtu, they had to land on the crude, under construction, 2-mile-long runways with inadequate unloading and maintenance facilities. Once the XX Bomber Command, the operational component of the 20AF, had arrived in the CBI and were ready to commence operations, a major weakness in *Matterhorn* became evident. The huge tonnage of fuel, bombs, supplies, and spare parts that had to be flown across the Hump for the operation to be self-sustaining could not be attained by the C-87s, C-109s, and C-46s and needed to be augmented by the XXBC's own B-29s delivering fuel to China. To be used as flying tankers, each carrying 7 tons of fuel, the B-29s were stripped of nearly all combat equipment. To build up a reserve of enough gasoline for one B-29 to fly a mission against Japan; that B-29 had to make seven round trip flights, offloading gasoline in China, and then having only enough fuel to return to India for another trip. Other supplies had to be flown forward as well, and in all 12 round-trip flights over the Hump were required to support one combat sortie for one B-29.

On 5 June 1944, 98 B-29s flew their first combat mission on a raid on Bangkok's Makasan rail center. It was a very inauspicious start as damage was light with fewer than 20 bombs falling on the target area. Five B-29s were forced to ditch, 14 others aborted early, and one crashed on take-off. From June 1944 to January 1945, approximately 800 tons of bombs were dropped by China-based B-29s on Japanese targets but these attacks were of insufficient weight and accuracy to yield any significant results, except to demonstrate to the Japanese that it could be done. XX Bomber Command failed to achieve the strategic objectives intended for *Operation Matterhorn*, mainly because of logistical problems, and also because of the bomber's mechanical difficulties, the vulnerability of Chinese staging bases, and the extreme range required to reach key Japanese cities. Although the B–29s achieved some success, Maj. Gen. Claire Chennault considered the XXBC to be a liability and thought that its supplies of fuel and bombs could have been more advantageously used by his 14AF in support of Lt Gen. Joseph Stilwell's Chinese and Allied armies. The XXBC had consumed almost 15 per cent of the Hump airlift tonnage per month during *Matterhorn*. Lt Gen. Albert Widmeyer, who replaced Stilwell as American senior commander in the China Theater, agreed with Chennault. Both generals were pleased to see the War Department withdraw the B-29s from China in early 1945 to fly from the newly captured Marianas bases where

Transferring fuel into a C-109 for *Operation Matterhorn*, the Hump fuel supply for 20AF B-29s flying from Chinese airfields to bomb Japan. (*ATC*)

C-109 44-49059, *The White Angel/Donna K*, of the 2nd Air Transport Squadron, flaunts camel symbols denoting 156 Hump crossings before this mishap. (*ATC*)

operations there would profit from the organization and improved tactics developed in the CBI and seaborne fuel and materials supply. Because of the dangers faced on a Hump trip, the B-29 crews were given credit for a combat mission and C-87s and C-109s for a supply mission, as denoted by a camel symbol below the cockpit. Support of *Matterhorn* greatly increased the amount of tonnage being hauled across the Hump by the India-China Division. The Division received a windfall when XX Bomber Command agreed to assign its C-87s and C-109s to the Air Transport Command when it transferred to the Marianas.

The *Fireball Express* to India

As an offshoot of the Hump operation, Gen. Harold George instituted the *Fireball Express* in September 1943, which was to be a weekly C-87 express flight (26,000 miles in ten days) by the 26th Transport Group carrying critical spare parts from the Air Service Command Depot at Fairfield, Ohio, to the ATC Service Depot at Agra, India. This supply was critical as due to the isolation and the lower priority of the CBI Theater, there was a lack of engines and spare parts, meaning there were seldom more than 18 transport aircraft available to fly the Hump. Flight crews were often sent into the Himalayan foothills to cannibalize aircraft parts from the numerous crash sites.

Previously, contract carriers operated these flights, chiefly Pan Am, as Craven & Cates' *The Army Air Forces in World War II* (Office of Air Force History, 1983) explained: 'Only a few military crews had been trained for four-engine aircraft because, up to this point (June 1943), nearly all the C-54s and C-87s assigned to the command were operated by the contract carriers, which were responsible for their own operational crew training.' To expedite shipments to the Asian and African war zones, Pan Am formed a new Africa-Orient Division and began its famous *Cannonball Route* stretching 11,500 miles from Miami to South America, across the Atlantic to Africa and from there to India. It became the longest, fastest, large-scale air transport route in history and an important supply line for the entire Far East.

To begin to fly this route independently, the ATC established an operational training unit at Homestead, Florida, specializing exclusively in four-engine instruction for a number of C-87 and B-24 crews and later C-54 crews. In November 1943 the Ferrying Division opened the *Fireball Express Route* from Florida to India in which C-87s (stripped of their camouflage paint to give them an extra 5mph of airspeed) and later C-54s were employed. The *Fireball* paralleled Pan Am's *Cannonball Route* that had begun a year earlier and more than tripled the capacity of the flyway between America and the Far East, expediting the shipment of critical cargo along with passengers and airmail.

B-24 Tactical Liberators Fly the Hump to Supply Liberator Groups

The 308th Bomb Group deployed to Kunming Airport, China, on 31 March 1943, becoming the heavy bombardment arm of the new 14AF in the CBI. Once based in China, the group had a difficult time becoming established because of the fuel and supply shortage and monsoon weather, and it began two months of 'reverse Hump' operations. Its B-24 bombers and C-87s flew round trips to India airlifting the gasoline, oil, bombs, spare parts, and other materiel it needed to stockpile for the group to prepare for and then to sustain its combat operations. The group's B-24 bombers were converted into fuel transports using kits developed by the South India Air Service Command Depot. The 308th used Chabua Airfield, already crowded with more than 80 ICW transports, and soon its lightly constructed runway deteriorated under the weight of the B-24 transports. Jorhat had sturdier runways, but its taxiways were unpaved, making it unsuitable for four-engined aircraft. Both Sookerating and Mohanbari were due to have strong concrete runways capable of handling all aircraft, but neither was yet paved, and monsoon rains made them inoperable. Once the monsoon ended and airfields became serviceable, the group established an impressive record, especially since that all gas, bombs, ammunition, and other supplies had to be flown over the Hump in its own aircraft, thus making it necessary to fly about three Hump flights for every combat mission.

In May 1945, once Burma had been retaken by the Allies and the 10AF had met its tactical goals, Gen. George Stratemeyer, the senior American air officer in the CBI, and his staff had decided that, as the ATC effort had fallen short of its April allotment by more than 4,000 tons, the cost in fuel of conducting heavy bomber operations from bases in China was prohibitive and that the four-engine B-24 Liberators of the 7th and 308th Heavy Bombardment Groups would be more productive in fuel and cargo transport operations than in tactical operations. Consequently, these two B-24 groups, the 433rd Troop Carrier Group, and the 3rd and 4th Combat Cargo Groups, were taken off combat operations and assigned to the operational control of the India-China Division of the ATC for Hump airlift operations. These troop carrier and combat cargo groups, which had been supporting combat operations with twin-engine transports, were reassigned to ATC to complement a distribution system moving cargo from the main bases to smaller fields in the Chinese interior where the four-engine transports could not make their deliveries.

After cessation of their tactical missions, groundwork for their transport missions consisted of conferences with the operations officers of ATC and Air Traffic Control groups and a 'special training session'. These bomber and troop carrier combat crews were not happy about their new assignment, particularly when they learned that ATC General 'Tonnage Tunner' had required a week of special training flights under the supervision of ATC personnel in preparation for Hump transport operations. This caused resentment among these crews, all of whom were veterans of months and sometimes years of Hump operations, especially since they had been transporting considerably more tonnage across the Hump than ATC (in March 1945, delivering twice the tonnage transported during the same period by ATC).

In their new transport role the two bomb groups would fly a direct route across northern Burma, south of the established routes of ATC. These routes were designated

After their combat requirements waned, Gen. George Stratemeyer decided to reassign B-24 tactical units to Hump supply and fuel transport operations as the ATC had not met its assigned obligations. (*AAF*)

to not interfere with other traffic across the Hump and flying was limited to daylight hours because of crew navigation inexperience, high gross loads, and the rainy season. To keep a continuous flow of gasoline to China, all squadrons were scheduled at first for five and later seven sorties daily. Each crew was reduced to seven men instead of ten and a number of officers were placed on temporary duty to speed turnarounds in China. Each aircraft was assigned its own maintenance crew. The Liberators were modified by removing their bombsights and to reduce weight 75 per cent of ammunition (the Japanese air threat was nil) and the ball turret were removed. The armor plate and nose, waist, dorsal, and tail guns remained for future use. Three droppable bomb bay tanks and two 75-gallon tanks were carried, giving a total fuel capacity of about 4,000 gallons. Initially all aircraft made flights direct to Kunming and Chengkung, taking off with all gas possible and returning to India the same day. The minimum fuel requirements to return were set at 1,300 gallons. When it became necessary to haul gasoline to more distant eastern China, it was decided to fly direct, unload to minimum of 800 gallons, and return to the Kunming area for RON (Remain Over Night). To relieve congestion at Kunming, Lüliang and Chengkung were also used as overnight stops and refueling points. Group records show on an average more than 90 per cent of scheduled flight days were flown, with weather cancelling the others. Despite the friction between the combat crews and the ATC personnel, the combat units began hauling cargo, dramatically increasing tonnage flying across the Hump.

Hump Final Accounting

After its last full month of wartime operations during July 1945, Hump operations officially ended after three and a half years on 15 November 1945. Military supply operations were discontinued in August 1945 and the final months of operations provided for the closing of China Hump bases and the moving of support personnel from China to India for transportation home.

Gen. Tunner's final report stated that the airlift 'expended' 594 aircraft with 'at least' 509 American and 41 CNAC aircraft known lost from all causes, with 1,314 air crewmen and passengers killed. In addition, 81 more aircraft were never accounted for, with their 345 personnel listed as missing. Another 1,200 personnel had been rescued or found their way back to base on their own.

Between 1 December 1943 and 31 August 1945 the Hump airlift flew 156,977 trips, logging 1.5 million hours of eastbound flight time that carried 685,304 gross tons of cargo eastbound, including 392,362 tons of gasoline and oil, with nearly 60 per cent of that total delivered in 1945. In addition to cargo, 33,400 personnel were transported, in one or both directions. Between 1942 and 1945, CNAC pilots made the important contribution of 75,000 tons (about 12 per cent) flying 77 C-47s and 23 C-46s. The airlift ultimately operated from 13 bases in India and six bases in China, with the main terminus at Kunming, which became one of the busiest airports in the world. Though supplemented by the opening of the Ledo Road network in January 1945 and by the recapture of Rangoon, the airlift's total tonnage of 650,000 net tons dwarfed that of the Ledo Road (147,000 tons).

So demanding were the Hump missions that the AAF awarded an Air Medal to crews completing 25 successful missions and a Distinguished Flying Cross to those making 25 round trips. On 2 March 1944, ATC personnel serving in the CBI were awarded the Presidential Unit Citation for their efforts. The India-China ferrying operation was the largest and most extended strategic air bridge (in volume of cargo airlifted) in aviation history until it was surpassed in 1949 by the Berlin Airlift, an operation also commanded by Gen. Tunner.

Chapter 7

B-24 ETO Trucking and Supply Drop Operations

Introduction

After the Normandy Beachhead breakout, the Allied advance across France became so rapid that a severe supply situation arose during which various factions clamored for fuel, supplies, and weapons. Among these factions were isolated French Forces of the Interior (FFI) and the French Maquis partisans, Patton's armored forces racing across France. Then there were American airborne forces participating in *Operation Market Garden* in Holland during September, followed by the resupply of American (*Operation Varsity*) airborne forces as part of *Operation Plunder*, Montgomery's ambitious crossing of the Rhine during March 1945.

FFI and Maquis Air Supply

After the Normandy Breakout, the Allies relied on the FFI and the Maquis to hamper the movement of German reinforcements through direct attacks and sabotage. Supplying them was the assignment of Liberators under *Operation Carpetbagger*, which had been ongoing since January 1944 but the scope of French operations now increased greatly, as did their need for arms and munitions. To augment the B-24 *Carpetbaggers*, SHAEF ordered B-17s of the 3AD to begin 4 large daytime supply drop missions: 180 B-17s on 25 June; 324 on 14 July; 194 on 1 August; and 79 on 9 September.

B-24 Used for Bulk Gasoline Shipment

To convert Liberators borrowed from combat units into fuel transporters it was necessary to reduce their gross weight before installing the additional fuel-carrying tanks so that the maximum quantity of gasoline to be carried did not exceed the gross weight limitations for safe landings. To reduce their weight, the bombsight and bombsight stabilizer, armor plate, ammunition cans and ammunition, waist guns, the ball turret, and loose equipment throughout the bomber were removed so that the total landing weight was reduced from 59,000 to 57,000lb. A result of this gross weight reduction was that the Center of Gravity location was moved to a more advantageous location for its new transport duty. Three B-24 Fuel Load Plans were used, depending on the availability of bomb bay tanks.

B-24 Fuel Load Plans

Load Plan #1 (50 per cent Usage)	Capacity
2 wing tip tanks (standard equipment)	450 gallons
1 forward bomb bay tank	390 gallons
1 P-47 fighter belly tank in the forward bomb bay	108 gallons
4 P-47 fighter belly tanks in the rear bomb bay	432 gallons
1 P-38 fighter belly tank at the waist windows	165 gallons

Total: 1,545 gallons

Load Plan #2 (25 per cent Usage)	Capacity
2 wing tip tanks (standard equipment)	450 gallons
2 forward bomb bay tanks	780 gallons
4 P-47 fighter belly tanks in the rear bomb bay	432 gallons

Total: 1,662 gallons

Load Plan #3 (25 per cent Usage All *Carpetbagger*)	Capacity
2 wing tip tanks (standard equipment)	450 gallons
3 bomb bay tanks	1,170 gallons
2 P-47 fighter belly tanks in rear bomb bay	216 gallons

Total: 1,836 gallons

Most Advantageous (Not Used) Loading Plan	Capacity
2 wing tip tanks (standard equipment)	450 gallons
4 bomb bay tanks	1,560 gallons

Total: 2,010 gallons

Use of 5-gallon Jerry Cans
Some first-line combat B-24s were used to carry fuel in 5-gallon Jerry cans, which were hand loaded and mostly stacked on a makeshift plywood-covered bomb bay floor, the usual total being 218 cans (1,090 gallons/4,126 liters)

Use of Bomb Bay Tanks
The bomb bay tanks were installed in the forward bomb bay on each side of the catwalk and were secured by two straps encircling it horizontally and by another vertical strap installed as a bottom support turnbuckle on the horizontal straps that connected the end and side sections so that they could be tightened after the cells were mounted. When fuel cells were installed in the bomb bay, the bomb shackles were removed from the vertical racks in that bay and stowed elsewhere in a canvas bag. The capacity of each bomb bay tank was 390 gallons (1,476 liters) for a combined total capacity of 780 gallons (2,953 liters). On later-model Liberators, the two auxiliary bomb bay cells were factory installed and had a combined capacity of approximately 780 gallons (2,953 liters).

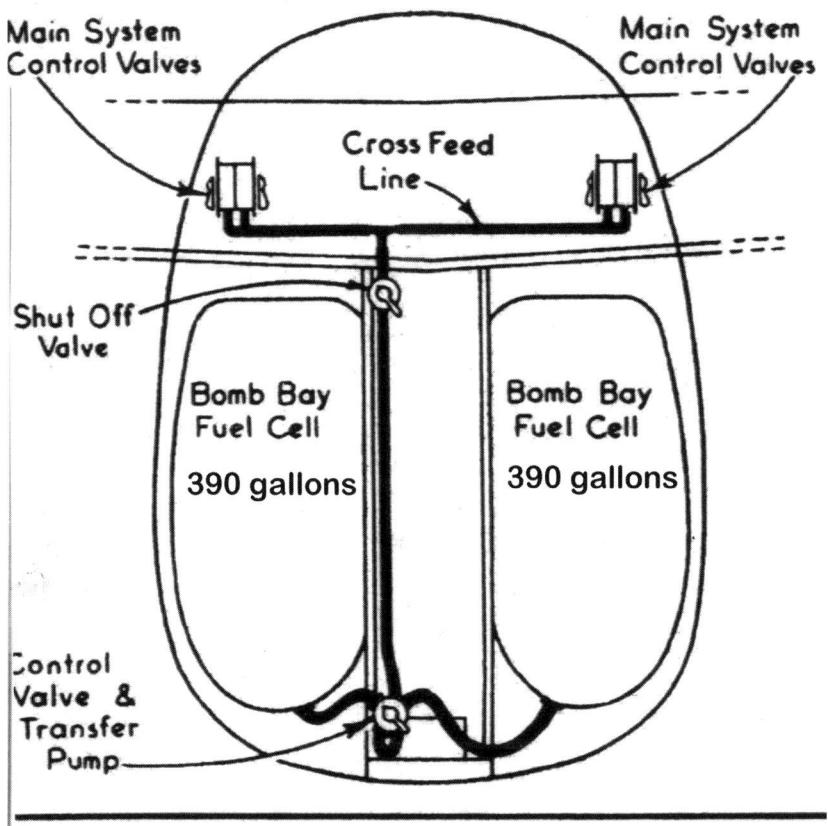

Bomb Bay Auxiliary Fuel System

Use of Fighter Belly Tanks

Neither the bomb bay nor belly tanks presented an installation problem and ideally the maximum number of bomb bay tanks were to be used but these were in short supply at the time and so metal, not the paper composite substitute, fighter belly tanks were to be used. The fighter belly tanks could be easily modified for mounting on the bomb racks and then could be readily removed once installed. The use of multiple fighter belly tanks caused a pumping difficulty because the suction hose had to be changed too often, causing air locks in the lines and pipeline system. The use of belly tanks with greater individual capacity would have greatly reduced the air lock problem. The 200 gallon (757-liter) auxiliary fuel tanks in the bomber's wings were isolated from the main fuel system and fuel tank filler caps, noted as so in white, so that it could carry 80 octane automotive (tank and truck) fuel as the B-24 operated on 100 or 115/120 octane fuel. The aircraft used as fuel tankers could not be returned immediately to combat operations as their wing and bomb bay tanks were contaminated with 80 octane non-aviation fuel and the replacement or purging of these was necessary, which was the purpose of using second-line B-24s.

P-38 and P-47 drop tanks were placed in the Liberator's bomb bays and waist areas to carry fuel to Patton's fuel-starved armored units. Two 108-gallon P-47 fighter belly tanks are being filled in this B-24 rear bomb bay. (*AAF*)

Carpetbagger Liberators Transport Fuel

Carpetbagger Liberators were better suited for fuel transport as they already had their combat equipment (turrets, guns, etc.) removed. *Carpetbagger* Liberators were used to fly gasoline directly to newly captured continental forward airfields, with personnel at RAF Harrington in Northamptonshire, UK, working non-stop to convert the B-24s into flying fuel bowsers. Two 400-gallon (1,514-liter) tanks were installed into the bomb bays and the auxiliary wing tank feed pipes were sealed off, enabling them to be used after first having painted the filler caps white to reveal that they had carried non-aviation fuel. Six P-51 or P-47 belly tanks, each holding 108 gallons, were installed in the fuselage, with three more fixed over the Joe hole; all the tanks being vented outside.

Trucking Operations for Patton

After finally devastating the German forces at Caen and in the Falaise Gap followed by the breakout at Saint-Lô, Allied ground forces were racing across northern France. Gen. George Patton's Third Army, in particular, was advancing so quickly that the special Red Ball Express truck convoy system was established to bring in fuel and supplies. It began operating on 25 August 1944, manned primarily by African American truck drivers, and at its peak operation, the Express operated 5,958 vehicles and carried

Filling a B-24 tanker from underground storage in the UK. (*AAF*)

about 12,500 tons (12.5 million kg) of fuel and supplies per day. Despite these impressive statistics, the system became overloaded, and a supplement was needed. At the time the IX Troop Carrier Command was unable to contribute its fleet of transports as from late August it was either awaiting or participating in the Arnhem–Nijmegen *Market Garden* airborne operations in Holland, which also needed to be supplemented by converted Liberator transports.

On 29 August 1944, Liberators of the 93rd, 446th, and 448th Bomb Groups began their first supply mission; flying empty to a supply depot in southern England, where Royal Artillerymen loaded the Liberators with urgently needed food, medical, and other supplies. Once loaded, they crossed the Channel and then flew on the deck and landed on the newly captured airfield at Orléans-Bricy, 70 miles from Paris. These missions continued until

Once the B-24 tankers landed at advanced bases on the Continent, their gasoline was transferred to 55-gallon drums to be transported by trucks to supply Patton's waiting armored units. (*AAF*)

9 September, with 43 B-24s delivering 130.2 tons (130,200kg), including medical supplies (27.2 tons/27,200kg) and food (55.7 tons/55,700kg).

On 9 September, the Combined Air Transport Operations Room (CATOR) ordered the 302nd Transport Wing to suspend its supply to the air forces, except for basic mail and passenger services, and to allocate its transports to the supply of Patton's Army, which was continuing its race across France. At the same time, the 8AF was directed to transport 345,000 gallons of fuel to the 12th Army Group, in a fuel supply operation nicknamed *Trucking*. All four B-24 bomb groups of the 96CBW – the 458th, 466th, 467th, and the redesignated 492nd (*Carpetbagger*) – and several groups from the 2BD were to be involved. The 492nd ceased its *Carpetbagger* operations to begin the fuel-hauling ops and afterward only the 856BS would resume *Carpetbagger* operations. The *Carpetbagger* Liberators and second-line war-weary B-24s with five-man reserve crews were used for these missions as much as possible. The first *Trucking* mission was flown on 12 September but afterward the B-24s were stood down and flew practise missions over southern England in preparation to support *Market Garden* operations on the 17th.

Market Garden Trucking Support

On 17 September the *Trucking* B-24s were joined by B-24s from the 14th and 20th Wings to support *Operation Market* (airborne) *Garden* (ground forces), which was a bold and ambitious plan that was hastily designed by the usually cautious British Gen. Bernard Montgomery. The plan called for 35,000 American, British, and Polish paratroops to be dropped into the Netherlands and to hold several bridges in successive towns, Nijmegen, Eindhoven, and Arnhem, allowing British armored XXX Corps to drive 40 miles on a dangerous single-tracked road, linking each paratroop unit and finally to break into Germany's vital industrial Ruhr Valley: thus, skirting the Siegfried line, the German defense line guarding the Rhine River. Ultimately, *Market Garden* resulted in an Allied setback as the paratroop units were unable to link up and the operation would prove to be 'one bridge too far'.

During the night of 16 September, trucks had delivered supplies to Liberator bases, and each was loaded with 2.5 tons (2,500kg) in 20–21 bundles to be dropped under the supervision of personnel from the 9th Troop Carrier Command. Of these bundles, 12 were loaded in the bomb bay, five or six around the ball turret well, and three near the rear ventral hatch. These Liberators had their existing ball turrets or the turret fairings of previously removed balls removed so that the bundles could be dropped through metal chutes (already removed as Joe holes on *Carpetbagger* B-24s). So-called 'indestructible' items were to free-fall while the remainder were parachute-assisted. After loading 782 tons (782,000kg) of supplies, 252 B-24s, including 6 Liberators carrying 9,300 gallons (34,826 liters) of gasoline for Patton, headed for France for the first full-division *Trucking* mission.

During the early afternoon of 17 September, the aircraft took off from airfields in Norfolk and Suffolk but the mission began to unravel almost immediately as leading

During the initial *Market Garden* operation on 18 September 1944, 252 Liberators dropped 782 tons of supplies to airborne troops on the ground (note landed gliders). (*AAF*)

German troops on the ground directed almost constant small-arms fire at the low-flying Liberators and 7 were shot down, while 154 were damaged. (*AAF*)

Most of the supplies dropped by the Liberators reached the Allied airborne troops below despite most of the Liberators encountering heavy small-arms fire and some having to make three runs over the dropping zone, a few releasing their supplies miles short. (*AAF*)

elements of the 20th Wing were forced to make a 360-degree port turn to evade an oncoming C-47 unit. The maneuver then befuddled the following groups and the 448BG became separated from the main force in the sea haze and continued on alone, while five 93BG Liberators returned to base. The continuing Liberators descended to 400ft (122m) to find checkpoints over Holland, which was very difficult, as the coastal area had been completely flooded by the retreating Germans. At the initial point the 20th Wing Group was unable to receive recognition signals because of the failure of the radio beacon. Two escorting P-47 strafing groups were unable to suppress the almost constant small-arms fire that was directed at the low-flying bombers. Seven Liberators were shot down while 154 were damaged and one crewman was KIA, 61 were MIA, and 26 were WIA. The 446BG and 448BG each lost three Liberators and had many more damaged, including 25 of 36 based at Bungay. Nonetheless, these Liberators entered the dropping zone at Grosbeek near Nijmegen in formation. Despite some 453BG Liberators having to make three runs over the dropping zone and the 448BG releasing its supplies about 5 miles (8km) short, the First Allied Airborne Army recovered about 80 per cent of all supplies dropped by the 20th Wing. Meanwhile, the 14th Wing, led by the 491BG, received heavy small arms fire on its dropping zone at Best, Holland, but was able to drop its supplies more successfully.

B-24 Transport of Supplies and Bulk Fuel, 12–30 September 1944

First Phase: UK Bases: Storage and Transportation of Supplies

Liberators of the 96th Combat Bomb Wing and 2nd Bombardment Division initially flew empty from their various UK bases to load supplies at advanced UK stations. Initially rations, medical supplies, and gasoline carried in Jerry cans were loaded onto wooden bomb bay platforms at Aldermaston, Membury, Ramsbury, Welford, Greenham Common, and later at Beaulieu and French bases at Clasters, Lille, and Saint-Dizier. This phase encountered major difficulties such as maintenance, servicing, messing, housing, briefing, weather, communications, etc. B-24s dispatched to these bases often found that loading personnel there were too few and sometimes absent, or that there were no supplies to be loaded. At no time was there enough personnel available to load more than ten aircraft per hour and the 2AD finally had to send its own operational and maintenance detachment to these advanced bases and to provide messing and living accommodations. During the initial phase of supply, operational liaison was not set up and it was impossible for this headquarters to receive any detailed information on the project other than daily commitments from the Eighth Air Force. These problems led headquarters to firmly recommend that any future operation be carried out with the delivery of cargoes directly to the home bases, eliminating the need of the advanced bases.

Second Phase: UK Loading and Transport of Bulk Gasoline to Terminal Stations in France

UK Stations: Loading and Transport of Bulk Gasoline

The Petroleum Board was responsible for the daily delivery of 84,000 gallons (318,000 liters/70,000 imperial gallons) of 80 octane fuel to the 2nd Air Division UK stations and 120,000 imperial gallons per day to USAAF Station Harrington. The 2AD Headquarters maintained operational control only by the units to conduct the missions. Briefing (weather and control) and dispatching (movements, clearance, and the establishment of corridors) were implemented by the designated wing.

There was adequate gasoline and transport aircraft available to meet the Petroleum Board's requirements. The main problem at the UK bases principally concerned the temporary storage of 80 octane motor vehicle fuel and 100 octane aviation fuel as underground storage facilities could not be used due the incompatibility of the two fuel types and the continued requirement to use these 100 octane tanks for ongoing air operations. To remedy the storage and handling difficulties at the stations, it became necessary to provide each station within the Eighth Air Force with temporary bulk storage facilities. Also, when using fighter belly tanks for vehicle fuel transport, the fueling crews had to change hoses often and carefully to avoid contamination.

Advanced Storage Terminals: Discharge and Storage of Bulk Gasoline

French terminal stations were advanced Allied airfields captured from the Luftwaffe and needed to be extended and repaired as they had been bombed and were mostly minimally maintained by their former beleaguered tenants. Their initial and hasty repair and extension was for the operational use of Allied fighter and fighter bomber units that supported the Allied advance across France, but these fields remained marginal for the landing of the heavily loaded Liberator haulers. As these bomber haulers joined the fighters and fighter bombers, these terminals became congested and disordered but after a small 2AD control and maintenance detachment arrived at each location, operations proceeded more smoothly. During this critical time, sufficient Liberators could be posted from the UK to fulfill the fuel transport requirement; however, the terminal stations in France, at Clasters, Lille, and Saint-Dizier, did not have adequate unloading facilities. The initial fuel unloading method used small, slow portable pumps and/or hand pumps to unload the fuel to trucks parked near the fuel tanker or to slowly pump the fuel directly into 5-gallon Jerry cans or 55-gallon drums for storage, but both systems were unsatisfactory and inefficient. The next method in improving fuel unloading at these terminals consisted of using more faster dedicated pumps, provided with unloading suction lines that unloaded one aircraft each at a time, but subsequently all the pumps connected more than one aircraft and these could be unloaded simultaneously into a large bulk storage tank, from which the drums and Jerry cans could be filled independently of the aircraft unloading operation. It was necessary for units of the 2AD to provide personnel at terminal stations to conduct the operational, communications, and housekeeping functions. The operational personnel at the terminal stations consisted of flying control (including airdrome controllers), an operational section of two officers and two clerks, communication personnel consisting of one officer and three enlisted men, while the housekeeping personnel usually consisted of approximately two officers and ten men, including cooks and orderlies. The 2AD also found it necessary to provide and transport tents, cooking equipment, cots, blankets, water storage facilities, firefighting equipment, and two Jeeps from the home base. At times when the weather prevented the Liberators from returning to their UK bases the crews had to spend the night in France. Since there was no additional accommodation on these fields, the crews had to either sleep inside their aircraft or under their wings. Since the B-24 was normally notorious for retaining gasoline fumes, this trait was even more noticeable during gasoline *Trucking* missions and sleeping outside was preferable.

During this second phase of operations in September 1944, it was vital that direct liaison was established between the hauling units at headquarters, 9th Air Force, Advanced, Communications Zone and General Omar Bradley's 12th Army Group, receiving the supplies. But these advanced bases initially lacked the necessary communications requirements for safe air supply operations, which included: airfield HF and VHF control facilities, navigational aids (radio beacons, etc.), radio link with home base or headquarters, and local telephone facilities.

During the 13 days of the operation (there were 3 days during which only 2 missions were flown), 494 were aircraft dispatched with 456 effective, and these delivered 727,160 gallons (2,752,600 liters) of fuel. Instead of painting bomb symbols to signify the mission, crew chiefs painted flour sacks and oil freight cars on the noses of their Liberators. Even though the men considered these fuel transport missions with the huge amount of fuel on board as dangerous as some of their combat missions, they received no combat credit for these missions toward their 'going home' mission credits.

Gasoline *Trucking* Missions Supplying Patton

Date	A/C	Gallons	Destination
12 Sep 1944	12	13,080	Clasters
18 Sep 1944	6	9,270	Clasters
19 Sep 1944	24	38,016	Clasters
20 Sep 1944	11	16,896	Clasters
21 Sep 1944	29	45,858	Lille*
22 Sep 1944	14	22,332	Clasters
22 Sep 1944	13	20,787	Lille
23 Sep 1944	9	14,375	Clasters
23 Sep 1944	29	46,326	Saint-Dizier
25 Sep 1944	67	107,727	Lille
26 Sep 1944	35	57,234	Lille
26 Sep 1944	6	9,738	Clasters
27 Sep 1944	45	72,333	Lille
28 Sep 1944	56	90,498	Lille
29 Sep 1944	49	79,566	Lille
30 Sep 1944	51	83,124	Lille
Total	456	727,160	

At the end of these missions several B-24s had been lost by straying too close to German AA positions, by navigational errors, and mainly through crashes on take-off and landing on the newly captured airfields in France.

All Trucking Fuel and Supply Missions

Date	A/C
12 Sep 1944	36
18 Sep 1944	96
19 Sep 1944	?
20 Sep 1944	40
21 Sep 1944	84
22 Sep 1944	108

23 Sep 1944	162
24 Sep 1944	47
25 Sep 1944	176
26 Sep 1944	165
27 Sep 1944	163
28 Sep 1944	194
29 Sep 1944	190
30 Sep 1944	116

Most of the *Trucking* operations occurred during September 1944, when the 2nd Air Division and the 492nd Bomb Group delivered critically needed gasoline, food, and medical supplies to forward areas. During September 2,205 supply sorties were flown that delivered 8,225.9 gallons (31,138 liters) of gasoline, 154.1 tons (154,100kg) of medical supplies, 1,229.3 tons (1,229,300kg) of food, and 14.5 tons (14,500kg) of miscellaneous supplies for a total of 9,635.4 tons (9,635,400kg). After this time the number of *Trucking* missions decreased dramatically, with only 75 sorties carrying 263.4 tons (263,400kg) of miscellaneous supplies being flown during the next seven months until VE-Day.

Supply Drop for *Operation Varsity*: Crossing of the Rhine

On 24 March 1945 *Operation Varsity* began as the largest single-day airborne operation in history. The 2nd Air Division's Field Order stated:

> *Varsity* can be considered the most important combined operation since the Invasion of France. 2AD's mission is the D-Day supply of assault and airborne forces which will have landed on the German side of the Rhine shortly before our crews drop supplies to them. The magnitude of an operation of this sort makes it essential that for its complete success each part of the job by each force participating must be carried out with exactitude. 2AD is committed to drop supplies in the places designated.

American, British, and Canadian airborne and glider troops were to be transported behind German lines across the River Rhine by nearly 1,600 towing aircraft and gliders, which also carried large ordnance such as artillery and vehicles. Fifteen minutes after the troop drop, an air task force comprised of B-24s from the 2nd, 14th, and 20th Combat Bomb Wings was to drop ammunition, ordnance, grenades, rations, tents, blankets, medical supplies, etc. Half the bundles were to be for American use and half for British use, with the drop zones about 4 miles apart.

A few practise missions were flown in France and special intelligence briefings were held with sandbox mock-ups of the Rhine and drop areas. During the early morning on the day of the mission the crews of the nine participating groups had received a thorough four-mission briefing to ensure that they understood the complicated flight plan.

Squadron element and wing men were instructed to fly as loosely as possible without straggling with positions to be maintained reasonably well abreast with maximum lateral spread. The formation was to close up for the drop and to reach the initial point (IP) at 500ft (152m), let down to 300–500ft (91–152m) when releasing the bundles, while not exceeding 150mph (241km/h) at drop time so as not to damage the parachutes. Pilots could use 10–15 degrees flaps as needed but were not to lower the wheels. After the drop they were then to spread out on climb and withdraw after crossing the Rhine. On the previous low-level *Market Garden* supply mission to Holland on 18 September 1944, Army Air Transportation technicians were responsible for dropping the bundles from the aircraft but during this operation group crews were to throw out or release the bundles. They had been instructed by the 490th Quartermaster Depot Company on the loading and dropping of each type of bundle. Loads would be dropped from the bomb bays, the empty ball turret well, and the emergency escape hatch near the tail. The heaviest and bulkiest items were packed in A-5 bundle pods loaded on to the bomb bay racks and had a static line attached to the bomb shackle so that a parachute would be deployed when the shackle released. To land in the drop zones, all bundles needed to be jettisoned in less than 20 seconds after hearing the bail-out warning bell. After the pods were dropped, a crewman was to go into the bomb bay and pull the dangling static lines back into the aircraft so that the bomb bay doors could be closed. This proved to be dangerous, as due to limited space in the bomb bay, a crewman could not wear a parachute while reaching out into space for the static line. The bundles at the other two locations were pushed out by gunners. The plan was for the 240 B-24s to be over the drop zones as closely as possible behind the 300 C-47s carrying paratroops and the 1,300 towing gliders carrying troops or large ordnance. In support of the operation the 8AF would dispatch 1,749 bombers, escorted by more than 1,300 fighter escorts, to strike Luftwaffe airfields to suppress enemy fighter interceptors. Meanwhile, RAF Bomber Command and the US 15th Air Force in Italy would attack targets deeper in Germany, while their multitudes of fighter escorts would further occupy Luftwaffe fighters. The 445BG would lead groups from the 2nd and the 14th Combat Wings for drops to US troops at drop point SDW-W. The 20CW along with some 14CW squadrons would drop supplies for British troops at SDP-B. During the Wesel resupply mission, the 14th Combat Wing dropped 4,856 bundles of supplies weighing 598 tons (598,000kg), with 100 per cent of the American loads dropped in the target area. Intense flak near the British drop zone resulted in only 85 per cent of those loads being on target. Of the 240 Liberators dispatched, 122 supplied the American assault area with 312 tons (312,000kg) of supplies and 118 supplied the British assault area with 270.3 tons (270,300kg).

Preceding the drop, Allied AA batteries were to be warned of the low-flying Liberators in their area and powerful anti-flak air operations were carried out by Allied fighter bombers that intended to destroy most of the German flak guns. The Liberators were most vulnerable to flak on their straight and level approach but after the drop they were to descend as close to the deck as possible and to recross the Rhine and Allied lines as quickly as possible. On their turn around back over the Rhine the Liberator pilots

Operation Varsity on 24 March 1945 was the largest single-day airborne operation in history, during which Allied paratroops were dropped on the German side of the Rhine. Parachute bundles are seen being loaded on to Liberators in the UK. (*AAF*)

A total of 240 B-24s were to arrive over the drop zones as closely as possible behind the 1,500 C-47s carrying paratroops and the 1,300 gliders carrying troops to parachute supply canisters. (*AAF*)

were advised not to bank too steeply as this gave the numerous light German AA and small arms gunners a larger target. Despite the flak danger, mission planners considered that small arms fire from the estimated 25,000 German troops on the ground would the greatest danger to the bombers, which was the case. The losses were heavy, with 14 Liberators destroyed, 103 damaged, and 5 crew KIA, 116 MIA, and 30 WIA.

A week after this mission, Gen. William Kepner, 2nd Air Division Commander, relayed this message to his groups:

I am highly gratified and pleased to transmit to you the following message from Lt Gen. Brereton, 1st Allied Airborne Army to Lt Gen. Doolittle concerning the operations of 24 March in which 2nd Air Division played so vital and successful a part: 'I should like to express my appreciation for the excellent support given by your Air Forces to the First Allied Airborne Army in its operation across the Rhine, 24 March 45. The attacks by your bombers of enemy airfields and their interdiction program and the fighter sweeps, and the armed recces provided were largely responsible for the success of the operation. Bomber resupply on D-Day (24 March) beautifully carried out. As in our operations in Holland, your Air Force has been of outstanding assistance. Many thanks to you and all those under your command'.

Chapter 8

Trolley Missions

Rhineland Tour

Within days of the 8th Air Force flying its last combat mission on 25 April 1945, a series of six *Trolley Missions* were being planned 'to provide all ground personnel with an opportunity of seeing the results of their contribution in the strategic air war against Germany … Only by flying over areas that had been bombed by the 8th Air Force or attacked by Allied land forces could the ground crews really understand what their dedication and skill had helped achieve.' The Liberator *Trolley Missions* were mainly flown by B-24s of the 2nd Air Division from 7 through 12 May. The route for the first four missions, 7–10 May, called the *Rhineland Tour*, was flown from the 2AD base to Southwold, then over Ostend, Mannheim, Aschaffenburg, Frankfurt, Bingen, Koblenz, Bonn, Cologne, Düsseldorf, Brussels, Ostend, Southwold, and return to base. The route for the last two missions, called the *Northwest Germany Tour*, was flown from their base to Great Yarmouth, then over Katwijk aan Zee, Arnhem, Münster, Osnabrück, Bremen, Hamburg, Brunswick, Hanover, Bielefeld, Hamm, Essen, The Hague, Great Yarmouth, and back to base. In addition to the B-24s there were also a large numbers of B-17s cruising the area (on 10 May, 670 8AF bombers flew *Trolley Missions*, including 379 B-17s and 291 B-24s).

A set of guidelines were established for these missions, which were actually 'sightseeing' trips. Group commanders were instructed to 'accord special attention to the selection of the most responsible and experienced pilots'. Safety was stressed with the 'responsibility of the pilot to his crew and passengers … and … the deplorability of needless loss of life to carelessness, particularly now that hostilities in Europe are at an end'. The B-24s were to have a minimum crew of five (pilot, co-pilot, navigator, engineer, and radio operator) and carry ten passengers (these were dedicated bombers, not C-87s). The passengers were to wear parachutes and Mae Wests and were to be instructed on bail-out and ditching procedures and the use of the interphone. For the six-to-seven-hour flights, group messes were to provide sandwiches, while co-pilots were given bags of candy for the passengers and crew. Before each mission an S-2 officer would brief the enlisted passengers on the route, showing Balopticon slides of each target before and after the attacks along with the importance of the target and the group's part in their destruction. Target Strike Reports were discussed assessing damage to the targets.

Combat air crews complained about not being allowed to go on these missions, but the High Command responded that air crew members 'had seen plenty already'. The crews argued back that there was a difference in what they saw from bombing at high altitude and at the low altitudes of these sightseeing missions but to no avail.

The aircraft were to take off in elements of three, and within each group there was to be an interval of 10 minutes between the take-off of the first and last aircraft. Once assembled, the elements would depart in trail at one-minute intervals and maintain an altitude of 1,000ft for the entire flight with no buzzing or circling. To enforce these rules an observer aircraft flew with each wing. If weather conditions did not permit that approved altitude, the entire mission was to be cancelled. Despite these precautions, accidents did occur. On 7 May, a 389BG Liberator, possibility buzzing the area, crashed into the Engers Bridge over the Rhine near Cologne, killing 19 men, and on 10 May, a B-17 was lost during a collision over the UK with no survivors.

Despite the earlier flight warnings, the 2AD added new instructions on 10 May: 'All personnel are to be briefed on the danger of throwing objects from a/c during flight. Nothing is to be jettisoned during the flight.' Buzzing became so blatant that the 2AD warned that 'any violations reported of low flying will be subject to severe disciplinary action' and announced that five pilots were up for court martial for buzzing the previous day. The pilots protested that they thought the 1,000ft rule only applied their flight over England. However, once the observer aircraft was out of sight the pilots flew over the Continent at between 200 and 300ft in order to give their passengers a good look at everything possible.

There was an anecdote that a 577BS pilot flew very low over a field occupied by German PoWs and as they flew over, a few of the prisoners taunted the fliers with Nazi salutes; galling both crew and passengers. On his next *Trolley Mission*, the crew and passengers dropped trash on these prisoners. Rolls of toilet paper unraveling in flight and flares were the favorite objects to be dispensed. Of all the sights on these trips the memorable was the majestic Cologne Cathedral, still standing with little, if any, obvious damage, amidst the surrounding utter destruction. The numbers of 2nd Air Division B-24s on each mission was large. On the first, 7 May mission, 362 aircraft were dispatched and since this mission occurred the day before VE Day, some crews included a gunner. On 9 May, 330 2AD aircraft were dispatched with only 186 on the sixth and last *Trolley Mission*.

Cook's Tour

On 10 May, the 14th Combat Wing conducted the first *Cook's Tour*, which was 'an opportunity for outstanding crew chiefs and other maintenance personnel who had received the Legion of Merit or Bronze Star to visit bombed areas in Germany'. Unlike other *Trolley Missions* where aircraft were not allowed to land on the Continent, these aircraft landed with their passengers, who were then allowed to tour the German city, Duisburg, on foot to observe the damage. Each visitor would carry one steel helmet, one carbine or rifle per enlisted man or .45 pistol per officer, and K-rations for one day.

Aircraft for these special tours took off from each group base at 0700 on 10 May and then continue each following day until all scheduled personnel had flown and toured. The bombers would fly from their base to Southwold, then over Ostend, Brussels, Liege,

Post-war *Trolley Missions* were organized to show non-combat ground personnel the damage their charges had inflicted on the Reich. (*AAF*)

Probably the most well-known example of Allied bombing proficiency was Cologne Cathedral, still standing among the surrounding utter destruction. (*AAF*)

As part of their *Cook's Tour* the sightseers landed at Venlo, Holland, and were transported overland to Duisburg, Germany, where they could walk around at their leisure to observe 8AF bombing destruction and have lunch. (*AAF*)

Düren, Cologne, and Frankfurt (via the Rhine) and then land at Station Y-55 at Venlo, on the border between south-east Holland and Germany. From Venlo, the men would be transported overland to Duisburg, where they could walk around at their leisure and have lunch. During the war Duisburg endured 299 bombing raids that almost totally destroyed the historic city center and 80 per cent of all residential buildings had been destroyed or partly damaged. Ironically, most of the damage was caused by RAF bombers. Upon their return to Y-55, they flew to Brussels, Ostend, Southwold, and back to base.

Post-War B-24 Use to Return Troops to the US

After originally flying combat with the 44BG on the Ploieşti oil refinery raids and afterward with the 576BS/392BG, the war weary *Minerva* (41 23689) became the first 392BG Assembly Ship. However, it was badly damaged in 1944 and salvaged by the 93BG in October. At the end of the war *Minerva*, now a long-standing veteran, was part of one final experiment to test the viability of carrying troops back home in bombers. She successfully jammed an astonishing 52 soldiers on board and took off, but the idea was abandoned. Perhaps this foreshadowed today's low-cost airlines.

Minerva had several reincarnations during her wartime career: bomber, war-weary assembly ship, and badly damaged and repaired and then test aircraft. (*AAF*)

Commemorative Air Force: The Last Liberator Hauler

The Commemorative Air Force (CAF) operates the oldest B-24 type in existence. This Liberator (40-2366) was the 25th of more than 18,000 built and the 18th LB-30 of an order of 20 for Great Britain. On a training flight from Eagles Nest Airport, New Mexico, prior to its delivery to England, AM927 suffered a landing accident with damage severe enough that the aircraft was returned to San Diego for repairs. It was then deleted from the UK order and was converted to a transport aircraft, serving as an example for the C-87 (which is now mistakenly advertised as the prototype for the C-87 transport, which was actually B-24D 42-40355 *Pinocchio*). It then served as a flying test bed for further development of essential B-24 features, such as modifying the control surfaces to develop lighter pilot control forces. It then undertook scheduled flights between San Diego, Fort Worth, and New York, becoming known as *Ol' 927* from its serial AM927. This Liberator carried critical parts between San Diego and the Fort Worth plant along with the domestic transport of various company personnel, and also American and foreign dignitaries.

After the war, the aircraft was sold to the Continental Can Company, which operated it as an executive transport for about ten years. Then it was sold to Mexico's national oil company, Petroleos Mexicanos (PEMEX), and flown in Latin America until the CAF acquired it in 1969. In 1971 she was painted in the colors and markings of the 98th Bomb Group, *Pyramiders* of the 9th Air Force in North Africa, and was named *Diamond Lil*. A major conversion project began in 2006, to restore her to her original 1941 B-24A bomber configuration using the factory camouflage paint scheme and *Ol' 927* nose art. During April 2012, the *Diamond Lil* configuration was returned.

Diamond Lil. (*CAF*)

Ol' 927. (*CAF*)

Bibliography

Magazine, Newspaper, and Internet Articles
Consairway, *Flight Deck*, 1943–1945 (various issues)
Sloat, Chuck, 'The Unknown Liberator: RY-3', *Warbirds International*, May/June 1988

Books
Blue, Allan, *B-24 Liberator: A Pictorial History*, Ian Allan, UK, 1976
Bond, Steve & Forder, Richard, *Special Ops Liberators*, Grub Street, UK, 2011
Bowers, Peter, *Boeing Aircraft since 1916*, Putman, UK, 1966
Bowman, Martin, *100 Group (Bomber Support)*, Pen & Sword, UK, 2006
Bowman, Martin, *B-24 Liberator: 1939–1945*, Wensum, UK, 1979
Bowman, Martin, *Combat Legend: B-24 Liberator*, Airlife, UK, 2003
Bowman, Martin, *Consolidated B-24 Liberator, Crowood*, UK, 1990
Bradley, Robert, *Convair Advanced Designs, Specialty*, MN, 2010
Campbell, John & Donna, *Consolidated B-24 Liberator,* Schiffer, PA, 1993
Carty, Pat, *Secret Squadrons of the Eighth*, Allan, UK, 1990
Churchill, Winston, *The Second World War: The Hinge of Fate: Volume IV (History of the Second World War),* Houghton Mifflin, NY, June 1953
Clarke, Ron, *The 802/492 Bomb Group: The Carpetbaggers*, Carpetbagger Museum, 2001
Cleveland, Reginald, *Air Transport at War*, Harper & Bros, NY, 1946
Craven & Cates, *The Army Air Forces in World War II,* Office of Air Force History, Wash. DC, 1983
Dmitri, Ivan, *Flight to Everywhere*, Whittlsey House, NY, 1944
Dorr, Robert, *Air Force One,* MBI, MN, 2001
Freeman, Roger, *B-24 at War,* Ian Allan, UK, 1983
Freeman, Roger, *Mighty Eighth War Manual, Janes*, UK, 1984
Feuer, A.B., *The B-24 in China*, Stackpole, PA, 1992
Glines, Carroll, *Bernt Balchen: Polar Explorer*, Smithsonian, Wash. DC, 1999
Glines, Carroll, *Chennault's Forgotten Warriors*, Schiffer, PA, 1995
Gunston, Bill, *World Encyclopedia of Aero Engines*, Patrick Stephens, UK, 1986
Halley, James, *Squadrons of the Royal Air Force,* Air Britain, UK, 1980
Harrington, Janine, *RAF 100 Group: Birth of Electronic Warfare*, Fonthill, UK, 2016
Hendrie, Andrew, *Cinderella Service: RAF Coastal Command: 1939–1945,* Pen & Sword, UK, 2006
Herman, Arthur, *Freedom's Forge*, Random House, NY, 2013
Howell, Fred, *The Snoopers*, Vantage, NY, 1991
Hutton, Stephen, *Squadron of Deception: 36th Bomb Squadron in WWII,* Schiffer, PA, 1999
Jackson, Robert, *The Secret Squadrons*, Robson, UK, 1983
Johnsen, Frederick, *Bombers in Blue: PB4Y-2 Privateers and PB4Y-1 Liberators*, Bomber Books, WA, 1979
Johnsen, Frederick, *Consolidated B-24 Liberator: Combat History and Development of the Liberator and Privateer*, Motorbooks, MN, 1993
Johnsen, Frederick, *Consolidated B-24 Liberator (Warbird Tech #1)*, Specialty, MN, 2001
Johnson, E.R., *American Military Transport Aircraft since 1925*, McFarland, NC, 2013
Jones, Lloyd, *U.S. Bombers, 1928–1980s*, Aero, CA, 1984

Jones, W.E., *Bomber Intelligence*, Midlands, UK, 1988

Kinzey, Bert, *B-24 Liberator in Detail, Squadron/Signal*, TX, 2000

Kostenuk, S. & Griffin, J., *RCAF Squadrons and Aircraft*, Canadian War Museum, Canada, 1977

Larkins, William, *Surplus WWII US Aircraft*, BAC, CA, 2005

Lloyd, Alwyn, *Liberator, America's Global Bomber*, Pictorial Histories, MT, 1993

Moyes, Philip, *Bomber Squadrons of the RAF and Their Aircraft*, MacDonald, UK, 1977

Moyes, Philip, *Consolidated B-24 Liberator (Early Models)*, Vintage Aviation, UK, 1979

Moyes, Philip, *Royal Air Force Bombers of WW2: Vol.1*, Doubleday, NY, 1968

Nelmes, Michael, *Tocumwal to Tarakan, Australians and the Consolidated B-24 Liberator*, Australia, Banner Books, 1994

Nelson, Donald, *Arsenal of Democracy: The Story of American Production*, Harcourt, Brace, NY, 1946

O'Leary, Michael, *Consolidated B-24 Liberator*, Osprey, UK, 2002

Oliver, David, *Airborne Espionage*, Sutton, UK, 2005

Parnell, Ben, *Air Commandos: Saga of the Carpetbaggers in WWII*, ibooks, NY, 1993

Parnell, Ben, *Carpetbaggers: America's Secret War in Europe*, TX, Eakin Press, 1987

Pentland, Geoffrey & Malone, Peter, *Aircraft of the RAAF 1921–71*, Kookaburra, Australia, 1971

Perrone, Stephen, *B-24 Snoopers*, NJSG, NJ, 2001

Rickenbacker, Eddie, *Rickenbacker*, Prentice Hall, NY, 1967

Robertson, Bruce, *British Military Aircraft Serials, 1912–1969*, Ian Allan, UK, 1969

Serling, Robert, *When the Airlines Went to War*, Kensington, NY, 1997

Shacklady, Edward, *Consolidated B-24 Liberator*, Cerebus, UK, 2002

Spight, Edwin & Jeanne, *Eagles in the Pacific: Consairway*, Historical Aviation, NY, 1980

Streetly, Martin, *Aircraft of 100 Group*, Robert Hale, UK, 1984

Streetly, Martin, *Confound and Destroy*, McDonald & Janes, UK, 1978

Swearngin, Philip, *Carpetbagger Project: Secret Heroes*, Create Space, US, 2009

Swedish Aviation Historical Society, *Sweden: Haven of Refuge*, SAHS, Sweden, 1976

Tanner, Stephen, *Refuge from the Reich*, Sharpedon, NY, 2000

Vincent, Carl, *Canada's Wings 2: Liberator and Fortress*, Canada's Wings, 1975

Wagner, Raymond, *American Combat Planes*, Doubleday, NY, 1982

West, Bruce, *The Man Who Flew Churchill*, McGraw Hill, NY, 1975

Manuals

AAF, Erection & Maintenance Instructions for Army Models B-24D, G, H, and J. RB-24C and E/Navy Model PB4Y-1/British Models, AN 01-5E-2, 25 October 1944

AAF, Parts Catalog for the Army Models B-24D and J Airplanes, Navy Model PB4Y-1, and British Models, AN 01-5E-4, 25 July 1944, 1 December 1944

AAF, Erection & Maintenance Instructions for Army Models C-87 and C87A/Navy Models RY-1 and RY-2 Airplanes, AN 01-5CA-2, 10 February 1944

AAF, Pilot's Flight Operating Instructions for Army Models C-87, C87A, and C-87B and Navy Models RY-1 and RY-2 Airplanes, AN 01-5CA-1, 15 December 1943

AAF, Operation and Flight Instructions for the Model LB-30 Liberator II Airplane, 30 December 1941

Bureau of Aeronautics, Pilot's Handbook of Flight Operating Instructions: Navy Model RY-3 Airplane, AN 01-5CB-1, 1 December 1944

Consolidated Aircraft Company, Handbook of Erection & Maintenance for the Consolidated Liberator LB-30 'Liberator II' Bombardment Airplane, 15 April 1941

Consolidated Aircraft Company, Pilot's Notes for the Liberator II Airplane, 21 May 1941

Reports, Letters, Memorandum, Studies, and Analyses

USAAF Board, 'Tactical Application, and Test of Refueling in Flight of Heavy Bombardment Aircraft,' Project No. T-9, 10 March 1944

USAAF Engineering Division Memorandum, 'Appendix V: Sample Flight Plan Employing Flight Refueling (MX-204),' Report No. ENG-50-914, 20 July 1943

USAAF Materiel Command, Appendix II: 'Operation of the Flight Refueling Equipment during Flight Tests at Eglin Field (MX-204),' USAAF Materiel Command Engineering Division, 20 July 1943

USAAF Materiel Command Flight Section, 'Memorandum Report on Pilot's Comments on Refueling Project (B-24D),' ENG-19-1609-A, 18 June 1943

Index

Dear Reader,

We hope you have enjoyed this book, but why not share your views on social media? You can also follow our pages to see more about our other products: facebook.com/penandswordbooks or follow us on Twitter @penswordbooks

You can also view our products at www.pen-and-sword.co.uk (UK and ROW) or www.penandswordbooks.com (North America).

To keep up to date with our latest releases and online catalogues, please sign up to our newsletter at: www.pen-and-sword.co.uk/newsletter

If you would like a printed catalogue with our latest books, then please email: enquiries@pen-and-sword.co.uk or telephone: 01226 734555 (UK and ROW) or email: uspen-and-sword@casematepublishers.com or telephone: (610) 853-9131 (North America).

We respect your privacy and we will only use personal information to send you information about our products.

Thank you!